Human Resources Management
in the
Hospitality Industry

David K. Hayes, Ph.D.

Jack D. Ninemeier, Ph.D.

WILEY

John Wiley & Sons, Inc.

Copyright © 2009 by John Wiley & Sons, Inc. All rights reserved
Published by John Wiley & Sons, Inc., Hoboken, New Jersey.
Published simultaneously in Canada.

For general information on our other products and services, or technical support, please
contact our Customer Care Department within the United States at 800-762-2974, outside
the United States at 317-572-3993 or fax 317-572-4002.

Wiley also publishes its books in a variety of electronic formats. Some content that
appears in print may not be available in electronic books.

For more information about Wiley products, visit our Web site at http://*www.wiley.com.*

Library of Congress Cataloging-in-Publication Data:
Hayes, David K.
  Human resources management in the hospitality industry / David K. Hayes,
Jack D. Ninemeier.
    p. cm.
  Includes index.
  ISBN 978-0-470-08480-9 (cloth)
  1. Hospitality industry—Personnel management. I.   Ninemeier, Jack D. II.   Title.
  TX911.3.P4H39 2008
  647.94068—dc22
                                                                          2007021312

Printed in the United States of America
10 9 8 7 6 5 4 3 2 1

Contents

Preface

Today's hospitality professional must be an expert at managing many functions. Ask successful hospitality managers working at all levels of the industry to identify their most daunting tasks, however, and you will find that these tasks relate to people management. In every segment of the hospitality industry, finding, training, and retaining outstanding staff members are always challenging tasks, but every manager must master them.

Rising labor costs, increased competition for quality staff, changing workers' attitudes, increased customer expectations, and a proliferation of new laws related to what Human Resources (HR) managers may and may not do legally are among many factors that point out the importance of effective HR management education. To help meet the challenges of teaching professional HR management, *Human Resources Management in the Hospitality Industry* has been painstakingly developed.

As the text's authors, we are especially pleased with the result and believe it will be well received by instructors, students, and those industry practitioners who are in the trenches of day-to-day hospitality operations. Some might argue that the concepts that should be taught in an HR management course are universal, thus a text useful for managers in general business, manufacturing, or other service industries would also be appropriate for those students studying to enter the field of hospitality. The authors counter that the needs of hospitality students are different and that the teaching of HR management to these students demands the availability of an excellent hospitality-specific text. We believe this to be true for three important reasons:

1. **Organizational structure of hospitality business.** Many HR texts describe the operation of an organization's HR department. In the hospitality industry, the on-site manager *is* that unit's HR department in all except the largest of operations. Thus, it is extremely important that hospitality managers be well versed in HR management, including employee recruitment and selection, training, compensation, performance appraisal and discipline, safety, and other key areas in which they will be personally called upon to make critical decisions. Therefore, this text asks the reader to assume the role of that decision maker.

2. **Diversity of employees.** The management of a hospitality unit requires managers to be adept at understanding the HR-related concerns of a wide range of employees with differing experience and skill levels. The backgrounds of workers found in hospitality operations range from those who are entry level to others who are highly educated and proficient in advanced management areas such as finance, marketing, production, and revenue management. As a result,

hospitality managers must be equally able to compute the overtime wages of tip-credit eligible hourly employees and to understand how the Sarbanes-Oxley Act affects the work of the financial staff they supervise. This book recognizes that diversity.

3. **Complexity.** There is no doubt that successful hospitality managers must be particularly skilled and knowledgeable. For example, they serve as both manufacturing and retail managers. A professional hospitality manager is unique because all of the functions of product sales, from item conceptualization to product delivery, are in the hands of the same individual. The result is that these managers must understand much more than how they will interface with an HR department. Instead, they must realize that, in the eyes of their employees, fellow managers, company owners, and their guests, they *are* the HR department, and thus must be aware of the legal (and many other) consequences of their decision making. As a result, the examination of complex legal implications of HR management is a dominant theme throughout this book.

Text Concept and Content

As we identified the content for this hospitality-specific HR text, we continually recognized the distinction between HR management and supervision. Historically, many hospitality students have been taught how to supervise employees. The reasoning was simple: good managers become recognized as such by first being good supervisors. In today's litigious society, however, managers (and students) who do not understand the legal requirements and responsibilities that must underpin their actions are greatly disadvantaged. For example, hospitality supervisors and managers may know what they want to do to build an effective workforce; however, at the same time, they must not lack an understanding about what they are legally allowed to do, required to do, or even prohibited from doing! Those who have been teaching how to supervise human resources now, with the publication of *Human Resources Management in the Hospitality Industry,* have the preferred option of teaching their students how to legally manage those resources.

With the goal of effectively aiding in the teaching of HR management, the authors created a manuscript with 13 chapters, divided among the following four major parts.

PART I: OVERVIEW OF HUMAN RESOURCES MANAGEMENT

Part I introduces readers to the topic of HR management in hospitality and contains the following chapters:

1: Introduction to Human Resources in the Hospitality Industry

2: The Legal Environment of Human Resources Management

3: Human Resources Management: Policies and Procedures

In this critical foundation section, readers will learn about the diversity of the hospitality industry's workers, the important labor-related legislation they must know to manage these workers, and the key aspects of legal compliance, policy documentation, and record keeping required of successful HR managers.

PART II: SECURING HUMAN RESOURCES

Part II of the text examines the important topics of legally recruiting, hiring, and orienting hospitality employees. It contains the following key chapters:

    4: Employee Recruitment and Selection
    5: First Impressions and an Ethical Foundation

In this section, readers are introduced to many key employee selection concepts, including legal recruitment, interviewing, and selection, as well as negligent hiring, employee orientation, handbooks, ethics, and social responsibility.

PART III: HUMAN RESOURCES IN ACTION

Part III of this text introduces readers to specific activities implemented by effective HR managers. Critical chapters included in this section are:

    6: Planning Training Programs
    7: Delivering and Evaluating Training Programs
    8: Compensation Programs
    9: Performance Management and Appraisal
    10: Employee Health and Safety

Because of its detailed treatment of employee training, this part of the text, perhaps more than any other, illustrates the distinctive approach to HR management. Effective HR managers must understand and implement training principles. With the large number of unskilled positions to be filled, employee turnover rates that often approach 100 percent or more per year, a labor pool that grows increasingly diverse, and increasing job complexity, employee training is the key to quality guest service and operational profitability. For this reason, the text examines the key HR concepts of job descriptions, job breakdowns, and task analysis in this section (rather than in employee recruiting). This content organization approach is consistent with the concept that, in the overwhelming number of cases, newly hired hospitality employees must be trained to do their new jobs. Thus, hospitality job content can best be understood, not in terms of the skills potential employees must bring to the workplace, but rather in terms of the training required to prepare qualified employees for their positions.

Other critical HR activities addressed in this text part include the legal aspects of compensation management, wages, salary, and benefit administration, as well as nonfinancial employee compensation. Additional topics of importance included are performance appraisal, discipline, and separation. This section concludes with an examination of the importance of employee health and physical safety, including a thorough examination of harassment, a topic increasingly recognized as one important to the physical safety (as well as the physical and mental health) of employees of diverse gender, race, religion, and sexual orientation.

PART IV: SPECIAL HUMAN RESOURCES CONCERNS

In the concluding section of the text, special concerns of HR managers in hospitality are addressed. Chapters included in this section are:

11: Role of Human Resources in Strategic Planning and Organizational Change

12: Critical Issues in Human Resources Management

13: Human Resources: Planning for Global Expansion

This section contains a range of topics and information important to HR managers. Key sections included are those addressing change, employee empowerment, and strategic planning. In addition, employee labor unions in hospitality are thoroughly examined in this section, as are the topics of succession planning, cross-generational management, and downsizing strategies. Chapter 13, the text's concluding chapter, illustrates a final point of differentiation for this text. Globalization of the hospitality industry is now occurring at an increasingly fast pace. For American companies, expansion will, in the future, occur as frequently outside U.S. borders as within them. As a result, those professionals entering the industry must understand the unique challenges of managing HR resources globally as well as locally. It is our firm belief that in today's world, a global view is the only approach to take.

Text Features

From a reader's perspective, the features of a textbook often are as important as its content. Thoughtfully designed textbook features make the content presented easy to read, easy to understand, and easy to retain. You will find that **Human Resources Management in the Hospitality Industry** is especially reader friendly. The following strategically designed features help readers learn:

- *Chapter Outline.* The two-tier chapter outline at the beginning of each chapter shows the context for each topic and provides a simple way to quickly find material within the chapter.

- *Checklist of Learning Objectives.* This list of measurable learning objectives helps readers anticipate the skills or knowledge they will acquire upon completing the chapter. A unique feature of this text's design is that these learning objectives are listed a second time in their exact chapter location, allowing readers to be prepared for and excited about what they will be able to achieve when all of the chapter's material is successfully mastered.

- *Impact on Human Resources Management.* Each chapter utilizes this short feature to explain, in clear terms and before any content is presented, exactly *why* the chapter's topic is important. This feature makes it easy for readers to see what the chapter is about and what they will learn by reading it.

- *Human Resources Terms.* As is true with many areas of specialization within hospitality management, HR managers speak their own language. In recognition of this fact, more than 300 special HR-related terms are defined within the text (an alphabetical glossary of these terms is available on the text's Web site: *www.wiley.com/college/hayes*).

- *It's the Law!* Reinforcing its emphasis on the legal aspects of HR management, this feature is included in every chapter. It explains, in detail, how current or proposed legislation directly affects the topics presented and the resulting HR management-related actions that are, and are not, legally allowable or advisable.

- *Human Resources Management: Current Events.* This feature, included in each chapter, and taken from current industry news, trends, and issues, illustrates how concepts presented in the text are played out in the real world. For example, employee and guest smoking in the workplace is an important HR issue. It becomes an even more pressing HR issue, however, when local regulatory bodies propose the legislation of facility-wide smoking bans. The examination of in-the-news HR-related topics provides the content of this attention-getting feature.

- *Human Resources Management Issues.* Each chapter contains several of these real-world mini-cases designed to make readers think about how they would personally use the information they have learned to respond to HR-related situations they will likely encounter in their jobs. Questions are included at the end of every case to help stimulate classroom discussion.

- *List of Human Resources Terms.* Readers often need help in remembering key concepts that should be mastered after reading a section of a book. Thus, the *Human Resources Terms* are listed again at the conclusion of each chapter and in the order in which they were presented in the chapter, to provide a helpful study aid.

- *For Your Consideration.* These end-of-chapter questions about the chapter's content are excellent for reader review. They are designed to be effective in stimulating classroom dialogue, team activity assignments, and/or for homework assignments.

- *Chapter Ending Case Study.* Case studies in **Human Resources Management in the Hospitality Industry** are unique. They present real-life situations and then ask readers to examine that same situation from varying HR perspectives. For example, a case study examining the declining performance of an aging, but long-term hospitality employee asks readers to consider the issue from three distinct perspectives: (1) the appropriateness of the employee appraisal system in use; (2) the importance, to an organization, of maximizing employee performance; and (3) an employer's responsibility to its long-term employees. Several questions are asked, focusing on multiple dimensions of the case study to emphasize critical thinking.

■ *Internet Activities.* The importance of the Internet as a learning tool cannot be overlooked in any field of study. In this text, the *Internet Activities* feature that concludes each chapter not only identifies pertinent Web sites to visit, but it also gives readers specific instructions about what they should do, consider, and learn when they visit the site.

We know that students learn best when concepts and practices are illustrated through many examples and features designed to engage their interest. Each of the special text features utilized in this edition meet that criterion. The result is an effective text that is concise and informative as well as highly readable.

ADDITIONAL RESOURCES

To aid students in retaining and mastering hospitality human resources, there is a *Study Guide* (ISBN: 978-0-470-14060-4), which includes learning objective reviews, study notes and chapter outlines, key terms and concept reviews, and quizzing exercises.

Instructor support materials supplied by Wiley are among the very best available, and that is true for this text as well. The accompanying *Instructor's Manual* (ISBN: 978-0-470-25398-4) for this text includes extensive chapter outlines, chapter quizzes suitable for in-class use, and an extensive bank of examination questions and answers.

A *Companion Website* (www.wiley.com/college/hayes) provides readers with additional resources as well as enabling instructors to download the electronic files for the *Instructor's Manual,* Power Point slides, and Test Bank.

WebCT and Blackboard online courses are available for this book. Visit www.wiley.com/college/hayes and click on Blackboard or Web CT buttons in the center of the page for more information, or contact your Wiley representative.

Acknowledgments and Dedication

Human Resources Management in the Hospitality Industry has been designed to be the most comprehensive, technically accurate, and valuable teaching resource available on the topic. We acknowledge the many individuals who assisted in its development. Special mention is appropriate for those professionals who reviewed the original draft outlines of each chapter and for those readers who carefully reviewed each chapter draft as it was written and rewritten. We also want to recognize those hospitality practitioners and instructors who participated in a thorough review of each chapter's final version. For comment, collaboration, and constructive criticism on the manuscript, we thank our reviewers: Michael Barnes of SUNY Delhi, David Brower of SUNY Delhi, Michelle Crabtree of Northern Virginia Community College, Misty Marie Johanson of Georgia State University, Harry Lenderman of the University of Delaware, Richard Patterson of Western Kentucky University, Janet Shaffer of Lake Washington Technical College, Steve Siegel of Niagara University, Deanne Williams of Virginia State University, and Larry L. Williams of Scottsdale Community College. Additionally, Allisha A. Miller of Panda Pros Hospitality served as an invaluable reviewer and contributor, and her efforts are most appreciated. The authors wish to thank Dr. A. J. Singh, Associate Professor, The School of Hospitality Business, Michigan State University, for contributing Chapter 13, Human Resources: Planning for Global Expansion. Dr. Singh's knowledge of and experience in International hospitality management provides chapter readers with insights that are crucial to understanding human resources dimensions in the global industry.

Experienced authors know the value of a quality publisher in the development of a manuscript. We were impressed but not surprised at the tremendous effort devoted to this project by JoAnna Turtletaub, Wiley Vice President and Publisher, and Melissa Oliver, the text's Acquisition Editor. Julie Kerr, Senior Developmental Editor for this book, deserves special recognition because her efforts illustrate well the commitment of Wiley toward this project. She served as the authors' guide to reviewer input, and she scrutinized each word, concept, and even photo caption of the manuscript. Julie's efforts, as much as any individual working on the project, helped ensure that this text met the high standards Wiley sets for its own publications and, by doing so, helped the authors contribute their very best efforts as well. To the extent the text is a success, the many individuals mentioned here deserve all of the credit; for any shortcomings in the text, the authors willingly accept full responsibility.

Finally, we wish to dedicate this text to Professor H. B. Meek, who, in 1954, founded Cornell University's School of Hotel Administration, and without whose dedication and vision, the discipline of hospitality education would be greatly diminished. Just as Professor Meek understood the uniqueness and importance of hospitality education as a separate discipline, we hope he would approve of our efforts to continue the enhancement of the field by this contribution to hospitality human resources management. To the degree that he would approve of our efforts, we will have succeeded as much as we hope those students reading this resource succeed in their own careers.

David K. Hayes, Ph.D.   Jack D. Ninemeier, Ph.D.
Okemos, MI   *Hilo, HI*

PART ONE

Overview of Human Resources Management

CHAPTER ONE

Introduction to Human Resources in the Hospitality Industry

CHAPTER OUTLINE

Overview of Hospitality Industry
Managing Human Resources in the Organization
Human Resources Activities
External Influences
Internal Influences
Diversity in the Hospitality Workplace
Overview of Diversity
Implementing Diversity Initiatives
Specific Human Resources Responsibilities
Human Resources Terms
For Your Consideration
Case Study: Human Resources Management in Action
Internet Activities
Endnote

CHECKLIST OF CHAPTER LEARNING OBJECTIVES

As a result of successful completion of this chapter, readers will be able to:

1. Provide a brief overview of the hospitality and tourism industries, and emphasize the importance of effective human resources management to all organizations within them.

2. Explain how human resources management relates to the management of a hospitality and tourism organization.

3. Present an overview of human resources activities, and explain external and internal influences that affect them.

4. Review the importance of diversity in the hospitality workplace, and tell basic procedures important in planning and implementing a valuing-diversity emphasis.

5. List specific human resources responsibilities important in most hospitality and tourism organizations.

Impact on Human Resources Management

While the hospitality industry is broad and diverse, organizations within it share some things in common. One is the need for staff members with a variety of knowledge, skills, and experience to produce the products and services that are needed or desired by consumers. The industry has often been described as a "people business." In this context, the people typically referred to are both the employees who produce the products and services, and those who purchase and consume them. In this book, we will be focusing on one of the two groups of people just noted: employees.

The need to devote an entire book to procedures to facilitate the work of staff members in the hospitality industry is easy to defend. Almost without exception, hospitality managers in all types and sizes of organizations and in locations around the world consistently note concerns about recruiting and retaining personnel at all organizational levels. Their goal is to employ persons with the attitudes and abilities required to best meet the needs of those being served. This chapter provides an overview of and the context within which the management of human resources in the hospitality industry will be presented.

Overview of Hospitality Industry

1. **Provide a brief overview of the hospitality and tourism industries, and emphasize the importance of effective human resources management to all organizations within them.**

Hospitality industry: The range of for-profit and not-for-profit organizations that provide lodging and/or accommodations including food services for people when they are away from their homes.

The **hospitality industry** is one part of the larger travel and tourism industry that, in addition to hospitality, consists of transportation services organizations and retail businesses. The for-profit and not-for-profit operations in the hospitality segment share a common goal: to provide lodging and/or accommodations including food services for people when they are away from their homes. Many people think of hotels and restaurants when they think of the hospitality industry, but it comprises numerous types of organizations. Figure 1.1 identifies three segments of the travel and tourism industry.

As you review Figure 1.1, note that the travel and tourism industry can be divided into three segments: transportation services, hospitality, and destination businesses. This text concerns one segment: hospitality. Lodging organizations within the hospitality segment include hotels, conference centers, destination resorts, camp and park ground facilities, and inns. The foodservices segment can

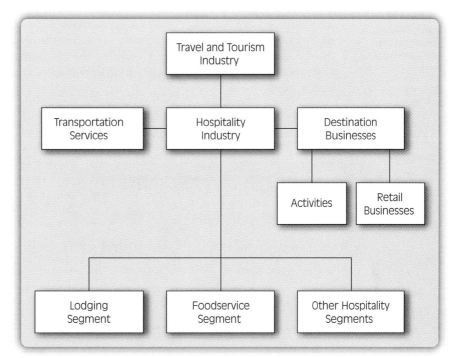

FIGURE 1.1: Overview of Hospitality Industry

be divided into two general components. For-profit operations include hotels, restaurants, caterers, and retail operations such as grocery stores and service stations that provide prepackaged sandwiches, beverages, snacks, and other items. The other component, not-for-profit operations, includes food services offered by educational facilities, healthcare institutions, the military, business/industry organizations, religious and charitable groups, correctional facilities, and transportation companies. These not-for-profit organizations may operate their own food services or, alternatively, may contract with a foodservice management company to do so. Other hospitality segments include organizations such as private clubs, sports and recreational foodservice operations, cruise ships, casinos, vending businesses, and amusement and theme parks.

Organizations in the hospitality industry tend to be **labor-intensive.** Technology cannot provide the level of service that is integral to the expectations of many consumers. Even the phrase, *hospitality*, refers to the friendly treatment of one's guests, and this human touch must be provided by the organization's staff members.

Hospitality and tourism organizations require employees; the greater their level of **revenue** and the more consumers they serve, the more staff members these

Human resources management (HRM): Processes used by a hospitality or tourism organization to enhance its performance by effectively using all of its staff members.

operations require. Success requires a full complement of staff members from owners/managers to entry-level employees who consistently attain required quality and quantity standards. In this industry, the emphasis must be on **human resources,** and leaders must practice **human resources management** principles and practices.

Human Resources Management: CURRENT EVENTS 1.1

HOW CAN THE HOSPITALITY INDUSTRY SUCCESSFULLY COMPETE FOR ITS EMPLOYEES?

Historically, the number of hours worked in the average workweek has been decreasing. However, many managers in the hospitality industry work long hours and, unfortunately, many of these hours are late at night and on weekends and holidays when others are with their families and friends.

Conditions in some industries lend themselves to opportunities for employees to work at home for all or part of their jobs, to fulfill work responsibilities during hours that are best for the employee, and to job-share (as when two persons divide up tasks for a single job).

Although the latter approach (job-sharing) can be used in hospitality and tourism organizations, it is difficult to deliver service without an employee to do so, and it is also difficult to sell a service at times other than when consumers desire it. How can service organizations compete with those in other industries for the very best management talent?

Some organizations have found creative alternatives that allow selected persons to become **intrapreneurs**. These persons manage a specific part of the business and receive a specified part of the profits from its successful operation. This may be a motivator for those with an entrepreneurial spirit. One example occurs when a bonus is paid to a hospitality manager based on performance that exceeds specified financial goals. Other organizations offer creative profit-sharing plans to staff members for whom money is a motivator. When revenues and expenses for a specific venue, such as a food or beverage outlet or a gift shop in a hotel, can be specifically allocated, additional opportunities for intrapreneurial arrangements become possible.

Human resources–related challenges will continue to be a priority for most hospitality and tourism operators in the foreseeable future. What can be done to meet the task of recruiting and retaining staff members? As this and related questions are successfully addressed, organizations will enjoy a competitive edge over their counterparts who do not deal with this important concern.

Intrapreneur: An employee of an organization whose compensation, in whole or in part, is based on the financial performance of the part of the business for which the person is responsible.

Management process: The process of planning, organizing, staffing, supervising, controlling, and appraising organizational resources to attain goals.

Regardless of the industry segment in which they work, most employees have the same basic wants and needs. They share the same basic concerns about how they are treated by their employers, which impacts their work performance and length of employment. Much of a person's attitude about work is affected by interactions with other management and nonmanagement employees. However, human resources concerns ranging from compensation and benefits to opportunities for training and professional development, as well as beliefs about how they fit into the organization, are important to many staff members.

Some human resources managers begin their careers in operating positions in a hospitality or tourism organization and then move into a specialized human resources position. Others begin in hospitality human resources and spend much of their career in progressively more responsible positions in that discipline. Still others with hospitality human resources duties move into similar positions in other industries. These and other options are possible because of the similar concerns shared by most employees in all organizations and industries. These basic issues and concerns and the ways they can be addressed are among those topics discussed in this book.

Managing Human Resources in the Organization

Resources: What an organization has available to achieve goals. Examples include people (human resources), money, time, machinery, processes and procedures, energy (utilities), and products such as food, beverages, and supplies.

Managers: Staff members in the organization who direct the work of supervisors.

Supervisors: Staff members in the organization who direct the work of entry-level personnel.

2. **Explain how human resources management relates to the management of a hospitality and tourism organization.**

The staff members of every hospitality and tourism organization are its most important resource. How their work is managed (facilitated) directly impacts the success or failure of the organization. The basic **management process** is the same in almost any type of organization, and it consists of six basic functions that relate to all **resources,** including staff members. These functions are listed in Figure 1.2, which also provides an example of human resources responsibilities applicable to each function.

Figure 1.2 suggests that, while the responsibilities within each management function narrow from top-level **managers** to **supervisors,** each person with management responsibility has obligations relating to each function. Top-level managers tend to have longer-term, big-picture responsibilities, managers have more specific departmental-related duties, and supervisors serve as linking pins to connect upper levels of management with entry-level staff members in day-to-day operations.

	LEVEL OF MANAGEMENT		
Management Function	**Top-Level Manager**	**Mid-Level Manager**	**Supervisor**
Planning	Analyzes the number of persons needed for key management positions in the future (succession planning).	Considers estimated costs of departmental training programs for an upcoming budget period.	Schedules employees for the following week.
Organizing	Determines reporting relationships as a hotel front office department is reorganized.	Determines tasks to be part of a specific position.	Revises a work task based on work simplification tactics.
Staffing	Recruits and hires employees for a healthcare dietary services operation.	Provides input about a hire or fire decision.	Provides input to **job descriptions** used for employee recruitment.
Supervising	Directs the work of managers.	Directs the work of supervisors.	Directs the work of entry-level employees.
Controlling	Establishes labor standards for a quick-service restaurant.	Compares estimated and actual labor cost data, and takes corrective actions as necessary.	Ensures that procedures used to control costs are in use.
Appraising	Determines the extent to which human resources goals, including labor costs, professional development programs, and performance improvement, are met.	Evaluates the work of department staff.	Determines whether revised work procedures that address a problem have corrected it.

FIGURE 1.2: Basic Management Functions Involve Human Resources Responsibilities

Job descriptions:
A list of tasks that a person working within a specific position must perform.

The Role of Human Resources Is Broader Than Just Filling Positions

Effective human relations procedures must be used to recruit and select staff members. However, human resources responsibilities extend beyond this and further than other stereotypical duties such as planning staff parties, approving employee vacations, and collecting paperwork when new employees are hired.

Numerous federal and state laws relating to hiring and employment practices must be understood and implemented in every hospitality and tourism organization. The extent of compliance has a significant impact on how affected managers make personnel-related decisions and on whether significant time and financial resources must be committed to issues that could have been avoided if labor laws were followed.

The management of human resources is of strategic importance to the organization. Goals cannot be attained without the best people in the appropriate position who consistently attain standards needed to deliver products and services of the correct quality. At the same time, those with human resources responsibilities must represent and advocate for the employees. When the **corporate culture** encourages them to do so, employees working at all organizational levels can provide ideas and creative energies to give the organization a competitive advantage. Those with human resources responsibilities are at the forefront of helping to develop, implement, communicate, interpret, and enforce the policies and procedures that help ensure that the organization's most important resources (employees) are empowered to help the organization achieve its goals.

Managers with human resources responsibilities also realize that labor costs must be controlled. They must help ensure that the labor-related expenses incurred are actually **value-added** dollars that are worth more to the hospitality organization than what is spent for the labor.

Human Resources Activities

3. **Present an overview of human resources activities, and explain external and internal influences that affect them.**

Corporate culture: Shared beliefs, experiences, and norms that influence how things are done within an organization.

Large hospitality and tourism organizations typically have **human resources departments** with **staff specialists** whose primary responsibilities focus on human resources concerns. Managers in small organizations function as generalists, and they assume human resources concerns in addition to numerous others as part of their job. Most organizations in the hospitality industry are small. Therefore,

Human Resources Management:
CURRENT EVENTS 1.2

THE BIGGEST CHALLENGE IS HUMAN RESOURCES!

Just ask any manager in any type of hospitality or tourism organization about his or her most significant challenge, and the answer is likely to be "not enough qualified help." Labor shortages are an ongoing challenge, and much of a manager's time is often spent in recruiting and training new employees and in correcting defects caused by employees who don't care before they resign and by newly hired personnel who are concerned, but who have not completed training in proper work procedures. Reasons for labor shortages vary by location but typically include an inadequate number of persons desiring to work in the industry, perceived low compensation, and, unfortunately, very high **employee turnover** rates.

Managers can use three basic strategies to address labor shortages, and each has human resources implications:

- *Keep the people currently employed; reduce the turnover rate.* Selecting the right people and using tactics to retain staff members are examples of ways to accomplish this goal.
- *Increase productivity.* When increased output that meets required standards is generated with the same or reduced number of labor hours, fewer personnel will be needed. Again, selecting the right persons is helpful, as is providing well-thought-out orientation, training, and professional development programs for interested staff members.
- *Recruit from nontraditional labor markets.* Many hospitality and tourism managers enjoy great success when they employ "empty nesters" (parents of grown children), older workers seeking part-time employment to complement retirement income, and other persons with physical and mental challenges who can become proficient at performing many necessary tasks.

Value-added: The concept that the benefits of money spent on something are worth more to an organization than the amount of money that is spent on its purchase.

managers in these operations will be responsible for making staff-related decisions without the benefit of the specialized assistance that their counterparts in larger organizations receive. *Note*: This book has been written from the perspective of managers in small organizations, and it discusses basic human resources concerns that these managers must address as they facilitate the work of their staff members.

Figure 1.3 reviews basic human resources activities and indicates the external and internal influences on these activities.

Managers and supervisors who practice human resources skills can reduce employee turnover rates and the associated productivity and service quality problems that occur when there is a revolving door of new employees. *Courtesy PhotoDisc/Getty Images*

Human resources department: The department within a large hospitality or tourism organization with the responsibility for recruiting, screening, and developing staff members. Persons in this department also administer compensation and benefit programs, coordinate safety practices, implement labor law requirements, and, if applicable, administer collective bargaining agreements.

Staff specialists: Persons with technical expertise in an area such as human resources that provide advice to, but do not make decisions for, managers in the organization's chain of command.

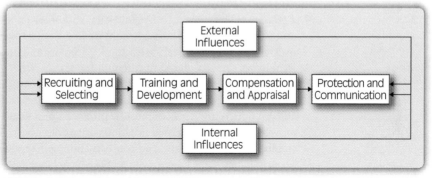

FIGURE 1.3: External and Internal Influences on Human Resources Activities

Let's review Figure 1.3 by noting the human resources activities:

■ *Recruiting/selecting.* These tasks include tactics and procedures to attract applicants to the organization (recruiting) and choosing the very best persons among them (selecting). These activities will be discussed in detail in Chapter 4.

■ *Training and development.* Preparing new staff members to do required work, updating their experienced peers, and providing opportunities for all interested staff members to assume more responsible positions are integral to the efforts of most organizations to attain goals and address competitive pressures, if applicable. These topics are discussed in Chapters 6 and 7.

- *Compensation and appraisal.* Personnel should receive pay and benefits commensurate with their contributions to the organization. Performance appraisal provides input to help employees attain the on-job success that can yield promotions with higher compensation levels. These topics are examined in Chapters 8 and 9.
- *Protection and communications.* Safety and security concerns are of obvious importance to all employees. Many laws and regulations mandate safety procedures, and numerous other tactics that top-level managers should do (and not do) impact employee safety. Many legal and procedural issues with safety implications are addressed by those with human resources responsibilities. These topics are discussed in Chapter 10. In addition, effective communication that flows up, down, and across the organization helps ensure that staff members know about issues that affect them. These topics are discussed in Chapters 3 and 5.

EXTERNAL INFLUENCES

Figure 1.3 indicates that human resources activities are impacted by external influences. These include:

- *Legislation.* The impact of federal, state, and other laws on the hiring process and their influence on management decisions affecting personnel cannot be overstated. Chapter 2 addresses the legal environment, and numerous other legal issues are considered throughout the text.
- *Consumer preferences.* What consumers desire must be identified and supplied by hospitality and tourism organizations. What are business/operating volumes? What products and services must be produced, and when are they needed? The answers to these and related questions drive employee recruiting and selecting, training and development, and compensation and appraisal activities.
- *Demographics.* The characteristics of the local labor market and the guests are of obvious concern. Income levels in a community affect wage and salary rates, and they also impact the ability and interest of consumers to purchase the organization's products and services. Young persons are the foundation of employees in many organizations; are they available?
- *Global issues.* Many hospitality and tourism organizations exist to serve travelers. Business volumes impact human resources activities, and these are affected by international and national events that encourage (e.g., sporting events and special commemorations) and discourage (e.g., violence and disease threats) travel.
- *Economy.* The financial well-being of world markets and the country, state, and community in which the hospitality organization operates impact business volumes and, therefore, the need for human resources.
- **Employee unions.** Staff members may belong to an *employee union* that represents their interests in numerous aspects of the human resources activities noted in Figure 1.3.

INTERNAL INFLUENCES

Policy: Rules and regulations established by an organization that specify how applicable staff members should act.

Figure 1.3 also suggests that there are internal organizational influences on human resources activities:

- **Policies.** A *policy* can greatly influence how an organization feels about staff members. In the absence of laws that regulate specific actions, employers have

---

Human Resources MANAGEMENT ISSUES   (1.1)

"**T**his would be a great place to work if only the human resources department was on our side," said Jonathon as he spoke to Emma, another manager at the Ocean Edge Hotel. "They send us job applicants who are not qualified; they don't do an adequate job of orienting new employees to our hotel; they have no role in train- ing; and they issue so many policies (many of which are ridiculous!) that I simply can't keep up with everything."

"You're right that communication could be better, and there is probably a need for our human resources people to really know exactly what we do," replied Emma, "but before I came here, I spent five years working for a much smaller property that didn't have a human resources department. Each manager had to do whatever the General Manager wanted. Some of the GMs wanted a lot—and others wanted only a little—responsibility for the human resources function."

"You know," continued Emma, "That really wasn't a good situation either. Like everywhere else, the managers had primary work responsibilities that involved a specific cost or revenue center. And they had to be concerned with many human resources details that impacted their employees. I'll tell you, Jonathon, the world of human resources management is full of legal, technical, and other concerns that are pretty far removed from helping guests, preparing and serving meals, and cleaning guest rooms."

"I guess I never thought about that," said Jonathon, "I've been here for a long time, and it's always been a 'them versus us' relationship between operating managers and the human resources people. Do you suppose there is no ideal situation and, because of this, the organization, its managers and employees, and the guests often lose?"

QUESTIONS

1. What appears to be the primary problem at the Ocean Edge Hotel? What tactics might address the problem you have identified?
2. What are the pros and cons for managing human resources in a small property and for working in a larger property with human resources specialists?
3. How can managers in small operations keep up with legal and other current events that impact human resources?

Work procedure:
A course of action or
steps to be used to
accomplish an
objective; usually
developed to
describe how a work
task should be
accomplished.

Empowerment:
The act of authoriz-
ing employees to
make discretionary
decisions within their
areas of responsibility.

Downsizing:
Activities implemented
to eliminate jobs in
order to generate
greater efficiencies
and cost savings.

significant discretion in establishing protocols that may affect the attitudes of staff members toward the organization.

▪ **Work Procedures.** *Work procedures* that are designed with (or without) input from applicable personnel, the extent to which equipment is used to ease physical work tasks and the amount of employee **empowerment,** if any, impact how work is done and, in turn, required human resources activities.

▪ *Corporate culture.* The perceived worth of employees to the organization is an integral part of its culture. It drives the philosophies and attitudes about employees and their roles in the organization, and human resources activities.

▪ *Long- and short-term plans.* Longer-term plans such as expansion or **downsizing** and shorter-term plans such as rolling out a new program or service impact employees and affect recruiting, selecting, and training activities.

▪ *Management judgment and experience.* Managers and human resources specialists (in large organizations) bring their own judgment and experience to the decision-making process. This input affects the policies, procedures, and plans already discussed and influences other decisions about human resources issues.

Diversity in the Hospitality Workplace

4. **Review the importance of diversity in the hospitality workplace, and tell basic procedures important in planning and implementing a valuing-diversity emphasis.**

Diversity: The broad range of human characteristics and dimensions that impact the employees' values, opportunities, and perceptions of themselves and others at work.

Diversity has received a great deal of attention in modern organizations.[1] To some, it means providing equal opportunities to persons of selected characteristics such as age, gender, mental/physical abilities, sexual orientation, race, or ethnic heritage. To others, the concept implies responses to legal concerns such as for equal employment opportunities. To still others, diversity connotes equalizing the percentage of employees (and, sometimes, an organization's suppliers) with selected demographics of the general population in, for example, the community in which the operation is located.

OVERVIEW OF DIVERSITY

The hospitality and tourism industry has typically employed a large number of minorities as well as other persons who are seeking a short-term job (not a career). Hotels, restaurants, clubs, foodservices operators in noncommercial facilities, and others compete with potential employers in other industries for persons without specialized knowledge or skills to work at beginning wage rates in entry-level positions. This, in turn, has led to a commonly held, but incorrect, stereotype that industry employees can only work in low-paying and dead-end positions. However, the industry in general, and many organizations more specifically, have implemented and publicized efforts to upgrade the industry's reputation by making genuine efforts to offer career opportunities, with all of the advantages that accrue to them, to all interested persons. Many exemplary organizations have invested significant time, money, and creativity into these efforts.

Increasingly, then, the definition of *diversity* is being revised. It is being defined in the broadest possible way so all employees in an organization are included and so all employees' diversity will be valued because of their contributions to their employer.

A reasonable definition of *diversity* might separate the entire population into the six characteristics noted earlier: age, gender, mental/physical abilities, sexual orientation, race, and ethnic heritage. These factors do influence how one experiences the world; however, numerous secondary dimensions also shape one's values, expectations, and experiences. These include education, family status, organizational role and level, religion, first language, income, geographic location, and numerous others. Every person is unique and brings special qualities to the job that influences his or her attitudes about it and opportunities to contribute to it.

Equal Employment Opportunity Laws and Affirmative Action Programs Are Different from Valuing-Diversity Efforts

Equal Employment Opportunity laws (see Chapter 2) address the prevention and/or correction of employment practices that discriminate against individuals based on age, color, disability, Vietnam-era veteran status, national origin, race, religion, and gender. Affirmative Action programs are implemented to address these types of discrimination. Their goal is to close gaps by establishing targets and time frames to modify race and gender profiles in organizations. Many organizations that are exempt from these requirements also implement programs to better match the profile of their employees to that of the external labor pool.

Hospitality and tourism organizations that implement valuing-diversity efforts move beyond race and gender concerns and attempt to provide an environment that is welcoming and rewarding for every staff member. The goal is to move beyond satisfying legal requirements to addressing environmental concerns, improving productivity, and increasing morale—in other words, to creating a corporate culture in which diversity is desired because it yields the full utilization of the diverse talents of every staff member.

Many persons argue that a diversity effort should be implemented and kept ongoing because it is the right thing to do, but it is also possible to make a strong business case for a diversity effort, and several benefits of a successful diversity emphasis impact human resources concerns:

- A welcoming and rewarding work environment encourages excellent job performance.
- The changing makeup of the U.S. labor force increasingly requires the employment of those with diverse personal dimensions.
- When all employees are valued, turnover and absenteeism are minimized and associated costs are reduced.
- A culture of understanding, respect, and cooperation encourages teamwork with its benefits.
- Diverse backgrounds create more creative alternatives as decisions are made and as problems are resolved.
- Many consumers are attracted to businesses that employ staff members who reflect the diversity of those consumers. The result is increased sales volume, which, in turn, improves the financial viability of the organization.

IMPLEMENTING DIVERSITY INITIATIVES

How is a valuing-diversity effort implemented? It does not just happen because top-level officials require it, because human resources specialists have been asked to make it happen, or because a manager in a specific department desires it. It is not a program in which a committee decides what to do and an employee training effort follows. Instead, valuing diversity represents a significant organizational culture change that must have the ongoing commitment (in other words, an emphasis that never ends!) from those mentioned. It must also have buy-in from employees in every department throughout the organization.

Basic changes in management strategies may well be required to successfully implement a valuing-diversity emphasis. People typically respond to new ideas in predictable ways based on the extent to which they tolerate perceived risks. Those who perceive little or no risk in valuing diversity view it as a creative opportunity and will be among the first of their peers to endorse the concept. Those who are more cautious about exploring new ideas will likely view diversity to be desirable only after it has been proven beneficial to the organization. Other staff members with the highest level of perceived risk will see diversity as changing the status quo (how things have always been). They will mistrust it and will be very interested in keeping things as they are.

Strategies to implement a valuing-diversity effort should begin by involving those who see its value and should also recognize that employees who are anxious about and/or fearful of it are not likely to change their attitudes quickly. There are no quick-fix implementation plans to convince employees that a valuing-diversity mindset is useful. Instead, it involves lifelong learning, personal commitment, and ongoing self-improvement. In other words, it requires a change in attitude.

Hospitality and tourism employees who value diversity have some basic beliefs that form the framework for their mindset:

- Valuing diversity requires a change in corporate culture, and these change efforts never end.
- When diversity is valued, benefits accrue to employees and to the organization.
- Efforts to implement diversity efforts should include everyone, because every staff member brings diverse attitudes, backgrounds, and experiences to the job.

Hopefully, you now realize that top-level managers cannot simply tell the human resources department (in a large organization) or a specific manager (of a small property) to start a diversity program. Instead, a leadership team comprising representatives throughout the organization who believe in the concept, who have some knowledge about multicultural issues, and who desire and have the time to become involved should be brought together.

Group members have a formidable task in most organizations. They must:

- Obtain input from numerous internal and external sources.
- Identify and consider cultural diversity implementation concerns.
- Arrive at objective conclusions about the readiness of the organization to adapt to cultural change.
- Develop specific and useful plans.
- Assign tasks and monitor their completion.
- Communicate effectively with leaders about diversity issues.
- Plan ongoing activities that promote diversity and its benefits to the organization's staff members.

It typically takes much longer than diversity proponents initially believe to change the corporate culture. Attitudes that have developed over many years and that have passed down through generations must be changed. Even when it becomes an accepted organizational goal, it will take a long time for many employees to value diversity, and some staff members are unlikely to ever accept it.

Diversity goals recognize simple issues. Those who support the concept believe that all staff members want to:

- Be recognized for whom they are and appreciated for what they do.
- Feel comfortable with whom they work.
- Believe that their input is valued and that they have some impact on the decisions that affect them.

As the importance of diversity is better recognized and addressed in the hospitality and tourism workplace, the basic human needs of all staff members will be better recognized.

IT'S THE LAW!

You'll learn about many laws that affect human resources management throughout this book. One that affects many hospitality and tourism organizations—and, perhaps, yourself—concerns the minimum wage.

The United States Fair Labor Standards Act (FLSA) covers most private and public employers and requires that employers pay at least a federal minimum wage. In July 2008, the wage was $6.55 per hour, (with a planned increase to $7.25 in July 2008) but tipped employees could be paid less per hour if their tips, combined with their employer's payment, equaled the federal minimum hourly rate. (To the extent they did not, the employer was required to make up the difference.) If states have a higher minimum wage rate than the federal minimum, then the state wage rate is applied.

Wages paid are of significant (perhaps primary) concern to many job applicants, and for those seeking employment in entry-level positions, even relatively small differentials can impact employment decisions.

Some hospitality associations have typically opposed increases in minimum wage rates for numerous reasons. First, there is the honest belief that higher wages reduce profits, threaten business closures, and limit their constituents' abilities to create and maintain jobs. Second, they point out that many persons who receive the minimum wage are working for spending money and not to support themselves or their families. Third, they note that many of their members employ persons without "world of work" skills who might otherwise be unemployed. Association representatives also correctly indicate that many states require wage rates above the federal minimum, that many organizations pay higher rates than the mandated minimum, and that employers incur significant mandated and voluntary labor-related costs in addition to wages. Finally, they suggest that those working in minimum-wage positions have opportunities for higher wages and salaries through job advancement.

Minimum wage rates, like many other aspects of human resources management, can be viewed from different perspectives. Unfortunately, like many other aspects of human resources management, the issues are complicated and do not suggest easy answers or offer right or wrong approaches. They do, however, have a significant impact on employers, employees, and those being served. Those with human resources responsibilities must stay current with applicable laws, must interpret and apply them correctly, and must be able to communicate their organizations' positions about all matters, including compensation, that affect their employees.

Specific Human Resources Responsibilities

5. **List specific human resources responsibilities important in most hospitality and tourism organizations.**

What tasks are involved in the management of human resources in a hospitality or tourism organization? The short answer is, "almost everything involved in the relationship between staff members and the organization." A composite response suggesting the range of human resources responsibilities is found in Figure 1.4.

You'll note a wide variety of job tasks in the composite job description shown in Figure 1.4. It is unlikely that any human resources director in any hospitality or tourism organization is responsible for every one of these tasks. It is also possible that additional responsibilities are integral to the job descriptions of top-level human resources personnel in other organizations. However, the job description suggests the wide variety of activities of concern to those with human resources responsibilities.

A quick first glance at Figure 4.1 may lead one to think, "How can any single person do all of these things?" In fact, large organizations may have a director of human resources with one or more professional associates to whom some tasks can be delegated. A more significant question that arises is, "How can the unit manager and his or her staff in a small hospitality and tourism organization without human resources specialists do all of these things?" The answer is: "They probably can't, so they will need to rely on external specialists, and it is likely that problems can arise when there is a lack of time and/or expertise to address all of these issues."

Most hospitality and tourism organizations are too small to enjoy the services of one or more human resources specialists. In that case, managers have only a few options available:

- The general manager must assume responsibility for some of these tasks.
- A decentralized approach may be used in which department heads are responsible for the personnel-related issues relevant to their specific staff.
- Basic policies and procedures are implemented, and a qualified attorney is contacted when issues arise that appear to be outside the boundaries that they impose.
- Unfortunately, other tasks may not be accomplished or may be done incorrectly.

Just as no single person can probably perform all of the tasks identified in Figure 1.4, one book cannot address all of the necessary human resources issues in the proper depth needed to minimize the possibility of problems. However, the goal of managers in small operations should be to address the most important topics likely to cause the most significant problems.

Executive committee: A group comprising department heads who serve as the organization's key management team and who, in this capacity, are responsible for the overall management of the organization.

Human Resources Department

I. Position:
Director of Human Resources

II. Job Summary:
Assists department management staff with recruitment, selection, and orientation of new staff members. Administers payroll records, directs the processing of wage and salary payments, and ensures that all applicable federal, state, and local wage and hour, worker's compensation, and other labor laws are consistently complied with. Implements data collection systems and manages the organization's health, employee protection, retirement, and other benefits programs. Conduct labor analyses, staff planning, and other studies as requested. Serves on the organization's **executive committee.**

III. Job Tasks:
1. Administers employee compensation, benefits, performance management systems, and safety and recreation programs.
2. Advises managers about organizational policies and recommends needed changes.
3. Develops and places recruitment ads, plans recruitment strategies, screens applicants, and makes hiring recommendations.
4. Conducts and reviews wage and benefit surveys, and proposes employee benefit modifications to the general manager.
5. Analyzes data and reports to identify and determine causes of personnel-related problems, and develops recommendations for improvement.
6. Analyzes training needs and designs applicable employee development, language training, and health and safety programs.
7. Conducts exit interviews to identify reasons for employee termination.
8. Maintains organization's policy manual, and communicates policy changes to applicable staff members.
9. Develops, administers, and evaluates applicant tests.
10. Coordinates all employee (personnel) recordkeeping functions.
11. Continually reviews and assists in updating the organization chart and employee handbook.
12. Manages the organization's group insurance, unemployment, and related benefits programs; communicates benefits information to staff, and ensures compliance with legal requirements.
13. Maintains records and compiles statistical reports concerning personnel-related data such as hires, transfers, performance appraisals, and absenteeism rates.
14. Negotiates collective bargaining agreements, helps interpret labor contracts, and administers the formal labor relations program with unionized staff.
15. Oversees the evaluation, classification, and rating of occupations and job positions.
16. Undertakes special projects relating to job description and specification updates, performance appraisal improvements, wage and salary comparison surveys, long-range staff planning, and other personnel issues.
17. Keeps abreast of laws and regulations relating to employees, ensures compliance with these laws and regulations, and advises managers as necessary.

FIGURE 1.4: Composite Job Description for Director of Human Resources

18. Advises line managers about discipline, discharge, and related employment matters.
19. Manages educational and referral programs for alcohol and substance abuse.
20. Assists department heads in planning professional development and training programs for employees.
21. Develops forecasts of short- and long-term staffing needs.
22. Coordinates transfer, promotion, and layoff strategies.
23. Benchmarks employee recruitment and selection processes with others in the industry, and explores new strategies as appropriate.
24. Develops and maintains a library of training resources specifically designed for each position.
25. Plans and implements employee motivation, recognition, and retention programs.
26. Organizes employee activities such as the holiday party and other activities as appropriate.
27. Provides current and prospective employees with information about policies, job duties, working conditions, wages, opportunities for promotion, and employee benefits.
28. Provides terminated employees with outplacement or relocation assistance.
29. Represents the organization at personnel-related hearings and investigations.
30. Oversees all work-related injury claims to ensure integrity, ongoing case management, and reporting compliance.
31. Recruits, hires, trains, supervises, schedules, and evaluates staff members in the human resources department.
32. Works with payroll personnel to ensure that all forms required of new employees are completed.
33. Conducts preliminary employment interviews with position applicants.
34. Investigates and reports on accidents for insurance carriers.
35. Meets with employee relations committee on a regular, scheduled basis.
36. Maintains OSHA-related logs and reports.
37. Coordinates, monitors, and suggests improvements for employee performance appraisal system.
38. Schedules and conducts employee safety meetings.
39. Recommends drug-testing procedures for employee applicants.
40. Interacts with the general manager and department heads to investigate employee violations of policies and to recommend correction actions, if necessary.
41. Interacts with organization's attorney relative to personnel legal issues involving concerns about EEOC, harassment, and lawsuits.
42. Attends staff meetings as scheduled.
43. Serves as a member of the organization's executive committee.

IV. Reports to:
General Manager

V. Supervises:
Human Resources Associates

FIGURE 1.4: (*Continued*)

Human Resources MANAGEMENT ISSUES   (1.2)

"I don't know how you do it, Alice," said Maureen. "I manage a Nutrition Services department in a large hospital and continually receive lots of advice from our human resources department about a wide variety of special concerns that otherwise I would never know about."

Maureen was speaking to her old college classmate, Alice, who worked in the same city as manager for a fast-paced casual-service restaurant.

Alice's reply was expected: "Keeping up with legal issues and finding time to address a wide variety of other human resources concerns is a real problem. I try to do the best I can, but there are always fires (emergencies) that must receive a priority. Then, unfortunately, many things that are nice to know and do must be placed on the back burner."

"How do you stay out of trouble, then, Alice?" asked Maureen. "There are always legal concerns, benefits cost issues, and compensation studies, for example, that I would assume are necessary. There also must be lots of things that your employees want and deserve that require some attention," replied Maureen.

"Maureen, you're right! As a manager of a property in a multiunit chain, I do get some support from corporate officials, and I belong to several professional associations and attend meetings and receive updates from that source. I've learned some other tactics along the way, but obviously it's not possible to spend all of the time on human resources concerns that I would like to."

QUESTIONS

1. What additional practical tactics can Alice use to obtain necessary human resources-related information?
2. What information applicable to Maureen's nutrition services employees will likely be relevant to all hospital employees? What specific concerns might Maureen have?
3. What tactics do you think single-unit restaurant operators without corporate-level assistance can use to cope with the less-than-ideal human resources information they probably have easily available to them?

HUMAN RESOURCES TERMS

The following terms were defined in this chapter:

Hospitality industry	**Corporate culture**
Labor-intensive	**Value-added**
Revenue	**Human resources department**
Human resources	**Staff specialists**
Human resources management	**Employee union**
Employee turnover	**Policy**
Intrapreneur	**Work procedure**
Management process	**Empowerment**
Resources	**Downsizing**
Job descriptions	**Diversity**
Manager	**Executive committee**
Supervisor	

FOR YOUR CONSIDERATION

1. Review Figure 1.2 in the chapter (Basic Management Functions Involve Human Resources Responsibilities).
   a. What additional examples of each management function applicable to human resources might be the responsibility of top-level managers, mid-level managers, and supervisors?
   b. While all of these management functions are important, which do you think are the most important? Why?
2. Review Figure 1.3 in the chapter (External and Internal Influences on Human Resources Activities).
   a. What are additional examples of external and internal influences on each of the basic human resources activities discussed in the chapter?
   b. How might a staff human resources specialist in a multiunit organization assist a property manager with the basic human resources activities noted in Figure 1.3?

CASE STUDY: HUMAN RESOURCES MANAGEMENT IN ACTION

Pedro and Felix were good friends who worked out regularly at the Muscle Man's Gym in their community. By coincidence, Pedro was the Dining Room Manager in an upscale restaurant in a local hotel, and Felix was the Director of Housekeeping at a resort with a similar business volume within easy commuting distance of the community where both men lived. Not surprisingly, their jobs were a frequent topic of conversation after they completed their workouts.

"Felix, we've talked about this so many times before," said Pedro. "It's hard to believe that our employers are in the same basic business, and hire the same types of people, and yet their philosophies about human resources are so different."

"I agree," said Felix. "At my resort the emphasis is on, first, the guests, second on maximizing profit, and third on the employees. We churn through a lot of staff members who start out with a positive attitude about their work and whose morale then goes quickly downhill as they are confronted with things that really shouldn't happen."

"Give me an example," replied Pedro. "Some of your stories are really fascinating."

"Well," responded Felix, "my most recent stories are really the same old thing. We use out-of-date job descriptions to recruit employees and, many times, there's little resemblance between what new staff think they're going to be doing and what they will actually do. Orientation sessions are done whenever there is time, training is done on-the-run, and if the staff members don't learn quickly, top-level managers conclude that it's because they don't care, not because they haven't been properly trained."

"A lot of our supervisors have been there for a long time and really don't care about the organization or their staff members. They sure don't treat staff the way they would want to be treated themselves."

"Performance appraisals focus on what staff members do wrong, not on what they can do right and how they can improve. There is an ongoing emphasis on job rather than on career, and many employees seem to just mark their time until there is a position vacancy at your hotel."

Pedro had heard Felix talk about these issues many times before. His hotel was, in fact, an employer of choice where many persons in the community did want to work and, subsequently, where employee turnover rates were low. In fact, Pedro had long ago agreed to let Felix know if and when the Executive Housekeeper position vacancy at the hotel became available.

Pedro wondered why Felix's employer didn't seem to be concerned about the problem and wasn't doing anything to address the concerns. To Pedro, they seemed like commonsense issues that had relatively simple fixes. He realized, however, that attitudes were much more difficult to change than procedures were to revise.

After thinking about it for a moment, Pedro said, "Felix, things are going to have to change at the resort, aren't they? You've mentioned that business is getting slower. Maybe it's because employees aren't treated well and they, in turn, are less concerned about the guests. We both know that we'll soon have another hotel in town, and the human resources people there will be aggressively searching for new staff members. If things don't change at your property, things will get even worse than they are now."

"You're right about that, Pedro," said Felix. "Our highest-level managers should already know that they are hurting themselves with their current employee practices. The point will really be driven home, and it will happen a lot sooner than they think."

Dimension: Strategic

1. How are the results of strategies used to manage human resources at Felix's hotel affecting the business?
2. What are possible reasons that top-level managers at Felix's property do not recognize the problems that a lack of focus on human resources concerns are creating?

Dimension: Tactical

1. What could Felix, as a department head, do within his own level of responsibility to improve the management of human resources within his department?
2. What might Felix do to alert others at his resort about the human resources problems that he senses?

Dimension: "The Friendly Competition"

1. What can Pedro's hotel do to capitalize on the human resources problems accruing at Felix's resort?
2. What tactics can Pedro's hotel use as it faces competition for its employees from the new hotel that will soon be opening in the community?

INTERNET ACTIVITIES

1. Numerous Web sites provide current information about the world of human resources management. These can be helpful as one studies the topic or works within the hospitality and tourism industry. Check them out!

Hospitality-Related Sites

- Hotel-online.com: *www.hotel-online.com* (Type "labor" in the site's search box).
- Restaurants & Institutions: *www.rimag.com* (Type "human resources" in the site's search box).
- Council of Hotel & Restaurant Trainers (CHART): *www.chart.org* (Click on "resources," and then "research").
- Hospitality Net: *www.hospitalitynet.com* (Type "human resources" in the site's search box).

General HRM-Related Sites

- KnowledgePoint: *www.knowledgepoint.com*
- Workforce Management: *www.workforce.com*

■ Society for Human Resources Management: *www.shrm.org*
■ World Federation of Personnel Management Associations: *www.wfpma.com*
■ Business and Legal Reports: *www.hr.blr.com*

2. The Educational Institute of the American Hotel & Lodging Association (AH&LA) offers a certification program for hospitality human resources professionals. To learn about the program, go to: *www.ei-ahla.org.* When you arrive at the site, click on "Certification," then "Professional Certification Descriptions," and then "Certified Human Resources Professional."

ENDNOTE

1. This section is adopted from: Marilyn Loden, *Implementing Diversity.* Boston, MA: McGraw-Hill, 1996.

CHAPTER TWO

The Legal Environment of Human Resources Management

CHAPTER ## OUTLINE

CHECKLIST ## OF CHAPTER LEARNING OBJECTIVES

As a result of satisfactory completion of this chapter, readers will be able to:

1. Define and describe "employment law," the legislation directly addressing employer–employee relations.

2. Recognize the importance of the government's role in establishing legal requirements affecting HR management.

3. List and briefly describe selected labor-related legislation enacted in the United States by the federal government.

4. Identify the unique issues facing hospitality companies that operate units in countries with legal systems different from that of the United States.

5. Recognize and appreciate the unique HR-related responsibilities of the hospitality unit manager.

Impact on Human Resources Management

In most cases, hospitality unit managers serve as their own on-site legal counsel. As a result, these individuals are looked upon by their employers as well as those reporting to them to make the legally appropriate decisions in a wide variety of work situations. These range from selecting and disciplining employees to preventing harassment in all of its forms, to employee compensation, employee appraisal, termination, and a myriad of other HR concerns.

Hospitality managers responsible for HR management must fully understand that the wrong HR decision can subject their companies (and themselves!) to significant legal liability. Multimillion-dollar jury awards levied to penalize those companies found to be guilty of improper employment practices are common in the United States. As a result, it is critical that those hospitality managers responsible for HR management recognize, and follow, all of the laws that affect their daily HR-related decision making.

Employment Law

1. Define and describe "employment law," the legislation directly addressing employer–employee relations.

Employment law: The body of laws, administrative rulings, and precedents that addresses the legal rights of workers and their employers.

Hospitality managers responsible for HR activities at either the unit or company level must understand the importance of **employment law** to their daily activities and decision making.

Employment law in the United States arose, in most cases, as a result of the demands of workers for better working conditions and the right to organize. Whenever these worker demands were deemed reasonable by a majority of society or the courts, legislation was enacted and became part of the accepted employment practices of the country.

Today, employment laws are still proposed by various segments of society in an effort to ensure fairness in the workplace. The societal view of what actually constitutes fairness in the workplace, however, is often controversial and always changing. For example, some employment-related legislation that would have been considered quite radical in the 1800s is today commonly accepted. For example, the now-accepted concept that the rights of female employees should be equal to those accorded to men was certainly not the norm in the 1800s (recall that it was 1920 before women in the United States gained the right to vote!).

In other cases, the citizens of individual states or cities may vary greatly in their own views of what constitutes fairness in employment. Not surprisingly then, employment laws that vary greatly are likely to be enacted in those states and cities.

As a result, you as a hospitality manager must be keenly aware of the individual employment laws that directly affect you, your operation, and your employees. In this text, the legal consideration of many HR practices will be examined, because the impact of employment laws on those practices is so significant.

In this chapter, you will learn about a variety of employment laws that directly affect the management of a hospitality organization's HR efforts, as well as the management of individual restaurants, hotels, and other hospitality operations. In some cases, the laws directly related to employment in the hospitality industry are general (e.g., the federal laws relating to the rights of workers to unionize). In other cases, the laws related to employment may best be understood in the context of a particular segment of HR management. As a result, laws related specifically to employee recruiting (see Chapter 4), compensation (see Chapter 8), performance appraisal (see Chapter 9), and employee safety and security (see Chapter 10) will be closely examined in those individual chapters.

Hospitality managers, even those working full-time in HR management, are not expected to be attorneys. A lack of understanding about HR-related law, however, can easily produce problems that result in those managers requiring the services of an attorney! Experienced managers know that lawsuits and litigation are expensive and time consuming. Most would also agree that the negative publicity associated with highly publicized lawsuits can be a real detriment to their business (and even their careers). For these reasons, hospitality managers at all levels should take great care to ensure that their actions do not inadvertently create legal issues for themselves and their companies.

The Law and Human Resources: Prevention Is Better Than a Cure

In the medical fields, it is widely agreed that it is better to prevent a serious illness beforehand than to treat it after the fact. For example, doctors would advise that it is preferable to prevent a heart attack through proper diet, exercise, and the elimination of smoking than to perform a bypass operation on a patient after a heart attack has occurred. In the case of prevention, the doctor advises the patient, but it is largely up to the patient to put into practice the physician's recommendations. In a similar vein, it is far better for hospitality managers to understand the laws that relate to HR management than to expose their organizations to the fines and litigation that can result from violations of the law. Therefore, a basic understanding of how employment law is enacted, as well as how current law affects HR management, is absolutely essential.

IT'S THE LAW!

"**D**eb," a food and beverage server, is accused of stealing money from the purse of a peer in the food and beverage department. Management is convinced that Deb took the cash, but she denies it. Can Deb be required by management to submit to a lie detector test? In most cases, the answer is no.

Societal views about what should be legal at work change constantly. In most cases, issues related to the rights of workers and employers seek to balance the best interests of each group. In some cases, the resulting legislation is, at best, a tenuous compromise. For example, the Employee Polygraph Protection Act of 1988 (EPPA) generally prevents employers from using lie detector tests, either for preemployment screening or during the course of employment, with certain exemptions.

Employers generally may not require or request any employee or job applicant to take a lie detector test, or discharge, discipline, or discriminate against an employee or job applicant for refusing to take a test or for exercising other rights under the Act. In addition, employers are required to display the EPPA poster in the workplace for their employees.

Should employers have the right to require employees to take lie detector tests? Since 1988, they have not, nor will they have it *again* unless and until the societal view supports such a right. Regardless of your position on this specific issue, it is very clear that employment laws will continue to directly influence what those in HR management can and cannot do in all segments of the hospitality industry. As a result, an understanding of laws such as this one is critical!*

*The EPPA prohibits most uses of lie detectors by employers on their employees and job applicants. The Employment Standards Administration's Wage and Hour Division (WHD) within the U.S. Department of Labor (DOL) enforces the EPPA. For more information, call 1-866-4USWAGE or go to *www.dol.gov*.

The Government's Role in the Management of Human Resources

2. **Recognize the importance of the government's role in establishing legal requirements affecting HR management.**

If you manage a hospitality business, you have many partners in your HR-related activities and decision making, because the hospitality industry is regulated by a variety of federal, state, and local governmental entities. They enforce the many regulations that spell out the ways you must operate your businesses, as well as how you are required to carry out your HR efforts.

Hospitality managers interact with governmental entities in a variety of different ways, and they must observe the procedures and regulations established by the government. Managers must fill out forms and paperwork, obtain operating licenses, maintain their property to specified codes and standards, provide a safe working environment, and, when required, even open their facilities for periodic inspections.

It should come as no surprise that a society, working through its governmental structures, will implement and often revise its rules of employee–employer conduct and responsibility. Society is in a constant state of change, and that has significant implications for those working in business, especially in the hospitality industry. To illustrate, consider the hospitality industry in the United States in 1850. At that time, you would certainly not find a law requiring a specific number of automobile parking spaces to be designated for a restaurant's or hotel's disabled workers.

The world of the 1850s contained neither the automobile nor (importantly) the inclination of society to grant special parking privileges to those who were disabled. In today's society, we have both. What changed? First, the physical world changed. We now have automobiles and the necessity of parking them. More significant, however, is the fact that society's view of how disabled individuals should be treated has changed. Parking ordinances today require designated "Disabled" parking spaces, which are generally located close to the main entrances of buildings to ensure easy access. Not only is it good business to employ those with disabilities, but current laws mandate that the hospitality manager must do so. In this case, employment of the disabled (and parking requirements) grew out of a law created by the federal government, the Americans with Disabilities Act (ADA). It is mentioned here to illustrate that laws evolve just as society evolves. It is important to know current law, but it is just as important to understand that you must keep abreast of changes in the law to ensure that facilities you operate are managed legally.

Just as the federal government has played and will continue to play an important regulatory role in the hospitality industry, so too do the various state governments. It is important to understand that the states serve both complementary and distinct regulatory roles. The roles are complementary in that they support and amplify efforts undertaken at the federal level, but they are distinct in that they regulate some areas in which they have sole responsibility.

The administrative structure or specific entity name will vary by state, but the regulatory process will be similar. It is also important to note that state and locally passed employment law and regulations may affect the actions of hospitality managers even more often than will federal regulations. Codes and ordinances established at the state or local level can often be very strict and may be strictly enforced. The penalties for violating these laws can be just as severe as those at the federal level.

Generally, each state regulates significant parts of the employee–employer relationship occurring within its borders. Items such as worker-related **unemployment compensation** benefits, worker safety issues, and at-work injury compensation fall to the state entity charged with regulating the workplace. In addition, in most states, this entity will also be responsible for areas such as employment assistance programs for both employees and employers.

Unemployment compensation: A benefit paid to an employee who involuntarily loses his or her employment without just cause.

Workers' compensation: A benefit paid to an employee who suffers a work-related injury or illness.

Garnish (ment): A court-ordered method of debt collection in which a portion of a worker's income is paid directly to one or more of that worker's creditors.

Regardless of the state in which you will be working, it will be important to know and follow your state's regulations related to workplace safety and for properly documenting and reporting any work-related injuries. In each state, worker safety and **workers' compensation** will usually be monitored by a workers' compensation agency, commission, or subdivision of the employment security agency.

In most communities, some agency of the court system (sometimes called a "Friend" of the court) will have the responsibility of assisting creditors in securing payment for legally owed debts. These debts can include a variety of court-ordered payments, such as child support payments. In cases such as these, a hospitality manager can be ordered by the court to **garnish** an employee's wages.

The importance to the hospitality industry of local and city governments can be illustrated by examining the actions of the Santa Fe, New Mexico city council. In 2006, the city of Santa Fe initiated the nation's highest minimum wage rate: a city-wide mandated $9.50 per hour. Santa Fe's wage covers all businesses with 25 or more employees. The city's minimum wage is scheduled to rise to $10.50 per hour in 2008, pending another vote by the same city council that overwhelmingly supported the increase to $9.50. By contrast, the federal and New Mexico minimum wages are both lower. The city has had the United States' highest minimum wage since establishing the rate at $8.50 per hour in 2004. Regardless of the local hospitality industry's initial support of, or opposition to, this specific piece of employment legislation, its impact on the Santa Fe hospitality industry is clearly significant.

As you have now learned, employment laws in the United States may be enacted at the federal, state, or local levels. At each of these levels, the laws reflect the desires of citizens and, ultimately, their elected officials and courts. Most hospitality professionals would agree that all workers are best protected when employers, employees, and governmental entities work together to protect wages, benefits, pensions, safety, and health. In most cases, that is the societal intent when passing and enforcing employment-related legislation.

Today, there are literally hundreds of thousands of laws that affect the operation of a hospitality property, and the number increases annually. These laws are implemented and enforced by a variety of governmental entities. In the next portions of this chapter, you will learn about some of the most historically significant of these many employment rules and regulations.

A Manager's Review of Significant Employment Legislation

3. List and briefly describe selected labor-related legislation enacted in the United States by the federal government.

In the view of many historians, the beginnings of the most significant employment legislation passed at the federal level can be traced largely to the New Deal era of the 1930s. However, several important pieces of legislation were passed in the very

Labor union: An organization that acts on behalf of its members to negotiate with management about the wages, hours, and other terms and conditions of the membership's employment.

Interstate commerce: Commercial trading or the transportation of persons or property between or among states.

early 1900s. One of the most noteworthy was the Clayton Act of 1914, which legitimized and protected workers' rights to join **labor unions.** Then, in 1926, Congress passed the Railway Labor Act (RLA), requiring employers to bargain collectively and prohibiting discrimination against unions. It applied originally to interstate railroads but, in 1936, it was amended to include airlines engaged in **interstate commerce.** The Norris-LaGuardia Act, passed in 1932, was the first in a series of laws passed by Congress in the 1930s that gave federal sanction to the right of labor unions to organize and strike.

Perhaps the most important labor legislation of the 1930s was the National Labor Relations Act (NLRA) of 1935, more popularly known as the Wagner Act, after its sponsor, Sen. Robert F. Wagner (NY-D). The NLRA was applicable to all firms and employees engaging in activities affecting interstate commerce. The law's impact included coverage of hotel and restaurant workers, and they and most other workers were guaranteed the right to organize and join labor movements, to choose representatives and bargain collectively, and to strike. It also expressly prohibited employers from:

- Interfering with the formation of a union
- Restraining employees from exercising their right to join a union
- Imposing any special conditions on employment that would discourage union membership
- Discharging or discriminating against employees who reported unfair labor practices
- Refusing to bargain in good faith with legitimate union leadership

The NLRA spurred the growth of unions, whose total membership grew from 3,584,000 members in 1935 to 10,201,000 by 1941 (the eve of World War II).

THE CIVIL RIGHTS ACT OF 1964 (TITLE VII)

Perhaps the single most significant piece of legislation affecting the workplace was passed in the aftermath of a true American tragedy. The assassination of John F. Kennedy in November 1963 resulted in the Lyndon Baines Johnson presidency. On November 27, 1963, addressing the Congress and the nation for the first time as president, Johnson called for passage of a wide-sweeping civil rights bill as a monument to the fallen Kennedy. "Let us continue," he said, promising that "the ideas and the ideals which [Kennedy] so nobly represented must and will be translated into effective action." In June 1964, Congress passed the Civil Rights Act of 1964, the most important piece of civil rights legislation in the nation's history and, on July 2, 1964, President Johnson signed it into law.

Title VII: The specific section of the Civil Rights Act of 1964 that outlaws discrimination in employment in any business on the basis of race, color, religion, sex, or national origin.

This Civil Rights Act of 1964 contains several sections, but for hospitality employers, the most important of these is **Title VII.** Title VII of the Civil Rights Act of 1964 outlaws discrimination in employment in any business on the basis of race, color, religion, sex, or national origin. Title VII also prohibits retaliation against employees who oppose such unlawful discrimination.

Human Resources Management:
CURRENT EVENTS 2.1

THE HOTEL AND RESTAURANT UNION

Hospitality workers in the United States have a long history of unionization. Although the hospitality industry as a whole is not, nor has it ever been, heavily unionized, the Hotel Employees and Restaurant Employees Union (HERE), a U.S. labor union representing workers of the hospitality industry, first formed in 1891.

In 2004, HERE merged with the Union of Needletrades, Industrial, and Textile Employees (UNITE) to form UNITE HERE. Major employers contracted in this union include several large casinos (e.g., Harrah's, Caesars, and Wynn Resorts), hotels (e.g., Hilton, Hyatt, and Starwood), and Walt Disney World. HERE and later UNITE HERE were affiliated with the AFL-CIO until September 2005, when the General Executive Board of UNITE HERE voted to leave the AFL-CIO and join with the Change to Win Coalition.

Congress passed the Fair Labor Standards Act (FLSA) in 1938. The main objective of this act was to eliminate "labor conditions detrimental to the maintenance of the minimum standards of living necessary for health, efficiency and well-being of worker." The act established maximum working hours of 44 per week for the first year, 42 for the second, and 40 thereafter. Minimum wages of 25 cents per hour were established for the first year, 30 cents for the second, and 40 cents over a period of the next six years. Interestingly, as of July, 2009, employers must pay covered employees a minimum wage of not less than $7.25 per hour. Hospitality employers may pay employees on a piece-rate basis and, under specific conditions, may consider tips as part of wages (see Chapter 8).

The Fair Labor Standards Act also prohibited child labor in all industries engaged in producing goods in interstate commerce. The act set the minimum age at 14 for employment outside of school hours in nonmanufacturing jobs, at 16 for employment during school hours, and at 18 for hazardous occupations.

Equal Employment Opportunity Commission (EEOC): The entity within the federal government assigned to enforcing the provisions of Title VII of the Civil Rights Act of 1964.

In 1972, the passage of the Equal Employment Opportunity Act, a revision to the Civil Rights Act of 1964, resulted in the formation of the **Equal Employment Opportunity Commission (EEOC).** The EEOC enforces the antidiscrimination provisions of Title VII. The EEOC investigates, mediates, and sometimes even files lawsuits on behalf of employees. Businesses that are found to have discriminated can be ordered to compensate the employee(s) for their damages in the form of lost wages, attorney fees, and other expenses. Title VII also provides that individuals can sue their employers on their own. In most cases, an individual must file a complaint of discrimination with the EEOC within 180 days of learning of the discrimination or lose the right to file a lawsuit.

The following general areas fall under the enforcement jurisdiction of the EEOC:

- Race/color discrimination
- Age discrimination
- National origin discrimination
- Pregnancy discrimination
- Religious discrimination
- Portions of the Americans with Disabilities Act
- Sexual harassment

The impact of the EEOC on the daily tasks of the hospitality manager is clear. Consider, for example, the hotel manager who seeks to schedule a Christian worker on Christmas Day when, of course, the hotel is open. The question that may arise is whether the needs of the manager, who must staff the hotel, should take precedence over those of the worker, who desires a day off on the basis of his or her religious convictions.

Title VII prohibits employers from discriminating against individuals because of their religious beliefs when hiring and firing. It also requires employers to, when possible, accommodate the religious practices of an employee or prospective employee, unless doing so would create an undue hardship on the employer. Flexible scheduling, voluntary substitutions or swaps, job reassignments, and lateral transfers are examples of ways to accommodate an employee's religious beliefs. The question of whether a manager could reasonably accommodate the request of a Christian worker to be off on Christmas Day is complex. The point to be remembered, however, is that managers are not free to act in any manner they desire. The federal government, through the requirements of the EEOC, plays an important role in the HR-related actions of management. Title VII and additional laws enforced by the EEOC are listed in Figure 2.1.

In the late 1970s, courts began holding that **sexual harassment** is also prohibited under the Act, and in 1986, the Supreme Court held in a lawsuit (*Meritor Savings Bank v. Vinson*, 477 U.S. 57 (1986)) that sexual harassment is sex discrimination, and

Sexual Harassment: Unwelcome sexual advances, requests for sexual favors, and other verbal or physical conduct of a sexual nature.

Laws Enforced by the Equal Employment Opportunity Commission

- Title VII of the Civil Rights Act
- Equal Pay Act of 1963
- Age Discrimination in Employment Act of 1967 (ADEA)
- Rehabilitation Act of 1973, Sections 501 and 505
- Titles I and V of the Americans with Disabilities Act of 1990 (ADA)
- Civil Rights Act of 1991

FIGURE 2.1: Laws Enforced by the Equal Employment Opportunity Commission

thus is prohibited by Title VII (more detail about this human resource issue is provided in Chapter 10).

Title VII has since been supplemented with legislation prohibiting pregnancy, age, and disability discrimination (see the Americans with Disabilities Act of 1990). Title VII only applies to employers who employ 15 or more employees for more than 19 weeks in the current or preceding calendar year.

The Civil Rights Act of 1964 makes it illegal for employers to discriminate in hiring and in setting the terms and conditions of employment. Labor unions are also prohibited from basing membership or union classifications on race, color, religion, sex, or national origin. The law also is clear in its prohibition of employers retaliating against employees or potential employees who file charges of discrimination against them, refuse to comply with a discriminatory policy, or participate in an investigation of discrimination charges against the employer.

Affirmative action: A federally mandated requirement that employers who meet certain criteria must actively seek to fairly employ recognized classes of workers. (Some state and local legislatures have also enacted affirmative action requirements.)

In later amendments, the Civil Rights Act was expanded to include **affirmative action** requirements. Affirmative action constitutes a good-faith effort by employees to address past and/or present discrimination through a variety of specific, results-oriented procedures. This is a step beyond an equal opportunity law such as Title VII that simply bans discriminatory practices. State and local governments, federal government agencies, and federal contractors and subcontractors with contracts of $50,000 or more, including colleges and universities, are required by federal law to implement affirmative action programs. For those foodservice and hotel managers working in colleges, universities, hospitals, and many other settings, affirmative action plans are required.

Hospitality employers can utilize a variety of techniques for implementing their affirmative action plans. These include:

1. Active recruiting to expand the pool of candidates for job openings
2. Revising selection tools and criteria to ensure their relevance to job performance
3. Establishing goals and timetables for hiring underrepresented groups

Bona fide occupational qualification (BFOQ): A specific job requirement for a particular position that is reasonably necessary to the normal operation of a business, and thus allowing discrimination against a protected class (e.g., choosing a male model when photographing an advertisement for beard trimmers).

Originally, affirmative action activities were intended to correct discrimination in the hiring and promotion of African Americans and other people of color. Now, affirmative action protections are being applied to women, and some government jurisdictions have extended affirmative action provisions to older people, the disabled, and Vietnam-era veterans. The goal of most affirmative action programs is to broaden the pool of candidates and encourage hiring based on sound, job-related criteria. The intended result is a workforce with greater diversity and potential for all.

In some very limited cases, Title VII permits a **bona fide occupational qualification (BFOQ)** to be used to discriminate among workers.

In a rather famous case, Hooters Restaurants came under fire after the EEOC made allegations that it had violated Title VII of the Civil Rights Act by discriminating against men. In 1992, seven men argued that Hooters discriminated against them when it refused to hire them as wait staff. It was true that Hooter's chose to hire only female servers, bartenders, and hosts. As a defense, Hooters attempted to use female sexuality as a BFOQ. Hooter's, however, markets itself primarily as a restaurant. In this case, the courts looked at the essential nature of the business. Hooters portrays itself to the public as a restaurant; therefore, Hooter's BFOQ did not hold up in court, because being female is not a requirement for the job of serving food. It is important to understand that the government, through the EEOC, and not an individual hospitality business, can authorize the legal use of a BFOQ.

In addition to the Civil Rights Act of 1964, many states also have their own civil rights laws that prohibit discrimination. Sometimes, state laws are more inclusive than the Civil Rights Act, in that they expand protection to workers or employment candidates in categories not covered under the federal law (such as age, marital status, sexual orientation, and certain types of physical or mental disabilities). State civil rights laws may also have stricter penalties for violations, including fines and/or jail time. For example, it is illegal in California for an employer to discriminate against an employee because of that employee's sexual orientation or perceived sexual orientation.

The Civil Rights Act of 1964 does not specifically prohibit this type of discrimination. It is important to remember that HR managers working in the hospitality industry must be aware of all civil rights laws in effect in the location where they are working. While a state or local law is not permitted to take away employee rights granted at the federal level, they are allowed to add to them. Thus, as in the California example, an employee group not protected by federal law may be granted protection by a more favorable (to the employee) local law.

It is important for hospitality managers to understand that, in the general case, federal (as well as many state and local) laws are intended to define and prevent inappropriate **disparate treatment** of employees based on a non-job-related characteristic.

Disparate treatment is a basic concept in employment discrimination cases. Lawyers classify employment discrimination cases as either disparate treatment cases or **disparate (adverse) impact** cases.

In a disparate treatment case, the employee's claim is that the employer treated him or her differently than other employees who were in a similar situation. For example, both Sara and Randy are late for work one day, and the employer fires Sara but does not fire Randy. If the reason Sara was fired is that she is female, then the employer has engaged in disparate treatment because of sex, which would be a violation of Title VII. If, however, Sara had been late ten times in the last ten days, and Randy had not previously been late despite having worked for the company for five years, the termination (because it was job related) would be lawful.

In a disparate impact case, the claim is that the employer has a practice that has a much bigger impact on one group than on another. For example, the employer won't hire janitors unless they are high school graduates. This might have a much bigger impact on selected minority group candidates as a whole than on whites as a whole and may not truly be a job-related requirement. Disparate impact policies are also illegal and point to the importance of HR managers carefully reviewing all employment policies to ensure they do not inadvertently lead to charges of disparate treatment or disparate impact.

Disparate treatment: The claim that, in the same situation, one employee was treated differently than other employees.

Disparate (adverse) impact: The claim that an employer's action, though not intentionally discriminatory, still results in unlawful discrimination. Also known as *adverse impact*.

Human Resources MANAGEMENT ISSUES (2.1)

" I'm sorry, Danielle," said Jetta Goh, the owner and manager of the Golden Dragon restaurant. Ms. Goh had placed a classified ad for a server in the employment section of the local newspaper. The response was good, and Danielle Hidalgo, the daughter of a Mexican citizen and an American citizen who was born and raised in the United States, had applied, as well as many others. Danielle was an excellent server with an outstanding work history. She was learning, via the telephone, however, that another candidate of the same ethnic background as Ms. Goh had been selected for the job.

Ms. Goh continued: "You know, Danielle, people come to the Golden Dragon for an Asian dining experience; they expect Asian servers. That's why I only hire a certain type person for front of the house positions, but there could be a spot for you in the back of the house. Are you interested?"

1. Do you think Ms. Goh has violated the Civil Rights Act of 1964?
2. Would your opinion change if Ms. Goh maintained that she did not discriminate because of race because she had, in the past, hired Chinese, Korean, Hmong, and Vietnamese workers as servers?
3. As an HR specialist in hospitality, what would you advise Ms. Goh to do in the future? What would you advise Ms. Hidalgo to do now?

THE AGE DISCRIMINATION IN EMPLOYMENT ACT OF 1967

The Age Discrimination in Employment Act of 1967 (ADEA) was initially passed to prevent the widespread practice (at that time) of requiring employees to retire at age 65. As worker life spans increased, it made little sense for employees to be forced to retire when many could and wanted to remain on the job. The ADEA originally gave protected-group status to those workers between the ages of 39 and 65. Since 1967, the act has been amended twice; once in 1978, when the mandatory retirement age was raised to 70, and then again in 1986, when the mandatory retirement age was removed altogether.

The ADEA now protects individuals who are 40 years of age or older from employment discrimination based on age. The ADEA's protections apply to both employees and job applicants. Under the ADEA, it is unlawful to discriminate against people because of their age, with respect to any term, condition, or privilege of employment, including hiring, firing, promotion, layoff, compensation, benefits, job assignments, and training. It is also unlawful to retaliate against an individual for opposing employment practices that discriminate based on age or for filing an age discrimination charge, testifying, or participating in any way in an investigation, proceeding, or litigation under the ADEA.

In 1986, an important amendment to the Age Discrimination in Employment Act eliminated the mandatory retirement age. *Courtesy PhotoDisc/Getty Images*

The ADEA makes it unlawful to include age preferences, limitations, or specifications in job notices or advertisements. As a narrow exception to that general rule, a job notice or advertisement may specify an age limit in the rare circumstances where age is shown to be a bona fide occupational qualification (BFOQ) reasonably necessary to the operation of the business. For example, airline pilots may still be required to retire at a certain age because of evidence that increasing age causes a decline in piloting abilities. Customer preference is not a rationale that will result in the granting of a BFOQ by the EEOC. Thus, for example, a male bar owner who determines that his customers like young (and attractive) servers better than older ones would not be allowed to hire only young servers. He would also not be allowed to terminate servers as they became older, even if the bar owner honestly believed it would be good for business.

In fact, the ADEA does not specifically prohibit an employer from asking an applicant's age or date of birth. In the hospitality industry, for example, it may be legally necessary to establish an applicant's age prior to hiring him or her to serve alcohol or to operate certain types of potentially dangerous kitchen equipment. It is important to understand, however, that because such inquiries may deter older workers from applying for employment or may otherwise indicate possible intent to discriminate based on age, requests for age information will be closely scrutinized by the EEOC to make sure that the inquiry was made for a lawful purpose, rather than for a prohibited purpose.

The Older Workers Benefit Protection Act of 1990 (OWBPA) amended the ADEA to specifically prohibit employers from denying benefits to older employees. This law was passed to prevent the practice of reducing employment benefits such as medical insurance based on an employee's age. An employer may reduce benefits based on age only if the cost of providing the reduced benefits to older workers is the same as the cost of providing benefits to younger workers. The ADEA applies to employers with 20 or more employees, including state and local governments. It also applies to employment agencies, labor organizations, and the federal government.

THE PREGNANCY DISCRIMINATION ACT OF 1978

The Pregnancy Discrimination Act of 1978 is actually an amendment to Title VII of the Civil Rights Act of 1964. As a result, discrimination on the basis of pregnancy, childbirth, or related medical conditions now constitutes unlawful sex discrimination under Title VII. Women affected by pregnancy or related conditions must be treated in the same way as other applicants or employees with similar abilities or limitations. An employer cannot refuse to hire a woman because of her pregnancy-related condition as long as she is able to perform the major functions of her job. Also, an employer cannot refuse to hire her because of prejudices against pregnant workers or the prejudices of coworkers, clients, or customers.

An employer may not single out pregnancy-related conditions for special procedures to determine an employee's ability to work. However, an employer can use any legal procedure utilized to consider other employees' abilities to work. For example, if an employer requires employees to submit a doctor's statement concerning their inability to work before granting leave or paying sick benefits, the employer may require employees affected by pregnancy-related conditions to submit the same type of statements.

Pregnant employees must be permitted to work as long as they are able to perform their jobs. If an employee has been absent from work as a result of a pregnancy-related condition and recovers, her employer may not require her to remain on leave until the baby's birth. An employer may not prohibit an employee from returning to work for a predetermined length of time after childbirth, nor can a company refuse to allow a "reasonable" amount of unpaid leave time after a baby's birth. Although the law did not specifically establish a definition for "reasonable" time off after a baby's birth, many organizations consider six weeks to be reasonable, and that time frame has been supported by the EEOC. Pregnancy leave does not have to be paid leave, unless the company has a policy of paying employees who are on medical leave. If it does, then the law requires that the pregnant employee be treated identically to an employee on leave for non-pregnancy-related medical reasons.

Employers must hold open a job for a pregnancy-related absence the same length of time that jobs are held open for employees on sick or disability leave. Any health insurance provided by an employer must cover expenses for pregnancy-related conditions on the same basis as costs for other medical conditions. Employers must also provide the same level of health benefits for spouses of male employees as they do for spouses of female staff members.

The Pregnancy Discrimination Act also requires that pregnancy-related benefits cannot be limited to married employees. If an employer provides any benefits to workers on leave, the employer must provide the same benefits for those on leave for pregnancy-related conditions. In summary, hospitality organizations, as well as any other employer, must treat an employee's pregnancy exactly the same as other temporarily disabled employees for accrual and crediting of seniority, vacation calculation, pay increases, and temporary disability benefits. It is also important to understand that where no benefits are offered to employees, the employer is not required by this law to provide benefits for those who are or become pregnant. The law simply states that, where employee benefits are *already* offered, they must be uniformly offered to those employees who are or become pregnant.

Human Resources MANAGEMENT ISSUES (2.2)

"I don't get it," said Tonya Zollars, the new HR Director for Clubs International, a company that specialized in the operation of golf, city, and other private clubs. Tonya had just finished reading the annual evaluation for Naomi Yip, the sous chef at one of the private city clubs managed by her company. Naomi had been with the organization for five years and was considered one of the company's best and brightest culinary artists. Every evaluation she had received since joining the company was excellent. However, her current supervisor did not, at the end of the evaluation, check the box "Ready for Promotion" that each of her previous supervising chefs had checked.

"Well," said Thomas Hayhoe, the executive chef who completed the evaluation, "You know Naomi's gonna have a baby. She's due in five months. I like Naomi a lot, but maybe it would be better for her right now not to take on the added responsibilities a promotion would require. She told me she's looking forward to spending as much time as possible with her baby, and you know as well as I do that at the next level, 60-plus hours weekly for the executive chef's job are the norm around here."

Clubs International has just been awarded the contract to operate a new and lucrative account, the Hawk Hollow Golf Club. Assume you were advising the company's vice president of operations about the new executive chef's position there.

1. Should Tonya recommend offering Naomi the promotion to executive chef at Hawk Hollow?
2. Based on Chef Hayhoe's evaluation, what would you advise Tonya to say if her own boss opposed her recommendation?
3. Do you feel it would be appropriate to inform the new client (Hawk Hollow) of Naomi's condition so their input could be considered?

THE WORKER ADJUSTMENT AND RETRAINING NOTIFICATION (WARN) ACT OF 1989

The Worker Adjustment and Retraining Notification Act (WARN) is sometimes called the Plant Closing Act. It was enacted in August 1988 and became effective in February 1989. WARN offers protection to workers by requiring employers to provide notice 60 days in advance of the closing of an employment site or in the event of a mass layoff. This notice must be provided either directly to the affected workers or their representatives (e.g., a labor union) and to the appropriate unit of local government. One intent of the law is to allow workers to seek alternative employment options when their employer is committed to closing their employment sites. In most cases, employers are covered by WARN if they have 100 or more employees, not counting employees who have worked less than 6 months in the last 12 months, and exclusive of employees who work an average of less than 20 hours per week. Private, for-profit employers and private, nonprofit employers are covered. Employees entitled to notice under WARN include hourly and salaried workers, as well as managerial and supervisory employees. Business partners such as vendors and suppliers, however, are not entitled to notice under the Act.

An employer must give notice if an employment site will be shut down, and the shutdown will result in an employment loss for 50 or more employees during any 30-day period. In the hospitality industry, many restaurants are too small to be covered by WARN. In many cases, limited-service hotels also employ too few workers to be covered. An exception, however, is common in the case of the sale of larger full-service hotels. Often, the sale will result in partial or full closure of a property to rebrand the hotel with a new **franchisor.** These situations are covered by the WARN Act.

Franchisor: The business entity that has sold or granted a franchise.

When a covered property is sold, the following requirements apply:

1. In each situation, either the buyer or the seller is, at all times, the employer responsible for giving notice.
2. If the sale by a covered employer results in a covered employment site closing or a mass layoff, employees must receive at least 60 days' notice.
3. The seller is responsible for providing notice of any covered employment sites closing or a mass layoff that occurs up to and including the date/time of the sale.
4. The buyer is responsible for providing notice of any covered employment sites closing or a mass layoff that occurs after the date/time of the sale.
5. No notice is required if the sale does not result in a covered employment site closing or a mass layoff.
6. Employees of the seller, on the date of the sale, become, for purposes of WARN, employees of the buyer immediately upon completion of the sale. This provision preserves the notice rights of the employees of a business that has been sold.

"Employment loss" as defined by the WARN Act includes:

1. Termination, other than a discharge for cause, voluntary departure, or retirement
2. A layoff exceeding six months
3. A reduction in an employee's hours of work of more than 50 percent in each month of any six-month period

An employee who refuses a transfer to a different employment site within reasonable commuting distance is not considered to have experienced an employment loss. An employee who accepts a transfer outside this distance within 30 days after it is offered or within 30 days after the employment site closing or mass layoff also is not considered to have experienced an employment loss.

There are some allowable exceptions to the 60-day notification rule. These are:

1. *Faltering company.* This exception covers situations where a company has sought new capital or business contracts to stay open and where giving notice would ruin the opportunity to get the new capital or business. This applies only to property closings.
2. *Unforeseeable business circumstances.* This exception applies to closings and layoffs that are caused by business circumstances that were not reasonably foreseeable at the time notice would otherwise have been required.
3. *Natural disaster.* This applies where a closing or layoff is the direct result of a natural disaster, such as a flood, earthquake, drought, or storm (e.g., New Orleans hotels during Hurricane Katrina in 2005).

If an employer provides less than 60 days' advance notice of a closing or layoff and relies on one of these three exceptions, the employer bears the burden of proof that the conditions for the exception have been met. The employer also must give as much notice as practicable. An employer who violates the WARN provisions by ordering an employment site closing or a mass layoff without providing appropriate notice is liable to each affected employee for an amount including back pay and benefits for the period of violation (up to 60 days).

THE AMERICANS WITH DISABILITIES ACT (ADA) OF 1990

In July 1990, the Americans with Disabilities Act (ADA) was enacted. It now applies to those private employers, state and local governments, employment agencies, and labor unions employing 15 or more workers. The ADA prohibits discrimination against people with disabilities in the areas of public accommodations, transportation, telecommunications, and employment. The ADA is a five-part piece of legislation, but Title I of the Act focuses primarily on employment.

Three different groups of individuals are protected under the ADA:

1. An individual with a physical or mental impairment that substantially limits a major life activity. Some examples of what constitutes a "major life activity" under the Act are seeing, hearing, talking, walking, reading, learning, breathing, taking care of oneself, lifting, sitting, and standing.
2. A person who has a record of a disability
3. A person who is "regarded as" having a disability

Reasonable accommodation: Any modification or adjustment to a job or the work environment that will enable a qualified applicant or employee with a disability to participate in the application process or to perform the job's essential functions.

Employers cannot reduce an employee's pay simply because he or she is disabled, nor can they refuse to hire a disabled candidate if, with **reasonable accommodation,** it is possible for the candidate to perform the job.

Not surprisingly, one of the significant issues regarding ADA is the practical application of the word *reasonable*, when considering how to best accommodate a disabled job candidate or employee. Therefore, a basic understanding of the U.S. court system's continuous defining and refining of the term is critical for hospitality managers.

For example, the courts have held that restructuring a job to shift a minor (nonessential) responsibility for a task from a disabled to a nondisabled employee is a reasonable accommodation. In addition, allowing disabled workers extra unpaid leave when it does not present a hardship to the business is considered a reasonable accommodation. It is important to note, however, that an employer is not required to provide a disabled worker with more paid leave than the employer provides its nondisabled workers.

Modified or part-time schedules are considered reasonable accommodations when they do not cause the employer undue hardship. A modified schedule may involve adjusting arrival or departure times, providing periodic breaks, altering when certain job tasks are performed, allowing an employee to use accrued paid leave, or providing additional unpaid leave.

Certain things are not considered reasonable accommodations and are, therefore, not required. For example, an employer does not have to eliminate a primary job responsibility to accommodate a disabled employee. In addition, an employer is not required to lower productivity standards that are applied to all employees, but the employer may be required to provide reasonable accommodation to enable an employee with a disability to meet the productivity standard. An employer is also not required to provide a disabled worker with personal-use items such as a prosthetic limb, a wheelchair, eyeglasses, hearing aids, or similar devices. In other words, an employer is not required to make a reasonable accommodation when that accommodation would cause an undue hardship on the employer.

Generally speaking, an undue hardship occurs when the expense of accommodating the worker is excessive, or when it would disrupt the natural work environment. Unfortunately, the law in this area is vague. Therefore, any employer who maintains that accommodating a worker with a disability would impose an undue hardship should be prepared to document such an assertion. After investigation, the EEOC will ultimately issue a "right to sue" letter to an employee if it feels an employer is in violation of the ADA.

An employee's request for a reasonable accommodation or the granting of a reasonable accommodation is typically a matter to be discussed only between the employer and the employee. An employer may not disclose that a disabled employee is receiving a reasonable accommodation, because this usually amounts to a disclosure that the individual has a disability. (The ADA specifically prohibits the disclosure of an employee's medical information except in very limited situations, which never includes disclosure to coworkers.)

As a hospitality employer, you may be faced with questions from your nondisabled employees about why a coworker is receiving what is perceived as different or special treatment. The best response to questions of this type is to emphasize that all employees' special needs are accommodated when it is possible to do so. You may also find it helpful to point out that many of the workplace issues encountered by employees are personal and that, in these circumstances, it is your company's policy to respect employee privacy. You may be able to make this point even more effectively by reassuring the employee asking the question that his or her privacy would similarly be respected if it was necessary for him or her to request some type of workplace change for strictly personal reasons. There may not be any pressure from the employer to do so, but employees with a disability may voluntarily choose to disclose to coworkers that they are receiving a reasonable accommodation.

Even with the passage of the ADA, an employer does not have to hire a disabled applicant who is not qualified to do a job. The employer can still select the most qualified candidate, provided that no applicant was eliminated from consideration because of a qualified disability.

Although the law in this area is changing rapidly, the following conditions currently meet the criteria for a qualified disability and are protected under the ADA:

- AIDS
- Cancer
- Cerebral palsy
- Tuberculosis
- Heart disease
- Hearing or visual impairments
- Alcoholism

Conditions that are not currently covered under the ADA include:

- Kleptomania
- Disorders caused by the use of illegal drugs
- Compulsive gambling
- Sexual behavior disorders

Employers are required to post notices of the ADA and its provisions in a location where they can be seen by all employees. One reason is that the ADA has changed the way employers may select employees. Questions on job applications and during interviews that cannot be asked include:

1. Have you ever been hospitalized?
2. Are you taking prescription drugs?
3. Have you ever been treated for drug addiction or alcoholism?
4. Have you ever filed a workers' compensation insurance claim?
5. Do you have any physical defects, disabilities, or impairments that may affect your performance in the position for which you are applying?

One very important ADA provision of which foodservice employers should be aware concerns employees and job applicants who have infectious and communicable diseases. Each year, the U.S. Secretary of Health and Human Services publishes a list of communicable diseases that, if spread through the handling of food, could put a foodservice operation's guests at risk. Employers have the right not to assign or hire an individual carrying one of the identified diseases to a position that involves the handling of food, but only if there is no reasonable accommodation that could be made to eliminate such a risk.

Accommodating Disabled Employees

To reduce the risk of an ADA noncompliance charge related to reasonable accommodation, the following steps can be of great assistance.

Steps for ADA Reasonable Accommodation

1. Can the applicant perform the essential functions of the job with or without reasonable accommodation? (You can ask the applicant this question.)

   If "no," then the applicant is not qualified and is not protected by the ADA.
   If "yes," then go to question 2.

2. Is the necessary accommodation reasonable? To answer this question, ask yourself the following: Will this accommodation create an undue financial or administrative hardship on the business?

   If "yes," you do not have to provide unreasonable accommodations.
   If "no," then go to question 3.

3. Will this accommodation or the hiring of the person with the disability create a direct threat to the health or safety of other employees or guests in the workplace?

   If "yes," you are not required to make the accommodation and have fulfilled your obligation under the ADA.

THE FAMILY MEDICAL LEAVE ACT OF 1993

The Family and Medical Leave Act (FMLA) was enacted in February 1993. This law allows an employee to take unpaid leave due to pregnancy, illness, or to care for a sick family member. It was one of the first major bills signed by President Bill Clinton in his initial term. Prior family leave bills had either failed in Congress or been vetoed by the previous President George H. W. Bush. Understanding the FMLA is important for at least two reasons: (1) the actual content and impact of the law; and (2) the history of the FMLA provides managers with a recent (and continuing) example of how employment laws in the United States are proposed, debated in the public arena, and, in many cases, enacted in some form or another.

Currently, the FMLA requires employers of 50 or more employees (and all public agencies) to provide up to 12 weeks of unpaid, job-protected leave to eligible employees for the birth and care of a child, for placement with the employee of a child for adoption or foster care, or for the serious illness of the employee or an immediate family member. For purposes of the FMLA, an immediate family member is defined as a spouse, child, or parent of the employee.

Employees may elect (and employers can require) that any accumulated paid leave due to employees (e.g., paid vacation time or paid personal days off) be used before the employee begins unpaid leave. In all cases, employees are required under the FMLA to make a reasonable effort to schedule any medical treatment so as not to disrupt their employer's business. They must also, when possible, give their employer 30 days' notice of their intent to take FMLA-mandated time off.

Under the FMLA, employers can require that a request for leave be certified as necessary by the healthcare provider of the eligible employee or of the child, spouse, or parent of the employee, as appropriate. When the employer requests it, the employee is required to provide, in a timely manner, a copy of the certification to the employer.

In most cases (there are some very limited exceptions for extremely critical or key positions), an employer must allow the employee to return to the same position he or she held when the leave commenced, to an equivalent position, or to one virtually identical to the employee's former position in terms of pay and working conditions, including status and benefits. Also, the fact that the employee took the leave may not be held against the employee in other ways, including when determining pay increases or during the employee's performance reviews.

Perhaps it is not surprising that the FMLA has proved popular with employees but less popular with employers. According to recent data from the U.S. Department of Labor, 42 percent of workers who have taken unpaid time off under the FMLA have done so to care for their own serious illness; 26 percent have taken time off to care for a new child or for maternity disability reasons; 13 percent have taken time off to care for a seriously ill parent; 12 percent have taken time off to care for a seriously ill child; and 6 percent have taken time off to care for a seriously ill spouse. In some cases, employers have maintained that employees have abused the law by requesting time off for frivolous reasons or in ways that are disruptive to their businesses.

It is highly likely that changes to the current FMLA will be proposed or enacted. The language of the FMLA was originally drafted by the National Partnership for Women and Families (formerly known as the National Women's Defense Fund), a nonprofit organization that seeks to promote "fairness in the workplace, quality health care, and policies that help women and men meet the dual demands of work and family." Groups such as this and others who feel strongly about the issue currently support efforts to expand the provisions of the FMLA. Consider your reactions to some of the suggestions that have been proposed to modify the FMLA:

1. Allow covered and eligible employees to take up to 24 hours of leave per year to participate in their children's academic school activities or literacy training. (Currently, the FMLA allows leave for serious health needs of family members, but it does not give parents unpaid leave and job protection to address their children's educational needs.)
2. Lower the eligibility threshold for employers from 50 employees to 25 or more.
3. Lower the eligibility threshold for employers from 50 employees to 15 or more.
4. Include FMLA benefits for victims (female and male) of domestic violence.
5. Provide federal money to the states to fully or partially replace the lost family income of those individuals who requested and took advantage of the unpaid time off provisions of the FMLA.

Alternatively, business groups also have ideas for modifying the FMLA. They suggest ways to make the law more equitable and to better serve the needs of society (and not just those of the immediately affected workers).

Regardless of your personal position on the value that the FMLA brings to workers and employers, the dialogue on it and other issues related to the workplace and the public interest will continue. The outcome will ultimately shape what HR managers in the hospitality industry and others can do as they operate their facilities.

In future chapters, you will learn about more laws that affect the HR decisions of hospitality managers. As the workplace continues to evolve, legislation affecting it will also likely continue to evolve at the federal, state, and local levels. Therefore, hospitality managers with HR responsibilities should stay informed about pending legislation and actively take part in the public opinion debates that help shape governmental policies. It is for those reasons (obtaining information and making their voices heard) that many hospitality managers become active in one or more professional trade associations.

Figure 2.2 summarizes some of the most important labor-related legislation passed in the United States in the last 75 years. The effects of legislative changes on the manner in which businesses and workers must be managed is significant.

Purpose of Legislation	Bill	Enacted
Legalize labor unions	Wagner Act	1935
Require overtime pay	Fair Labor Standards Act	1938
Mandate equal pay for equal jobs	Equal Pay Act	1963
Prohibit discrimination based on selected worker characteristics	Civil Rights Act	1964
Prohibit age discrimination	Age Discrimination in Employment Act	1967
Protect workers' health and safety	Occupational Safety and Health Act	1970
Allow workers access to their personal files	Privacy Act	1974
Require documentation of legal status prior to employment	Immigration Reform and Control Act	1986
Allow continuation of selected benefits after job loss	Consolidated Omnibus Budget Reconciliation Act (COBRA)	1986
Mandate employee notification prior to business closing	Plant Closing Bill	1989
Prohibit discrimination based on workers' disabilities	Americans with Disabilities Act	1990
Allow workers unpaid leave for selected medical and family matters	Family and Medical Leave Act	1993
Mandate personal responsibility for financial reporting of business results	Sarbanes-Oxley Act	2002

FIGURE 2.2: Selected Significant Labor-Related Legislation

The International Legal Environment for Multinational Hospitality Companies

4. Identify the unique issues facing hospitality companies that operate units in countries with legal systems different from that of the United States.

As a hospitality organization grows from one that operates within a single country (and, therefore, within a single legal environment) to one that operates internationally, the HR management function must also grow to consider a new and broader perspective. As a hospitality company expands, first with single operations (and, perhaps, franchise partners) in other countries to multiunit management on multiple continents, the legal environment in which that company must operate will become increasingly complex.

The rise of global expansion should be no surprise to hospitality managers, because travel, tourism, and an interest in international cuisines have historically been integral parts of the industry. As cooking methods and menu items that are popular in one culture are introduced to another, their popularity often expands. Examples in the U.S. foodservice industry include Coca-Cola, the Atlanta, Georgia-based soft drink company, and McDonald's, the Oak Brook, Illinois-based franchisor and restaurant operator. In the hotel segment, companies such as Hilton and Marriott have long operated hotels internationally.

To more closely examine just one international success story, consider Ray Kroc, who opened the first McDonald's restaurant in Des Plaines, Illinois, in 1955. Today, McDonald's restaurants are operated in 115 countries worldwide and serve more than 50 million customers per day. McDonald's operates or franchises more than 13,500 restaurants in the United States, but an even larger number of stores now exist *outside* the United States. Figure 2.3 presents only a *partial* list of countries in which you could visit one of the more than 30,000 McDonald's restaurants worldwide.

Clearly, the HR function at McDonald's, as well as many other hospitality companies, has significant international dimensions. As the U.S. hospitality business continues to grow, it is natural that more companies will look beyond their own

Argentina	Ecuador	Kuwait	Singapore
Australia	Egypt	Lebanon	Slovakia
Austria	Finland	Malaysia	Slovenia
Bahrain	France	Mexico	South Africa
Belgium	Germany	Netherlands	Spain
Brazil	Greece	Oman	Sweden
Bulgaria	Guatemala	Paraguay	Switzerland
Canada	Hong Kong	Pakistan	Taiwan
Chile	Hungary	Peru	Turkey
China	India	Poland	United Arab Emirates
Colombia	Ireland	Portugal	United Kingdom
Croatia	Italy	Qatar	United States
Cyprus	Japan	Romania	Uruguay
Czech Republic	Jordan	Russia	Yugoslavia
Denmark	Korea	Saudi Arabia	

FIGURE 2.3: Selected McDonald's Locations Worldwide

Human Resources Management:
CURRENT EVENTS 2.2

WOMEN'S RIGHTS IN SAUDI ARABIA

The rights of women as professional hospitality managers in Saudi Arabia are very different from those enjoyed by women in the United States. In a society where women constitute the majority of the population and account for more university graduates than men, they have few of the rights that most of Western society usually grants. Women are not allowed to study any subject they desire; law and engineering, for example, are closed to them. In addition, they continue to be barred from jobs that are deemed not suitable to their nature. They cannot vote, travel without the explicit approval of their husband or a male guardian, drive, or work in most government offices. Even when hired in a private office, they usually work in a separate room from men. What has perhaps most attracted the attention of the human rights and feminist groups in the West is the fact that Saudi women must wear an *abayas* (a neck-to-ankle black robe) and cover their hair with a black scarf. Many Saudi women, however, say what they need most is not a debate over what they can or cannot wear. Instead, they want to gain social respect and political equality. Some other women say they prefer the status quo because of their own cultural and religious views.

Regardless of their personal opinions on the issue, it is clear that, for U.S. citizens (male or female) assigned by their companies to work in Saudi Arabia, that Middle Eastern society's view of appropriate roles for working women is an example of the many cultural differences faced by international hospitality managers.

country's borders for expansion and growth. This trend is certainly likely to continue in the areas of restaurants, hotels, and contract and healthcare food services.

Many hospitality professionals work at some point in their careers with a company that does business internationally. There are a variety of reasons why you might be assigned the responsibility of HR management in your company's international operations. These include:

- Your education and past work history give you the experience you need to succeed in the job.
- No local staff (in the foreign country) is currently qualified to assume the responsibility.
- Your responsibilities include the training of local HR staff.
- Local persons are being trained for positions that will ultimately replace the need for your assistance, but they are not yet qualified to assume 100 percent responsibility.

- Your employer wants you and other managers to gain a global perspective.
- It is in the company's best long-term interest to improve the cultural understanding between managers and employees in the company's various international components.
- An international assignment is considered an integral part of your professional development process.
- There is an interest in obtaining tighter administrative control over a foreign division or addressing and correcting a significant problem.
- There are HR operating or public relations issues that require long-term on-site management direction to properly address the issues.

How different are HR-related issues (and their management) in other countries? Consider an item as straightforward as accrued vacation time. In this area, the expectations management may have for its workers and the expectations these workers have for management can differ widely. To illustrate, Figure 2.4 details the amount of paid vacation earned by employees who have worked at least one year in several different countries in which U.S. companies typically do business.

The quality of training and the availability of qualified numbers of employees can be problematic HR issues in many areas of the world. Also, employee and management attitudes toward gender equality, appropriate dress, work ethic, religious tolerance, and minorities' rights are additional areas that can present significant challenges to international HR managers. As you have learned, individual societies create laws that reflect their cultures and values and, because cultures vary, HR-related laws in different cultures are also different.

It is also important to understand that the introduction of U.S. cultural values that are so valued by U.S. citizens does not ensure that individuals working in other countries will readily embrace those values. Some people believe that the expansion of U.S. companies such as Coca-Cola, McDonald's, KFC, Pizza Hut, and others to foreign countries has had an overall negative effect on the local culture of the areas in which they are located. Others, however, believe that the impact of international expansion and development in terms of economic benefits (job creation and the expansion of local entrepreneurship) is extremely positive.

Both groups would likely agree, however, that the past need not dictate the future. International companies may or may not have done all they should have in the past to ensure a positive impact on their operations. All should agree that these companies, through enlightened HR practices, can shape the future through positive activities to improve their own profitability and the quality of life in the communities where they are located.

Expatriate manager: A citizen of one country who is a working manager in another country.

These HR issues require **expatriate managers** to seriously reexamine their personal views of fairness and even morality.

For example, assume that you, as a restaurant manager in a foreign country, pay wages that are considered to be very good in that country, but that are significantly less (in U.S. dollars paid per hour) than those granted to U.S. workers who are doing the same job. Some observers would say your restaurant is providing valuable local jobs at fair wages; others might accuse your company of injustice because of the disparity in wage rates paid. Add to this challenge the fact that, in

Country	Vacation Time Earned
Argentina	14 calendar days
Australia	No law, but 4 weeks is standard
Belgium	20 days with premium pay
Bulgaria	20 business days
Canada	At least 2 weeks, as determined by provincial law
Chile	15 days
China	0
Czech Republic	4 weeks
France	5 weeks
Germany	4 weeks
Hong Kong	7 days
Hungary	20 days
Ireland	4 weeks
Israel	14 days
Italy	Mandated vacation; length determined by employment contract
Japan	10 days paid time off
Mexico	6 days
Poland	18 days
Puerto Rico	15 days
Saudi Arabia	15 days
Singapore	7 days
South Africa	21 consecutive days
South Korea	10 days
Spain	30 days
Sweden	5 weeks
Taiwan	7 days
The Netherlands	4 weeks
Turkey	12 days
UK	European Community directive (4 weeks annual leave)
Ukraine	24 calendar days
US	No national requirement; 2 weeks is common but not mandatory
Venezuela	15 paid days

FIGURE 2.4: Annual Earned vacation time

many cultures, it is traditional to pay men more than women for doing identical work, and you can easily see the type of HR difficulties you may face. It is beyond the scope of this text to address and comment on all of the legal issues of wage and gender inequities and business variations due to the cultures that are routinely

Human Resources Management: CURRENT EVENTS 2.3

SMOKING OR NONSMOKING?

Restaurant managers in the United States have, for the past several decades, been required to provide separate dining space for smokers and nonsmokers. Their employees often could smoke in designated smoking areas or in specially designated employee break rooms.

Effective June 1, 2006, smokers across much of eastern Canada (including those working in the hospitality industry) are only permitted to smoke outside. Prior to that time, smoking was already banned from most workplaces across Canada, but the ban in Ontario and Quebec extended the ban to public places in general, including bars, restaurants, and schools. The ban also required employers to close designated employee smoking areas.

Canada is considered a global leader in its efforts to reduce smoking. It was the first country to require graphic warnings on cigarette packages. Nine of the country's 13 provinces and territories have now passed smoking bans prohibiting cigarettes in the workplace and public buildings, bars, and restaurants. The law is wide-reaching but still falls short of the efforts of Ireland, Norway, New Zealand, Bhutan, Uruguay, Scotland, Bermuda, and Puerto Rico, (as well as New York City) all of which have total smoking bans in restaurants and bars.

The diverse opinions about smoking held by those in the hospitality industry mirror those of society in general. Beginning with Westin Hotels and followed by Marriott, Comfort, Hyatt, and others, complete hotel-wide smoking bans are increasingly becoming standard practice in the United States. It is clear that managers who operate properties in different parts of the world (and even in different communities within the United States) will encounter variations in employment-related laws. The smoking versus nonsmoking issue is just one example.

experienced by expatriate managers. It is important to remember, however, that those expatriate managers who most succeed do so by demonstrating a genuine knowledge, respect, and understanding for the legal culture of their host country.

It is important for those working in HR to understand that U.S.-based employers who employ U.S. citizens in locations outside of the country are still subject to the majority of employment laws designed to protect those workers. The antidiscrimination (and many other) laws of the United States will not, however, apply to noncitizens of the United States who work in facilities operated outside of the United States.

Conversely, multinational companies based outside of the United States with properties inside the United States are subject to the same U.S. employment laws as are U.S. employers. As a result, in many cases, a significant HR role to be played by U.S. managers is that of teaching internationally trained expatriate managers working *in* the United States about the important components of U.S. employment law.

The Special Role of the Hospitality Unit Manager

5. Recognize and appreciate the unique HR-related responsibilities of the hospitality unit manager.

Unit manager: The individual with the final on-site decision-making authority at an individual hospitality operation.

Regardless of whether a hospitality manager's assignment is within his or her own country or outside its borders, **unit managers** are perhaps the single most important factor affecting an operation's short- and long-term profitability and success. These managers are generally the on-site leaders of their operating units and are held directly responsible for the actions of the employees and supervisors who report to them. In fact, the unit manager's job in the hospitality industry is so important that the primary focus of this text is the HR-related information that must be known and applied by the individuals holding these key positions.

Hospitality management has always been a challenging profession. Whether in a casino, a school lunch program, a five-star hotel, a sports stadium concession program, or a myriad of other environments, hospitality managers are required to have a breadth of skill not found in many other areas of management. Hospitality managers are in charge of securing raw materials, producing a product or service, and selling it—all under the same roof. This makes them very different from their manufacturing counterparts (who are in charge of product production only) and their retail counterparts (who sell, but do not manufacture, the product). Perhaps most important, hospitality managers have direct contact with guests, the ultimate end user of the products and services supplied by these managers' operational teams.

The hospitality industry is also unique because the first industry job for many managers was often an entry-level, hourly paid position rather than a salaried management assignment. For example, in the table service restaurant segment, nine out of ten salaried managers started as hourly employees. Hospitality unit managers are also a diverse group. According to the U.S. Department of Labor, "eating-and-drinking" places employ more minority managers than any other industry. Three out of five first-line supervisors of food preparation and service workers are women, 16 percent are of Hispanic origin, and 14 percent are African American. In 2003, more than one-quarter (26 percent) of foodservice managers were foreign born. As you can see, a very diverse group of unit managers are responsible for the key aspects of ensuring that operations adhere to a company's policies and the employment laws that pertain to them.

In this chapter, you have learned how evolving employment legislation reflects an American society that has changed the way in which employers manage employees. The often mentioned "social contract" between employer and employee is—most hospitality industry professionals would agree—exactly that: a contract.

Like all contracts, it spells out the obligations undertaken by all contractual parties. Hospitality personnel at the unit management level represent their company in this contract, and they must understand it. Because contracts are legal documents, violations typically result in repercussions for one side or the other. In the business world, this can mean loss of job for an offending employee. For employers, violations can create adverse publicity, the loss of significant time and money to address legal issues, or, in egregious cases, the closure of their businesses. A major goal of this text is to provide unit managers with up-to-date information they need to responsibly fulfill their HR-related obligations to their employers, employees, society, and, most important, to themselves.

Historically, most students of hospitality management have been taught how to supervise employees. The rationale was that, by better understanding and motivating staff members, a better workforce would emerge. The reasoning is that good managers become recognized as such by first being good supervisors. It is true that some concepts, including communications, motivational theory, and team building, that have traditionally been addressed using this supervisory approach to human resources management have value. However, those unit managers and others who do not understand the legal requirements and responsibilities that underpin these concepts are at a huge disadvantage to their peers who recognize these and related legal issues. For example, managers may know exactly what they want to do to build an effective workforce, but they may lack an understanding about what they are legally allowed to do, required to do, or even prohibited from doing! The result can be that, time after time, well-intentioned unit managers may unwittingly create difficulties for their organizations and themselves because they do not understand the ever-changing terms of the employment contract.

Written company policies can be fairly easily relayed to unit managers, but it is simply not possible for you as a unit manager to know every governmental regulation that could affect your segment of the hospitality industry, and some laws change regularly. Changes in major federal laws are typically well publicized, but you cannot be sure that the policies of all federal agencies, state regulators, and local governments will be readily known. As a result, hospitality industry journals and publications (many of them delivered online) can be of real assistance in helping you follow legislation at the national level. Reading about the hospitality industry will not only make you a better unit manager, but will let you keep up with changing regulations as well. For those managers employed by a national chain or management company, the company can be an excellent source of information on changing regulations. One valuable service provided by franchisors to franchisees is regular updates on regulatory agencies and their work.

As a hospitality manager, it is important for you to stay involved in the hospitality trade association that most closely represents your industry segment. The National Restaurant Association (NRA), the American Hotel and Lodging Motel Association (AH&LA), the American Dietetics Association (ADA), and others like them regularly provide their membership with legislative updates. Many of these organizations have state, regional, or local chapters that can be invaluable sources of information. On a local level, chambers of commerce, business trade associations, and personal relationships with local police, fire, and building officials can help a unit manager keep up-to-date with changes in municipal regulations.

As a professional hospitality manager, it is also critical that you take an active role in *shaping* the regulations that affect your industry. As you have learned in this chapter, societies will, through their governments, pass regulations that they believe are in the best interests of the communities they represent. Problems can arise, however, when those who do not understand the hospitality industry propose legislation that will result in costs or infringement upon individual rights that far exceed the societal value of implementing the proposed regulation. In these cases, all hospitality professionals must make their own views known.

Human Resources MANAGEMENT ISSUES   (2.3)

"**S**o that's it," said Tom Bollenbeck, the regional manager for Boston Blackie's, a chain of barbecue houses popular in the Southeastern United States. Tom had just explained to Travis Ware that the Boston Blackie's restaurant Travis had managed for the three years since it opened would be closed in eight weeks.

"You have done a great job here, Travis," said Tom. "And, like I said, when we finish construction of the new store in Crossville, you will have the manager's position there. Bigger store, more money! But I need you to keep this store operating well until the end of the month when our lease runs out."

Travis was troubled when he left the meeting with Tom. His employees, he knew, were one of the major reasons his boss was so pleased with his work. They were a great team, but the new store in Crossville was 100 miles away—much too far for them to commute. Travis also knew that if he told his current employees about the impending closure of their restaurant, the best of them would immediately start looking for other jobs, and they would easily get them. That would mean real difficulties during the final weeks his store was to operate.

QUESTIONS

1. Assume Travis's restaurant is too small to be covered by the Worker Adjustment and Retraining Notification Act (WARN). Does he have a legal obligation to inform his employees of the impending restaurant closing?
2. Consider the following statement: "An action can be legal, but still not be ethical." Do you agree? Why or why not?
3. Assume that you were Travis, and you knew that your restaurant was large enough to be covered by WARN. Assume also, however, that your boss specifically instructed you not to announce the closing to your employees. What would you do?

Human Resources Terms

The following terms were defined in this chapter:

Employment law	Bona fide occupational
Unemployment compensation	qualification (BFOQ)
Workers' compensation	Disparate treatment
Garnish (ment)	Disparate (adverse) impact
Labor union	Franchisor
Interstate commerce	Reasonable accommodation
Title VII	Expatriate manager
EEOC	Unit managers
Sexual harassment	

For Your Consideration

1. Some business persons believe that the government is too intrusive in the operation of business. Consider the employment-related laws presented in this chapter. Are there any that you believe should not have been passed? Is so, what legislation? Why? Is there any employment-related legislation you believe should be passed? If so, identify it and explain the reason for your support.

2. The Family Medical Leave Act was controversial at the time of its passage and remains so today. Do you consider the Act an undue burden on employers? Assume you are an executive in the governmental relations department of the National Restaurant Association (NRA). Do you think the NRA's membership would want you to actively lobby to expand or to contract its current provisions? What would you do in such a situation?

3. Assume you are responsible for the HR function at a 300-room franchised hotel that employs 90 staff members and that, in this situation, the WARN Act does not apply. Assume also that you were informed by the general manager and owners that the property would be closed in 90 days for conversion to a condo hotel (a process that would involve closing the property completely for one year). However, it was important to remain open and operating normally for that 90-day period. What would you advise the hotel's owners and the general manager to do regarding giving notification of the hotel's closing to the property's employees? Explain your plan in detail.

4. In many cases, Americans working internationally are viewed as not having respect for local laws and customs of their host countries, including those related to employer–employee relations. Assume you were an international manager and you encountered an employment practice that would be illegal and discriminatory in the United States but was commonly accepted where

you were working (e.g., the remnants of the now technically illegal caste system in India). Explain how you would respond to clear-cut instances of local but society-approved discrimination when operating your hospitality business in such a setting.

CASE STUDY: HUMAN RESOURCES MANAGEMENT IN ACTION

Donna Moreau was employed for nine years as a room attendant for the Windjammer Hotel. Her work and attendance during that period were considered excellent. The hotel was moderately busy during the week, and then typically filled with tourists on the weekends.

In accordance with a hotel policy requiring two weeks' notification, Donna submitted a "day off" request on May 1, for time off on Saturday, May 15, to attend the 1 P.M. high school graduation ceremony of her only daughter. The hotel was expected to be extremely short of staff on the weekend of May 15 due to some staff resignations and terminations, as well as a forecasted sell-out of guest rooms.

Donna's supervisor, Tara Roach, denied Donna's request for the day off, stating the housekeeping department needed her to work that entire weekend. Donna was visibly upset when the schedule was posted and she learned that her request had been denied. She confronted Tara and stated, "I *will* be attending my daughter's graduation. I've been a single parent to my daughter for 17 years, and there's no way I am going to miss that day!" Tara replied that she was very sorry, but all employee requests for that weekend off had been denied, and Donna was to report to work as scheduled.

On the Saturday of the graduation, Donna, in accordance with written hotel policy, called in "sick" four hours before her shift was to begin. The hotel was extremely busy and, due in part to Donna's absence, each room attendant who did show up at work was assigned a heavier than average workload, causing a great deal of departmental tension.

Tara, who was angry at what she saw as willful disregard for supervisory authority, and recalling the earlier conversation with Donna, recorded the employee's call-in as an "unacceptable excuse" and completed a form stating that Donna had, in fact, quit her job voluntarily by refusing to work her assigned shift. Tara referred to the portion of the employee manual that Donna signed when joining the hotel. The manual read, in part:

"Employees shall be considered to have voluntarily quit or abandoned their employment upon any of the following occurrences;

1. Absence from work for one (1) or more consecutive days without excuse acceptable to the company
2. Habitual tardiness
3. Failure to report to work within 24 hours of a request to report

Donna returned to work the next day to find that she had been removed from the schedule. She was also informed that she was no longer an employee of the hotel. Donna filed for unemployment compensation. In her state, workers who voluntarily quit their jobs were not typically eligible for unemployment compensation. Those who are terminated do typically receive the benefit (which is ultimately paid for by the hotel).

Dimension: Societal Reaction

Review the actions described in the case:

1. What do you think those outside the hospitality industry would think about Tara's decision to terminate Donna?
2. Assume that accurate information regarding this situation were to become well-known in the local community surrounding this hotel. Would this information likely increase or decrease the interest of other professional housekeepers in working at the Windjammer in the future?
3. The concept of "unacceptable excuse" can be difficult to define. Despite that, define it in terms you believe Donna and other employees would use. Define the term in a manner that Tara and other supervisors would likely use.

Dimension: Company Procedure and Decision Making

Review the actions described in the case:

1. What do you think of the "time off" request system in use at the Windjammer?
2. If you were the hotel's general manager, would you support the actions of your housekeeping supervisor?
   a. If your answer is "yes," how would you respond to Donna if she maintains (accurately) that she has not called in "sick" in the past 15 months, and in fact has frequently been called in to work on her days off because other employees called in sick fairly often?
   b. If your answer is "no," how would you respond to Tara if she maintains (accurately) that allowing employees to set their own schedule in her department would lead to severe difficulties that would result in poorly cleaned guest rooms and, ultimately, unhappy guests who were very likely to complain to the general manager or even directly to the hotel's owners? In addition, Tara is adamant that if you do not support her decision making on this issue, her credibility as a departmental supervisor will be severely diminished.
3. Were Tara's actions in the best interests of the hotel? Explain your answer.

Dimension: The Unemployment Compensation Hearing

Assume you were called to an administrative court hearing to defend the Windjammer's contention that Donna was not fired, but rather that she quit (and thus is not eligible for unemployment compensation). Review the actions described in the case:

1. If you were an Unemployment Compensation Administrative Hearing Judge in this case, would you initially be more likely to side with the employee or the hotel?
2. How would you likely answer the following specific questions asked by the Administrative Hearing Judge?
   a. Is there a distributed list of "unacceptable" reasons for calling in sick? Who decides what is "unacceptable"?
   b. Have, in the past six months, all employees who followed the hotel's policy of calling in sick four hours before their shift ultimately been documented as "resigned" from their job?
   c. Assuming the answer to the above question is "no," what was the hotel's basis for treating Donna differently from:
      - Males in the hotel
      - Those of a different ethnic background (the hearing officer explains that this is asked simply to ensure that the hotel is not guilty of a civil rights violation)
3. How important would it be to be very familiar with the state's unemployment compensation laws if you were:
   a. The person representing the hotel at the administrative hearing?
   b. The hotel's general manager?
   c. Tara?

INTERNET ACTIVITIES

1. Staying abreast of legal trends in the hospitality industry is important. HospitalityLawyer.com is one resource that is readily available to you. Operated by Stephen Barth, a hospitality professor at the University of Houston's Conrad Hilton College of Hotel and Restaurant Management, it contains the most current legal information (including employment law) related to the hospitality industry. To review it, go to: *www.hospitalitylawyer.com.*
   a. Review the 12 subsections of hospitality law listed in the Legal, Safety and Security Solutions Center for the Hospitality Industry.
   b. Identify the date and location for this year's Hospitality Law Conference.
   c. Subscribe to the free newsletter.
   d. Bookmark the site if you feel it will be an asset in your future management efforts.
2. If you are responsible for the management of a hospitality operation in another country, you will likely have access to a variety of resources that will help you familiarize yourself with that country's specific labor-related laws. However, in some cases, you may be responsible for finding your own

learning aids. For this exercise, go to *www.amazon.com*, and type in the book title *International Labor & Employment Law: A Country by Country Look at Legal Issues in Human Resources in Major Markets Around the Globe* (ISBN 158762379X).

a. List at least 12 specific countries whose employment laws are reviewed in the text.

b. Identify the text's authors. Comment briefly on their credibility.

c. List at least three specific labor-related topics that are explored in the book.

d. Comment on the selling price of the text. Do you feel it is excessive? Explain your position.

3. In many cases, you simply will not know some of the applicable employment laws of a state until you are actually assigned to work there. Identify a state (or one of the states) in which you are most likely to work when you graduate. Then, proceed to "Google" or your favorite search engine and enter the name of that state and the words "unemployment claims." Select the agency that is responsible for processing unemployment claims and determine the following:

a. The number of weeks for which employees in that state are typically eligible for unemployment compensation

b. The maximum amount of weekly compensation allowable

c. Specific reasons for which unemployment compensation will be denied

CHAPTER THREE

Human Resources Management: Policies and Procedures

CHAPTER | **OUTLINE**

HR Policies and Procedures Activities
 Policy and Procedure Development
 Areas of Policy and Procedure Development
Steps in HR Policy and Procedure Development
Review for Legal Compliance
Applying Advanced Technology to HR Policies and Procedures
 Information Dissemination
 Information Storage
HR Policies and Procedures Documentation and Record Keeping
Human Resources Terms
For Your Consideration
Case Study: Human Resources Management in Action
Internet Activities

CHECKLIST | **OF CHAPTER LEARNING OBJECTIVES**

As a result of satisfactory completion of this chapter, readers will be able to:

1. Recognize and describe the difference between the HR policies and HR procedures utilized by employers.

2. Identify the steps managers use to develop HR management policies and procedures.

3. Understand the importance of seeking legal counsel and/or review prior to implementing HR policies and procedures.

4. Recognize and appreciate the role advanced technology is currently playing, and will continue to play, in the process of HR-related policy and procedure development.

5. Recognize the most significant reasons why HR managers must develop, implement, and maintain effective HR recordkeeping systems.

Impact on Human Resources Management

Just as culinarians in the hospitality industry know that standardized recipes will help them turn out a quality menu item every time the recipe is followed, those managers working in the HR field recognize that consistency in their own policy-related actions is critical to the smooth operation of their units.

Employees and managers alike want to know that all of the policies and procedures applied to them at work will also be applied, in the same manner, to each of their coworkers. If they do not believe this is true, charges of bias, favoritism, cronyism, sexism, and even racism can result. Therefore, experienced HR managers know they must (1) carefully design and implement any operating policies they wish to utilize, and (2) reliably document their fair and consistent application of those policies.

HR Policy and Procedures Activities

1. **Recognize and describe the difference between the HR policies and HR procedures utilized by employers.**

POLICY AND PROCEDURE DEVELOPMENT

As you have learned, the responsibilities for HR management issues may lie with unit-level managers (in smaller properties) or full-time specialists (in larger hospitality organizations). Assume you have taken a position in which you are ultimately responsible for the HR management issues related to the operation of a newly constructed 45,000-square-foot water park with an attached 400-room hotel and supporting foodservice operations. The facility will ultimately employ more than 300 full- and part-time staff members. Assume also that the facility has yet to open. In such a situation, you will soon be required to make decisions about many employee-related issues and policies. The policies you design must address many topics. Just a few examples include:

1. Employee selection criteria
2. The accumulation and use of employees' vacation time
3. Dress and uniform codes
4. Attendance and tardiness
5. Performance evaluation
6. Termination

The actual procedures you will use to operate your own department must also be developed. These procedures would likely address a variety of issues related to the policies you developed, such as:

1. Who is responsible for selecting employees?
2. How is employee vacation time accrued and recorded?
3. What are the penalties for dress code violations?
4. Who will record employee absences and tardiness?
5. How frequently will employee performance reviews be undertaken? Who will do them?
6. What written documentation will be required in cases of employee termination?

HR policy(ies):
A course of action selected from alternatives and designed to guide future decision making.

HR procedures:
The methods or steps used to effectively develop and apply HR policies.

Note that there is an important relationship between what your business will do (its **HR policies**) and exactly how you will do it (its **HR procedures**).

Consider the HR policy and procedure examples presented in the water park example. Figure 3.1 shows some ways in which these example policies and procedures are related to each other. For purposes of this chapter, the term "policy" will be used to refer to *what* a business operation has determined it should do, while the term "procedure" will refer to *how* it will do it. These procedures may spell out rewards for policy compliance, penalties for noncompliance, and steps required for policy implementation. In most cases, a single policy will require multiple supporting procedures. Some examples of the specific procedures required to support operation policies are illustrated in Figure 3.1.

In some cases, the line between what businesses do and how they do it can be a fine one. However, it is important to remember that, to be effective, HR policies must be supported by procedures that, when followed, ensure the fair and consistent application of the policy.

Policies: What We Will Do	Procedures: How We Will Do It
1. Select employees	1. Use standardized application forms.
2. Grant employees paid vacation	2. Record accrued vacation time biweekly.
3. Implement employee dress codes	3. Impose consistent penalties for noncompliance.
4. Monitor attendance and tardiness	4. Record employee arrival and departure times daily.
5. Conduct performance evaluations	5. Schedule annual employee reviews and designate the reviewers.
6. Terminate employees	6. Develop standards for documenting (in writing) employee terminations.

FIGURE 3.1: HR Policy and Procedure Relationship

Human Resources Management:
CURRENT EVENTS 3.1

ENGLISH-ONLY OR SOLO INGLES?

Can a U.S. employer mandate that English is the only language that may be spoken in the workplace? The EEOC recently (2006) announced that it settled a lawsuit against a New York City hotel. The hotel was accused of discriminating against 13 Hispanic employees and ultimately forcing them to resign for speaking Spanish in the workplace. The settlement was $800,000. In addition, the hotel agreed that:

- It is prohibited from maintaining an English-only rule for its employees.
- It will train its managers and employees in equal employment law.
- It will regularly report to the EEOC about any new discrimination complaints it receives.
- It will require its senior vice president to undergo three hours of one-on-one training, which must be reviewed and approved by the EEOC. At a minimum, the training will address the topics of discrimination, retaliation, harassment, diversity, and sensitivity.

Discrimination on the basis of "national origin" is clearly prohibited by Title VII of the Civil Rights Act of 1964 (see Chapter 2). Those employers considering the adoption of an "English-only" at-work policy must be ready to face healthy skepticism on the part of the EEOC. In most cases, a rule requiring employees to speak only English at all times in the workplace will be presumed to violate Title VII and will be closely scrutinized by the EEOC.

An employer may have a rule requiring that employees speak only English at certain times where the employer can show that the rule is justified by business necessity. For example, a server taking an order from diners who speak only English can be required to speak English. If the employer believes the English-only rule is critical for business purposes, employees should be told, in advance (and in writing!), when they are required to speak only English and the consequences of violating the rule. If the company does not do so, its English-only policy will likely be deemed discriminatory if it is challenged.

A better HR policy for hospitality managers may well be the subsidized support of on-site English as a Second Language (ESL) courses for those employees who need and want to improve their English skills. An ESL policy, demonstrating real support for staff needs, sends the right signal to workers, guests, and the community. Not only is it the smart thing to do, it's the right thing to do.

IT'S THE LAW!

In Chapter 2, you learned about employment laws that affect some of the policies that businesses are, and are not, allowed to implement. Can a business organization that has developed and implemented a perfectly legal employment policy still be sued because of the policy, and ultimately lose the case? Absolutely. It happens all the time when the procedures the managers used to support the policy were flawed, deficient, or both.

A policy or action that is perfectly legal must still be applied in a legally coherent (fair) manner, or the courts will simply not support its use. For example, can a hotel, restaurant, casino, or other hospitality operation lay off or terminate employees because of declining sales? In most situations, clearly it can. However, consider the recent real case of an organization that elected to lay off six employees, of whom five were African-American women and one was a Caucasian man.

The women were called into the manager's office and informed they were being laid off effective immediately. They were told to collect their belongings and leave within 30 minutes. In full view of their coworkers, managers monitored them as they cleaned out their lockers. The monitoring was such that coworkers thought they were being observed to prevent stealing. They did not have an opportunity to say goodbye to their coworkers, some of whom cried because they would miss them and felt badly for them.

This was in stark contrast to the treatment the white male received upon his termination. He was given a month's advance notice of his layoff. He was allowed to come to the operation at his convenience to receive his termination notice. He was not monitored as he cleaned out his work area, and he was permitted to walk around the building freely to say goodbye to his coworkers. In this case, the Court of Appeals held that the *manner* in which the layoff was conducted was discriminatory, and the women won their case. They should have.

Despite some popular misconceptions, employers in the United States still enjoy a tremendous amount of freedom (more than in many other economically advanced countries) regarding how they operate their businesses. Can employees be laid off or terminated when business warrants it? Yes, they can. Can an employer (as in this case) do it so poorly that the courts will refuse to support it and, in fact, punish the employer? Yes. Terminations and layoffs are emotional situations in the best of times. Managers must conduct them professionally and with respect. The number-one rule to prevent claims of discrimination related to terminations and layoffs is simple: "be fair and be consistent"! That rule is a good one to apply to all of your HR policies and procedures.

AREAS OF POLICY AND PROCEDURE DEVELOPMENT

Not all of a hospitality operation's policies and procedures relate to HR. To continue our example of the HR manager of a water park resort, many issues would not be under your control. How frequently the pools' filters are cleaned, the proper number of cloth napkins to regularly be held in the food and beverage inventory, and the establishment of the ideal selling price of guest rooms on a given weekend are not decisions made by the HR manager. HR policy and procedure development will, however, have a direct effect on all areas of the resort, as they will on all areas of any other hospitality operation. As experienced managers know, it is not possible to identify all of the subjects within every hospitality operation that require written policies and procedures. Clearly, the policy and procedures needs of a large, multinational hospitality organization will be very different from the needs of a small, independently owned sandwich shop.

Despite differences in size and need, all hospitality organizations undertake HR-related activities that can be readily identified. There are a variety of ways to classify these activities and the policy and procedure making related to them. Figure 3.2 lists one way to categorize the areas of policy and procedure responsibility

Assigned Area/Activity	Requires Policies and Procedures Related To
Staffing the Organization	Operational planning and needs analysis Recruiting Interviewing Selecting
Developing Staff	Employee orientation Training Employee development and career planning Managing and implementing organizational change
Motivating Staff	Job design Employee evaluation Compensation Employee benefits Employee recognition
Maintaining Staff	Employee health Employee safety Employee-related organizational communications

FIGURE 3.2: HR Policy and Procedure Development Areas and Activities

commonly assigned to the HR function. It categorizes the areas of HR policy and procedure development as related to:

- Staffing the organization
- Developing staff
- Motivating staff
- Maintaining staff

As you read about the following tasks normally assigned to those responsible for HR management, consider the policies and procedures development and implementation efforts needed to address these tasks.

Staffing the Organization

The recruitment and selection of employees is probably the area that most hospitality managers think of first when they consider the work of the HR department or the HR manager. Prior to recruiting and selecting employees, however, the HR manager must carefully assess the operation's needs. If, for example, the executive chef of a large convention hotel informs the HR department that an additional chef is needed, the specific skills of that needed individual must be identified. Clearly, if the skills of a **garde-manger** are sought by the executive chef, the recruitment and selection of a **patissier** or **saucier**, regardless of their ability and skill level, will be inappropriate.

In nonhotel operations, but in much the same manner as the previous example, before employees can be recruited, their skill requirements must be established. As a result, even at the smallest of local restaurants, the manager of the operation must still identify the specific skills, knowledge, and abilities of the employees needed by the restaurant. Additionally, it is important to recall that the specific requirements of current labor law mandate that managers thoroughly understand the specific skills required for the jobs they advertise. Identifying and documenting those specific skill sets effectively helps limit the potential legal liability that could be incurred if particular groups of employees are ultimately excluded from the search process. Excluding potential employees on the basis of identified and legitimately required job skills is legal, whereas excluding potential candidates for non-job-related reasons is typically illegal.

After the most critical characteristics related to a job's successful candidates have been carefully identified (see Chapter 6, "Position Analysis" discussion), the two most important staffing-related tasks facing the HR manager are:

- Ensuring an adequate pool of qualified applicants to maximize the operation's chances to hire an outstanding candidate
- Providing enough job information to discourage unqualified job applicants to help prevent the organization from wasting time and resources in the interviewing process

Garde-manger: Pantry chef. Responsible for cold food production, including salads, salad dressings, cold appetizers, charcuterie items, terrines, and similar dishes.

Patissier: Pastry chef. Responsible for all baked items, including breads, pastries, and desserts.

Saucier: Sauté station chef. Responsible for all sautéed items, including most sauces.

The policies and procedures related to employee recruitment and selection are among some of the most important to any organization. In Chapter 4, you will learn how hospitality managers develop policies that help ensure fair hiring practices.

After an adequate number of qualified candidates has been identified, it is the HR manager's job to refer those candidates to the individual who will make the hiring decision (typically in large organizations) or to make the actual selection (in most small organizations). In both situations, candidate testing and/or other assessment steps may precede the actual job offer.

Identifying qualified candidates and *offering* positions to them is only a part of the professional HR manager's job because, in a tight labor market, qualified and talented applicants are very likely to be sought by a variety of organizations. Therefore, the HR manager must also encourage the desired candidate to ultimately *accept* the position. To do this, the HR manager will typically provide the candidate with a good deal of job-related and organization-related information. Topics such as organizational culture, growth plans, and performance expectations are all notable areas that could influence an individual's acceptance decision, and these should be fully discussed with the candidate. Information related to these subjects should be accurate and help the candidate make an appropriate career decision that is best for the candidate and the hospitality organization.

Developing Staff

After new employees are selected, orienting these new employees to the organization becomes an important HR function. Even experienced employees who need little or virtually no skill training will still need to learn much about their new employer. Information about items such as organizational rules, regulations, and goals of the organization, department, and work unit will need to be communicated. Procedurally, questions of who will do the orientation, when it will occur, and what specific topics will be addressed are all HR policy and/or procedure issues.

In some cases, employees may be qualified for the job they have secured but will require facility-specific skill training. For example, even housekeepers with many years of experience cleaning rooms will likely still need to be shown "how we do it here" when they begin work with a new employer. Minor variations in housekeeping procedures, such as the preferred manner of folding terrycloth items (for guest room towels, hand towels, washcloths, and the like) must be taught. In a similar manner, even experienced service staff, if newly hired, will likely need to be instructed on a restaurant's specific table setting, order taking, guest check recording, order pickup, food delivery, and check presentation procedures.

As an employee's career within an organization progresses, that employee may need to acquire new skills. In many cases, changes in the employee's work unit or in the goals and needs of the organization may dictate that additional training is needed. It is also important to remember that many employees hope to advance within their employing organization. The HR manager should provide those employees, to the greatest degree possible, with opportunities to do so. This may take the form of providing employees with advanced skills training related to their present jobs, training in jobs they may hold in the future, or cross-training employees in new skills to prepare them for different jobs.

The best of HR managers, whether serving the dual role of unit manager or heading a large HR department, know that planning for the future staffing needs of their organization is an ongoing process. The competitive nature of the hospitality industry requires that most organizations have the ability to rapidly add products (such as new menu items) or services (such as those related to providing guests wireless Internet access in hotel rooms) that directly impact that organization's employees. Newly added menu items will likely require additional food production skills training. Adding the feature of wireless Internet access to a hotel's guest rooms will likely require that one or more hotel employees receive additional training in computer-related technology. Regardless of the individual within the organization who will actually do the training, it remains the HR manager's role to ensure that the training is provided and to develop the legally defensible policies and procedures required to do so.

Motivating Staff

The task of motivating employees to do their best is one of the most studied, talked about, and debated of all HR-related topics. The question of how to motivate employees to do their best (or even if it is possible for management to do so) will continue to be discussed. However, one helpful way to consider the role of HR managers in policy and procedure development related to employee motivation is to consider two factors that are commonly agreed to affect worker motivation. These are an employee's:

- Ability to do a job
- Willingness to do a job

The ability of an employee to effectively do the job is affected by the employee's skill level, the availability of effective training, and the worker's access to the tools or information needed to properly complete assigned tasks.

The willingness of employees to work efficiently has long been the subject of study by motivational theorists. Figure 3.3 briefly summarizes five of the most popular and widely discussed theories of employee motivation. Interested managers will be able to readily find additional information about each of these views of employee motivation via a basic Internet search (*google.com*). Regardless of the motivational philosophy adopted by a manager or a hospitality organization, adequate policies and procedures related to its implementation will be crucial to motivating employees.

Motivational Theorist	Motivational Theory	Theory Synopsis
1. Abraham Maslow	Needs Hierarchy	Assumes needs are arranged in a hierarchy and that some needs are more powerful than others. Workers seek to satisfy their needs in the following order: 1. Physiological (first) 2. Safety 3. Love/Belonging 4. Esteem 5. Actualization (last) The first four layers of Maslow's "pyramid" are called "deficiency needs" or "D-needs," because the individual does not feel anything if they are met, but feels anxious if they are not met.
2. Douglas McGregor	Theory X and Theory Y	States that managers tend to hold and act on one of two basic views (theories) about workers. Theory X assumptions are that: 1. The average person dislikes work and will avoid it if he or she can. 2. Most people must be forced with the threat of punishment to work toward an organization's objectives. 3. The average person prefers to be directed, to avoid responsibility, is relatively unambitious, and wants security above all else. Theory Y assumptions are that: 1. Effort in work is as natural as work and play. 2. People will apply self-control and self-direction in the pursuit of organizational objectives, without external control or the threat of punishment. 3. Commitment to objectives is a function of the rewards associated with their achievement.

FIGURE 3.3: Motivational Theorists, Theories, and Theory Synopsis

3. Frederick Herzberg	Motivation/ Hygiene Theory	Identifies two separate groups of factors affecting motivation. "Hygiene factors" cause feelings of dissatisfaction among employees. They include working conditions, pay, and job security. These do not motivate, but their absence adversely affects job performance. "Motivation factors," including concerns such as achievement, learning, and advancement, play a major role in positively influencing performance. Workforce motivation is not possible if hygiene factors are deficient.
4. David McClelland	Three-Need (achievement, affiliation, and power) Theory	States that workers have needs for achievement, affiliation, and power, each of which must be satisfied if they are to be motivated. The theory suggests that these three needs are found to varying degrees in all workers and managers. It also indicates that this mix of motivational needs characterizes an individual's management style in terms of being motivated, as well as in the management and motivation of others.
5. Victor Vroom	Expectancy Theory	Proposes that a worker's motivation is primarily influenced by the "expectation" that additional effort will lead to additional organizational rewards. If this expectation is not met, influencing an employee's motivation in a positive way will not be possible.

FIGURE 3.3: (Continued)

Maintaining Staff

Employee Assistance Program: The term used to describe a variety of employer-initiated efforts to assist employees in the areas of family concerns, legal issues, financial matters, and health maintenance.

Even the best of work teams require regular maintenance and care. Policies and procedures related to the maintenance of employees include those that help encourage quality workers to stay with the organization. Major areas of concern include worker health and safety, as well as the development and implementation of **Employee Assistance Programs (EAPs)**.

Additional areas of staff maintenance concern relate to communication efforts designed to keep employees informed about the work-related issues that are important to them. Other policies may identify opportunities for employees to

Human Resources MANAGEMENT ISSUES   (3.1)

"**B**ut, Larry, I just can't work on Sunday," said Shingi, a room attendant at the 800-room Courtplace Hotel.

Larry, the executive housekeeper, had just told Shingi that a storm in the area had delayed flights out of the regional airport and that a group that had been scheduled to leave the hotel on Sunday morning was now staying until Monday morning. The result was an additional 110 stayover rooms to clean Sunday, and Larry was hurriedly attempting to add eight housekeepers to the employee schedule.

"Why can't you work on Sunday?" Larry asked. Then, before Shingi could answer, he added, "You know when we hired you, we told you that our business can be unpredictable, and that all employees' work schedules are subject to change."

"I know," replied Shingi, "and I'd work if I could, Larry, because I really need this job. However, after you posted the schedule last week and I saw I was off Sunday, I told my boss it was okay to schedule me at my other job. They always work around my schedule here, but I know I'll get fired if I don't go in, and I need that job too. I'm sorry, I just can't work Sunday."

1. Many employees in the hospitality industry hold more than one job. What are some reasons why they do so?
2. How can Larry determine if the situation in his hotel warrants a "second job" (or moonlighting) policy?
3. As an HR specialist, what specific issues would you advise Larry to consider as he developed and implemented his policy?

have their voices heard by management. Staff meetings, bulletin boards, newsletters, and suggestion boxes are common examples of devices employers routinely use to encourage information exchange.

Now that you are familiar with many common areas in which HR managers develop polices and procedures, it is important for you to also know the process these managers use to properly develop and implement them.

Steps in HR Policy and Procedures Development

> 2. **Identify the steps managers use to develop HR management policies and procedures**.

It is generally a poor practice to make HR-related decisions based on momentary operational needs. Consider the case of the dining room manager who, because he was rushed and harried during a busy dinner period, "fires" an employee (busser) who (the manager feels) violated the dress code because the busser's shirt was untucked while clearing tables. In this case, the busser's shirt was indeed untucked. Therefore, it might seem the dining room manager's actions were reasonable. Experienced managers advising this dining room manager would likely, however, first ask a few relevant questions, such as:

1. Was the employee ever informed of the restaurant's "no untucked shirts" policy? Is that requirement specifically listed within the restaurant's dress code?
2. Is there *written* evidence that the employee received and understood (in his own native language) this specific policy?
3. How long has the employee been with the organization?
4. Is this the employee's first dress code policy violation?
5. Was the employee given a reasonable chance to explain the circumstances leading to his violation of the policy?
6. Have, in the past, all employees found to be in similar violation of this same policy been fired immediately? If not, what was the rationale for the firing of this specific employee?
7. Under the laws of the state in which the restaurant is located, will the employee likely qualify to receive unemployment compensation in this case?
8. Are the restaurant's employees unionized? If so, is the termination allowed under the terms of the union contract? Is the restaurant part of a chain? If so, was the termination consistent with the action that has, in the past, been taken by other dining room managers working within the chain?

When managers carefully develop and implement HR-related policies, the risk of expensive and time-consuming HR-related litigation is greatly reduced. *Courtesy PhotoDisc/Getty Images*

9. Has, in the past, this manager ever been accused, successfully or unsuccessfully, of discrimination in the hiring or firing of the restaurant's employees?

10. Given the circumstances of this incident, what message did the dining room manager seek to send to the restaurant's remaining employees? Does the manager feel that the message sent will help or harm the restaurant's long-term HR efforts?

Step	Rationale
1. Identify the HR issue to be addressed.	Policies and procedures typically are developed to address an important issue, establish a standard, or solve an identifiable problem.
2. Consider on-site factors affecting implementation.	Internal factors directly affecting the development of the policy or procedures are considered next. Examples include items such as the existence of a union contract, the objectives management seeks to achieve, and the time frame required for implementation.
3. Consider off-site factors affecting implementation.	Off-site factors that may need to be considered in the policy and procedure development process include overriding chain or franchise policies, local labor-related legislation, and competitor policies.
4. Draft policy and procedures and submit for (legal) review.	After a policy and the procedures required to implement it have been drafted, it is always a good idea to have the draft examined by a qualified legal expert. This step is important in helping to reduce potential litigation directly related to the policy.
5. Develop related documentation and recordkeeping requirements.	After a legal review has been undertaken and completed, managers will develop the recordkeeping procedures needed to ensure the consistent application of the policy, as well as the ability to prove it has indeed been applied consistently.
6. Communicate finalized policy and procedures to affected parties.	HR policies and procedures that have not been adequately communicated to those affected are difficult or may even be impossible to enforce. The final step in policy development and implementation is the policy's clear and timely communication to all affected parties, as well as the documentation of that communication.

FIGURE 3.4: Six-Step Policy and Procedure Development Process

As you can readily see from these questions, management is, in most cases, generally given broad powers to hire and terminate employees. However, today's legal environment, as well as the basic concept of fairness and quality employee relations, mandate that operators should carefully follow policies that they have thoughtfully developed when managing HR issues.

To help minimize the negative consequences that can be associated with improperly developing or applying HR policies, experienced managers should establish a basic policy and procedure development process. While this process will vary based on the size and type of hospitality operation involved, most will follow a series of important steps designed to ensure that only an appropriate development approach is utilized. These steps are shown in Figure 3.4.

In some cases, HR managers can save time by purchasing prewritten policies and procedures that can be utilized as is or modified to apply to their own operations (as well as disseminated to affected employees). To see an example of one such product, go to *www.policytech.com*.

Review for Legal Compliance

3. Understand the importance of seeking legal counsel and/or review prior to implementing HR policies and procedures.

Earlier in this chapter, you learned that a legal review was an important step in the policy and procedure development process. The reason why this step is critical for managers is readily apparent when you consider that it makes no sense to develop procedures to support an illegal policy. While experienced HR managers understand that the manner in which a policy is implemented can be flawed, a policy that is already flawed or illegal from the outset simply should not be implemented. In most cases, a legal review of a policy proposed by experienced managers will not indicate that the proposed policy is illegal. Rather, the legal review will more likely indicate potentially troublesome procedural areas to which HR managers should pay close attention.

To see how a legal policy, improperly applied, could create difficulties, and as a result, to illustrate the importance of a thorough legal review, consider the case of Latisha. She is a foodservice director for a local hospital. Latisha's operation prepares and serves more than 500 meals per day. Despite some managers' thoughts to the contrary, Latisha knows that the law allows her much discretion in setting appearance standards for her staff, and she wishes to do so by creating and implementing a department-wide dress code.

In nearly all cases, hospitality managers such as Latisha can (and often do) legally impose rules and guidelines that have a basis in social norms, such as those prohibiting visible tattoos, body piercings, or earrings for men. While tattoos and piercings may be examples of employee self-expression, they generally are not recognized as signs of religious or racial expression (and thus are not typically protected under federal discrimination laws). For example, in *Cloutier v. Costco Wholesale Corp.*, 390 F.3d 126 (1st Cir. 2004), the First Circuit Court considered whether an employer was required to exempt a cashier from its dress code policy prohibiting facial jewelry (except earrings) and allow her to wear facial piercings as a reasonable religious accommodation. The employee claimed that her religious practice as a member of the Church of Body Modification required she wear the piercings uncovered at all times.

This court accepted that the cashier was protected by Title VII of the Civil Rights Act, without specifically discussing the sincerity of her beliefs, and only ruled on whether her requested exemption from the dress code would impose an undue hardship on the employer. The court found that exempting the employee from the policy would in fact create an undue hardship for the employer because it would "adversely affect the employer's public image," and the employer had a legitimate business interest in cultivating a professional image. The employee's case was dismissed. Certainly, hospitality employers such as Latisha have the same legitimate business interest.

In most cases, a carefully drafted dress code that is applied consistently should not violate discrimination laws. Despite the wide latitude given to hospitality and tourism employers, it is possible that all or part of an implemented dress code can be found to be discriminatory. It is not uncommon for hospitality employees to challenge even well-designed dress codes on the basis of purported discrimination related to their sex, race, or religion.

Sex discrimination claims typically are not successful unless the dress policy has no basis in social customs, differentiates markedly between men and women, or imposes a burden on women that is not imposed on men. Thus, for example, a policy that requires female managers to wear uniforms while male managers are allowed to wear "professional attire," such as their choice of suit and tie, is likely discriminatory. However, dress requirements that reflect current social norms generally are upheld, even when they affect only one sex. For example, in a decision by the Eleventh Circuit Court of Appeals in *Harper v. Blockbuster Entertainment Corp.*, 139 F.3d 1385 (11th Cir. 1998), the court upheld an employer's policy that required only male employees to cut their long hair.

In most cases, race discrimination claims would be difficult for an employee to prove because the employee must show that the employer's dress code has a disparate (and unfair) impact on a protected class of employees. One limited area where race claims have had some success is in challenges to "no beard" policies. A few courts have determined that a policy that requires all male employees to be clean-shaven may discriminate if it does not accommodate individuals with pseudofolliculitis barbae (PFB), a skin condition aggravated by shaving that occurs almost exclusively among African-American males.

Employees have had the most success challenging dress codes on the basis that they violate religious discrimination laws. These charges occur most frequently when an employer is unwilling to allow an employee's religious dress or appearance. For example, a policy may be discriminatory if it does not accommodate an employee's religious need to cover his head or wear a beard. However, if an employer can show that the accommodation would be an undue hardship, such as if the employee's dress or grooming created a safety concern, it would not likely be required to vary to its policy. Interestingly, dress code claims also may be filed under the National Labor Relations Act (NLRA). For example, to comply with the NLRA, employers, even in nonunion workplaces, generally may not ban the wearing of union insignia.

As you have now learned, even in an area such as dress codes—where employers such as Latisha have wide latitude to manage their businesses as they see fit—the potential for legal difficulties can still exist. Virtually any of the areas in which policies and procedures are developed may be the source of litigation, but managers must be most careful in the areas related to the control of employee dress, expression of opinion, and behavior away from the worksite. As a result, experienced HR managers know that, in nearly all cases, a periodic legal review of an organization's overall policy and procedures manual, as well as a specific review each time it is significantly modified or revised, is a wise use of organizational resources.

A careful review for legal compliance is a critical step in the HR policy development process. *Courtesy Purestock*

Human Resources Management:
CURRENT EVENTS 3.2

THE EMERGING BLOGOSPHERE

Web logs, or "blogs," have become extremely popular in recent years, especially in the case of younger workers. In fact, blogging is so popular that it is estimated more than 1 million new blog postings are added to the Internet every day. Most of these are of a personal nature, but some, inevitably, have to do with the blogger's work. Just as inevitably, in some cases, the comments workers make about their workplace or their managers are, to put it gently, less than complimentary. It would be tempting for managers who become aware of derogatory blogs to seek to punish those workers who wrote them (especially if the posted statements are unfair or one-sided), but these managers need to tread very carefully.

As a result of "lawful conduct" statutes employees generally have rights to engage in lawful activities during nonwork hours. Blogging certainly is not illegal. Also, the NLRA grants employees rights that include those related to criticism of their companies and their managers. Furthermore, the NLRA generally protects from retaliation measures those workers who (even publicly) are critical of management.

It is just as important to note, however, that not all work-related speech is protected by the NLRA or laws related to free speech. Reckless or malicious lies, disclosure of confidential company information, and threatening and harassing statements are not typically protected forms of free speech.

Savvy HR managers will carefully watch the emerging blogosphere. If they elect to develop policies regulating blogging, they will also understand that they must carefully navigate the sometimes very fine line between their companies' rights and the rights of their employees.

Applying Advanced Technology to HR Policies and Procedures

4. Recognize and appreciate the role advanced technology is currently playing, and will continue to play, in the process of HR-related policy and procedure development.

Some managers in the hospitality industry view the application of technology to operational issues as a problem, rather than an opportunity. It is true that the technological systems used in restaurants, bars, clubs, hotels, and other hospitality operations are far more advanced and complicated today than those available only a short time ago, and these systems continue to advance rapidly. Rather than viewing technology applications as conveying impersonal, cost-savings-only attributes,

HR managers will find that advances in technology have made it easier than ever to do their jobs.

In most cases, two extremely important functions of HR and, as a result, two areas where HR-related technology can be effectively utilized include information dissemination and information storage.

INFORMATION DISSEMINATION

Consider the challenges and opportunities facing the management team of a ski resort that elects to implement a new HR policy about the specific procedures to request time off under the Family Medical Leave Act (FMLA, see Chapter 2). For the managers involved in this policy and procedure development process, one major hurdle they must overcome relates to informing the proper individuals about the new policy and any new procedures associated with it. In the recent past, the managers would have had limited options for disseminating the new information and, just as important, their options for documenting that dissemination would have been limited as well. As a result, changes in policies and procedures were typically accompanied by a **hard copy** document detailing the new policy and procedures. This hard copy would typically be distributed, signed by employees, and then a copy of the document with the confirming signature would be placed in the employee's **personal file**. In other cases, the information might be added to an existing **employee handbook** (or **employee manual**), which, after management had updated all of the affected sections, would be redistributed to employees.

It is important for managers to understand that the courts will generally allow employers wide latitude to enforce a variety of job-related policies and procedures. In most cases, however, those employers must first conclusively show that their employees were, in fact, informed about the policies and procedures. Therefore, documenting an employee's actual receipt of important policy and procedure information is imperative.

In many hospitality operations, the initial dissemination of and documentation that essential employment policies and procedures were received occurs when employees are hired and given an updated copy of the employee handbook. Documentation most often involves placing, in the employee's personal file, a signed document (or photocopy) with the employee's signature stating he or she did receive a copy of the manual. Figure 3.5 is an example of a document that can be utilized to verify employee receipt of an operation's employee handbook and its important policies and procedures.

Increasingly, because of advances in communications technology, the options available for information dissemination are much greater. HR managers can select from a wide variety of communication devices and approaches both for the initial dissemination of important policies and procedures information and for their later modification, additions, and deletions. Returning to the example of the ski resort managers seeking to implement new procedures for requesting time off

Hard copy: The common term for a document that has been printed on paper.

Personal file: A record of information about a single employee's employment. Typically, this file includes information about the employee's personal status, application, performance evaluations, and disciplinary warnings. Also known as a *personnel file.*

Employee handbook: A permanent reference guide for employers and employees that contains information about a company, its goals, and its current employment policies and procedures. Also often referred to as the *employee manual.*

Employee manual: Same as *employee handbook.*

Acknowledgment of Receipt of Employee Handbook

The Employee Handbook contains important information about (*insert company name* _____).
I understand that I should ask my supervisor, manager, or the HR administrator about any
questions I have that have not been answered in the handbook. I have entered into my
employment relationship with the company voluntarily, and understand that there is no
specified length of my employment. Either the Company or I can terminate the relationship
at will, at any time, with or without cause, and with or without advance notice.

Because the information, policies, procedures, and benefits described in this manual are
subject to change at any time, I acknowledge that revisions to the handbook may occur. All such
changes will be communicated through an official notice, and I understand that revised
information may add to, modify, or eliminate the company's existing policies.

Also, I understand that this handbook is neither a contract of employment nor a legally
binding agreement. I have been given the time needed to read the handbook, and I agree to
accept the terms in it. I also understand that it is my responsibility to comply with the policies
contained in this handbook and any revisions made to it.

I understand that I am expected to read the entire handbook. After I have done so, I will
sign two original copies of this Acknowledgment of Receipt, retain one copy for myself, and
return one copy to the company's representative listed below. I understand that this form will
be retained in my personal file.

Signature of Employee	Date
Employee's Name (Printed)	
Company Representative	Date

FIGURE 3.5: Sample Employee Handbook Signature Page

under the FMLA, Figure 3.6 summarizes some of the more popular information-related options available to these managers.

It is important to recognize that many employees in the hospitality industry have neither the language skills nor the computer skills and access required to take advantage of some of the communication options available today. Enlightened managers know that, ultimately, it is their responsibility, not that of their employees, to ensure and document that required policy and procedure information has been provided to those who need it.

Information storage: The processes, equipment, and documents that make up a company's records retention effort.

INFORMATION STORAGE

In addition to expanding the number of information dissemination options available to managers, advances in technology have increased the number of available **information storage** options.

Communication Device	Dissemination Characteristics	Documentation Characteristics
E-mail with attachment	Fast, inexpensive	Recipients can be asked to confirm e-mail receipt prior to opening
Web site posting	Permanent accessibility, but Web site modifications may be costly	Employees may be asked to sign in via an individually issued code prior to gaining access to protected Web site areas
CD	Less expensive, in many cases, than producing traditional hard-copy employee manuals	Employees may be asked to verify, via their signature (on paper copy or electronically), receipt of the CD
Toll-free number: telephone voice recording	Employees may access information via a numerically initiated options menu. Recordings may be made available in multiple languages.	Employees may be asked to verify, via their signature, receipt of the toll-free number allowing their access to the policy and procedure information
Electronic news posting/blog	Inexpensive and instantaneous updates	Employees may be asked to verify, via their signature, receipt of the address of the site/blog

FIGURE 3.6: Manager's Policy and Procedure Initial Dissemination and Documentation Options

In the fairly recent past, most HR-related records in the hospitality and tourism industry simply consisted of hard-copy (paper) files stored in the appropriate employee personal file, or in a file developed specifically for recordkeeping purposes. Thus, for example, information related to employees' requests for time off or paid vacation might be kept in the individual employee's file, or in files designed to track and record these types of employee requests. Obviously, in very large hospitality operations, with hundreds of employees, such a paper-based system could easily become unwieldy and cumbersome. Increasingly, even smaller restaurants, hotels, clubs, and other operations find that management of today's HR-related records and information requires the application of advanced technology hardware and software, partly because of the increases in recordkeeping requirements, as well as the challenges of maintaining accessibility (and security) of HR-related information.

Many HR managers actually find that information storage is one of their greatest challenges. To understand why this is so, consider the following areas for which data storage is of significant concern:

Employment applications

Résumés

Human Resources MANAGEMENT ISSUES (3.2)

"**B**ut that's nearly impossible!" said Trisha Sangus, general manager of the Plaza Intercontinental Hotel, the 750-room convention hotel located in the heart of downtown and adjacent to the city's convention center. "How can we do that?"

"I don't know, but that's what the e-mail from corporate says," replied Pam Cummings, director of human resources.

"So let me see if I get this straight," said Trisha. "We have to certify, in writing, that each of our employees has received, and understands, the information in our corporate employee handbook."

"That's right," said Pamela. "I've had my staff do some checking. With our current 430 employees, we would need a total of about 16 translations. You know, Russian, Portuguese, Korean, Polish, Croatian, and others. Plus Spanish, but corporate already has that translation, so I guess we really only need 15 more."

QUESTIONS

1. Do you believe it is the right of all employees to receive a copy of their work-related policies and procedures rules written in their native language?
2. What, if any, accommodation do you believe should be made for those employees who are not capable of reading any language?
3. What specific advice might you give Trisha and Pamela as they seek to comply with this directive from their corporate HR office?

Performance evaluations

Disciplinary records

Medical files

Insurance-related records and correspondence

Training records and documentation

Certificates, transcripts, diplomas

Military records

Governmental entity inquiry records

Lawsuit-related information

Other employee or employment-related correspondence

Hospitality managers who are responsible for designing effective recordkeeping systems also face a conflicting challenge. Stored records must be easily available for viewing, but they also must be kept secure and inaccessible to viewers who would compromise the confidentiality of the records. Fortunately, although the recordkeeping

Server: A central computer system that stores documents and information for input and retrieval.

CD: A **c**ompact **d**isc is a device capable of storing digital information. CD-ROM (read-only memory) means that once the data has been recorded onto the CD, it can only be read or played, but not revised.

DVD: Short for **d**igital **v**ersatile **d**isc or **d**igital **v**ideo **d**isc, the DVD is a type of optical disk technology similar to the CD-ROM. DVD-ROMs are commonly used as a medium for digital representation of movies and other multimedia presentations that combine sound with graphics. DVD-RAM (random access memory) discs can be recorded and erased repeatedly, but are only compatible with devices manufactured by the companies that support the DVD-RAM format.

requirements facing HR managers are greater than ever, the tools available to HR managers also provide greater options.

In addition to paper documents, HR managers can choose from a variety of advanced technology recordkeeping and retrieval systems. These systems often include components such as:

Security features. In many cases, HR managers develop information storage systems that allow for multiple levels of security to protect sensitive documents and files from unauthorized viewers. Each user has a security access level, and each document has a sensitivity level. Depending on the access level granted to the users, they will see only the lists of documents that are appropriate for their security access level.

Records-specific servers. A **server** can be readily designed to provide access to important HR-related data. Servers are often dedicated: they perform no other tasks besides their server tasks.

Document archival features. These components allow information or documents to be downloaded to a file server, tape, **CD**-ROM, **DVD**-ROM, or DVD-RAM.

High-speed image printing. This component of a recordkeeping and retrieval system is utilized to create hard copy of electronically stored information.

Continued advances in technology help HR professionals in the hospitality industry address their communication and documentation needs. *Courtesy PhotoDisc, Inc.*

Regardless of the sophistication level of the information storage and retrieval system they develop, HR managers must comply with the documentation and recordkeeping requirements imposed on them by their own companies as well as by governmental entities that mandate and monitor their compliance.

HR Policies and Procedures Documentation and Record Keeping

5. Recognize the most significant reasons why HR managers must develop, implement, and maintain effective HR recordkeeping systems.

Regardless of the level of technology they apply to the process, all HR managers must follow specific laws and regulations that address employment-related documentation and recordkeeping issues. In addition, businesses often develop some of their own in-house procedures for policy and procedures documentation and record keeping. As a result, HR managers must make decisions regarding their own record retention policies and procedures. For example, most HR managers agree that it is a good idea to keep a copy of all applications and résumés received when they advertise to fill an employment vacancy. The reasons for retaining these documents are many, but include the ability to monitor the quality of the available workforce, to help ensure that advertisements by the organization appeal to the broadest labor pool possible, and to help judge the workforce demand for the employer's position. Consider, however, the HR manager who must answer the following very specific question:

Are all individuals who submit résumés via the Internet considered applicants for recordkeeping and reporting purposes? If so, how shall these records be stored, and for how long? What if the candidates are clearly unqualified for the position?

Questions such as this may be difficult to address, but HR managers must still do so thoughtfully. Other examples of records-related questions that require policy and procedures decisions include those such as:

- How do regulations related to ADA, COBRA, FMLA, FLSA, and OSHA affect the length of time records should be kept? (*Note:* Specific record-related requirements of these agencies are addressed, where applicable, in the pertinent area of this text.)
- Should employees have access to their discipline records? Can they make copies? How long should a terminated employee's files be kept?
- Which personnel management-related documents should require actual (not electronic) signatures?

Regardless of how questions such as these are answered, HR managers must make significant decisions regarding the employment records that must be retained and the length of time to retain them. In some cases, employment-related legislation will dictate the full or partial answers to questions of this type.

Figure 3.7 lists selected recordkeeping requirements enforced by the U.S. government. Other requirements may be imposed at the state or local level.

HIRING AND EMPLOYMENT ACTIONS

Employee Record	FLSA, EPA	FMLA	ADEA	IRCA	Title VII, ADA	OSHA	Tax Laws
Employee name, address, Social Security number, gender, date of birth	3 years from last entry	3 years from last entry	3 years from last entry	3 years from hire or 1 year after termination	1 year after record created or personnel action taken	1 year after termination	4 years after tax due or paid
Position, job category	2 years after created		3 years from last entry				4 years after tax due or paid
Applications, résumés, recruitment notices, job orders, employment tests			1 year after related personnel action		1 year after record created or personnel action taken		
Date of hire					1 year after record created		
I-9 form				Later of 3 years after hire or 1 year after termination			
Work permits/age certificates for minors	While employed						
Dates and reasons for promotion, demotion, transfer, layoff, rehire, and termination			1 year after related personnel action		1 year after personnel action		

FIGURE 3.7: Selected Federal-Level Hiring and Employment Action: Recordkeeping Requirements

HIRING AND EMPLOYMENT ACTIONS

Employee Record	FLSA, EPA	FMLA	ADEA	IRCA	Title VII, ADA	OSHA	Tax Laws
Performance evaluations	2 years after created				1 year after record created or personnel action taken		
Training opportunities, agreements	Duration of training		1 year after related personnel action		1 year after personnel action		1 year after termination

Key Terms

FLSA, EPA	Fair Labor Standards Act, Equal Pay Act
FMLA	Family & Medical Leave Act
ADEA	Age Discrimination in Employment Act
IRCA	Immigration Reform & Control Act
Title IIV, ADA	Civil Rights Act, Americans with Disabilities Act
OSHA	Occupational Safety & Health Act

FIGURE 3.7: (Continued)

To further illustrate the practical importance of proper documentation and record keeping, consider the case of Tonya Walker, the director of food services at a large corporate dining facility. The facility is operated under contract by a nationally recognized foodservice management company that has employed Tonya for the past 15 years. Her operation serves more than 1,000 persons per day. Approximately 200 of her diners are salaried managers who eat in the executive dining room, while 800 are hourly workers who eat in a separate, larger dining area.

Tonya is an excellent manager, so she was surprised when Becka Larsen, the company's vice president of human resources, arrived at her operation to announce that the company had received a letter from the EEOC stating that an ex-employee had charged Tonya's operation with discrimination and **constructive discharge**.

Essentially, explained Becka, the EEOC's letter was sent to officially notify Tonya's company of the charges initiated by the former employee. The letter also included an **RFI**, which was the reason for Becka coming to see Tonya.

When questioned, Tonya explained to Becka that the employee making the charges was a dining room attendant who had, in fact, complained once about the sexually oriented nature of comments made by a fellow worker. That same employee had also complained once about some comments made by one of the diners in the executive dining room.

Tonya also explained that she, as the facility manager, had personally addressed both situations and, to further assist the employee, she had reassigned her from the executive dining room to the regular employees' dining area. Tonya finished by stating that, two or three weeks after the second complaint was addressed, the employee resigned because she had accepted a higher-paying job across town. Although this occurred more than five months ago, as Tonya now recalled the situation, no mention was made of any unhappiness at the time the employee resigned.

Cases such as this one are most often very complex. However, it should be apparent from the few details presented that, if Tonya's employer is to successfully defend itself and, if Tonya is to continue to be perceived as an effective manager, Tonya's HR policies, procedures, and documentation systems should conclusively show that:

1. An effective sexual harassment policy was clearly stated in the employee manual that Tonya issued to each employee when hired.
2. The employee making the charges in this case was given a copy of the manual as well as the opportunity to have it explained by management if any part of it were unclear.
3. The existence or absence of other, similar charges filed by Tonya's current or former employees have been documented.
4. Tonya responded to this ex-employee's complaints in a timely manner.
5. Tonya (or members of her management team) properly followed the specific investigation procedures proscribed in the sexual harassment complaint portion of the employee manual.

Constructive discharge: An employee-initiated termination of employment brought about by conditions that make the employee's work situation so intolerable that a reasonable person would feel compelled to quit. Also known as constructive *wrongful* discharge.

RFI: An official EEOC Request for Information. An EEOC requirement that the accused party submit all requested copies of personnel policies, the accuser's personnel files, the personnel files of other individuals, and any other information deemed relevant by the EEOC.

6. The measures Tonya took in response to the allegations were not only proper, but they were also fully documented, with precise detail about items including time, date, actions taken, and persons involved.

7. Relevant information related to those individuals accused of harassment by the ex-employee was recorded and is now available for review.

8. Management's resolutions of the complaints were fully explained, in a timely manner, to the ex-employee.

9. No changes in the former employee's employment status, work assignment, or employment conditions occurred that could be used to support or justify the constructive discharge allegation.

10. Tonya clearly followed her own company's internally mandated policies and procedures, as well as all applicable federal and state laws, when responding to the former employee's harassment charges.

The absence of records such as those indicated in the list will not definitively mean that Tonya's employer cannot successfully defend itself against the ex-employee's charges. However, the ability of Tonya's employer to successfully mount a valid defense to the ex-employee's charges will be greatly reduced, as will be Tonya's ability to support her own managerial action (or inaction) if any of these records are unavailable.

While this is just one example of the importance of proper record keeping, it is critical to understand that a great number of similar examples could be shown. Experienced HR managers agree that determining exactly which

The employee-related record-keeping requirements imposed by local governmental entities vary based on a business's size and location.
Courtesy PhotoDisc, Inc.

Human Resources MANAGEMENT ISSUES   (3.3)

"**H**ow many years back?", asked Josephine Cochsky, the manager of the Delta River Dinner Cruise Boat.

"Three years," answered Penny Cuthbert, Josephine's HR manager.

"Let me see if I understand," said Josephine. "We have to produce the actual time cards, for Anthony Graves, for the last three years. He hasn't even worked here for six months. Who's the letter from?"

"The State Board of Disability Appeals," said Penny, as she read the certified letter that had just been delivered. "I guess what happened," continued Penny, "is that Anthony got really hurt on his new job after he left here, and he is now applying for disability. The state wants us to confirm his wages during the two-year period he worked for us."

"Can't we just send them copies of his W-2 statements?" asked Josephine.

"I guess not," replied Penny. "According to the Board, state law requires we keep actual copies of our time cards or time sheets showing the specific days and hours worked for each of our employees for a period of five years. It's for tax purposes, but the Disability Board uses the same income database. I didn't know we were supposed to keep old time cards. We don't have them. I only keep them for a year. I think this could really be a problem!"

QUESTIONS

1. Do you feel it was Josephine's responsibility, or Penny's, to know the employee recordkeeping requirements that apply within their state?
2. If you operated the State Board of Disability, what penalties might you suggest for hospitality operators and others who maintain they do not know which employment-related laws apply to them and, therefore, do not comply with all laws that are applicable?
3. How can advances in technology help Josephine and Penny avoid the potential damage and fallout that could result from additional mistakes made in their operation's record keeping?

employment-related records to keep, and for how long, is one of their most essential tasks. Most hospitality managers would also agree that it is critical for large, multiunit operators to have well-documented employee-related policies and procedures in place, despite the enormity of the task. Even for very small hospitality operators, while the effort required to address the task may be lessened, in today's litigious society, its successful completion is no less critical.

HUMAN RESOURCES TERMS

The following terms were defined in this chapter:

HR policy(ies)	Personal file
HR procedures	Employee handbook
Garde-manger	Employee manual
Patissier	Information storage
Saucier	Server
Employee Assistance Program (EAP)	CD
	DVD
Hard copy	Constructive discharge

FOR YOUR CONSIDERATION

1. The debate about which theory of motivation is true has been a long-standing one. Review the various theories in Figure 3.3 of this chapter. Which theory most closely represents your own view of motivation? How do you think you came to hold your current view? Identify one event that helped shape the way you feel about this topic.
2. Employee Assistance Programs (EAPs) are increasing in popularity. Go to *www.compsych.com*. Select two programs that you, as a manager, believe employees would find to be important. Do you think these would be the same two EAPs that their employers would consider most important? Explain your answer.
3. Many managers are surprised to hear that they can be held personally responsible for damages resulting from HR-related events that happen in their workplace. What specific steps would you recommend individual hospitality managers take to minimize this liability?
4. HR recordkeeping activities must be well-planned, detailed, and undertaken consistently. What are some specific personality characteristics of individuals who would excel at these tasks? Do you think most hospitality managers have (or could acquire) these traits?

CASE STUDY: HUMAN RESOURCES MANAGEMENT IN ACTION

"This is a pain," said Sara. "And it doesn't make any sense."

"What doesn't make sense?" replied Dave Berger, the owner of the Golden Rose, the restaurant where Sara had begun working full time, splitting her duties between that of part-time accounting clerk and part-time HR assistant.

In her accounting role, Sara's job was to prepare the checks needed to pay the restaurant's bills, verify credit card receipts, and make cash deposits. In her role as HR assistant, her job was to total employee time cards and prepare the biweekly payroll, as well as to keep track of each employee's use of sick time, holiday, and vacation pay. Even though she was new, Sara was very good, very bright, and cared deeply about the restaurant and its employees. Because of that, Dave increasingly had come to value the talent she brought to her position, as well as the insightful opinions she was certainly not afraid to share.

"Full-time employees accrue two weeks of vacation per year, and part-time employees accrue about one week. Is that right?" asked Sara.

"That's right," said Dave. "I have always thought that part-timers who work regularly and who stay with the company should earn some vacation time also. It's in the manual."

"Right," said Sara. "It's right here. It says:

"A regular employee who works one-half time or more but less than full-time shall accrue vacation/annual leave prorated on the basis of their actual number of hours worked. An employee who is employed less than ten hours per week shall not be eligible to accrue vacation/annual leave."

"So, if I work 20 hours per week, I earn one week a year. And I use it or lose it. That is, employees are not allowed to carry vacation forward to the next year. Right?" asked Sara.

"That's right," said Dave. "I decided that would be our policy when I started the restaurant, because the idea is that an employee's vacation should be a time to relax and refresh. So it just makes sense to me that if we are going to give employees vacation time, they should take it every year."

"So, does the part-time person earn one week of 40 hours pay, or one week of 20 hours pay?" asked Sara.

"Well, they should be getting one of their regular weeks in my opinion. That is, if they only work 20 hours per week, they should only get paid for a 20-hour vacation week. If they average 30 hours, they should get a 30-hour paid vacation."

"That would make sense," replied Sara, "but your old accounting clerk wasn't doing that. She was recording 3.07 hours for each full-timer per pay period worked and 1.54 hours for each part-time employee."

"3.07 hours and 1.54 hours? Why?" asked Dave.

"Well," replied Sara, "with 26 pay periods per year, and 10 days, or 80 hours vacation accrual, it works out to 3.07 hours per pay period. One week a year is half that—1.535 technically. But rounding to 1.54 is darn close."

"Sounds like she took a shortcut and treated all of the part-timers the same," replied Dave. "We should be able to fix that."

"You could, but that's the problem," said Sara. "You have 52 full-time employees and 38 part-timers. Not all part-timers work every week, and not all of them work 20 hours. You want them to accrue time based on the hours actually worked, but your current record keeping doesn't match the policy. Your current system treats all part-timers as if they worked the same amount of time. To calculate each employee's actual time each week would be insane. Even worse, if they work less than ten hours one week, but 20 the next, you have a whole different problem. That's probably why the old accounting clerk did it this way."

"Well," replied Dave, "let's just change the way we record it. Make it more accurate."

"Dave," said Sara, "it already will take me nearly two hours every pay period just to update the vacation records on our 90 employees. That's 52 hours, or more than a week per year, just to have me track employee vacation time the way you do it now. Tracking it even more accurately would likely double the time, not to mention the time it already takes to record the employee's sick days earned and used, and their paid holidays. There's got to be a more efficient way to do this!"

Dimension: Workforce Enhancement

Consider the vacation policy Dave has implemented at the Golden Rose.

1. How do you think the restaurant's policy affects each of the following HR functional areas:
   a. Staffing the operation
   b. Developing staff
   c. Motivating staff
   d. Maintaining staff
2. Why do you think paid vacations are so frequently used by many businesses in an effort to motivate employees?
3. The hospitality industry employs a large number of part-time workers. Most do not accrue paid vacation time. Why do you think the industry has been so reluctant to grant paid vacations to this large segment of its workforce?

Dimension: Record Keeping and Documentation

Consider the recordkeeping system put in place by the former HR assistant.

1. Would you change the recordkeeping system that has been used?
2. What alternatives could Sara suggest to Dave that would help the restaurant save time and money in maintaining these records?
3. What role could advanced technology play in helping solve this problem? (*Hint*: Google "Vacation records software: employees" and report your findings.)

Dimension: Policy Development

Assume you were considering the development of vacation policies and procedures for an operation of your own.

1. Draft a two-paragraph statement explaining your policy for use in your employee handbook.
2. Draft a two-paragraph statement that would also be used in the handbook explaining the policy and procedure employees would utilize when requesting the use of their paid vacation time.
3. Draft a procedures summary that details how your operation will document granting employee vacation time requests in a manner designed to minimize any charges of bias or unfairness by your employees.

INTERNET ACTIVITIES

1. One of the most difficult areas of employee policies and procedure management relates to the amount of time you must spend creating and maintaining employee records. Fortunately, there are resources to assist you in determining which records you must keep and for how long. One such resource is G-Neil. You can visit their Web site at *www.gneil.com.*
   Click on "Employee Records." Then consider the following:
   a. What available materials and products do you think would be applicable to the hospitality industry?
   b. What types of hospitality operations could use the materials available?
   c. How could a hospitality manager evaluate the cost effectiveness of materials such as these?
2. Some nonprofit and for-profit entities advertise that they can readily provide managers with off-the-shelf policies and procedure checklists, which will save time and money for the organizations using them. One such entity is the Alexander Hamilton Institute. According to its Web site (posted July 1, 2006), "the Alexander Hamilton Institute has been helping executives manage their companies and their careers since 1909. We currently publish newsletters, booklets, and loose-leaf manuals targeted to top management, Human Resource directors, personnel managers, front-line managers, and supervisors at small-to-medium sized firms."
   Go to their Web site at: *www.ahipubs.com.* Consider the following:
   a. What is your assessment of the quality of their HR-related resources?
   b. What concerns might you have about the use of their products or any externally generated products?
   c. This chapter presented an argument for employing a legal review of all significant HR policies and procedures. If you purchased a preprepared policy or procedure product from AHI, or another entity like it, would you still seek a legal review of the product prior to using it? Why? or Why not?

3. In the past, some managers felt their employees were not sophisticated enough, nor had the financial resources, to really challenge policies those employees felt were discriminatory or unfair. It is not true today. Web sites such as Workplace Fairness provide significant assistance to any employee with access to the Internet. Workplace Fairness is a nonprofit organization helping to preserve and promote employee rights. According to its posted information, Workplace Fairness "provides information about job rights and employment issues around the country and in all 50 states. It is for workers, employers, advocates and anyone else who wants to better understand, protect, and strengthen workers' rights." To visit the site, go to *www.workplacefairness.org.*

   a. Note that the National Employment Lawyers Association (NELA) sponsors the site. Why do you believe they would do so?

   b. What specific resources are available on this site? List at least three such resources.

   c. What are some specific work-related issues you feel would compel an employee to seek out the type of information found on a site such as this one? How can hospitality managers best address these issues?

PART TWO

Securing Human Resources

CHAPTER FOUR

Employee Recruitment and Selection

CHECKLIST   ## OF CHAPTER LEARNING OBJECTIVES

As a result of satisfactory completion of this chapter, readers will be able to:

1. Identify the factors that HR managers must consider prior to planning and initiating their organization's employee recruitment efforts.

2. Differentiate between the actions HR managers take when electing to conduct internal, external, or outsourced searches for qualified employees.

3. List and explain the importance of applications, interviews, testing, background checks, and references—the five major activities that HR managers undertake when screening employees for possible selection.

4. Understand and explain the potential legal liability related to negligent hiring.

5. Describe the legal differences between a conditional job offer and a final job offer.

Impact on Human Resources Management

Exceptional hospitality management company leaders are often quoted as saying that "our people are our greatest asset." These managers are not simply paying lip service to the importance of employees. They know it is true. There are few trade secrets or barriers to entry in the hospitality industry that would stop new businesses from successfully forming and competing for customers. As a result, nothing can prevent highly innovative and service-oriented individuals from creating new businesses and achieving tremendous success. In the hospitality industry, people are critically important. In fact, one characteristic that has historically distinguished the hospitality industry from others is the ability of a single, innovative entrepreneur to make a remarkable impact. Examples such as Ray Kroc (McDonald's), Kemmons Wilson (Holiday Inns), Horst Schulze (Ritz Carlton), and Richard Melman (Lettuce Entertain You) are merely a few powerful reminders that a single individual (and often one whose entry-level job in the industry was modest indeed!) can have an incredible impact on the industry.

Most successful hospitality industry leaders will also state that they have little personal interest in making their companies the biggest or even the most profitable. They know that if they focus on providing outstanding guest service, growth and profits are the inevitable result. With great success, and more customers, however, comes the need to identify, train, and retain even more talented people. These people must be kept happy, focused on excellence, and committed to the organization's goals. That is why employee recruitment and selection efforts are so critical to the long-term success of every hospitality business and to all of the hospitality managers who direct their operation's recruitment and selection process.

Factors Affecting Recruiting Efforts

1. Identify the factors that HR managers must consider prior to planning and initiating their organization's employee recruitment efforts.

In the hospitality industry, successful managers focus on two very different, but related tasks. These are:

1. Securing and keeping an adequate customer base
2. Securing and keeping an adequate number of qualified employees to serve the customer base

If either of these two tasks is not successfully completed, a hospitality business will suffer either from a shortage of customers or the skilled employees needed to serve them.

Product and concept development, facility design and construction, product planning, marketing, and advertising are some of the activities directed at securing and keeping a customer base large enough to maintain a business. Employee **recruiting** and **selection** are the first two essential steps taken by businesses to identify and choose the right employees, with the right qualifications, to serve their customers.

Recruiting: The process of identifying candidates for current or future position vacancies.

Selection: The process of choosing an individual for a current or future position vacancy.

In most traditional HR textbooks, a discussion of employee recruitment and selection is introduced only after a detailed presentation of the job analysis process. Job analysis is simply the manner in which managers carefully study the specific tasks that need to be done in their operations, as well as the skills workers must have to complete those tasks.

Human Resources Management:
CURRENT EVENTS 4.1

THE CHANGING NATURE OF JOBS

Before employers can effectively choose their employees, they must identify the knowledge, skills, and abilities that those applying for their vacancies should possess. This is completed via a thorough analysis of what their workers do and how they do it. They must then find employees capable of being taught, "How we do it here." Thus, the examination and analysis of jobs is both a recruitment and training issue.

In Chapter 6, you will learn how hospitality managers conduct detailed position analyses and task breakdowns to identify precisely the skills their workers currently need and then create effective training programs to teach these skills. This is consistent with the approach of "Find the *right* people, and then teach them the *right* skills." In some cases, however, the skills identified for a position may be critical to the recruitment of future employees. When this is the case, information about these special skill requirements should be included in the position's recruitment material.

For many hospitality managers, and especially for those hiring entry-level employees, personal characteristics such as friendliness, punctuality, attitude, and personal grooming and others may be much more important than a candidate's background or prior experience. Any manager seeking to find pretrained employees simply by listing detailed skill requirements in their position advertisements are likely to be sorely disappointed, because in most hospitality operations, the manner in which work is completed varies greatly. In addition, how things are done today is likely very different from how they will be done tomorrow. As a result, a careful reading of current position vacancy announcements shows a trend to emphasize (properly) personal characteristics, ability to change, and willingness to work to a much greater degree than specific previous work experience or current skill levels gleaned from detailed job analyses.

This traditional view makes the reasonable assumption that managers must know the specific work-related tasks that job applicants will need to do before they can effectively seek them out. The authors of this text do not discount the importance of managers fully understanding the details of the jobs that must be done in their operations. In fact, an extremely thorough discussion of this topic is presented in Chapter 6. The reality for most hospitality unit managers is that even the experienced workers they hire will, in nearly all cases, require detailed training in how their specific tasks are to be completed. As a result, the ability to perform required job skills at the time of employment is sometimes less important than are a variety of other, more important factors.

IT'S THE LAW!

In the United States, the Department of Justice is headed by the U.S. Attorney General. Although the position of Attorney General has existed since the founding of the Republic, a separate Department of Justice was not created until 1870, bringing together under the authority of the Attorney General the activities of United States Attorneys, United States Marshals, and others. The Justice Department investigates and prosecutes federal crimes, represents the United States in court, manages the federal prisons, and enforces the nation's immigration laws.

Most hospitality managers interact with the Department of Justice in the area of immigration. The Immigration and Naturalization Service (INS) was created in 1891, and is headed by a commissioner who reports directly to the Attorney General. The INS requires that managers in all industries, including hospitality, must secure verifying worker identification documents from everyone they hire. This is mandated so that jobs will be given only to those people who are legally able to secure them. Under current law (that may change over time), employers are required to secure but not to independently verify the authenticity of identification documents supplied to them. The result, in some cases, is that those who do not have the legal status to work in the United States have been hired.

In many parts of the United States, immigrants make up a very large portion of the hospitality industry workforce. As a result, many leaders within the hospitality industry have taken very public stances in favor of easing immigration restrictions. Certainly this is their political right, and most would agree that any efforts to expand the pool of qualified applicants legally permitted to work in the hospitality industry are always a good idea.

It is also very important to recognize, however, that under current law, the fines for knowingly employing undocumented workers can be severe. This area of public debate is quite volatile. As a result, professional hospitality managers must carefully monitor changes in legislation related to the issues of immigration, worker documentation, and worker document verification in the years to come.

To illustrate this point, consider the case of an excellent server with 10 years' experience working in a family-style table-service restaurant. This worker would likely still need very operation-specific training if hired as a server by the manager of a fine-dining establishment. In a similar manner, young persons with no previous job experience, who are hired to be dishwashers, will need to learn a specific set of new job skills simply because they have no previous job experience. In these cases, as well as many others within the hospitality industry, the job skills workers need to do their jobs may not actually be present at the time of their hiring. That fact is merely one of many factors that make the hospitality industry unique. Despite this, effective unit managers can, when the proper workers are selected, readily provide the skills training needed to ensure that these new employees will meet job performance standards.

In most cases, hospitality managers will find that the hourly employees they hire must undergo specific skills training before they become fully productive workers. Servers, dishwashers, kitchen cleaners, counter workers, food preparation specialists, cashiers, housekeepers, and front desk staff are just a few of the many positions for which it is common (and because of worker shortages, even necessary) to hire workers who do not come to the operation with readily applicable job skills. What the best of new employees can bring to the operation is a sincere commitment to serve guests, a willingness to learn, and the work ethic needed to perform as a valued employee. When these characteristics are present in newly hired employees, the hospitality manager who selected them may have chosen an unskilled employee, but he or she will also have selected an employee who will be an excellent addition to the staff. For that reason, hospitality managers should understand and appreciate other, more important nonskill issues, when considering the factors that directly affect their employee recruitment efforts.

Those managers directly responsible for recruiting a qualified pool of candidates must be keenly aware of the varied constraints they face prior to developing their recruiting plans. In the hospitality industry, managers must recognize existing legal, economic, industry, organizational, and positions constraints, discussed as follows:

Legal constraints. As you learned in Chapter 2, local, state, and federal laws significantly affect a hospitality manager's efforts in recruiting employees. An employer can no longer seek out preferred individuals based on non-job-related factors such as age, gender, or physical attractiveness. Those that do so may be confronted with significant legal problems. For example, in the hospitality industry, it is simply inappropriate to view positions as being best suited for males or females. Historically, the hospitality and tourism industries have provided tremendous opportunities for employees of all backgrounds, and they will continue to do so, not only because it is the legal thing to do, but because it is the right thing to do.

Economic constraints. Economic constraints affect both the organization that is recruiting employees and the employees themselves. In many cases, the wages and salaries that can be paid to workers and managers are directly determined by the profitability of the operation for which they will work. If, for example, the operation must maintain a targeted, predetermined labor budget, or achieve its labor cost percentage goal, it will likely be restricted in the amount of money it can offer new employees. All organizations face such economic restraints, and thus this challenge is simply one more that can be addressed and overcome by professional hospitality managers.

Just as employers face economic constraints, employees may be attracted to or deterred from applying for a position because of the money they can earn. It is clearly in the best interests of both the employer and employee for each to understand the realistic range of compensation available for vacant positions before these positions are advertised and applied for. It is also very important to understand that rate of pay is only one of several critical factors (see Chapter 8) that good employees consider before applying for and accepting a new job.

Industry constraints. Some individuals truly do not understand the hospitality industry well. As a result, they view it as one in which opportunities for personal advancement are few, and the remuneration offered for working is low. In fact, the hospitality industry offers significant personal and financial rewards for workers with a variety of backgrounds, from those with limited formal education to those with advanced professional degrees. It is unlikely that any single HR manager will change industry perceptions, but it is important to understand that recruitment efforts should, when necessary, directly address potential candidate biases.

One of the best ways to directly address the constraints on recruiting imposed by the hospitality and tourism industry is to focus on its varied and positive characteristics. These include:

■ Stability of employment
■ Variety of work
■ Ability to utilize personal creativity
■ Team environment
■ Rewards of serving others
■ Pleasant work atmosphere

Each job for which an HR manager advertises will have its own positive features. In addition, specific industry segments will have their own unique and positive attributes. Experienced managers directly address industry-related constraints when publicizing their jobs by clearly stating the attractive features of the jobs they are offering. The goal is not to promise falsely, but rather to better educate those who do not fully understand the advantages of a career in the hospitality and tourism industries.

Organizational constraints. Just as some applicants will have a general reaction to jobs advertised within the hospitality industry, others may react to the specific organization for which the job is advertised. For example, foodservice managers operating school foodservice units may find that their jobs are perceived very positively because of an assessment by applicants that these jobs will have traditional hours, may come with above-average benefits, and allow the worker to be off-work in the summer. Alternatively, managers operating high-energy nightclubs in larger cities will likely find that their best potential applicants are drawn to the excitement of their operations, although most of their jobs will require them to work during nontraditional (extremely late-night) hours.

Just as HR managers must highlight the positive features of their industry, an individual organization must truthfully point out the specific employment advantages it offers. When an organization is perceived in its community as being a good place to work, the pool of qualified applicants who will want to work there increases. It is important that potential employees believe this perception to be true, and that current employees confirm it.

Position constraints. In the hospitality industry, some jobs are perceived as glamorous, while others are not. If the position a manager seeks to fill is unattractive to most workers, recruiting a large and qualified pool of applicants will likely be challenging. In recent years, more hospitality managers have been complaining about the difficulty of finding suitably qualified individuals for manual labor positions such as dishwashers, janitors, landscaping and grounds care, room attendants, and others. In job markets where the **unemployment rate** is low, and where a wide range of opportunity creates competition, a worker shortage may exist. In cases such as these, qualified applicants may be difficult to find, so managers must work diligently and creatively to locate potential applicants who can bring great value to their organizations.

The unemployment rate is defined as the number of persons in a community or other designated area expressed as a percentage of the defined area's entire labor force.

Unemployment rate: A government statistic that measures the percentage of workers who are not employed, but who are seeking work.

The Search for Qualified Employees

2. **Differentiate between the actions HR managers take when electing to conduct internal, external, or outsourced searches for qualified employees.**

Hospitality managers at all levels and in all sizes of organizations will continually find that they must actively recruit employees. From company presidents to the lowest-skilled **entry-level** employee, candidate recruitment will usually be an ongoing activity.

Although a variety of methods could be used to examine the employee search process, one way to categorize it is based on the approach utilized by the organization conducting the search. Using this method, an employee search may be categorized as being one of the following:

Entry-level: The position in which an individual starts his or her career with a hospitality organization. For example, the position of dishwasher might be an entry-level job in an upscale restaurant.

■ Internal search
■ External search
■ Outsourced search

INTERNAL SEARCH

An **internal search** is undertaken when a manager or organization believes that the best candidates for upper-level positions will be found among those employees who are currently employed by the organization.

Applied properly, a **promote-from-within** approach can be very effective. If, for example, when seeking a rooms inspector, an executive housekeeper conducting the search felt that the best job candidates would be found among the hotel's current room attendants (or other current hotel employees), an internal search could prove to be very effective.

Current employees may be informed about pending job openings in conversations with their supervisors or through the public posting of the information on employee bulletin boards, Web sites, or newsletters. The advantages associated with utilizing internal searches when seeking to fill positions are many, and include the facts that internal searches:

■ Build employee morale.
■ Can be initiated very quickly.
■ Improve the probability of making a good selection because much is already known about the individual who will be selected.
■ Are less costly than initiating external or outsourced searches.
■ Result in reduced training time and less training costs because the individual selected need not be trained in organizational topics with which he or she is already familiar.
■ Encourage talented individuals to stay with the organization.
■ Are looked upon favorably by the EEOC.

Despite the many advantages of internal searches, managers utilizing them to fill their position vacancies have also reported distinct disadvantages. These include:

■ Inbreeding and a lack of new ideas can occur when an organization relies only on its own current workers to fill advanced positions.
■ Resentment among employees can occur when one worker is chosen for advancement while others are not.
■ Increased recruitment and training efforts result when a position is filled internally because the position vacated by the promoted employee must also be filled with a new staff member (who must also be trained).

Despite the added training effort required, most experienced hospitality managers firmly believe that the advantages of a promote-from-within policy far outweigh this and the other disadvantages that can sometimes be associated with it.

While it is not, strictly speaking, an internal search system, the use of **employee referral** systems extends the network of potential applicants from an organization's own employees to those potential workers whom the employees recommend.

Employee referral systems tend to work well because employees rarely recommend someone unless they feel that person can do a good job and will fit well into the organization. Another advantage to having employees directed to the organization via an employee referral system is that these employees tend to have a more accurate view of the job to be done and the organization's unique culture. This information reduces unrealistic expectations and can help lead to reduced new employee turnover.

In some operations, employee referral systems provide a financial bonus to a staff member who recommends an applicant who is hired by the organization and remains with it for a specified time. Such a system financially rewards employees for their suggestions, and saves the operation time and money that would otherwise be invested in the search process.

Just as there can be disadvantages associated with internal searches, potential problems may exist with employee referral systems. In some cases, recommenders may suggest their own friends or relatives for positions regardless of their qualifications. It is simply human nature to want to work with those people whose companionship is also enjoyed outside of work. Therefore, hiring managers must remember to apply the same standards of employment consideration to those candidates referred by employees as they would to any other individual being considered for a vacant position.

Nepotism: Favoritism in employment based on kinship.

Nepotism, or the hiring of relatives, may also be viewed as a problem encountered by managers who encourage referrals. Many hospitality managers find that, especially in some lower-skill-level jobs, the hiring of nieces, cousins, aunts, and uncles of current employees results in positive benefits for their operations. Other managers have had less encouraging experiences and may prohibit the hiring of a current employee's close relatives.

It is important to understand that referrals of all types can be a valuable source of information about potential employees. Lower-level and supervisory jobs can often be filled by the recommendations of current employees. Upper-level positions such as unit manager, district manager, or even higher are more likely to be referred by a professional acquaintance than by a close friend. Therefore, many hospitality managers are active and visible in the professional associations directly related to their segment of the hospitality and tourism industries.

It is also important for managers to recognize that those employees who have been referred internally must, for hiring purposes, be treated the same as nonreferred employees. It is perfectly legal to hire new employees who have been referred by current employees, but as you learned in Chapter 3, even a lawful action can be improperly implemented. As a result, to minimize the potential for charges of bias or discrimination, the application, evaluation, interview, and selection procedures used for internally referred individuals should match exactly those procedures used with nonreferred employees.

Most employees working in the hospitality industry seek to do a good job and hope to improve their lives and the lives of their families through hard work and loyalty to their employers. Employers can reward this employee loyalty in a very visible and affirmative manner by, whenever possible, seriously considering current workers for higher-level job openings that can directly improve these workers' lives and paychecks.

EXTERNAL SEARCH

External search: An approach to seeking job applicants that focuses primarily on those candidates who are not currently employed by the organization.

Despite the advantages of internal searches, many managers find that an **external search** is a good way to help identify a pool of applicants who are qualified for their organizations' vacancies.

When organizations seek candidates externally, they rely on a variety of strategies, including advertisements, public and private employment assistance agencies, educational institutions, and unsolicited applications, discussed as follows:

■ *Advertisements.* Advertisements are perhaps the most commonly used means of seeking qualified job applicants. These can range from fairly simple "help wanted" postings placed in the classified ad section of most local newspapers to elaborate Web sites utilized by companies in their cyberspace recruiting efforts. In most cases, the type of job determines the best place to run an advertisement. It is important to bear in mind that advertisements work best when placed in locations that are frequently encountered by the targeted job applicant. As a result, HR managers seeking a regional vice president of operations would not advertise that vacancy in the same locations as they would a vacancy for a dining room server.

Blind ad: A job advertisement that does not identify the advertising organization. Also known as a *blind-box ad.*

Although job advertisements often contain specific information about who is looking for candidates and the jobs they wish to fill, in some instances, organizations find it best to place a **blind ad.** In a typical case, respondents are asked to reply to a post office box number. Blind ads are often used when an organization wishes to replace a current employee with a new one, but does not wish to let the current employee know a replacement search is underway. Another purpose arises when the manager does not want the general public to know about a large number of vacancies. Although the use of blind ads is common, some individuals may not respond to them because they are afraid the advertisement was placed by the organization that currently employs them. In other cases, potential candidates may be hesitant to respond because the actual name of the organization, and thus its reputation, is a key determinant of interest in the vacant position.

Advertisements placed in local or national newspapers, professional trade magazines, or on Internet job sites may include very detailed information about the qualifications sought by an employer. Figure 4.1 is an example of the type of detailed ad that might be developed by a hospitality organization seeking to fill one of its higher-level management positions.

In most cases, the more detailed the ad and the wider the distribution of it, the more it will cost. As a result, managers seeking to attract candidates

Executive Chef

Position
We are currently seeking an Executive Chef to assist in the development and implementation of budgets, culinary standards, marketing, inventory control, quality control, and food safety for all five of our foodservice locations.

Responsibilities
Develop and oversee all menu planning. Implement and develop new ideas and initiatives to improve and maximize customer satisfaction and drive operational results. Ensure compliance with OSHA, state, and federal regulations relating to health, sanitation, and safety. Ensure compliance with collective bargaining agreements and company policies and procedures. Identify training needs for the growth and development of all culinary staff.

Qualifications
Approximately five years' work experience as an Executive Chef in a multifunctional service department. Excellent supervisory and people management skills relative to successful operations and all areas of production goals involving preparation, quality standards, cooking methods, presentation, portion control, labor, training, coaching, resolving conflict, and food cost control. Approximately three years' work experience as a manager in a multifunctional foodservice department. Experience with off-premises catering and special events preferred, but not required. Excellent interpersonal, communication, and presentation skills. Planning, organizational, and coordination skills required.

Ability to plan work schedules. Ability to champion new ideas and initiatives. Expertise in menu writing, costing, and planning. Proven ability to develop teams, delegate effectively, and train staff. Willingness to interact with service staff and understand operations from a service point of view. Working knowledge of safety regulations, worker safety, and accident prevention management. Proficiency with reporting systems, including inventory, food cost, scheduling, time and attendance, and labor.

Come put your experience, talent, and commitment to professional excellence to work for a company that truly values and rewards your contribution. Submit résumé, salary history, and three letters of reference to:

(Insert employer contact information)

FIGURE 4.1: Sample Employment Ad

with paid advertisements must carefully consider the investment involved in utilizing this very effective recruiting tool.

Increasingly, companies advertise their position openings on their own Web sites. Such Web postings are low cost, can be rapidly updated (or removed), and can be easily accessed by nearly all job candidates. Current examples of Web sites that are popular among HR managers seeking job candidates are *www.HCareers.com*, *www.Monster.com*, and *www.hospitalityonline.com*.

The Internet is a great place to advertise position vacancies, but there are many other popular places as well. *Courtesy PhotoDisc/Getty Images*

There are also venues for placing advertisements that are either free or that can be posted at a very low cost. These include posting job vacancies in apartment complexes, child care centers, supermarkets, libraries, churches, community centers, and school newspapers. For those employers seeking candidates for whom English is not their primary language, it may be advisable to place ads in foreign-language no-cost or low-cost newspapers and newsletters.

■ *Public employment assistance agencies.* In every state, hospitality managers will find that a public employment agency is available to help the state's citizens find jobs. The main function of these agencies is usually related to **unemployment benefits,** and most states give unemployment benefits only to individuals who are registered with the state employment agency. The result is that many individuals listed on the public employment assistance agency's register of available workers may have limited skills and training. For hospitality managers, however, such lists may include a number of excellent candidates for entry-level or even some mid-level and higher-level jobs.

Unemployment benefits: Monetary and nonmonetary resources given to those who are jobless but who are actively seeking work.

Public employment assistance agencies do not charge either employers or potential employees for their services. The result is that advertising jobs as part of a public (city) or state agency's job listings is a very cost-effective way to communicate with candidates who are qualified for some job openings.

■ *Private employment assistance agencies.* The essential difference between private employment agencies and those that are public relate to fees charged for services provided. While public agencies are free to their users, private agencies charge for their services. It may or may not be true, but private agencies are often viewed as a source of higher-paying and more desirable jobs, as well as better-qualified job candidates, than their public agency counterparts. Private employment assistance agencies may also provide employers with additional services such as advertising jobs, screening applicants, and even providing money-back guarantees if the applicant provided does not meet the employer's expectations. The fees charged by private employment assistance agencies for their services may be absorbed by the employer, the employee, or split between both. Especially for some higher-level position vacancies, private employment assistance agencies may be an effective tool in identifying employees who can quickly make a positive contribution to an organization.

■ *Educational institutions.* Most educational institutions provide services to assist their graduates in finding jobs. Whether the job to be filled requires a high-school diploma, specific vocational training, an Associate's degree, a Bachelor's degree, or even an advanced degree, educational institutions are a source of qualified job candidates that hospitality managers should not overlook. Colleges and universities, technical schools, and secondary (high) schools in an employer's area typically offer employers the chance, at little or no cost, to assess the quality of their students.

■ *Unsolicited applications.* Every employer receives unsolicited applications or requests to be considered for job openings. These may arrive in the manager's office by letter, fax, or e-mail, or may be delivered in person. Even if a company has no current vacancies, these applications may be kept on file for future consideration. In the hospitality industry, however, unsolicited applications

In many cases, an individual's first job is acquired in the hospitality industry.
Courtesy PhotoDisc/Getty Images

submitted by the unemployed generally have a relatively short life span. When these individuals are job searching, they will typically continue their search until it ends successfully. As a result, when applications of this type are submitted, they must be acted on by management within weeks, days, or even hours. Therefore, many managers make the time to personally, and daily, review all unsolicited applications submitted. These managers may even arrange to conduct on-the-spot interviews with applicants when they find their labor markets are very tight and, as a result, quality candidates are scarce.

OUTSOURCED SEARCH

Outsourced search: A search for job candidates that is performed by a professional company specializing in employee searches

Executive search: A private employment agency that specializes in identifying candidates for management positions. Also known as head hunter firms.

In some cases, HR managers decide that an **outsourced search** is the best method they can use to find the candidates they are looking for. An outsourced search is one in which an organization chooses an **executive search** firm to find potential candidates for a job.

Executive search firms impose significant charges for their services, with typical fees ranging from one-third to approximately half of the annual wages that will be paid to the employee who will be hired. These fees are typically paid by the employer, not the employee.

Executive search firms make it their business to monitor executive-level talent so they can advise their clients about the best candidates available. In most cases, the executive search firm will identify potential candidates from their lists of contacts and do preliminary screening. These firms are adept at seeking out executives with proper skills and who fit well with the hiring organization. Even though outsourced searches rely heavily on the expertise of the private employment agency chosen, the final hiring decisions still remain with the employer, not the executive search firm.

It is important to understand that, in most cases, HR managers do not choose from among internal, external, and outsourcing as their sole method of recruiting. Rather, the best managers select the approach appropriate for the vacancy they seek to fill. In some cases, this will result in using more than one of the strategies, or even all three of them when seeking to fill a specific position.

Factors Affecting Selection Efforts

3. **List and explain the importance of applications, interviews, testing, background checks, and references—the five major activities that HR managers undertake when screening employees for possible selection.**

After HR managers have assembled a pool of qualified candidates, they must select the applicant they wish to hire. When choosing potential applicants for employment, hospitality managers generally will utilize some or all of the five major selection activities. These are:

1. Applications
2. Interviews
3. Pre-employment testing
4. Background checks
5. References

APPLICATIONS

The employment application is a document that should be completed by all candidates for employment. The application need not be complex. It will generally list the name, address, work experience, and related information of the candidate. The requirements for a legitimate, legally sound application are many, but in general, the questions asked on the application should focus exclusively on job qualifications and nothing else. Most hospitality companies have their employment application reviewed by an attorney who specializes in employment law. If, as a manager, you are responsible for developing your own application, it is a good idea to have the document reviewed by a legal specialist prior to using it.

It is also important that each employment candidate for a given position be required to fill out an identical application, and that an application be on file for each candidate who is ultimately selected for the position. In addition, it is also a good practice for the application to clearly state the **at-will** nature of the employment relationship.

In the hospitality industry, many applicants for jobs may have limited English speaking, reading, or writing skills. These limitations should not necessarily disqualify an applicant from being selected and doing an excellent job. Because of these possible language limitations, many hospitality employers find it helpful to provide assistance to job applicants when filling out their employment applications.

Figure 4.2 is an example of an employment application that is legally sound. Note specifically how questions are related to ability to work, previous work history, and job qualifications.

At-will (employment): An employment relationship in which either party can, at any time, terminate the relationship with no liability.

INTERVIEWS

From the employment applications (or résumés) submitted, some candidates would be selected for the interview process. In some situations, this process may entail more than one meeting. Thus, some companies may conduct a first interview with many candidates and then, based on the results of those interviews, select only those candidates in whom they have the most interest for second or even third rounds of interviews.

Lighthouse Restaurant

Application for Employment

It is the policy of the Lighthouse Restaurant to provide equal employment opportunity to all qualified persons without regard to race, creed, color, religious belief, sex, age, national origin, ancestry, physical or mental handicap, or veteran status.

Name: Last_____ First_____ Middle_____

Street Address

_____

City_____ State_____ Zip

_____

Telephone ( )_____ Social Security #_____

Position applied for

_____

How did you hear of this opening?

_____

When can you start?_____ Desired wage per hour_____

Are you a U.S. citizen or otherwise authorized to work in the U.S.? Yes_____ No_____

Are you capable of performing the essential functions of the job you are applying for with or without reasonable accommodation? Yes_____ No_____

If under 18, indicate date of birth:_____

If applying for a job involving the service of alcoholic beverages, are you over 21? Yes_____ No_____

Are you looking for full-time employment? Yes_____ No_____

If no, what days and hours are you available? (please list all that apply)

	Sun.	Mon.	Tues.	Wed.	Thurs.	Fri.	Sat.
From	___	___	___	___	___	___	___
To	___	___	___	___	___	___	___

Do you have dependable means of transportation to and from work? Yes_____ No _____

Do you have any criminal charges pending against you? Yes_____ No _____

Have you been convicted of a felony in the past seven years?* Yes_____ No_____

If yes, please fully describe the charges and disposition of the case:

_____

_____

* Conviction of a felony will not necessarily disqualify you from employment.

Education: School Name; Location; Year Completed; Major/Degree

High School _____

Technical School _____

College _____

FIGURE 4.2: Employment Application

Other _____

In addition to your work history, are there other certifications, skills, qualifications, or experience we should know about?

_____

Employment History: (Start with most recent employer.)

Company name _____ Location_____

Date Started _____ Starting Wage _____ Starting Position_____

Date Ended _____ Ending Wage_____ Ending Position _____

Name of Supervisor _____ May we contact? Yes _____ No _____

Responsibilities _____

Reason for leaving

_____

Company name _____ Location _____

Date Started _____ Starting Wage _____ Starting Position _____

Date Ended _____ Ending Wage _____ Ending Position _____

Name of Supervisor _____ May we contact? Yes_____ No _____

Responsibilities _____

Reason for leaving

_____

Company name _____ Location _____

Date Started _____ Starting Wage_____ Starting Position _____

Date Ended _____ Ending Wage _____ Ending Position _____

Name of Supervisor_____ May we contact? Yes _____ No _____

Responsibilities _____

Reason for leaving

_____

I state that the facts written on this application are true and complete to the best of my knowledge. I understand that if I am employed, false statements on this application can be considered cause for dismissal. The company is hereby authorized to make any investigations of my prior educational and employment history. I understand that employment at this company is "at will," which means that I or the company can terminate the employment relationship at any time, with or without prior notice. I understand that no supervisor, manager, or executive of this company, other than its owner has the authority to alter the at-will status of my employment.

I authorize you to make such legal investigations and inquiries into my personal employment, criminal history, driving record, and other job-related matters as may be necessary in determining an employment decision.

Signature _____ Date _____

Confidential Material/Property of Lighthouse Restaurant LLC.

FIGURE 4.2: (*Continued*)

Human Resources Management:
CURRENT EVENTS 4.2

APPLICANTS, APPLICATIONS, AND THE INTERNET

Most hospitality employers utilize application forms to establish a single, uniform document for use by all job candidates or groups of candidates. In addition to obtaining needed personal information, the use of a standardized application form helps show who is considered to be an applicant; a determination that is very important in complying with the federal government's record retention and reporting requirements. For example, Title VII of the Civil Rights Act requires covered employers to retain applications for employment and other documents pertaining to hiring for one year from the date the records were made or the last action was taken. Does that mean that an HR manager who receives, via e-mail, an unsolicited résumé from an individual seeking a job must keep that e-mail for one year? What if dozens or even hundreds of such e-mails are received weekly? Daily? Are they all really applicants?

The Equal Employment Opportunity Commission (EEOC) and the Office of Federal Contract Compliance Programs broadly define applicant to include any person who has indicated an interest in being considered for hiring, promotion, or other employment opportunities. This interest might be expressed by completing an application form, in writing or orally, depending on the employer's practice. The difficult job of determining which specific contacts create a job applicant for recordkeeping purposes has only increased with the proliferation of e-mail, online recruitment Web sites, and corporate and personal Web pages.

Fortunately, the EEOC has issued opinions to clarify recordkeeping requirements for applicants using the Internet and related cybertechnologies. The EEOC's guidance limits the definition of applicant (in the context of the Internet and related technologies) to those people who have indicated an interest in a specific position that the employer has acted to fill, and who have followed the employer's *standard procedures* for submitting an application. For this reason, many employers require that *all* job applicants (including those who have prepared résumés) submit a completed job application if they want to be considered for employment. As a result, employers must retain only those completed applications.

It is important for HR managers to understand that the types of questions that can be asked in the interview are highly restricted. This is because job interviews, if improperly performed, can subject managers to significant legal liability. If a candidate is not hired based on his or her answer to, or refusal to answer, an inappropriate question, that candidate may have the right to file a lawsuit.

The EEOC suggests that an employer consider the following three issues when deciding whether to include a particular question on an employment application or to ask it in a job interview:

1. Does this question tend to screen out minorities or females?
2. Is the answer needed in order to judge this individual's competence for performance of the job?
3. Are there alternative, nondiscriminatory ways to judge the person's qualifications?

As a manager, you must be very careful in your selection of questions to ask in an interview. In all cases, it is important to remember that the job dictates what is an allowable question. Questions to be asked of applicants should be written down in advance and carefully followed. In addition, supervisors, coworkers, and others who may participate in the interview process should be trained to avoid questions that could increase the liability of the operation.

Generally, age is considered to be irrelevant in most hiring decisions, and therefore, date-of-birth questions are improper. Age is, however, a sensitive pre-employment question, because the Age Discrimination in Employment Act protects employees 40 years of age and older. It is permissible to ask applicants to state their ages if they are younger than 18 years old (see Figure 4.2), because they are only permitted to work a limited number of hours each week. It may also be important when hiring bartenders, and other servers of alcohol, that these individuals' ages are at or above a state's minimum age for serving alcohol.

Race, religion, and national origin questions are always inappropriate, as is the practice of requiring that photographs of the candidate be submitted prior to or after an interview. Questions about physical traits like height and weight have been found to violate the law because they eliminated disproportionate numbers of female, Asian-American, and Spanish-surnamed applicants.

If a job does not require a particular level of education, it may even be considered improper to ask questions about an applicant's educational background. Applicants can be asked about their education and credentials if these are bona fide occupational qualifications. For example, it is allowable to ask a candidate for a hotel controller's position if he or she has a degree in accounting and which school granted that degree. Asking a potential table busser for the same information would be inappropriate.

It is permissible to ask applicants if they use illegal drugs or smoke, because either of these traits can be legally used to disqualify applicants. It is also allowable to ask candidates if they are willing to submit to a voluntary drug test as a condition of employment. Questions concerning whether an applicant owns a home potentially discriminate against those individuals who do not own their own homes, and thus may be discriminatory. In a similar manner, questions concerning the type of discharge received by an ex-military applicant are improper, because a higher proportion of other-than-honorable discharges are given to minorities.

Safe questions can be asked about a candidate's present employment, former employment, and job references. In most cases, questions asked on both the application and in the interview should focus on the applicant's job skills and nothing else. It is not possible to list all of the allowable and unallowable questions that may be asked in an interview setting, but Figure 4.3 contains some detailed guidelines for asking appropriate interview questions.

Questions about Name that should be avoided:

- Maiden name of a married woman
- Name of a spouse

Questions about Name that can be asked:

- Whether or not the applicant ever worked under another name or was the applicant educated under another name (allowable only when the information is needed to verify the applicant's qualifications).

Examples:

1. Have you ever worked for our company under any other name?
2. Is there any information relative to you changing your name that would help us in conducting an educational background check?

Questions about Birthplace and Residence that should be avoided:

- Birthplace of applicant
- Birthplace of applicant's parents
- Do you own a home, rent, board, or live with your parents?
- Citizenship
- Address of applicant's spouse and children who are dependents

Question about Birthplace and Residence that can be asked:

- Inquiry about address sufficient to facilitate contact with applicant

Questions about Creed/Religion that should be avoided:

- Inquiry concerning religious preference, denomination, or affiliations of applicant
- The name of the Church attended or religious holidays observed by applicant

Examples of discriminatory questions:

1. What is your religion?
2. What religious holidays do you observe?
3. Which church do you attend?
4. What do you do on Sundays?

FIGURE 4.3: Interview Questions That Should Be Avoided and Those That Can Be Asked

Questions about Creed/Religion that can be asked:

- This job requires people to work on weekends; can you meet this requirement? (Employers do have an obligation, according to EEOC guidelines, to make "reasonable accommodations" for employees whose religious convictions may conflict with scheduling requirements of the business.

Questions about Race or Color that should be avoided:

- Applicant's race
- Color of applicant's skin, eyes, hair, distinguishing physical characteristics, markings

Questions about Race or Color that can be asked:

- None legitimately allowed

Questions about Age that should be avoided:

- Date of birth or age of applicant, except when such information is needed to legally perform a job (e.g., to satisfy the provisions of either state or federal minimum age statutes)

  Examples of discriminatory questions:

  1. What is your age or date of birth?
  2. How old are you?
  3. Are you between the ages of 18–24, 25–34, etc.?
  4. Will you mind being the oldest one working here?

Questions about Age that can be asked:

- If hired, can you offer proof that you are at least 18 years of age?
- If hired, can you offer proof that you are at least 21 years of age?

Questions about Language that should be avoided:

- Applicant's mother tongue
- Language commonly used by applicant at home
- How the applicant acquired the ability to read, write, or speak a foreign language

  Examples of discriminatory questions:

  1. Is English your first language?
  2. What language did you speak as a child?

Question about Language that can be asked:

  Which languages do you speak fluently (only if job-related)?

Questions about National Origin that should be avoided:

- Applicant's lineage, ancestry, national origin, descent, birthplace, parentage, or nationality
- Nationality of applicant's parents or spouse

FIGURE 4.3: (*Continued*)

Examples of discriminatory questions:

1. Are you a United States citizen?
2. Of what country are you a citizen?
3. Where were you born? Where were your parents born?
4. What nationality are you?
5. What language did you speak as a child?

Questions about Citizenship that can be asked:

■ Whether applicant can be lawfully employed in this country because of visa or immigration status
■ Whether applicant can provide proof of legal right to work in the United States after being hired

Examples:

1. Can you show proof of your eligibility to work in the United States?
2. If you are not a United States citizen, do you have the legal right to remain/work here?

Questions about Marital Status that should be avoided:

■ Any inquiry as to whether an applicant is married, single, divorced, separated, engaged, widowed, etc.
■ Number of dependents; number of children
■ Spouse's occupation
■ With whom do you live?

Questions about Marital Status that can be asked:

■ None

Questions about Disabilities that should be avoided:

■ Any general inquiry as to whether applicant has any physical or mental disability. This includes an inquiry about the nature, severity, or extent of a disability.

Examples of discriminatory questions:

1. Are you disabled?
2. What is the nature or severity of your disability?
3. What kinds of problems does being disabled cause you?
4. Do you think you have the physical strength for the job?

Questions about Disabilities that can be asked:

■ Does applicant have any disabilities that would prevent him or her from satisfactorily performing the job? (Must be accompanied by mention of reasonable accommodation.)

FIGURE 4.3: (*Continued*)

Example:

Are you able to perform the essential functions of this job with or without reasonable accommodation? (Show or read the applicant the position description so he or she can give an informed answer.)

Miscellaneous Questions that can be asked:

- This job requires heavy lifting. Can you lift or move 50 pounds? This is legal only if it is a bona fide occupational qualification (BFOQ).
- Are there specific times that you cannot work or adhere to this proposed work schedule?
- What professional or trade groups do you belong to that you consider relevant to your ability to perform this job?
- "Our smoking policy is . . . (fill in your operation's policy)." Can you adhere to it?

FIGURE 4.3: (*Continued*)

Human Resources MANAGEMENT ISSUES (4.1)

" I like his personality a lot, but I don't know, I just didn't like his looks," said Mini, the cafeteria supervisor.

"What was wrong?" asked Teri Settles, the Dietitian in charge of the hospital foodservice operation where Mini worked.

Mini and Terri were discussing Josh, a 23-year-old man who had interviewed for a job bussing tables in the hospital's public dining room.

"It was his neck," replied Mini. "He had these black things that looked like geometric designs on his neck!"

"Tattoos?" asked Terri.

"Yes," replied Mini. "I don't understand these young people."

"I don't know, Mini. I'm not so sure they are all that much different than we were at that age," replied Terri.

1. Do you think Mini's reaction to Josh's tattoos is representative of the general public?
2. While it is perfectly legal to reject an applicant with a tattoo, do you personally think visible tattoos should be grounds for rejecting an otherwise qualified job applicant? Why or why not?
3. As an HR specialist in the hospitality industry, what ground rules (if any) would you develop for employee body adornment (including makeup, visible tattoos, and body piercings)? What factors might influence your decisions?

TESTING

Pre-employment testing is a common way to improve the employee screening process. Test results can be used, for example, to measure the relative strength of two candidates. In the hospitality industry, pre-employment testing will generally fall into one of the following categories:

1. Skills tests
2. Psychological tests
3. Drug screening tests

Skills tests were among the first tools used by managers to screen applicants in the employment process. In the hospitality industry, skills tests can include activities such as typing tests for office workers, computer application tests for those involved in using word processing or spreadsheet tools, and, for culinarians, food production tasks.

Psychological testing can include personality tests, performance predictor tests, or mental ability tests. For both skills tests and psychological tests, the important rule to remember is this:

"If the test does not have documented validity and reliability, the results of the tests should not be used for hiring decisions."

Pre-employment drug testing is allowable in most states, and can be a very effective tool for reducing insurance rates and potential worker liability issues. Many managers feel a drug-free environment tends to attract better-quality employment candidates, with the resulting impact of a higher-quality workforce. There are, however, strict guidelines in some states as to when and how people can be tested. If pre-employment drug testing is to be used, care must be taken to ensure the accuracy of the testing. In some cases, applicants whose erroneous test results have cost them a job have successfully sued the employer. The laws surrounding mandatory drug testing are very complex. If you elect to implement either a pre-employment or post-employment drug-testing program, it is best to first seek advice from an attorney who specializes in labor employment law in your state.

BACKGROUND CHECKS

Increasingly, hospitality employers are utilizing background checks prior to hiring workers in selected positions. It has been estimated that as many as 35 percent of all résumés and employment applications include some level of falsification. Because this is true, employers are spending more time and financial resources to validate information supplied by a potential employee. It is important to understand that, while many types of background checks are available, not all are advisable. Background checks should be specifically tailored to obtain only information that relates directly to each individual's suitability for employment. The applicant background checks most commonly performed include criminal history, credit reports, driving records, and academic credentials and licenses, discussed as follows:

Criminal History

As a general rule, criminal conviction records should be checked when there is a possibility that the person could create significant safety or security risks for coworkers, guests, or clients. Examples include employees who will (1) have close contact with minors, the elderly, the disabled, or patients; (2) have access to weapons, drugs, chemicals, or other potentially dangerous materials; (3) work in, or deliver goods to, customers' homes; and (4) handle money or other valuables, or have access to financial information or employee personal information. In addition, some states require a check for criminal convictions before hiring individuals as employees of healthcare facilities (including food services), financial institutions, or public schools.

Credit Reports

Credit reports typically include financial information such as payment history, delinquencies, amounts owed, liens, and judgments relating to an applicant's credit standing. Arbitrary reliance on the results of these checks, however, has, in some cases, been found to result in adverse impact discrimination against women and minorities. Accordingly, use of credit reports should be limited to situations where there is a legitimate business justification, such as for jobs that entail monetary responsibilities, the use of financial discretion, or similar security risks.

Driving Records

Motor vehicle records (MVRs) are available from state motor vehicle departments. They usually contain information about traffic violations, license status, and expiration date. MVRs should be checked for any employee who will drive a company vehicle or a personal vehicle on the employer's business.

Academic Credentials and Licenses

Academic information (such as schools attended, degrees awarded, and transcripts) should be verified when a specified level or type of education is necessary for a particular job. Similarly, proof of licenses (and their current status, expiration dates, and any past or pending disciplinary actions) should be obtained if a license is required for the position in question.

Using background checks as a screening device does involve some risk to employers, as well as some responsibility. Employers should only search for information that has a direct bearing on the position for which a candidate is applying. In addition, if a candidate is denied employment on the basis of

Human Resources Management: CURRENT EVENTS 4.3

PRINCIPLES OF EMPLOYEE BACKGROUND CHECKS

Regardless of the applicant background checks you choose to conduct, four key points should always be addressed to ensure that the checks are completed legally and effectively.

Principle 1: *Always obtain written consent before conducting any background check.* An explicit written authorization helps protect against invasion of privacy, defamation, and other wrongful act claims. It is also a good idea to expand the waiver language on consent forms to include the employer and those who assist with background checks (such as HR staff, former employers, and screening firms).

Principle 2: *Evaluate results fairly and consistently.* Avoid hasty rejections when negative information surfaces during a background check. Consider the negative information in the context of the job to be performed. For example, to reject an otherwise qualified front desk agent as a candidate because of a poor driving record is unwise if the job requires no business driving. Alternatively, it may be the only sensible action in the case of a van driver's position at the same hotel.

Principle 3: *Restrict access to information obtained in background checks.* Background check materials should be kept in secure confidential files and disclosed only on a strict need-to-know basis. Access to records relating to criminal or financial history should be limited as narrowly as possible.

Principle 4: *Do your checks as one of the last steps in the selection process.* There is no need to spend the time and money for background checks on a candidate until the decision has actually been made that you will likely offer the candidate a position.

information found in a background check, the employer should provide a candidate with a copy of that report. Sometimes, candidates can help verify or explain the content of their own background checks. Also, reporting agencies can make mistakes, and if you improperly rely on false information to make a hiring decision, it may put your organization at risk.

REFERENCES

In the past, employment references were a very popular tool for managers to use in the screening process. In today's litigious society, however, they are much more difficult to obtain. While many organizations still seek information from past employers about an employee's previous work performance, few sophisticated companies will divulge such information. In most cases, previous employers are willing only (if at all) to reveal a previous employee's start date and separation date. It is important to note that some employers have been held liable for inaccurate comments that have been made about past employees. The benefits to a past employer for being truthful about previous employees is widely thought to be heavily outweighed by the potential liability associated with such honesty.

It is important for HR managers to understand that it is now very easy for job seekers to employ the services of companies that specialize in providing their clients (the job seeker) with a confidential, comprehensive verification of the employment references given by the job seeker's former employers. Because that is true, employers are becoming ever-more cautious about supplying information on employees who have left their organization. The end result is that personal references have become a much greater recruiting tool than references from past employers. If references from past employers are to be sought, to help minimize the risk of litigation related to the reference checks, it is best to secure the applicant's permission in writing before contacting an ex-employer.

As an employer, you and your own organization must be extremely cautious in both giving and receiving reference information. Employers are usually protected if they give a truthful reference, but that does not mean you will be free from the time and expense of defending a **defamation** case brought by an ex-employee.

Defamation: False statements that cause someone to be held in contempt, lowered in the estimation of the community, or to lose employment status or earnings, or otherwise suffer a damaged reputation.

If, for example, an employer giving a reference states that an ex-employee was terminated because he or she "didn't get along" with coworkers, the employer may well have to be able to prove the truthfulness of the statement, as well as prove that all of the blame for the difficulties was the responsibility of the ex-employee.

To minimize your own risk of a lawsuit, you should never reply to a request for information about one of your ex-employees without a copy of that employee's signed release authorizing the reference check. How much you choose to disclose about an ex-employee is your decision, but your answers should be honest and defendable. Also, it is best never to disclose personal information such as marital difficulties, financial problems, or serious illness (because you could also be sued for invasion of privacy). As a result, many employers today give only the following information about past employees:

1. Employer's name
2. Ex-employee's name
3. Date(s) of employment
4. Job title
5. Name and title of person supplying the information

If a prospective employee provides letters of reference, always call the authors of reference letters to ensure that they wrote them. When possible, it is best to put any request for reference information in writing, and ask that the response be in written form. If a verbal response is all that can be obtained, document the conversation; write down as much of the dialogue as possible, including the name of the party you spoke to and the date and time the contact occurred.

Human Resources Management:
CURRENT EVENTS 4.4

RESPONSIBILITIES FOR EMPLOYMENT STATUS VERIFICATION

In many parts of the country, labor shortages are one of the most difficult challenges facing hospitality managers. Add to that situation the fact that many individuals illegally migrate to this country to seek employment, and the potential for knowingly or unknowingly hiring individuals who are unauthorized to work in the United States is real. HR managers need to know their current (but potentially changing) responsibilities for determining the legal status of potential workers.

All newly hired employees are required to fill out an Employment Eligibility Verification form (commonly known as an I-9 form) stating that they are authorized to work in the United States. U.S. Citizenship and Immigration Service regulations allow an individual 72 hours from the time of hire in which to complete Form I-9 (e.g., If hired on Monday, an individual has until the close of business Wednesday in which to complete the form). Current I-9s can easily be downloaded in PDF format at http://www.uscis.gov/files/form/i-9.pdf.

The form requires potential employees to verify both their citizenship status and legal eligibility to work. The manner in which an employee can document these two facts is varied and can be accomplished via an applicant-selected configuration of one or two documents from a list of 29 possible items, including U.S. passport, driver's license, Social Security card, and school identification card.

Employers *are not* required to verify the authenticity of the identification documents they are presented, but they do need to keep a copy of them on file. The documents must pass a good-faith test: That is, "Do they look real?" If so, the applicant may be hired. If an employee is later found to be unauthorized, the employer must terminate employment. Employers who do not end employment of unauthorized workers or who *knowingly* hire unauthorized workers may be fined up to $11,000 for each ineligible employee.

HR managers should never knowingly break the law. They should also continue to monitor this important area of employment law so that they can constantly be in compliance with it, as well as with all applicable, but ever-changing, U.S. immigration and employment laws.

Negligent Hiring

4. **Understand and explain the potential legal liability related to negligent hiring.**

Giving references for past employees, like pre-employment testing, can subject you and your operation to litigation if the comments made during the reference are challenged, or if the information secured during a test is false or used in a way that violates employment law. In addition, if the information is improperly disclosed to third parties, it could violate the employee's right to privacy. *Not* conducting background checks on some positions, however, can subject you to even more legal difficulty under the doctrines of **negligent hiring** and **negligent retention.**

Negligent hiring liability is usually found where an employee who caused injury or harm to another had a reputation or record that showed his or her propensity to do so, and this record would have been easily discoverable by that employer, had reasonable care (in this case, a diligent search) been shown. Similarly, if an employer, after hiring an employee, discovers information that would have disqualified the candidate from job consideration, and the employer does not remove the employee from the job, negligent retention may be charged.

How can employers show that reasonable care was used in the hiring process? All that is normally required is to thoroughly verify all pertinent information about each candidate prior to making a job offer. For example, it would be extremely difficult for anyone to argue that the employer knew or should have known that the information received was false if multiple references were contacted, and if all relevant credentials of an individual employee were verified to the best of an employer's ability. It would also be difficult (but not, unfortunately, impossible!) for a judge or jury to find that an employer had been negligent in its hiring processes if this standard of care were exercised prior to every hiring decision.

Negligent hiring: Failure on the part of an employer to exercise reasonable care in the selection of employees.

Negligent retention: Retaining an employee after the employer became aware of an employee's unsuitability for a job, thereby failing to act on that knowledge.

Human Resources MANAGEMENT ISSUES   (4.2)

Holly Rosencrans is the assistant general manager of a country club in Texas. She has been in charge of membership activities and services for three years. One of her areas of responsibilities is the selection of pool lifeguards, which are required in her facility by local statute.

Each lifeguard working at the country club must be certified in cardiopulmonary resuscitation (CPR). Ms. Rosencrans interviews a candidate who lists the successful completion of a CPR course as part of his educational background. Ms. Rosencrans does not verify the accuracy of the candidate's statement. Assume the death of a six-year-old child of a club member resulted because this lifeguard did not, in fact, successfully complete CPR training. As a result, he was not able to render appropriate aid to the drowning victim, who would otherwise likely have been saved.

1. Do you think Ms. Rosencrans could be guilty of negligent hiring?
2. Do you think a jury of 12 average citizens would find Ms. Rosencrans and/or her country club guilty of negligent hiring?
3. As an HR specialist, how will you determine which of your job positions may subject you or your company to potential charges of negligent hiring?

Job Offers

5. Describe the legal difference between a conditional job offer and a final job offer.

After you have legally selected an employee for your organization, it is a good practice to clarify the conditions of the **employment agreement** with that employee.

All employers and employees have employment agreements with each other. The agreement can be as simple as agreeing to a specific wage rate per hour worked and at-will employment for both parties. This can be true even if there is nothing in writing, or if work conditions have not been discussed in detail. Employment agreements may be individual, covering only one employee, or, as in a unionized operation, they may involve groups of employees. Generally, employment agreements in the hospitality industry are established orally, or with an **offer letter.**

Offer letters, when properly composed, can help prevent legal difficulties caused by employee or employer misunderstandings. As their name implies, offer letters detail the offer made by the employer to the employee. Some employers believe offer letters should be used only for managerial positions. To avoid difficulties, all employees should have signed offer letters in their personnel files. Components of a sound offer letter include:

1. Position being offered
2. Compensation included
3. Benefits included (if any)
4. Evaluation period and compensation review schedule
5. Start date
6. Location of employment
7. Special conditions of the offer (i.e., the at-will relationship)
8. Reference to the employment manual (see Chapter 3) as an additional source of information regarding employer policies that govern the workplace
9. Signature lines for both employer and employee
10. Date of signature lines

An offer letter may be either conditional or final. When putting forward a *conditional* offer letter, the employer tentatively, or conditionally, offers the job, but the offer is subject to the conditions that must be met by the applicant before the job offer is finalized. These conditions may include passing drug or other tests, background checks, or any other requirement identified by the employer. With a conditional offer letter, the legally binding employment agreement is not in effect until the employee accepts the terms of the offer letter and fulfills the requirements it identifies. A *final* offer letter, however, contains no conditions that must be met before acceptance. An enforceable employment contract is in effect at such time as the final offer letter is legally accepted by the job applicant.

To further illustrate the difference between a conditional and final job offer, consider the case of Antonio Molina. Antonio applies for the position of maintenance

Employee selection is one of a manager's most critical tasks, because how effectively it is done will directly affect how others view that manager's people skills. *Courtesy Purestock*

foreman at a country club. He is selected for the job and is given a conditional offer letter by the club's general manager. In the letter, a special condition of employment is that Antonio must submit to and pass a mandatory drug test. Antonio signs the letter when it is received, but his employment with the country club will not be finalized until he takes and passes the drug test.

HUMAN RESOURCES TERMS

The following terms were defined in this chapter:

Recruiting	Unemployment benefits
Selection	Outsourced search
Unemployment rate	Executive search
Entry-level (position)	At-will (employment)
Internal search	Defamation
Promote-from-within	Negligent hiring
Employee referral	Negligent retention
Nepotism	Employment agreement
External search	Offer letter
Blind ad	

FOR YOUR CONSIDERATION

1. Some hospitality managers emphasize skills and experience when hiring new employees, while others choose employees based on the candidates' personality and attitude. It would likely be best to choose employees that are viewed positively on all of these traits, but if you had to select a new staff member based on fewer than all of these traits, which do you feel is most important? Explain your answer.

2. In many hospitality organizations, physical attractiveness is unquestionably a factor used to select employees in such positions as front-of-the-house food servers and hotel front desk agents. What is your opinion of the advisability and legality of utilizing such a hiring factor? Explain your answer.

3. Many employers simply refuse to answer any questions about the prior employment status of individuals who previously worked for them. What, if any, legal or ethical responsibility does a past employer have to provide information about a previous employee? Defend your position.

CASE STUDY: HUMAN RESOURCES MANAGEMENT IN ACTION

"Tell me again," said Tammy Larson, executive housekeeper at the Comley Grand Plaza Hotel. "What did she write?"

"I told you," said Mike Brennan, the hotel's HR director. "Under the Have You Ever Been Convicted of a Crime section, the applicant put "Yes." Under the Explanation section, she put "Drug Possession, 1998. Served 3 months in county jail.""

Tammy and Mark were discussing Stephanie Bell, a female who had applied for a job as a housekeeper.

"It was over ten years ago," said Tammy.

"Right," replied Mike, "but does it concern you that she served three months' jail time? It must have been serious."

"We don't know the specific circumstances," replied Tammy. "The question is: does this keep me from considering her for the job? I really liked her, and we are short of room attendants right now."

Dimension: Societal Responsibility

Review the conversation described in the case:

1. Do you think Stephanie should be considered a viable candidate for the vacant housekeeping position? Why or why not?

2. Assume you were the on-site foodservices director in a large elementary school. Would you consider hiring Stephanie for your kitchen operation? Why or why not?

3. Some companies only ask applicants to list recent criminal activity (typically within the previous seven years) when completing job applications. Do you agree or disagree with such an approach? Explain.

Dimension: Company Procedures and Decision Making

Review the conversation described in the case:

1. What crimes, if any, do you feel would automatically disqualify an employee from job consideration?
2. What types of criminal activity, if any, do you feel would not automatically disqualify an employee from job consideration?
3. What personal factors do you believe would influence your or any other hospitality manager's responses to these two questions?

Dimension: Negligent Hiring

Review the conversation described in the case. Assume that the decision was made to hire Stephanie. Assume also that, nine months later, Stephanie was involved in a physical altercation (shoving match) with a fellow employee, in which both were slightly injured. During the investigation of the incident, and in keeping with company policy, both employees were required to undergo drug and alcohol use testing on the day of the incident. Stephanie tested negative for alcohol and positive for trace cocaine. The other employee tested negative for alcohol and positive for trace marijuana.

1. What, if any, actions would you take as Stephanie's supervisor? How would the absence or presence of a company-established Employee Assistance Program (EAP) affect your decisions?
2. Assume Stephanie's fellow employee was seriously injured in their shoving match, and the attorney representing that employee charged your company with knowingly hiring a person who could reasonably have been expected to pose a risk to others (negligent hiring). How would you respond?

INTERNET ACTIVITIES

1. The Internet has made just as large an impact on employee recruiting as it has on most other parts of business. In the hospitality industry, Hospitality Careers.com has emerged as one of the most widely used recruiting devices. Go to *www.hcareers.com.*
   a. Select the jobs and the geographic areas in which you would be most interested to work.
   b. Did you find the site easy to navigate?
   c. If you were an HR director seeking candidates for a job opening, would you utilize hcareers.com? Why or why not?
2. Executive search firms help HR managers fill jobs nationally and internationally. One such company that services North America is Global Hospitality. To visit their site, go to *www.globalhospitality.com.*

    a. Read their "Code of Ethics" under the "About Us" tab.

    b. What is your opinion of their ethics code?

    c. Do you think you would ever list your name with such a company? Why or why not?

3. Hospitality managers increasingly use pre-employment background checks to reduce their chances of being sued for negligent hiring. Companies such as American Background were formed to assist managers in checking applicants' backgrounds. To review their services, go to *www.americanbackground.com.*

    a. Click on their "Services" tab to review the services they provide.

    b. How important are employee background checks to the industry segment in which you seek to work?

    c. Would there be any areas of your own life in which you feel a background check would be inappropriate or intrusive? Why?

CHAPTER FIVE

First Impressions and an Ethical Foundation

CHECKLIST   ## OF CHAPTER LEARNING OBJECTIVES

As a result of satisfactory completion of this chapter, readers will be able to:

1. Review the basic concerns of new employees as they begin work in a hospitality organization.

2. Explain important procedures that should be used as employee orientation programs and procedures are developed and implemented.

3. Note the importance of employee handbooks, and list typical policy and procedure topics that might be included in them.

4. Identify basic concerns that should be addressed as employee mentoring programs are planned and implemented.

5. Discuss the role of ethics in the management of human resources.

Impact on Human Resources Management

You've probably heard the old expression, "You only have one opportunity to make a good first impression!" This commonsense observation sets the scene as we address a new employee's initial on-job activities and ethical considerations that should guide the organization and its employees as decisions are made.

As new employees participate in initial work experiences, they desire reinforcement that their decision to join the hospitality organization was a good one. What managers do (and don't do) will likely have a significant impact on the perceptions of new employees. A well-planned and consistently implemented orientation program is a great first step in efforts to help assure that new employees have favorable rather than unfavorable first impressions of their employer, workplace, managers, and team.

Managers should consider their own initial work experiences and the impressions that were created. Background information about the process by which new staff members adapt to a work situation establishes the context within which orientation programs are planned and implemented. The orientation process is important for both the new staff member and the hospitality organization. Therefore, it should be carefully planned and, once used successfully, its major components can be replicated for use as initial on-job activities for future employees are required.

Employee handbooks provide a wealth of information that is helpful as managers make decisions affecting employees. Handbooks also assist staff members when they want to know about work requirements that affect them. Managers and supervisors must be fair, and equitable treatment of employees is most assured when the same requirements apply to all employees all of the time. These requirements should be addressed in a current and well-organized employee handbook provided to new employees during their orientation process.

Mentoring programs are used by some hospitality organizations to provide ongoing guidance by experienced staff members to their younger (less experienced) counterparts. Mentors may not be assigned to employees until after orientation and initial training activities are completed. In fact, they are typically only available to those employees desiring this special assistance and/or to their peers who are fast-tracking in a career development program. However, their availability, their role that supports personalized guidance to staff members, and the mechanics of how the program operates are among applicable topics to be addressed during orientation sessions.

Ethics relates to concerns about what is right and what is wrong. Professional managers are ethical managers, and they consistently use procedures that incorporate ethical considerations. The best-run organizations are influenced by a culture driven by ethical concerns, and their managers role-model the practices that are appropriate for their employees. These staff members will likely treat guests in the same manner as they are treated, so the success is better assured when ethical concerns are at the forefront of the decision-making process.

The New Employee Adaptation Process

1. **Review the basic concerns of new employees as they begin work in a hospitality organization.**

Adaptation (to the organization): The process by which new employees learn the values of and what it's like to work for a hospitality organization during initial on-job experiences.

Managers have an important responsibility to help their new employees learn about and become comfortable working in the hospitality operation. Whether it is planned or just happens, all newly employed staff go through an **adaptation** process as they learn about the values of the organization and what it's like to work for it.

Effective managers realize that their efforts to meet employee needs, and to reduce turnover rates, begin the moment employees are selected. They understand that new staff members are anxious and, perhaps, even stressed because they do not understand specific job expectations nor how their performance will be judged. They are uncertain about relationships with supervisors and peers, about whether there will be unexpected work tasks, and if there will be unanticipated physical and/or mental challenges. Managers should address these concerns in their earliest interactions with new staff members.

EMPLOYEE ADAPTATION CONCERNS

For employees to work effectively, they must know what to do, and they must perform job tasks properly. These concerns should be addressed in training programs that begin after orientation concludes. However, new staff members will see, hear, and experience things as they begin work that set the context for more formal experiences that will follow. Contrast, for example, two greetings that might accompany the introduction of a new employee to an experienced peer: "So glad you're here; welcome to the team," and "Hey, we really need help; hope you stay here longer than the last guy." While a manager cannot write the script for what an experienced employee will say to a new employee, the manager's history of actions that impact the work environment will be easily and quickly seen as the new staff member begins work.

The cleanliness of work stations, conversations of employees between themselves and with guests, and behaviors of employees that represent their work attitudes will be observed by and will influence the attitudes and behaviors of new staff members.

New employees want to be accepted by their peers and to quickly become contributing members of their work team. While the socialization process takes time, it begins as workers are initially put at ease and as they are involved in hospitable interactions with their peers. These are additional examples of how an organization's culture and the environment influenced by the manager will impact what and how early interactions occur. Managers know that employees want to fit in with their peers and become effective team members rather than advocates of the "them versus me" culture that exists in some operations. Managers have a pervasive influence over the attitudes and actions of staff members. The precedence they have set with their employers and their ongoing interactions will impact staff members' interactions with new employees.

Experienced hospitality managers know that new staff members adjust to the new employment situations in similar ways, and this is the topic of the next section of this chapter.

Human Resources MANAGEMENT ISSUES   (5.1)

Cindy had been working at the Harbor View Hotel as a bartender for about two months. She liked her job (great tips!), and she appreciated the way her supervisor, Florence, treated her on the job.

Although Cindy never had any problems with Florence's leadership style, she had noticed that Florence had her favorites. Cindy was glad that she was one of them. However, Florence also had other direct reports she treated much less fairly and, sometimes, disrespectfully. Cindy also remembered times when Florence had spoken inappropriately about top-level managers, some of the regular hotel and lounge guests, and even about the hotel and the entire hospitality industry.

Florence was very opinionated (and everyone who disagreed with her was obviously wrong), and she frequently discussed the people she knew and the "real job" that her contacts would help her to obtain. Cindy had initially overlooked these aspects of Florence's workplace tactics and attitudes because they didn't directly affect her. However, she now began to think, "Why is Florence nice to me? Is this really a good place to work? I have lots of other options and really desire a career in the hospitality industry. Is it better to stay here, and learn what a supervisor should *not* do, or take another job to learn things that will help me in my career?"

QUESTIONS

1. What, if anything, would you do if you were Cindy when Florence began saying negative things about other employees, customers, and the hospitality organization and industry?
2. How might Florence be affecting the corporate culture of her department?
3. How is the corporate culture affecting Cindy?
4. What would you do, if you were Cindy, as you considered your relationship with the hotel, your interest in remaining an employee at the property, and your desire to learn as much as possible about the hospitality industry early in your career?

STEPS IN THE ADAPTATION PROCESS

Figure 5.1 provides an overview of the new employee adaptation process.

Let's review the steps in the new employee adaptation process shown in Figure 5.1:

- **Step 1:** When new employees are selected, they have basic perceptions and attitudes about the work and the organization. These are probably based on factors including (a) information learned during the employment interview; (b) advertising messages (if, for example, the new employee has experienced the company's advertising messages); (c) previous experience, if any, as a guest in the operation; and (d) feedback about the property from others in the community, including present or past employees.
- **Step 2:** Early on-job experiences including orientation and training may reinforce initial perceptions (Step 1), or they may prove them to be less than accurate. Some apprehension is typical, however, if there is a significant difference between what new employees perceived (Step 1) and what they actually experience (Step 2). New staff members must either make significant changes in perceptions and expectations or, perhaps more frequently, new employees are likely to become discontented and become additional turnover statistics. This is especially so when the new employee desires to work for an organization in a position that meets initial expectations (Step 1), and/or when the staff member has other employment opportunities, which often occurs when there are high unemployment rates.
- **Step 3:** Employees who begin to recognize and accept the culture of the organization and who want to become cooperating members of work teams will likely be accepted by their peers. They then want to become contributing members of the organization.

FIGURE 5.1: The New Employee Adaptation Process

■ **Step 4:** At this point, perhaps the most difficult challenge has been accomplished. The new staff member has a positive attitude about the organization and is willing to learn about and contribute to it. The initial orientation and training activities enable new employees to perform work meeting quality and quantity standards. Successful performance reinforces the employees' attitude about the organization, and they begin to experience and relate to cultural norms encouraging retention rather than turnover.

Many of the tactics required to successfully assist new employees to adapt to the organization relate to on-job leadership and supervisory concerns that extend beyond the scope of this book. However, they also suggest that a combination of big-picture human resources strategies and front-line supervisory procedures yield a workforce committed to partnering with the organization. In large organizations, human resource managers and their line department counterparts must work closely together to best assure that the work environment is favorable to staff members. In smaller organizations without human resources specialists, managers have the increased responsibility to plan, implement, and maintain work environments that encourage employee retention. This should be of obvious concern. However, hospitality managers are very busy and, unfortunately, may spend significant time addressing short-term challenges rather than longer-term actions that impact employee relationships.

Will the new staff member signing this letter of acceptance enjoy or become stressed about his or her initial job experiences? In large measure, the answer will depend on the quality of the orientation program that has been planned and implemented by concerned managers.
Courtesy PhotoDisc/ Getty Images

Orientation Programs and Procedures

2. **Explain important procedures that should be used as employee orientation programs and procedures are developed and implemented.**

Orientation: The process of providing basic information about the hospitality organization that must be known by all staff members in every department.

Orientation is the process of providing basic information about the hospitality organization that must be known by all staff members in every department. Implemented effectively, orientation efforts provide initial on-job experiences that help new staff members learn about the organization and its purposes, become comfortable with the work environment, and learn where they fit into it. In other words, orientation assists with the new employee adaptation process discussed in the previous section. Discussions about basic policies and procedures also help new staff members learn about matters of personal importance, such as their employer's expectations and job-related benefits. In effect, then, orientation and other initial work-related experiences help the new employees learn how the organizational culture views its staff members. It is critical that an effective orientation program be planned and implemented, because it significantly affects the relationship between the organization and its staff members.

Human Resources Management:
CURRENT EVENTS 5.1

MANY NEW EMPLOYEES MEAN MANY ORIENTATION SESSIONS

When the W. Dallas Hotel opened, it had 3,000 applications for 200 positions. Many people, including those without previous hotel experience, wanted to work for this stylish, upscale hotel. About 400 new employees participated in an intensive 10-day program to learn about the W brand's service style. As part of their training experience, they were able to experience the property as guests in the hotel and in its restaurants, bars, and spa.

The employees were empowered to go out of their way to assist guests with unexpected extras. Ross Cline, the president of W, refers to staff members as "experience engineers" and "talent," and new employees are easily caught up in the philosophy of "giving guests whatever they want, whenever they want it, unless it's illegal."

Suzanne Marta. "W. Dallas Had 3,000 Applications for 200 Positions"; "Whit, Whimzy Are Key Words for W. Staffers in Training." Retrieved June 10, 2006, from *www.hotel-online.com*.

GOALS OF ORIENTATION PROGRAMS

Goals of orientation include:

- *Provides an overview of the organization.* Many newly employed staff members want to know about their employer's history, size (e.g., number of locations and staff members), and the products and services it provides. They should learn about the results their new organization is attempting to achieve. Trainees may want to know how their organization adds value for its guests, to themselves, and to the organization's owners. Hopefully, a **mission statement** explains what the organization wants to accomplish and how it intends to do so. The mission statement should also serve as a guide for decision making and be used every day (and not just as an introductory page in an employee handbook or for a slogan on the managers' business cards).
- *Indicates the new staff member's role.* If you were a new staff member, would you like to see an organizational chart showing all positions including yours and the reporting relationships between them? Would you like to learn where you fit in and about promotion tracks if you perform well? You probably would, and new staff members do as well.
- *Explains policies, rules, and other information.* Staff want to know general guidelines, including days and hours of work, uniform requirements, break times, auto parking, and other similar information to help them feel more comfortable.
- *Outlines specific expectations.* Topics including responsibilities of the employer to the staff and of the staff to the employer should be addressed.
- *Provides details about employee benefits.* Staff members want information about nonsalary/nonwage compensation and the requirements to receive these benefits.
- *Motivates new staff members.* The enthusiasm and excitement exhibited by those providing orientation experiences are important. Orientation helps establish a solid foundation for the relationship between the organization, its managers and supervisors, and the new staff members.

Taken together, the benefits of effective orientation programs can eliminate confusion, heighten a new staff member's enthusiasm, create favorable attitudes, and, in general, make a positive first impression.

Properly conducted orientation sessions address many concerns of new staff members. Managers should encourage questions and recognize their role as they provide an appropriate welcome to the organization.

Orientation is the first step in training, and it must be well-planned and organized. In smaller organizations, orientation may be the responsibility of the new staff member's immediate supervisor. In large hospitality organizations, there will, hopefully, be a cooperative effort among staff (human resources) personnel and line department supervisors or others. The new employee's supervisor, for example, can assist in the orientation program as he or she reviews the organization chart and position description and previews the training program(s) in which the new

Mission statement: A strategic statement that indicates (provides an overview of) what the hospitality organization wants to accomplish and how it intends to do so.

IT'S THE LAW!

Employers are required by law to obtain some information from new employees, and this may be done during orientation. Examples include federal, state, and/or community withholding tax information, and immigration and naturalization documentation and age verification (for minors), if this was not provided (finalized) during the selection process.

Legal problems might be avoided if some information is provided to employees during orientation (or at another early time in their employment). Examples include information about the employer's sexual harassment complaint procedures and about Americans With Disabilities Act (ADA) concerns. (*Note:* Sexual harassment is discussed in depth in Chapter 10; ADA concerns are explored in Chapter 2.) Also, many hospitality operations that sell or provide alcoholic beverages begin their emphasis on responsible service during their orientation program. This helps establish a priority for their concern, and it establishes a record of consistent and ongoing emphasis that could be of significant help in defending the organization if lawsuits arise.

Effective Orientation Programs Address Staff Questions

Think about the types of questions and concerns you might have had when you began working for a new organization:

- Where do I fit into the organization?
- Where and how can I contribute my time and talents?
- What are my duties?
- What are my rights?
- What are my limits?
- How can I advance (and to what positions) within my new organization?

Effective orientation programs consider these and related questions to reduce the stress and anxiety that many new employees have during their first days on the job. In the process, orientation programs help establish a relationship between the new staff member and the organization that will have a significant impact on their subsequent on-job success.

Some large hotels conduct orientation sessions for many new staff members one or more times weekly. What do you think this says about the organization's initial and ongoing interactions with staff members? *Courtesy Purestock*

Adaptation and Orientation: What's the Difference?

This chapter began by discussing adaptation: the process by which new employees learn the values of and "what's it like to work for" the hospitality operation during initial job experiences. Adaptation, then, relates to an employee's internal concerns and how they are (or are not) addressed during early activities that include but are not limited to orientation. In contrast, orientation relates to the process used by the organization to provide basic information that must be known by staff members in every department. The best hospitality managers consider and, to the extent possible, address the adaptation concerns of new employees into their orientation programs. This important task becomes much easier when existing employees who have completed the property's orientation program (and who have had their adaptation concerns adequately addressed) help to pass on the desired perspectives to new hires.

staff member will participate. Regardless of property size, the basic concerns to be addressed by orientation are the same, because the basic needs and concerns of a new staff member do not differ when they are employed by large or small organizations.

USE AN ORIENTATION CHECKLIST

Careful planning of an orientation program is important. Figure 5.2 illustrates a checklist that identifies many concepts that can be addressed in an orientation program.

It is important to assemble all needed materials required before the orientation session begins. Some hospitality operations include these in an **orientation kit.** Examples of items that can be included in an orientation kit are listed in Figure 5.3.

ORGANIZATION INTRODUCTION
- ☐ Welcome new staff member(s)
- ☐ Present/explain mission statement
- ☐ Discuss history of organization
- ☐ Review types of guests served (if applicable)
- ☐ Note products and services provided
- ☐ Review current organization chart

STAFF MEMBER – RELATED POLICIES

- ☐ **APPEARANCE**
  - __ Hygiene standards
  - __ Name tag
  - __ Uniform including shoes
  - __ Jewelry

- ☐ **CONDUCT**
  - __ Attendance
  - __ Drug-free workplace information
  - __ Respectful behavior required
  - __ Harassment policy and discussion

- ☐ **JOB PERFORMANCE**
  - __ Position description
  - __ Work schedules

- __ Training programs
- __ Breaks
- __ Performance evaluation system
- __ Probationary period

- ☐ **EMPLOYEE BENEFITS**
  - __ Vacation
  - __ Leaves (personal, military, jury duty, emergency, other)
  - __ Sick leave
  - __ Education incentives
  - __ Insurance programs (medical, dentist, life, disability, other)
  - __ Workers' compensation
  - __ Meals/uniform allowances
  - __ Other: _____
    _____
    _____

- ☐ **COMPENSATION INFORMATION**
  - __ Salary/wage
  - __ Pay periods; pay day
  - __ Procedures for checking in and out of work shifts

FIGURE 5.2: Sample Orientation Checklist

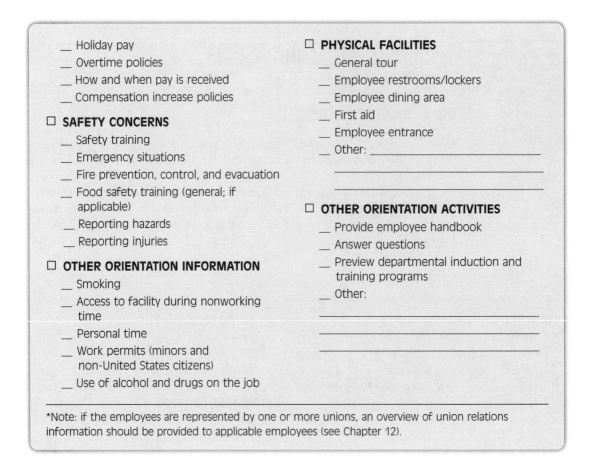

__ Holiday pay
__ Overtime policies
__ How and when pay is received
__ Compensation increase policies

☐ **SAFETY CONCERNS**

__ Safety training
__ Emergency situations
__ Fire prevention, control, and evacuation
__ Food safety training (general; if applicable)
__ Reporting hazards
__ Reporting injuries

☐ **OTHER ORIENTATION INFORMATION**

__ Smoking
__ Access to facility during nonworking time
__ Personal time
__ Work permits (minors and non-United States citizens)
__ Use of alcohol and drugs on the job

☐ **PHYSICAL FACILITIES**

__ General tour
__ Employee restrooms/lockers
__ Employee dining area
__ First aid
__ Employee entrance
__ Other: _____
_____
_____

☐ **OTHER ORIENTATION ACTIVITIES**

__ Provide employee handbook
__ Answer questions
__ Preview departmental induction and training programs
__ Other:
_____
_____
_____

*Note: if the employees are represented by one or more unions, an overview of union relations information should be provided to applicable employees (see Chapter 12).

FIGURE 5.2: (*Continued*)

Current organization chart
Copy of employee handbook
Copies of employee performance appraisal forms/procedures
Current copy of employee newsletter
Federal, state, and local tax law materials
Layout (maps) of facility (large properties)
Accident prevention guidelines

FIGURE 5.3: Sample Contents of Orientation Kit

When Does Orientation End?

Typical staff member orientation sessions require several (or fewer) hours or, perhaps, a half day (or longer). However, they generally conclude without follow-up sessions. Some hospitality organizations schedule additional orientation sessions several weeks or even longer after the initial session(s). By this time, staff members are familiar with their organization, department, and position. Based on their on-job experiences, the new employees can ask additional questions, participate in discussions, and learn about topics including guest service and teamwork that can be better addressed and understood with personal knowledge of the organization.

Human Resources MANAGEMENT ISSUES (5.2)

"I wonder what I'm getting into now," thought Daren, as he parked his car and walked through the parking lot. He had accepted a position as a cook in the foodservices department of a large hospital.

"I've cooked at several restaurants, and I have learned a few things: I like to cook, to be creative, and to work with a great team that feels like I do," were his next thoughts as he neared the entrance closest to the parking lot. "However, I've never worked for a healthcare facility. While it sounds good (e.g., great working hours, higher pay, and better benefits), I don't know about the environment with a lot of patients who are going to be depending on me."

As he walked closer to the building, he saw a sign: "Patient Entrance – Straight Ahead; Visitors' Entrance – Turn Left; Vendors Proceed to Purchasing Office."

"Well, what do I do now?" thought Daren. "I'm not a patient, I'm not a visitor, and I'm not selling anything. I guess employees know where to go, and they don't need a sign. So what should I do now?"

QUESTIONS

1. What would you do now if you were Daren?
2. What special orientation tactics can best help Daren and others without previous healthcare experience adapt to the unique environment?
3. Should an initial tour of the hospital include all areas, or just those in which Daren will be working? Why?
4. Assume the hospital's orientation process is excellent (except for the oversight about not telling Daren where to report to work). What do you think will be the major differences between this orientation program and a similar (excellent) one in a restaurant?

DEPARTMENTAL INDUCTION PROCEDURES

Induction: The process of providing new employees with basic information that everyone in their department must know that is unique to their department.

Induction relates to the process of providing new employees with basic information that everyone in their department must know that is unique to their department. For example, everyone in the hospitality operation must know about compensation policies and procedures and the importance of guest service. This information should be part of the orientation program. However, perhaps only food production personnel must know about kitchen workflow concerns, and, in a hotel, only front-office personnel may need to know about different classifications of hotel guests.

New employees should arrive at their department when there is time for an organized and orderly induction. Contrast this with the unfortunate situation that often arises when a new employee begins work during a busy shift and is expected to immediately become a productive member of the team. Our earlier discussion of the new employee adaptation process addressed the impact of initial experiences. An unplanned induction program can quickly destroy the benefits gained from an effective orientation program.

What concerns can be addressed in an induction program? Figure 5.4 presents a checklist of possible activities.

DEPARTMENT INDUCTION CHECKLIST
- ☐ Department introduction
- ☐ Department mission statement
- ☐ Review of department organization (positions and current incumbents of management/supervisory positions)
- ☐ How department impacts other departments

- ☐ Position duties and responsibilities
  - __ Provide/review current job description
  - __ Explain importance of position and its impact on other department positions
  - __ Review performance standards and evaluate methods
  - __ Work schedules (days/hours)
  - __ Overtime needs (if any)
  - __ When and how to request assistance

- ☐ Policies and procedures
  - __ Emergencies
  - __ Safety precautions and accident prevention

FIGURE 5.4: Sample Department Induction Activities Checklist

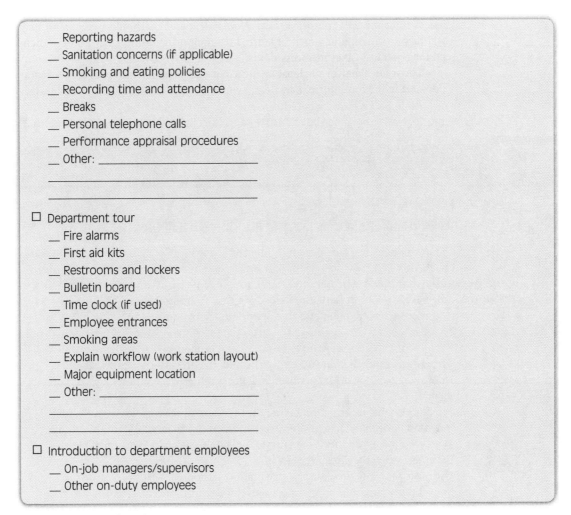

__ Reporting hazards
__ Sanitation concerns (if applicable)
__ Smoking and eating policies
__ Recording time and attendance
__ Breaks
__ Personal telephone calls
__ Performance appraisal procedures
__ Other: _____
_____
_____

☐ Department tour
__ Fire alarms
__ First aid kits
__ Restrooms and lockers
__ Bulletin board
__ Time clock (if used)
__ Employee entrances
__ Smoking areas
__ Explain workflow (work station layout)
__ Major equipment location
__ Other: _____
_____
_____

☐ Introduction to department employees
__ On-job managers/supervisors
__ Other on-duty employees

FIGURE 5.4: (Continued)

ORIENTATION FOLLOW-UP

Use of orientation and departmental induction procedures such as those outlined in, respectively, Figures 5.2 and 5.4 will take more time and effort than is spent by some hospitality organizations. However, a comprehensive program assists with an effective employee adaptation process that yields committed staff members.

Orientation follow-up activities are also important. It is not sufficient to say, "If you have any questions, just ask someone," or "Just assume you're doing okay unless someone tells you differently." New staff members should understand they will be participating in a well-organized training program designed to help them perform job tasks that meet standards.

The trainer may or may not be the same staff member who provided orientation and induction information. If so (which is typical in a small operation), this

Human Resources Management:
CURRENT EVENTS 5.2

BASIC ORIENTATION PRINCIPLES APPLY TO ALL HOSPITALITY SEGMENTS

The most important principles in facilitating the work of staff members are universal, although they do vary by industry segment or between industries. One reason is that people are people, and they have the same basic concerns and react in the same basic ways to the situations in which they find themselves.

Consider these keys to an effective orientation program:

- Plan the orientation program to ensure that it is organized and consistent.
- Prepare an agenda that includes meeting and greeting other coworkers.
- Inform current coworkers about new staff members. (E-mail messages are one tactic.)
- Provide essential information before the new employee's first day at work. Make new staff members feel comfortable by informing them about simple things: Where should they park? What entry door should they use? Who and where will they meet when they first arrive?
- Use more than one presenter for orientation sessions.
- Spread the orientation program over several days (or longer).
- Provide material that new staff members can take home to review, to reexamine, and to determine whether questions are appropriate.
- Solicit feedback about the evaluation process so the program can be continually improved.

Each of these principles represents a no- or low-cost procedure to help new employees feel welcome to and good about their recent employment decision.

Denise Moretti. "Corporate Orientation Programs: Retaining Great People Begins Before Day One." *Note:* The author represents the Hamister group, an organization that managed assisted living and healthcare properties before expanding into the hospitality industry. (To view the article, go to: *www.hotelnewsresource.com*. When you reach the site, enter the author's name into the search box.) A lesson to be learned: Human resources aspects of orientation in the healthcare industry are similar to those in the hospitality industry.

provides an opportunity for continuity as the orientation–induction–training processes evolve. When different staff members are involved (as is likely in a large organization), those involved in orientation and induction can still offer genuine enthusiasm and provide follow-up assistance as requested. They can regularly check back with the new staff member and answer questions that arise after the orientation and induction procedures have concluded.

You've learned that these early on-job experiences are important for the employee and the organization. Therefore, they should be evaluated to determine if they are cost effective (worth more than what they cost) and whether improvements are possible. Feedback from new staff members several months (or longer) after they have completed these initial on-job activities can help. Perhaps they can complete unsigned surveys or participate in interviews conducted for that purpose, or as part of more general efforts to receive employee input about operational improvements. Exit interviews of departing employees may also be helpful.

Employees will, one way or another, learn about the organization, their position, and their employer's expectations. It is better for them to acquire this information through a formal, planned, organized, and hospitable orientation effort than to pick it up in casual conversations with and by watching peers on the job.

Employee Handbooks

3. **Note the importance of employee handbooks, and list typical policy and procedure topics that might be included in them.**

Employee handbooks are personnel management tools used in hospitality organizations of all sizes.

EMPLOYEE HANDBOOKS ARE NECESSARY

As you learned in Chapter 3, an employee handbook is a centralized source of information detailing an employer's policies, benefits, and employment practices. It is typically distributed and discussed when new employees receive their general orientation. This enables staff members to review information presented during the orientation, and it provides other information that, because of time limitations, may be best presented in this manner.

Employee handbooks must be current (and kept current), and they must be correctly and professionally presented. Clean and current copies make a better statement about the hospitality organization and the importance it attaches to providing employee information than do handbooks that appear to be thrown together haphazardly. *Note:* Some organizations make their employee handbook

IT'S THE LAW!

Can policies contained in employee handbooks be considered a contract that must be followed without exception or, alternatively, are they guidelines that generally explain requirements and how staff members are normally treated?

Employee handbooks or policies in them might be considered a binding part of the employee relationship if the policy language is such that an employee could reasonably believe a contractual offer was being made. Careful wording is required to help assure that employees will not construe policies to be contractual promises.

One of the most significant legal concerns relates to the employment at-will relationship that exists when employers can hire any employee they wish, and dismiss that staff member with or without cause at any time. (The employee can also elect to terminate the work relationship anytime that he or she decides to do so.) Mixed messages can be created when, for example, handbook policies specify detailed discipline and discharge procedures that must be followed before termination. As well, if statements such as "our employees are our family" or similar messages are made, readers might perceive them to supersede at-will disclaimers.

available on the company's intranet. This makes it readily available (copies will not become lost) and easy to update.

Employee handbooks tell new and all other staff members about the organization. They detail all policies and procedures to which the employer and employees agree, and they can be referenced by courts seeking to define terms of the employment agreement if disputes arise.

Typically, employee handbooks should indicate that the hospitality operation has the right to modify, alter, or eliminate any or all contents at any time. Further, it is important to indicate within the manual that it is not a contract. The organization's attorney should be consulted as the employee handbook is developed and, most certainly, before it is circulated.

IMPORTANT POLICIES AND PROCEDURES ARE IDENTIFIED

Figure 5.5 lists a wide range of topics that might be applicable to hospitality organizations and that might be addressed in an employee handbook. However, not all topics are relevant or useful for all properties.

Absenteeism
Accessibility for Disabled
Accidents
Accrual of Vacation
Advancement
Alcohol Testing
Americans with Disabilities Act
Announcements of Openings
Appearance and Grooming
Appraisal
Attendance
Awards
Badges (name tags)
Benefits
Bereavement Leaves
Bids
Breaks
Call-Back Pay
Call-Out Pay
Changing Departments
Child Care Leave
Code of Ethics
Commendations
Commercial Driver's License
Compensation
Competence
Complaints
Compliance
Computer Use (Personal)
Concerns
Conferences
Confidentiality
Conflicts of Interest
Consultants (Use of)
Continuing Education
Controlled Substances

Conventional Standards of
    Workplace Behavior
Corporate Compliance
Counseling
Criminal Convictions
Customer Service
Dental Insurance
Department Transfer
    Questionnaire
Differentials
Disability Insurance
Disciplinary Process
Discrimination Claims
Displacements
Dress Code
Drug Testing
Drug Use
Drug-Free Awareness
    Program
Drug-Free Workplace
Drugs
Educational Assistance
Educational Leave
Emergency Plans/
    Preparedness
Employee Assistance Program
Employee Badges
Employee File
Employee Identification
    Program
Employee of the Month/Year
Employee Performance
    Appraisal
Employee-at-Will
Equal Employment
Ethics
Evaluation

Exit Interview
Expenses, Noneducational
Extended Sick Pay
Family Medical Leave Act
Fitness for Duty
Funeral Leave
Gifts/Gratuities
Grant Employees
Grants
Grievance/Complaint
    Procedures
Harassment
Health Insurance
Hiring
Hiring of Family Members
Holidays
Hourly Associate Forum
Hours of Work
Identification
Industrial Injury
Integrity
Investigation
Job Evaluation
Job Opportunities
Job Postings
Job Qualifications
Job Rotation
Job Vacancies
Jury Duty
Layoffs
Leave of Absence
Leaves
Leaving Department
Leaving Employment
Lockers
Lost Time Claims

FIGURE 5.5: Sample Employee Handbook Topics

Meal Allowance/Periods	Qualifying Periods	Tax-Sheltered Annuity
Medical Claims	Recall	Telephone Calls (Personal)
Military Leave	Recording Work Time	Termination
Modified Duty	Recruiting	Time Off without Pay
Multiple Employment	Reference Checks	Training
New Jobs	Relationships (on-job)	Transfers
On-Call Pay	Resignation	Transportation Allowance
Orientation Period	Retirement Programs	Transportation Work Program
Overtime	Return of Organization's	Travel
Overtime Pay	Property	Tuition
Paid Holidays	Return to Work	Tuition Grant
Parking	Safety/Security	Tuition Reimbursement
Pay and Pay Periods	Salary	Uniforms
Payroll Deductions	Schedule Posting	Vacancies
Pension	Scheduling Vacation	Vacation Accrual
Personal Business	Seniority	Vacation Banking
Personal Code of Conduct	Seniority Calculation	Vacation Pay
Personal Holidays	Service Awards Recognition	Vacation Scheduling
Personal Leave	Program	Vacations
Personal Records	Severance Pay	Violence
Posting	Sexual Harassment	Voluntary Time Off
Probationary Employees/	Sick Pay	Wages
Periods	Sick Time Accumulation	Weapons
Problems	Sick Time Buy-Back	Weather (inclement)
Professional Dues	Smoking	Work Rules
Professionalism	Staff Reductions	Work Time
Qualifications	Suggestions	Workers' Compensation

FIGURE 5.5: (*Continued*)

Managers can use a questioning approach to help assess what topics could be useful. Do new or longer-tenured staff members have questions about issues related to the topic? Is there an inconsistent understanding about how, if at all, an issue is managed from the perspectives of subordinate staff? These and related questions, when answered affirmatively, may determine the need for new or revised policies and procedures.

Keep Employee Handbooks Current

To be useful, employee handbooks must be kept current. While this appears obvious, busy hospitality managers sometimes replace written policies and procedures recorded in an employee handbook with understandings based on "how we've done things lately." Changes typically begin with small breaks in or small discrepancies with procedures that go unchallenged. For example, a restaurant's uniform code requires solid-toed shoes for kitchen workers to prevent punctures from dropped knives and burns from spilled hot liquids. However, a cook occasionally, then frequently, and then always arrives at work in canvas tennis shoes. Bending the rules the first time may have no immediate consequences, but it establishes the precedent that this policy is not always necessary or, at least, that it is not important.

Small lapses in policies and procedures can lead to larger ones. They can send the message that policies and procedures can be disregarded when it is convenient to do so, and that they involve personal interpretation. Policies and procedures should be designed for a specific purpose and, if they are not necessary, they should be discarded or revised. They should, therefore, be consistently followed. To help prevent the inconsistent application of policies and procedures, several tactics can be used:

- Insist that standards be respected. Policies and procedures should be followed all the time, and their expectations should be consistently met.
- Have managers, supervisors, and employees role-model examples for their peers.
- Inform staff members about the reasons for the policies and procedures.
- Present information about the most important policies and procedures during orientation. Other policies can be discussed on an ongoing basis as part of in-service or other training programs.
- Educate staff members that compliance with reasonable policies and procedures is part of the agreement with, and relationship between, their employers and themselves.

Mentoring Programs

4. Identify basic concerns that should be addressed as employee mentoring programs are planned and implemented.

Mentoring is a relationship in which an experienced staff member provides professional advice to a less-experienced staff member. These activities can arise informally when a relatively inexperienced person solicits advice from an "old-timer"

Mentoring: A formal or informal relationship in which an experienced staff member provides advice and counsel to a less-experienced staff member.

about how the organization works. Mentoring relationships can also be more formal, such as when experienced volunteers receive training in mentoring activities and then interact with staff selected for participation in fast-track"career development programs. Sometimes a mentoring relationship lasts for a short while, or it can last for many years.

BACKGROUND

Several advantages can accrue to organizations with effective mentoring programs:

- Junior staff can more quickly learn about the organization's culture and how to act within it.
- Mentorees may have increased commitment to the organization because they are better assimilated into the corporate culture.
- Higher levels of job satisfaction can occur with the decreased chance that those being mentored will leave the organization.
- Problems that hinder the mentoree's current performance can be addressed.

Advantages can also accrue to mentors:

- *Enhanced self-esteem.* A mentor will likely feel good about the opportunity to provide advice and to make a difference.
- *Increased knowledge.* Mentors learn as they interact with mentorees.
- *Seen as good citizens.* Mentors may receive special consideration as their own careers are evaluated.
- *Helps to train successors.* Sometimes mentors cannot be promoted until someone is available to assume their position, and this can be the mentoree.

An effective mentor can serve several roles in interactions with mentorees:

- *Trainer.* Mentors who are queried about specific on-job performance issues can provide applicable assistance and serve as an informal trainer.
- *Coach.* Mentors can provide positive reinforcement about desired performance, and they may advise against actions that may lead to on-job difficulties, just as a supervisor does when coaching a staff member.
- *Counselor.* Counselors do not make decisions for another person but, rather, discuss the pro and cons of a situation. They ask open-ended questions to learn what the other person is thinking and, in the process, allow the other person to more clearly think things through. A counselor provides benchmark information that can help one to evaluate personal perspectives.
- *Guide.* Just as a guide safely leads someone who is unfamiliar with a geographic area to a destination, so can a mentor help a mentoree to move on to interim locations on the way to a longer-term destination (career).

Phases of Mentoring Relationship

It is not typical that a senior staff member begins to interact with a less-experienced counterpart and immediately gives free advice. Instead, time is required for a relationship of mutual respect to evolve and for the mentoree to appreciate and trust the mentor's judgment. The relationship between a mentor and mentoree can involve the same steps as building a friendship:

- *Introduction.* A mentoring relationship can begin by chance as two persons meet on the job, or it can begin more formally when a senior staff member is paired with a less-experienced person in a planned career development program.
- *Cultivation.* Time is needed for both individuals to get to know each other, to understand each other's position, and for the mentor to understand the context within which the mentoree is soliciting advice.
- *Redefinition.* Few relationships on the job remain the same. They typically grow stronger or weaker, and they sometimes end. At some point, the junior staff member may not require or desire advice. Conversely, mentors may have a lessened desire to continue in the mentoring role. By contrast, relationships can become stronger and evolve into lifelong (or, at least, career-long) opportunities to share information and to enjoy a mutually rewarding relationship.

- *Role model.* The old saying, "Actions speak louder than words," suggests that mentorees can learn much from their mentors just by observing them as they interact with others in the organization.
- *Advocate.* A mentor in a senior position can emphasize the strengths and abilities of a mentoree to those at higher organizational levels.

How exactly can a mentor assist a mentoree? Examples of mentoring activities include:

Career ladder: A progression of increasingly more responsible positions within an organization or an industry.

- Helping the mentoree to develop a **career ladder**
- Advising about development activities that can assist the mentoree to move toward career ladder goals
- Evaluating alternative education and training programs and courses of action to address on-job concerns
- Providing applicable reading materials
- Suggesting alternative courses of action that address on-job problems
- If applicable, making special assignments and arranging for special training
- Providing ongoing counseling

Ten steps can be used in implementing a formal mentoring program, which are outlined in Figure 5.6.

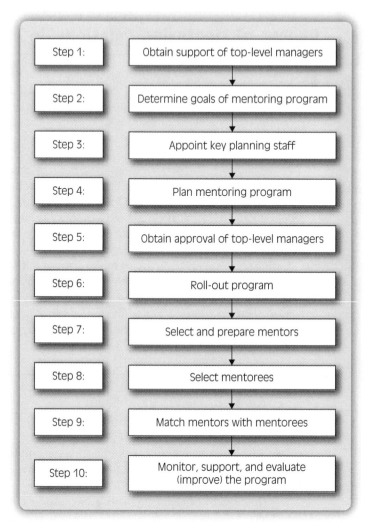

FIGURE 5.6: Steps to Implement a Formal Mentoring Program

Let's look at each of these steps more closely:

■ *Step 1: Obtain support of top-level managers.* Human resources personnel, managers, supervisors, and others who support the need for a formal mentoring program should serve as its advocates to top-level officials. A discussion of the benefits noted earlier may help yield approval.

- *Step 2: Determine goals of the mentoring program.* Numerous goals including benefits to the organization, the mentors, and mentorees noted previously are likely to be among desired results.
- *Step 3: Appoint key planning staff.* Those interested in developing a mentoring program are likely candidates. The project could also be appropriate for consideration by a **cross-functional team** of persons who could bring differing perspectives to the planning process.
- *Step 4: Plan mentoring program.* Decisions will be required about how mentors and mentorees will be selected and paired, their responsibilities, the mechanics of how and when the parties will interact, topics for which mentoring discussions are appropriate, and how the program will be announced, administered, and evaluated.
- *Step 5: Obtain approval of top-level managers.* Interim input from these officials may have been provided; if so, approval is likely to be easier and faster. The mentoring program should be seen as beneficial, inexpensive to implement, and with few disadvantages that will require consideration as an approval decision is given.
- *Step 6: Roll-out program.* Program announcements, staff meetings, organizational newsletters, information in orientation programs for new staff, and conversations among managers, supervisors, and staff members are among promotion possibilities. The availability of and procedures for the mentoring program should also be an integral aspect of applicable career development programs.
- *Step 7: Select and prepare mentors.* Effective mentors are usually successful, high-performing staff members. They have a track record of successful performance over many years and, probably, in several (or more) positions. However, they may need to learn basic mentoring skills. The knowledge, skills, and abilities of effective mentors frequently include:
  - The desire to assist mentorees
  - An ability to think creatively and to suggest problem-solving alternatives to mentorees
  - The ability to motivate mentorees
  - Effective oral communication skills, including the ability to present, explain, organize, and defend suggestions
  - An interest in assisting the organization and the mentoree
  - An understanding of and ability to apply change management principles
  - An understanding of the organization's culture, and the ability to use this knowledge to explain, defend, and justify suggestions
  - Detailed knowledge of business and operating principles applicable to the organization

  How should mentors be prepared for their role? Topics to be addressed in training sessions can include a discussion of:

  - Mentoring goals of the organization and for the mentor and mentoree
  - Critical attributes of the mentoring relationship

- ■ Suggestions for determining the mentoree's needs and for generating alternatives that address them
- ■ Training and career development opportunities within the organization. If applicable, a special emphasis should be placed on fast-track and other programs that include a formal mentoring component.
- ■ Training in communication skills including active listening techniques
- ■ Relationship skills
- ■ Effective coaching tactics
- ■ Problem-solving and conflict resolution suggestions
- ■ *Step 8: Select mentorees.* In informal mentoring programs, less-experienced staff may simply request that a more-experienced counterpart discuss issues of concern. Some organizations have mentor open-door policies, where any staff member with a question or concern can seek out a more-experienced person on an ad hoc or continuing basis. In a more formal model, fast-track staff are assigned a mentor, and this input is an integral part of their planned career development program.
- ■ *Step 9: Match mentors with mentorees.* Considerations in matching mentors and mentorees can include close proximity (same location) and the extent to which the mentor has held similar positions to that of the mentoree. In some

Ground Rules for a Mentoring Relationship

The environment within which an effective mentoring relationship exists is one of mutual respect and trust, productivity, and safety (comfort). Ground rules for managing the mentoring partnership can help ensure that this environment continues. Examples of mentor and mentoree agreements can include:

- How and when meeting times are established.
- How discussion topics are determined.
- How disagreements, if any, should be resolved.
- What, if any, contact should occur between scheduled meetings.
- Statement of confidentiality: Neither the mentor nor the mentoree should share each other's confidences without mutual approval.
- Meetings are treated as a priority, and each person's full attention is concentrated on them.
- Honesty is important.
- Humor, if used, is respectful and appropriate.
- Anecdotes of past mentoring and learning experiences are shared.
- The mentor is supportive, not controlling.

instances, gender match and/or a common ethnic, racial, class culture, or class background may be judged to reduce barriers that hinder trust. As well, observers typically suggest that mentors not be a staff member's immediate supervisor or trainer.

- *Step 10: Monitor, support, and evaluate (improve) the program.* Mentoring efforts, once implemented, should be evaluated to ensure that they are cost effective and that they are achieving planned results. Also, like many other programs, continuous quality improvement (CQI) efforts are helpful to ensure that the mentoring effort better meets the needs of the organization, the mentors, and the mentorees as it evolves.

Human Resources and Ethical Concerns

5. Discuss the role of ethics in the management of human resources.

WHAT ARE ETHICS?

Ethics: A set of rules or principles that define what is right and what is wrong as decisions are made that affect others.

Business ethics: Refers to the practice of ethical judgment by managers as they make decisions affecting the organization.

Behavior, ethical: Actions in concert with generally accepted social concerns relating to the impact of decisions on others.

Behavior, unethical: Actions not in concert with generally accepted social concerns relating to the impact of decisions on others.

The concept of **ethics** relates to a set of rules or principles that define what is right and what is wrong. Unfortunately, these definitions can vary considerably based on the individual making the determination. Society, through its body of laws, does not become involved until something is illegal. It is clear that something illegal is also unethical, but something can be legal and unethical. For example, it is legal for a human resources manager to show some favoritism toward a specific employee when determining who should attend a convention in a desirable out-of-town location, and the same manager might legally assign undesirable projects to an employee he or she dislikes. However, disregarding the morale and supervisory implications of these decisions, are they ethical?

It is important that persons make ethical decisions in their personal lives, but the practice of **business ethics** is of important concern to hospitality managers. Professional managers consistently practice **ethical behavior** and avoid **unethical behavior.**

The American public has probably always been concerned about ethics. However, today, after recurring news events about numerous business organizations and political corruption and abuses at all governmental levels that most persons believe to have serious ethical consequences, these concerns have never been more significant.

While ethical conduct is required at all times, the difference between what is right and what is wrong is sometimes difficult to distinguish. Consider the following examples:

- A purchasing agent for a large hotel receives some free tickets to a sporting event from a regular supplier. Does this illustrate a situation where the purchasing agent benefits and no one loses? Can the purchaser's future decisions about product purchases be affected?

- Top-level managers are offered (and accept) significant salary increases, while wages for hourly staff are kept minimal because of the organization's financial difficulties.
- Organizations increase employee benefits, but eliminate many full-time staff, and begin to utilize more part-time workers who do not qualify for the benefits.

Can these issues be addressed ethically, and can (or should) the social responsibilities inherent in the situations be considered? Perhaps so—but perhaps not—and the answer depends on the individuals confronted by the situation. The availability of a code of ethics can guide them but, unfortunately, ethical codes are disregarded in many cases.

Some writers have offered ethical principles for hospitality managers that should be followed when decisions are made. These include:

- *Honesty.* Don't mislead or deceive others.
- *Integrity.* Do what is right.
- *Trustworthiness.* Supply correct information, and correct any information that is not factual.
- *Loyalty.* Avoid conflicts of interest, and don't disclose confidential information.
- *Fairness.* Treat individuals equally; be tolerant of diversity.
- *Concern and respect.* Be considerate of those impacted by decision making.
- *Commitment to excellence.* Do the best you can do.
- *Leadership.* Lead by example.
- *Reputation and morale.* Work to enhance the company's reputation and the morale of employees.
- *Accountability.* Accept responsibility for decisions that are made.[1]

Other writers address factors that can serve as ethical norms.[2] For example, one or more of the following factors can be considered as decisions are made:

- *Utility.* To what extent does a specific act generate benefits for those affected?
- *Rights.* To what extent are the rights respected of persons involved as decisions are made?
- *Justice.* Is a decision fair?
- *Caring.* Does a decision consider the responsibilities that individuals have to each other?

As one reviews these recommendations, it becomes clear that it is much easier to make the statement, "Hospitality human resources managers must be ethical, and they do so by consistently practicing ethical behavior," than it is to define more specifically what the statement actually means. Given this significant limitation, most top-level hospitality leaders claim that their organizations give a priority to making ethical decisions.

An organization's culture may support and reward its members for making decisions that reflect ethical concerns or, alternatively, it may provide no benefit to those who do so. In extreme instances, the culture may even reward those who make unethical decisions. Examples include some organizations that have, historically, ignored protections mandated under Equal Employment Opportunity Commission (EEOC) laws, and some lodging organizations that have emphasized expansion in remote geographic locations without regard for the affected citizens of the area or the environmental impact of their expansion.

Human resources managers should recognize that their behavior often speaks more loudly than the philosophy expressed in their organization's mission statement. Consider managers who specify food portions that violate truth-in-menu laws, their peers who raise hotel room rates in times of emergencies in states where it is legal (but perhaps not ethical) to do so, and managers in all segments of the hospitality industry who exaggerate benefits in marketing and advertising messages. Might employees think that, "If the manager does those things to our guests, he or she will also do it to me?" At best, this is likely true and, at worst, it encourages staff members to violate commonly recognized ethical standards. These management actions may (or may not!) be effective in the short term, but they will likely be ineffective over longer time periods. Consumers and employees desire to, respectively, purchase products and services from, and to be employed by, hospitality organizations that are genuinely committed to doing what is right for all of their constituents.

This chapter began by emphasizing the importance of helping new employees adapt to their new work environment because it was the right thing to do for the staff member and the best tactic for use by the hospitality operation. This provides an example of how concerns for others benefit the organization and, if necessary, provides an incentive to do so. When employee concerns are addressed in the culture of the organization, numerous benefits arise, and no disadvantages are likely to accrue. A paradox arises, however: ethical behavior benefits the organization, but some hospitality operations do not recognize the importance of ethical behavior when considering staff members.

CODES OF ETHICS

Code of ethics: A statement used by a hospitality organization to outline broad concepts to guide ethical decision making.

Many hospitality organizations develop and implement a **code of ethics** to provide broad statements to guide ethical decision making. As such, their intention is to provide a framework for decision making rather than to specify exactly what should or should not be done in a specific situation.

Hospitality organizations typically develop codes of ethics for several reasons, including:

- To identify a foundation of acceptable behaviors.
- To promote standards that should guide decision making.
- To provide a benchmark that can be used to evaluate potential decisions.
- To support the responsibility and obligations that decision makers have to constituents and to society.

The most effective codes of ethics exemplify the ethical commitment of the organization and how it will interact with others as it conducts business (in commercial organizations) or provides products and services to its constituencies (in noncommercial operations).

The best codes of ethics are developed specifically for the organization, and they utilize input from the staff members who will be expected to utilize the codes. Organizational leaders should identify the employee groups that will be bound by the code of ethics being developed, and they frequently include staff members at all organizational levels. Input should also be solicited from investors, vendors, and perhaps even other organizations in the community. Those who assist in the code's development should understand the organization's mission and be concerned about its commitment to a positive professional and community image. The support of top-level leadership is of obvious importance as codes of ethics are developed. They should be reviewed by legal counsel, and formal approval from the highest levels in the organization is required.

The tactics used to implement and educate staff members about a code of ethics are important. For example, an exhibit of the code that is hung on the walls at the headquarters office and used as a preamble for an employee handbook will do little good unless it is integrated into and actually guides the culture of the organization. It is also important to consider enforcement concerns that are applicable if or when the code is violated. A code of ethics is important, and its emphasis should last forever. It is not a program that begins and ends at specified times. All staff members should be held accountable for the behavior described in the code of ethics.

What topics might be included in a code of ethics? Figure 5.7 identifies typical concerns addressed in many codes of ethics.

Following are examples of topics commonly addressed in codes of ethics:

■ Importance of guests
■ Respect for individual staff members
■ Need for honesty
■ Relations with suppliers
■ Compliance with the law in all matters
■ Avoiding conflicts of interest
■ Use of the organization's assets
■ Confidentiality of proprietary information
■ Political contributions
■ Relations with competitors
■ Reporting financial operating results fairly and honestly
■ Business entertaining, gift acceptance, and bribes

FIGURE 5.7: Topics in Codes of Ethics

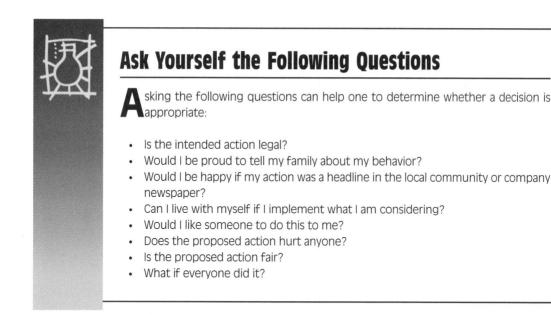

Ask Yourself the Following Questions

Asking the following questions can help one to determine whether a decision is appropriate:

- Is the intended action legal?
- Would I be proud to tell my family about my behavior?
- Would I be happy if my action was a headline in the local community or company newspaper?
- Can I live with myself if I implement what I am considering?
- Would I like someone to do this to me?
- Does the proposed action hurt anyone?
- Is the proposed action fair?
- What if everyone did it?

CORPORATE (SOCIAL) RESPONSIBILITY

Corporate (social) responsibility:
Relates to an organization's efforts to address its commitments to all of its constituencies, including guests, employees, other businesses including suppliers, investors, and society, and the community-at-large.

Stakeholders:
Groups, individuals, and organizations that are affected by an organization; also called *constituents*.

The concept of **corporate (social) responsibility** relates to the efforts of an organization to address its commitments to all of its constituencies, including guests, employees, other businesses including suppliers, investors, and society, and the community-at-large. These groups, also called **stakeholders,** are directly affected by the organization's action.

It is obvious that a hospitality organization must satisfactorily address commitments to its guests, employees, and investors. However, interactions with other businesses including suppliers should be carefully managed. (Recall the concern that codes of ethics should address supplier relationships.) It is also important that organizations act as good citizens in their specific communities and in society as a whole.

At this point, careful readers might be thinking, "While this is true, how exactly does corporate responsibility relate to the management of hospitality human resources?" The answer to this addresses two issues:

- *Cultural consistency.* Can an organization and its leaders be concerned about three constituencies (guests, employees, and investors) without being concerned about others? Doesn't the concept of business ethics noted earlier in this chapter apply beyond the organization itself? Those who shape an organization's culture in ways that attract and retain the most qualified staff members (the primary goal of human resources) will likely treat others in ways that mirror their concern for their staff members.
- *Employer-of-choice concerns.* Applicants are attracted to organizations within their community that have favorable reputations. In perhaps the most simple

example, networks of young people at high schools and colleges provide answers to questions for their peers such as "What's it like to work at specific restaurants, hotels, and/or other hospitality organizations within the community?" An organization's reputation is influenced by, and is known to, many persons beyond the market of current and potential employees. Consider, for

Human Resources Management:
CURRENT EVENTS 5.3

TOURISM CODE OF CONDUCT GUIDES BEHAVIOR RELATING TO SEXUAL EXPLOITATION OF MINORS IN BRAZIL

The Brazilian hotel sector's first code of conduct has been adopted by 140 hotels that are affiliated with Accor's six chains, located in seven South American countries. It addresses a pioneering concern about a worldwide problem, and it was developed in response to the 100,000 cases of exploitation of minors reported every year in Brazil that involve sexual abuse and commercial sexual exploitation.

The code is designed to help protect children and adolescents, is written in three languages (Portuguese, English, and Spanish), and complies with Brazil's federal constitution, its Statute of Children and Adolescents, and other international agreements of which Brazil is a signatory.

The code contains seven principles related to each Accor hotel's commitment to:

- Developing consistent policies addressing any form of sexual exploitation of minors
- Informing, educating, and guiding all staff members about the policy, company actions, and applicable laws
- Establishing guest accommodation agreement clauses that explicitly declare the rejection of any form of sexual exploitation of minors
- Rejecting advertising that encourages sexual exploitation of minors
- Training staff members
- Committing staff to take precautions against commercial relationships with any business that is involved with the enticement and sexual abuse of minors
- Informing guests and hotel visitors about the organization's commitment to the protection of children

Hotel-Online Special Report. "Accor Hotels Has Designed a Tourism Code of Conduct to Guide and Regulate Its Ethical Behaviour Concerning the Sexual Exploitation of Minors in Brazil; Adopted by Accor's 140 Hotels in South America." Retrieved from: *www.hotel-online.com*. October 3, 2005.

example, the impact of positive **publicity** that arises as organizations participation in community activities and assist with (or take a lead in) addressing broad societal concerns.

Everyone benefits when hospitality organizations assume corporate (social) responsibility for their actions. Is this factor the primary concern of a young person applying for an entry-level position in a hotel, restaurant, private club, or other hospitality organization? Probably not (although it might prompt an employment recommendation from a concerned parent). Do those employed by an organization feel good when they hear and/or read positive things about their organization? Probably so. Would employees of a hospitality operation like to contribute their time and even money to worthwhile causes sponsored or coordinated by their employer? Many would.

You can see, then, that the extent of an organization's corporate responsibility can have an impact on the management of its human resources.

Today's society increasingly emphasizes that its organizations be good corporate citizens, and businesses do so as they:

■ Assume a responsibility toward the environment by controlling (minimizing) the pollution of air, water, and land.

■ Accept a responsibility of concern toward guests by staying clear of unethical and irresponsible business practices relating to consumers' rights, unfair pricing, and being honest with advertising messages.

Some Examples of Corporate (Social) Responsibility

It makes good business sense for hospitality operations to help to improve their communities. They can do so in many ways including:

• Contributing time and money to worthwhile community projects and charitable causes.
• Providing products and services during times of disasters and other emergencies.
• Participating in environmentally friendly initiatives such as recycling, conserving energy, and utilizing environmentally "friendly" packaging.
• Coordinating activities for employees that provide volunteer services for the community.
• Investigating and correcting supplier abuses of employees in international locations.
• Recognizing animal welfare concerns in agreements with food suppliers.

HUMAN RESOURCES TERMS

The following terms were defined in this chapter:

Adaptation (to organization)	**Ethics**
Orientation	**Business ethics**
Mission statement	**Behavior (ethical)**
Orientation kit	**Behavior (unethical)**
Induction	**Code of ethics**
Mentoring	**Corporate (social) responsibility**
Career ladder	**Stakeholders**
Cross-functional team	**Publicity**

FOR YOUR CONSIDERATION

1. What is the impact of one's orientation experiences on his or her ability to perform work that meets required work standards?
2. What are some early-job experiences that you liked in previous positions you have held? Some that you disliked? How did each of these experiences impact your attitude about the organization, your manager/supervisor, and your position? What suggestions would you make to correct the things that you disliked about your early-job experiences?
3. How important do you think a code of ethics is for a small hospitality operation? How, if at all, is your response different for a very large hospitality organization?

CASE STUDY: HUMAN RESOURCES MANAGEMENT IN ACTION

"I guess there are advantages and disadvantages to being hired at the height of the busy season at a ski resort," said Sergio as he sat in the employee lounge with Patty during a well-deserved break. "I like my job in the maintenance department, especially the group I work with, and it's great to have all of the tools and supplies needed for routine maintenance. That has not been the case in some of my previous positions, and it really caused me to stress out!"

"We're all glad you're here," replied Patty, a housekeeping supervisor. "I didn't know what you would say now after I heard you talk earlier about your initial experiences with our resort that were less than perfect. I remember you telling me that you didn't know the location of the worksites for many of the maintenance tasks because the property is so large. I also remember you telling me how silly you must have looked to your peers because you didn't know specific maintenance tasks or the required tools for servicing some of our specialized equipment. In fact, you told me you had been here two weeks before you even met the department head."

"You're right," said Sergio. "The initial orientation process could have been much more organized and better delivered. If it was, I wouldn't have felt so awkward, and I could have better helped the resort by doing things right the first time without the need for lots of rework. I remember thinking a couple of times that they weren't treating me very well, and the fact that everyone appeared to be so busy, and they weren't doing it intentionally, didn't really soften my feelings. Since then, I guess I worked my way from a negative feeling to a neutral posture where I could take the job or leave it, to my present attitude that it's getting to be a better place to work."

"I don't think things would be very different in my housekeeping department," commented Patty, "if you started in the middle of the season. I guess I've always thought, incorrectly, that the excuse of being busy was accepted by new staff members. But now I can see that, as managers, we owe our staff members much more than promises that things will get better. I'm going to make some changes in my department and suggest to other department supervisors that they consider the need for changes in their departments as well. Thanks for the education, Sergio."

Dimension: Employer-of-Choice Concerns

1. How do you think most potential job applicants would react to the resort's reputation of "rough starts, but it gets better after you've been working there for a while"?
2. Many restaurant guests say almost nothing to friends if they have a good dining experience, but they say many things to contacts when they have inadequate dining experiences. Do you think the tendency to say a few nice things and lots of bad things is also true about one's experience with an employer? Why or why not?

Dimension: Human Resources Issues

1. Because the ski resort is so large, it likely has a human resources department. Is it possible that these specialists are not aware of their property's problems with orientation programs? If they are, what are reasons that they might not be more proactive in addressing issues? If they are not, what types of changes in the property's communication network might be appropriate?
2. What, if any, role should human resources personnel play in advising (improving) the orientation program? What should be the role, if any, of top-level managers?

Dimension: Employee Retention Issues

1. What impact, if any, do you think inadequate orientation programs have on employee retention rates?
2. How might you, as a department manager, better determine how, if at all, the quality of new employee orientation impacts the property's turnover rates?

3. Assume that you could prove a positive relationship between effective orientation programs and improved employee retention, and that it was cost beneficial to improve the orientation program. What potential responses might higher-level officials at this resort give in response to this information?

INTERNET ACTIVITIES

1. General business and management resources contain information applicable to the development and implementation of orientation programs for personnel in the hospitality industry. For a good reference, go to *www.workforce.com.* When you reach the site, type "employee orientation" into the search box.
2. Human resources managers can obtain much online assistance as they develop employee handbooks. They can, for example, review sample handbooks, analyze and/or purchase hardcopy and software guides to develop handbooks, and review sample handbook topics. See, for example, *www.hr-guide.com* and *www.humanresources.about.com/od/handbookspolicies/.*

You can also review Web sites of organizations that sell handbook development resources and provide customized services.

3. The hotel industry is increasingly concerned about managing in a way that is environmentally friendly. To review current information about this topic, go to *www.hotel-online.com.* Enter "green hotels" into the Web site's search box.
4. Environmental concerns are also very important to the restaurant industry. For example, type "restaurant environmental concerns" into your favorite search engine. You'll discover numerous reports focusing on environmental issues, including sanitation and the environment, waste reduction and recycling, no-smoking concerns, managing hazardous waste, minimizing water pollution and energy consumption, reducing water usage, genetic engineering, organic foods, and a wide variety of other topics. An excellent example is *The Better Restaurant and Café Guide, www.kbeap.org/Resources/restaurantandcafe.pdf.*

ENDNOTES

1. See, for example, Christin Jaszayn and Paul Dunk, *Ethical Decision Making in the Hospitality Industry.* Upper Saddle River, NJ: Pearson/Prentice Hall, 2006. (See Chapter 1.)
2. Ronald Ebert and Ricky Griffin, *Business Essentials,* 4th edition. Upper Saddle River, NJ: Pearson Education, 2003. (See Chapter 3.)

PART THREE

Human Resources in Action

CHAPTER SIX

Planning Training Programs

CHAPTER **OUTLINE**

Introduction to Training
What Is Training?
Benefits of Training
Obstacles to Training
Training Myths
Learning Principles Drive Training Principles
Focus on the Trainer
Use a Formal Training Process
Step 1: Define Training Needs
Step 2: Conduct a Position Analysis
Step 3: Define Training Objectives
Step 4: Develop Training Plans
Step 5: Develop Training Lessons
Step 6: Develop Training Handbook (file)
Step 7: Prepare Trainees
Human Resources Terms
For Your Consideration
Case Study: Human Resources Management in Action
Internet Activities

CHECKLIST **OF CHAPTER LEARNING OBJECTIVES**

As a result of satisfactory completion of this chapter, readers will be able to:

1. Define the term *training*, note its benefits, and discuss common obstacles to and myths about training.

2. Recognize basic learning principles that influence how training programs should be planned and implemented.

3. State characteristics that are important for an effective trainer.

4. Explain procedures required for use in the first seven steps in a formal training process:

   Define training needs
   Conduct a position analysis
   Define training objectives
   Develop training plans
   Develop training lessons
   Develop a training handbook (file)
   Prepare trainees

Impact on Human Resources Management

Training is important for all hospitality personnel because it is the best way to assure that staff members can make maximum contributions to the organization's success. This is critical because, in the labor-intensive hospitality industry, staff members are an organization's most important asset. Training is also important because managers have an obligation to help their employees achieve pride in their work and to enjoy doing so. These human concerns are met in a culture of respect that begins with training experiences that yield staff members who have the knowledge and skills necessary to be successful on the job.

Introduction to Training

1. **Define the term** *training*, **note its benefits, and discuss common obstacles to and myths about training.**

Training: The process of developing a staff member's knowledge, skills, and attitudes necessary to perform tasks required for a position.

Hospitality operations are labor intensive. While technology has reduced the need for staff in departments such as accounting and the front office, it has not generally affected the number of employees required to produce and deliver the products and services that guests desire. Recently employed staff must acquire the knowledge and skills needed to become proficient in their positions. Their more-experienced peers must obtain new knowledge and skills to keep up with an ever-changing workplace. Effective training is critical to attain these goals.

Performance-based (training): A systematic way of organizing training in efforts to help trainees learn the tasks considered essential for effective on-job performance.

WHAT IS TRAINING?

Training is a process that provides new and currently employed staff with the short- and longer-term knowledge and skills required to perform successfully on the job.

Hospitality managers are busy, and numerous responsibilities and tasks demand their ongoing attention. Those responsible for training are confronted with a dilemma: should nice-to-know or, alternatively, only need-to-know information and skills be emphasized? This question is best addressed by remembering that effective training is **performance-based**. It should be planned and delivered systematically to help trainees become more **competent** in the tasks that are essential for on-job performance. Then the success of training can

Competent: A description that means the staff member has been appropriately trained and is able to contribute to the achievement of desired results.

Performance-Based Training

The need for training to be performance-based can create a significant hurdle, because the following is required to do so:

- All **tasks** in a position must be identified. *Note:* A task is an observable work activity performed within a limited time period that leads to a product, service, or decision.
- The specific knowledge and skills required to perform each task must be known.
- Training that addresses all of the knowledge and skills required for each task must be developed.
- **Competencies** (standards of knowledge, skills, and abilities required for successful performance) must be known in advance. These should be shared with the trainees to help them understand what the training program will accomplish.
- A formalized evaluation process is needed. The worth of training represents the difference between what trainees know and can do before and after the training.

Task: A specific and observable work activity that is one component of a position and that has a definite beginning and end. For example, one task performed by a cook may be to prepare sandwiches using a standardized recipe.

Competency: Standards of knowledge, skills, and abilities required for successful job performance.

Cost effective: A term that indicates that something such as training is worth more than it costs to provide it.

Feedback: Response provided to a question or larger-scale inquiry such as a customer survey.

be demonstrated by considering the extent to which knowledge and skills improve as a result of the training.

Training must also be **cost effective:** the improved performance gained as a result of training must be greater than the costs of training.

Typically, performance-based training is best delivered at the job site in one-on-one interactions between the trainer and trainee. Conceptually, this is much better than group training. Why? The trainer can focus on what the individual must learn, **feedback** can be immediate, and training can be delivered at the best pace for the individual trainee.

BENEFITS OF TRAINING

Numerous benefits to effective training include:

- *Improved performance.* Trainees learn knowledge and skills to perform required tasks more effectively, and their on-job performance can be improved. They become **value-added** employees who can consistently achieve desired results.
- *Reduced operating costs.* Improved job performance helps reduce errors and rework, and associated costs can be reduced. Persons performing the job

Does Training Affect Attitudes?

At the beginning of this section, training was defined as "the process of developing a staff member's knowledge, skills, and attitudes necessary to perform tasks required for a position." Can a good trainer modify an employee's **attitudes** as a result of training? Maybe so, but maybe not! The **morale** of staff members generally improves when they recognize their employer's interest in helping them to work in a way that best serves the organization and its guests. Many staff members are also impressed with an employer's ongoing commitment to provide training that will allow advancement to more responsible, higher-paying positions. In these and related ways, training can have a positive impact on attitudes.

Now consider someone who does not care about his or her organization and/or position. In this instance, it is unlikely that training will yield improved work methods. Here's an example: Assume a training program is developed with the goal of ensuring that food safety (sanitation) concerns are a priority for food production personnel. Aspects of the training related to knowledge (why this is important) and how food safety concerns can be incorporated into the position (physical skills required to produce food) are included in the training. A knowledge assessment that requires the trainee to answer questions and a skills test to allow him or her to demonstrate proper practices can help evaluate whether knowledge and skill objectives were successful. However, will the cook consistently incorporate the safe food handling practices that he or she has learned and can now perform as a result of the training? If the trainee wants to do so (has a positive attitude), the training will be successful. If, however, the trainee is not motivated to do so (has a less-than-positive attitude), then the training will not be successful even though the why and how aspects of training were learned.

Value-added: The concept that something is worth more than it costs, that output is consistently correct, and that behavior or the product is changed. Value-added training occurs when it is cost effective, because desired output (service and/or products) is acceptable and better than without the training.

correctly will be more productive, fewer staff and/or labor hours will become necessary, and this, in turn, can help reduce labor costs.

■ *More satisfied guests.* Training can yield staff members who are more service-oriented and who will know what their guests desire and require.

■ *Reduced work stress.* Persons who can correctly perform the activities that are part of their positions will likely feel better about doing the job. Stress created by interactions with supervisors who are upset about improper work outputs, with peers who must take the time to do rework created by the employee's errors, and/or with frustrated guests about service and/or quality defects will be reduced.

Can Training Address Everything?

Effective training programs address the knowledge and skills needed to perform basic job tasks. However, they cannot consider everything that may confront employees on the job. Unique requests may be made of employees with guest service responsibilities. They and their peers in other positions may be confronted with unanticipated issues related to employee interactions, safety, or other atypical operating concerns not addressed in training. One's on-job experience may provide appropriate responses to these situations, as can common sense (a great personal attribute that is difficult to assess at the time of selection and during formal training).

Another tactic, problem solving, can be critical in these situations, and its basics can be taught. What are examples of times when one's supervisor should be alerted, and when is it permissible for an employee to solve a problem without supervisory assistance? Trainers teach trainees how to think on their own when they teach the basics and emphasize standards and the need to please guests. They also allow experienced staff to have some discretion, and provide an ongoing invitation to seek assistance whenever the employee recognizes the need to do so.

Attitude: Positive or negative feelings, beliefs, and values about something that influence a person to act in certain ways.

Morale: The total of one's feelings about his or her employer, work environment, peers, and other aspects of the employment.

Turnover rate: The number of employees who leave an organization each year expressed as a percentage of the average number of workers employed by the organization.

- *Increased job advancement opportunities.* Who is most likely to be promoted to a more responsible and higher-paying position: a competent or an incompetent employee? Training can assist staff in attaining their promotion goals.
- *Improved staff relationships.* Persons who can do their jobs are more likely to work in a team effort, and all will do their fair share of required work in the correct way. Staff members who are trained to perform tasks beyond the scope of their normal position can also help peers in other positions.
- *More professional staff.* Professionals want to do their job as best they can, and this is only possible with appropriate training.
- *Fewer operating problems.* Busy managers can focus on priority concerns, and they will not need to address routine operating problems caused by inappropriate training.
- *Lower turnover rates.* Labor shortages confront most hospitality operators. Fewer new staff members become necessary as **turnover rates** decrease. Those who are properly trained and rewarded for successful performance are less likely to leave, and managers have less need to recruit new employees in increasingly tight labor markets.
- *Increased morale.* Training can help staff members feel good about themselves and their employers. These positive attitudes can have a significant influence on one's overall perceptions of the workplace.

- *Higher levels of work quality*. Effective training identifies quality standards that help define acceptable product and service outputs. Trained staff members are more interested in operating equipment correctly, in preparing the right products, and in properly interacting with guests.
- *Easier to recruit new staff*. Satisfied staff tell their family and friends about their positive work experiences, and their contacts may become candidates for position vacancies that arise. Hospitality operations that emphasize training can evolve into **employers of choice** that provide first choice rather than last choice employment opportunities.
- *Increased profits*. It makes sense that, if guests are more satisfied and revenues increase and, if labor and other operating costs are reduced, there is a significant potential for increased profits. In the long run, training must be value-added. In other words, it must be worth more than it costs. This can be measured by the difference between the increased profits and the added training costs. While this measurement is not easy to make, most

Employer of choice: An organization with a reputation of offering a desirable place to work and with recruiting efforts made easier because of this perception.

IT'S THE LAW!

Hospitality managers may be legally mandated to provide training on some topics in many states. Examples include responsible service of alcoholic beverages and food safety (sanitation) training as a prerequisite to obtaining food handlers' permits. Other training including the avoidance of sexual or other harassment is required by the insurers of many hospitality operations.

Numerous other common practices in the hospitality industry are impacted by laws and regulations that require training to ensure compliance. Examples include room occupancy limits established by fire safety codes, dishwater washing temperatures required by applicable food codes, and guest nonsmoking areas mandated by local governing agencies.

Employee training is absolutely critical to minimize the possibility of lawsuits that can arise when staff members are not trained or are improperly trained. Consider, for example, the potential legal liabilities if employees are not trained to properly operate dangerous equipment, to handle dangerous chemicals, and to follow safe work practices mandated by Occupational Safety and Health Administration (OSHA) regulations.

Lawsuits filed by guests can also arise when they have been harmed by untrained employees. Consider examples of foodborne illness caused by food preparation personnel without appropriate food safety training, and preventable slips and falls caused by untrained maintenance or housekeeping staff who improperly (and unsafely) clean floors and sidewalks in public areas.

industry observers believe that, if training is done correctly, it will always win in the comparison.

OBSTACLES TO TRAINING

Despite the stated benefits, training does not always receive the proper priority in many hospitality operations. Numerous obstacles to effective training can include:

- *Insufficient time* for managers, supervisors, and/or trainers to plan for and deliver the training
- *Too much time* for trainees to be away from their positions to participate in the training
- *Lack of financial resources* to compensate for the trainer's and trainees' time and to acquire necessary training resources
- *Insufficient trainers' knowledge and skills.* Persons must be taught how to train, just as they must be taught to perform any other unfamiliar task. Formal train-the-trainer programs are not provided by many hospitality organizations.
- *Lack of quality resources available for training.* No manager or supervisor has the time, knowledge, and ability to develop training videos and/or to prepare extensive or sophisticated training resources or training evaluation tools. If these materials can't be developed in-house, are they available **off-the-shelf?** Resources addressing generic topics such as supervision tactics, sanitation, and safety can be purchased. However, excellent trainers are creative, and they would never elect to not train because supplemental resources were unavailable. The alternative is to take time to develop several basic training tools, including those described later in this chapter.
- *Scheduling conflicts.* When can front desk agents meet to learn a new way to perform a task? When can dining room servers be brought together for a group training session on guest service?
- *Turnover.* In many hospitality operations, some staff members leave within a few months (or less) of initial employment. Managers may think, "Why train employees if they don't remain on the job long enough to use what they have learned?" In fact, as noted previously, effective training can reduce turnover rates, and property managers who do not train are likely contributing to their unacceptably high turnover rate.
- *Insufficient lead time between one's* **hire date** *and the time when he or she must be on the job.* Hopefully, a **warm-body syndrome** is never used as a recruitment and/or selection tactic. Instead, staff are trained for expanded position duties, and recruitment tactics begin for new employees before an incumbent leaves and a position vacancy has occurred.
- *Difficulty in maintaining training consistency.* When individual trainers plan and deliver training activities based on what they think staff must know, the what and how of training will likely be inconsistent. Then those who train

Off-the-shelf: Generic training materials, typically addressing general topics of concern to many trainers, that are available for use if company-specific resources are not available.

Hire date: The effective date that a new staff member begins work.

Warm-body syndrome: The selection error that involves hiring the first person who applies for a position vacancy.

Although scheduling can be a challenge, effective managers find time for staff training sessions. *Courtesy Purestock*

may begin to think that "We tried to train, and it hasn't worked very well. There must be a better problem resolution alternative than training. What else can we do?"

■ *Trainer apathy.* There should be reasons for trainers to want to train. Benefits for successful training duties can include special privileges, compensation increases, advancement consideration, educational opportunities, and/or recognition. By contrast, when trainers must assume these duties in addition to other tasks, if they do not receive train-the-trainer training and/or if there is no (or little) support for training, why should trainers want to do so?

TRAINING MYTHS

Myths (untruths) about training can create obstacles. Examples include:

■ *Training is easy.* In fact, when training only involves a trainee tagging along with a more-experienced staff member, it is easy. However, the lack of planning and the increased possibility that basic training principles will be disregarded increases the likelihood that this type of training will be ineffective.

■ *Training costs too much.* Hospitality operations with a history of inadequate training that has yielded unsatisfactory results are unlikely to invest the resources required to plan and deliver more effective training. "Been there; done that; let's try something else" is a philosophy that can easily evolve.

■ *Training is a staff function.* Staff positions are manned by technical specialists who provide advice to, but do not make decisions for, people in chain-of-command line positions. Training is a line function that is too important to delegate to staff human resources personnel, if available, who may assist with recruitment, selection, and orientation tasks.

■ *Only new staff need training.* New employees do need training, but so do their more-experienced peers when, for example, operating procedures are revised because of technology or when new equipment is purchased. Employees with a wide range of experience may also want to participate in **professional development programs.**

■ *There is no time for training.* Many priorities compete for the limited time available to hospitality managers. In this context, training is often deemphasized, and available time is allocated to other tasks.

Professional development programs: Planned educational and/or training activities to prepare one for successively more responsible positions in an organization or industry.

Human Resources MANAGEMENT ISSUES (6.1)

"I don't understand it," said Ralph. "What's the big deal about training? Maybe you and I are smarter than the kids coming to work at the hotel today. But I remember watching and listening and following along with people who taught me everything I needed to know about the job."

Ralph and Lorine were supervisors who were talking about the hotel department staff meeting they had just attended. The department head had announced that all staff would be expected to participate in two training programs: one on guest service and the other on technology updates.

"You're right about what was done in the past, Ralph," said Lorine. "But you and I can cite a million (or more!) problems at our hotel. I wonder if proper training would reduce their occurrence? I wonder if things do need to change to remain competitive and to make sure we keep our good employees?"

"It's easy to keep the employees; just pay them more," replied Ralph. "You and I are good employees, and we became good by learning and watching. I think that's good enough today because it was good enough yesterday."

QUESTIONS

1. What are your reactions to Ralph's thoughts about training?
2. What role do you think effective training can play in remaining competitive and retaining employees?
3. What do you think about Ralph's comments regarding compensation and employee turnover?

When you consider the many training obstacles and myths just noted, a picture of training in many hospitality properties begins to emerge. Top-level managers may not commit resources to training because they are unaware of its benefits and/or because they have had previous negative training experiences. Lack of resources, training knowledge, and training plans work against training priorities and/or minimize its effectiveness when it is offered. Employee resistance can also arise when training must occur within the already limited time frame available to perform required work.

Learning Principles Drive Training Principles

2. Recognize basic learning principles that influence how training programs should be planned and implemented.

Those who believe in the numerous benefits of training share an old saying: "An organization pays for training even if it doesn't offer it!" They recognize that developing and delivering training takes time to do well, and costs are incurred to do so. However, they also know that, in the absence of training, wasted time and money occurs because of errors and rework. Without effective training, guests are less likely to receive the proper quality of required products and services.

If one accepts the idea that managers will, one way or another, pay for training, it makes good business sense to implement effective training that returns benefits exceeding costs. A first step is to recognize that several basic learning principles should be considered as programs are planned and implemented. Their application puts the trainee at the forefront of the process and, in so doing, lays the foundation for successful training. Basic learning principles include:

Learning Principle 1: Trainees Must Want to Learn and Need Motivation to Do So

The old adage, "You can lead a horse to water, but you can't make it drink," applies here. Trainees must want to learn and, for this to occur, they must recognize its worth. "Because the boss says it is necessary" is not a meaningful reason from the perspectives of most staff. By contrast, noting that "This training is a step in a career-long professional development program to help you become eligible for promotion" will be of interest to many trainees.

Learning Principle 2: Training Should Consider the Trainees' Life and Professional Experiences

Many hospitality employees are adults with many useful personal and work-related experiences. Good trainers establish a benchmark of what trainees already know and can do and build on this foundation of knowledge and skills. They maximize the worth of training by emphasizing the most important subject matter with which the trainee is unfamiliar.

Fortunately, one-on-one training is frequently the training method of choice, and it allows a skilled trainer to focus on what the trainee doesn't know instead of repeating what he or she does know.

Learning Principle 3: Trainees Require Time to Learn

Training takes time. This principle, while seemingly obvious, is sometimes violated. Consider, for example, that some managers expect a new staff member to learn necessary tasks by tagging along with an experienced peer. What happens when there is no dedicated training time and, instead, both parties are continually interrupted by ongoing operational demands?

Learning Principle 4: Trainees Should Know the Training Requirements

Experienced trainers often use a preview, present, and review sequence. They tell the trainees what they are going to say (preview), they tell them the information (present), and they tell them once again (review). This tactic helps minimize surprises and reduces trainee apprehension.

Learning Principle 5: Training Should Consider the Trainees' Attention Spans

Several short training sessions are generally better than one long session. When planning an entire program, consider the complete range of subject matter to be presented. Then break the total training requirement down into manageable (short) parts to be facilitated in a single session.

Learning Principle 6: Learning Should Be Paced

Closely aligned with the previous principle, paced learning allows trainees to practice and improve on basic skills in a focused way. They can concentrate on one or several skills rather than on all skills and, in the process, better learn the correct way to perform all of them.

Learning Principle 7: Learning Speed Varies for Trainees

Individualized training allows the trainer to incorporate what the trainee knows into and to exclude what the trainee doesn't know from the training process. The pace of training can then be individualized.

Application of these fundamental learning concepts allows those planning training to focus on the trainees as programs are planned and implemented. It then becomes important to consider some training-specific concepts to best assure that the trainees (not the training content) continue to remain the focal point of the activity. Several training principles apply to the largest and smallest hospitality operations regardless of location, type of guests served, or financial objectives being pursued.

Training Principle 1: Trainers Must Know How to Train

Who trains in most hospitality properties? Frequently, it is a supervisor and/or a peer of a new staff member being trained. In the former case, the supervisor may have been a good employee who is rewarded for effective performance by a promotion. Supervisors, however, must perform many tasks that are not part of their previous position, and one of these is often training. A serious problem is that one does not become an effective trainer by default. Instead, a person must be taught how to train, and train-the-trainer programs are needed to provide necessary knowledge and skills.

This principle also applies equally to an entry-level employee's peer who will conduct training. If training fails because the trainer doesn't know how to do it properly, the problem rests with the manager, not the trainer. Why? Because the manager did not recognize that effective training requires more than just one's willingness to do so.

Training Principle 2: Training Must Focus on Real Problems

Frequently, problems (challenges) are encountered that must be resolved, and training is a useful tactic to do so. It would seem that this principle is frequently used, but think about the content of some training programs such as detailed motivational theories in a supervisory session. Effective trainers constantly consider whether and to what extent training should address nice-to-know or need-to-know issues. While the latter topics must be included in the training, the former may (or may not) be needed. Trainers must consider and address these issues in the context of the specific training program being planned.

Training Principle 3: Training Must Emphasize Application

Most people learn best by doing. For example, hands-on training using an individualized training program is typically the best way to teach an entry-level housekeeper to properly perform guest room cleaning duties.

You have learned that most training should be performance-based. However, training can also be used to present information that extends beyond one's position or department. For example, shouldn't all staff members learn about their property's values, vision, and mission? How much, if any, of the organization's long-range plan should be explained? What about the organization's philosophy and policies relative to guest service? Perhaps these topics are addressed during orientation. Ongoing formal and informal training opportunities to consider these issues may be planned for more experienced staff. Fortunately, basic training principles apply to these situations as well as to more traditional task-focused activities.

Training Principle 4: Training Should Be Informal

To the extent possible, training should be personalized, conducted in the workplace, and allow the trainer to interact with the trainee. It should be designed for delivery at the pace that is best for the trainee and should address the trainee's specific questions and needs as they arise during the training. Individualized training methods make it easier to personalize the process.

Training Principle 5: Training Should Employ a Variety of Training Methods

Do employees learn when a trainer quickly shows them how to do something but doesn't allow them to practice immediately after the training? By contrast, training that allows for demonstration, practice, and comparison of written information (e.g., standards or procedures) with how tasks are actually done is more likely to be effective. Group training that uses case studies, small group interaction, video followed by discussion, and other interactive techniques will likely be better received by trainees than will a lecture-only format.

Training Principle 6: Training Focus Should Be on Trainees

Good trainers want to address trainees' needs. Trainers do not try to impress trainees with their knowledge or skills, nor do they make training more difficult than necessary because everyone should "learn it the hard way." Failure to teach a training point "because everyone should know it" is another error that trainers should avoid. Using difficult language including **jargon** can create problems, as can teaching advanced before basic skills. Addressing the question, "How would I like to be trained?" often reveals suggestions about tactics that should (and should not) be used.

Training Principle 7: Trainers Should Allow Trainees to Practice

Hospitality staff in every department and position must have significant knowledge and skills. Few skills can be learned by reading a book, listening to someone talk through a task, or watching someone else do it. Rather, skills are typically learned by observing how something is done and then by practicing the activity in a step-by-step sequence. After the task is learned, time and repetition are often required to enable the trainee to perform the task at the appropriate speed.

Jargon: Terminology used by and commonly known only to persons who are familiar with a topic.

It is just as important for service staff to receive training that addresses the needs of these residents in a retirement center as it is for those serving guests in a commercial restaurant.
Courtesy PhotoDisc/Getty Images

Training Principle 8: Trainers Require Time to Train

Assume that four employees are needed for a specific shift, and a new person must be trained. Can the four experienced staff do their work and, additionally, train the new person? Even worse: what happens when the four persons are reduced to three because of unexpected turnover? Can they do the work of four peers and still train another person? Training takes time that must be scheduled, and the resources required for it must be allocated.

Training Principle 9: Training Environment Must Be Positive

The stress created in the previous situation provides an example of a training environment that is *not* positive. Another example: consider someone given training responsibilities who does not enjoy the task (perhaps because there is no incentive to be a good trainer). These issues can quickly lead to a hostile environment that lacks the interpersonal respect that is another pre-requisite for effective training.

Training Principle 10: Trainees Should Be Treated as Professionals

Experienced staff training their peers should recognize that they will be peers with the trainees after the training is completed, and their responsibility is to use their training skills to help trainees learn.

Training Principle 11: Trainees Need Encouragement and Positive Feedback

Most employees want ongoing input about how their boss feels about their work. Trainees typically feel the same way: they want to know how the trainer evaluates their performance during and, especially, after training is completed.

Training Principle 12: Trainees Should Not Compete Against Each Other

Contests in which, for example, one trainee wins and other trainees lose do not encourage the teamwork that is required for a successful hospitality operation. An alternative is to develop contests in which all trainees who attain specified standards can win.

Training Principle 13: Trainees Should Be Taught the Correct Way to Perform a Task

It does little good for a trainer to show a trainee how something should *not* be done. Unfortunately, this can occur when a trainer notes that "Here's how many employees do it, even though it's the wrong way to do it." Instead, tasks should be taught using the correct work methods on a step-by-step basis, with trainer presentation followed by trainee demonstration.

Training Principle 14: Train One Task at a Time

Hospitality employees must typically perform many tasks in their positions. Tasks should be taught separately, and each should be broken into steps taught in proper sequence.

Training Principle 15: Train Each Task Using a Step-by-Step Plan

Consider the task of checking in a hotel guest. The trainer may begin by demonstrating the proper way to perform the task for one type of guest (such as airline crew). Then, beginning with the first step in the task, the trainer presents correct procedures, and the trainee is encouraged to demonstrate the procedures. Trainer feedback helps the trainee identify where performance improvements could be helpful. After the trainee successfully demonstrates the step, this process is repeated until all steps are presented to and successfully demonstrated by the trainee. The trainer demonstrates the correct way to do the entire task again, and the trainee repeats the correct procedures. He or she then practices each step as necessary to yield the appropriate speed for task performance.

Human Resources MANAGEMENT ISSUES (6.2)

"Its been a long day," said Ralph to Lorine as they walked to the hotel's parking lot. They had just participated in a two-hour rollout program about customer service training that would soon begin for entry-level staff.

"You're right, Ralph," replied Lorine. "It was a long day because we basically had to do everything expected of us during a regular shift and, in addition, participate in the training. I like the content of the program, and I think there were lots of great ideas," she continued. "I also hope it will be a lot different than today's session, however: too much lecture, little chance for our input, long periods between very short breaks, and the unavailability of some training materials."

"Remember our conversation last week, Lorine, when we talked about the old days of training?" asked Ralph. "Why can't we just remind our staff to be nice to guests, give them some examples of how to do so, and then let the staff do their jobs?"

"I don't have the answers to that question, Ralph," said Lorine. "However, I have learned that it is one thing to develop great training content, and it's another thing to effectively deliver it."

QUESTIONS

1. What training principles appear to have been violated in today's session attended by Ralph and Lorine?
2. Assume the content of the training program was developed by a training content supplier (it is an off-the-shelf program) or by corporate-level trainers (if the hotel is part of a multiunit organization). What kind of train-the-trainer support is needed in this property to help supervisors like Ralph and Lorine become effective trainers?

Focus on the Trainer

3. State characteristics that are important for an effective trainer.

A new maintenance person has just been employed by a private club. Who should provide the training? Sometimes this question is easily answered by asking a few questions: Who is available? Who wants to do it? Who has the time? Who will complain the least if he or she is given the assignment? Who is a good people person who will be able to interact with the new staff member? All of these and related factors are important but, unfortunately, they are not among the most important.

Instead, here are twelve characteristics that are important for every good trainer:

- *Have the desire to train.* Good trainers want to train. There are several reasons why a trainer might desire to do so, including an interest in helping others, internal recognition for a job well done, and the knowledge that effective trainers are frequently promoted to higher-level positions within the department.

    Unfortunately, there are also reasons why training might not be an attractive assignment, including the expectation that the trainer must complete all regularly assigned tasks and also conduct training. Also, a trainer might want to do a good job but not be able to do so. This occurs when the staff member has not been taught how to train and/or because there is insufficient time, equipment, money, or other resources required to do so. Regardless of the reason, the resulting stress is a disincentive for the training assignment.

- *Have the proper attitude about the employer, peers, position, and the training assignment.* Hospitality organizations that emphasize the importance of staff members and that provide quality training opportunities to all employees at all levels will likely increase the morale of their trainers. Conversely, when training is just another and not-so-important responsibility, a less-than-willing attitude is likely.

- *Possess the necessary knowledge and ability (skills) to do the job for which training is needed.* Effective trainers must be knowledgeable about and have the skills necessary to perform the work tasks for which they will train others.

- *Utilize effective communication skills.* Trainers are effective communicators when they (1) speak in a language that is understandable to the trainee, (2) recognize that **body language** is a method of communication, (3) use a questioning process to learn the extent to which a trainee has learned, and (4) speak to communicate rather than to impress. For example, they don't use unfamiliar jargon, and they teach new staff members the meaning of unusual but commonly used terms.

- *Know how to train.* The importance of train-the-trainer programs should be obvious but often is overlooked.

Body language: The gestures, mannerisms, expressions, and other nonverbal methods that people use to communicate with each other.

- *Have patience.* Few trainees learn everything they must know or be able to do during their first exposure to training. Effective trainers have patience and understand that training steps must sometimes be repeated several times in different ways. They know that the goal is not to complete the training quickly; rather, it is to provide the knowledge and skills the trainee needs to be successful.
- *Exhibit humor.* Use of humor in good taste often provides a subtle message to a trainee: "I am enjoying the opportunity to provide training, and I hope you enjoy it as well. Learning can be fun, because the process is enjoyable."
- *Have time to train.* Effective training takes time, and it must be scheduled for the trainer and for the trainees.
- *Show genuine respect for the trainees.* This characteristic is driven by the need to treat trainees as professionals. You'll likely find that those whom you respect will also respect you. This mutual respect allows training to be more effective.
- *Be enthusiastic.* Newly employed staff members want reinforcement that their decision to join the organization was a good one. Initial experiences with an enthusiastic trainer help develop the foundation for successful training and for employees' long-term commitment. Trainers can reinforce the philosophy of more senior staff: "This is a good place to work: let's make it a better place to work, and this training will help us to do so."
- *Celebrate the trainees' success.* Have you ever heard the saying that "If a trainee hasn't learned, it is because the trainer hasn't trained?" A successful trainer is one who has successfully trained, and the reverse is also true: trainers have not

These area managers learning about a new initiative from corporate headquarters may not be aware of the wide variety of tactics this trainer is using to make the training as effective as it can be. *Courtesy Purestock*

been successful when their trainees have not learned. Take time to celebrate when learning occurs.

- *Value diversity.* Increasingly, hospitality organizations employ persons with a variety of backgrounds and cultures, and the property is strengthened because of the different perceptions that provide input into decision making. All staff share the need to be well-trained. An effective trainer accepts the challenge to develop all trainees to the fullest extent possible, even though training tactics might differ based on the trainees' cultural backgrounds. For example, group trainers may need to actively solicit question responses from trainees who don't readily participate in discussions, and trainees from some cultures may be embarrassed to participate in role-play exercises.

Use a Formal Training Process

4. **Explain procedures required for use in the first seven steps in a formal training process:**

   Define training needs

   Conduct a position analysis

   Define training objectives

   Develop training plans

   Develop training lessons

   Develop a training handbook (file)

   Prepare trainees

Traditional tag-along, shadowing, and follow-the-trainer programs typically do not work because they lack an organized and well-thought-out approach to determining training content and delivery. By contrast, the training model shown in Figure 6.1 identifies a sequence of activities that helps assure that training attains planned results.

The first seven steps identified in Figure 6.1 will be explored in the remainder of this chapter. Steps 8 and 9 are discussed in Chapter 7. *Note:* The training steps outlined in Figure 6.1 are universal. They can be used when training recently hired staff members in all tasks required for their new position, and for training experienced employees in revised job tasks, for ongoing training, and for problem resolution purposes.

STEP 1: DEFINE TRAINING NEEDS

Some hospitality managers might question why there should be an emphasis on defining training needs. Isn't the challenge to determine what training needs should be the priority? In fact, it is important to ensure that the dollars budgeted for training are spent on the most important priorities.

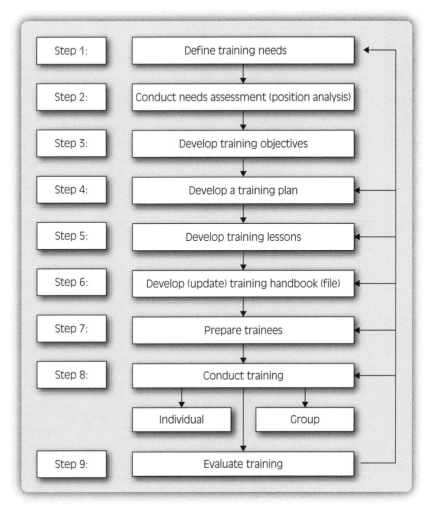

FIGURE 6.1: Overview of Training Process

These are typically long- and short-term training priorities. Examples of the former include:

- New staff members must be trained to perform all tasks in their new positions. While this appears to be a short-term training need, it really is not. Why? Training programs must be developed for those persons being recruited today and in the future.
- After planners identify necessary long-term courses of action, the role of training in attaining them can be considered.
- What are the staff's professional development needs? Hopefully, the corporate culture of the organization promotes education and training opportunities for those who are proficient in their current positions.

Training Never Ends!

There are numerous examples of short-term operating and other concerns that can be addressed by training programs. In the fast-paced hospitality industry, change is inevitable, and employee retraining is (almost) ongoing. New work methods, purchase of new equipment or technology, and/or implementation of cost-reduction processes may be continually necessary to enable the hospitality operation to do more with less. There may also be the need for more or different products and services to meet guests' needs.

Tactics to Identify Training Needs

Training needs can be determined in several ways:

- *Observation of work performance.* Those who manage by walking around may note work procedures that deviate from required standard operating procedures. *Note:* Hopefully, the required procedures were taught in applicable training sessions!
- *Input from guests.* Successful managers attempt to learn about their guests' needs and the extent to which they are met. Surveys can help identify problems, and ongoing interactions with guests can also be helpful.
- *Input from staff members.* Some managers use suggestion boxes, open-door policies, and frank input from performance appraisals and coaching sessions to identify problems that can be resolved with training.
- *Inspections.* Formal inspections such as those related to safety and informal inspections made by supervisors and others before, during, and after work shifts can suggest revisions in work processes that lend themselves to training.
- *Failure to meet performance standards.* Consider, for example, unacceptable scores on visits by franchisor's representatives. Will training help address these concerns?
- *Analysis of financial data.* Differences between budget plans and actual operating data may suggest negative variances traceable to problems with training implications. Consider the many reasons that labor or other costs can be excessive. After problems are identified, corrective actions including training may be implemented.
- *Performance/skills assessments.* Post-training evaluation may suggest that the training provided has not been successful and that additional (or, at least, different) training is needed.

■ *Exit interviews.* Formal or informal discussions with those who have resigned may identify training topics to help reduce turnover rates and to improve operations.

STEP 2: CONDUCT A POSITION ANALYSIS

Position analysis: A process that identifies each task that is part of a position and explains how it should be done with a focus on knowledge and skills.

Task list: A list of all tasks that constitute a position.

Task breakdown: A description of how one task in a task list should be performed.

Performance standards: Measurable quality and/or quantity indicators that tell when a staff member is working correctly.

Position description: A human resources tool that summarizes a position and lists the primary tasks that must be performed as part of it.

A **position analysis** identifies each task that is part of a position and explains how it should be done with a focus on knowledge and skills. As such, it becomes the foundation for developing training programs. *Note:* Position analysis (also called job analysis) is integral to many aspects of human resources management. For example, it defines job tasks that drive selection, training, ongoing work requirements, and performance evaluation. It is, therefore, a powerful tool that is critical to design and implementation of training and all other human resources functions.

Position analysis can also be done to study one task that requires revision because of changes created by new equipment or several tasks that are creating operating or guest-related problems. Training new persons in all tasks and experienced staff in new work methods becomes possible after position analysis activities are completed.

There are four basic steps in the position analysis process: (1) prepare a **task list,** (2) develop a **task breakdown,** (3) consider **performance standards,** and (4) write a **position description.** The sequence of these four components is illustrated in Figure 6.2 and discussed in the remainder of this section.

FIGURE 6.2: Components of Position Analysis Process

Prepare a Task List

A task list indicates all tasks included in a position. It focuses on how-to activities that a successful staff member must be able to do. Persons working in each position must perform several (or more) tasks that, in turn, typically require numerous **steps.**

Consider, for example, a dishwasher in a college and university foodservices operation. The tasks in this position are numerous and probably include those related to operating the dishwashing machine and washing dishes. To successfully wash dishes, the employee must complete several steps, including rinsing soil from plates, properly placing dishes in a rack, and removing and placing clean dishes in mobile carts after washing.

What is the complete list of tasks that the dishwasher must perform? The answer to this question is indicated in a detailed task list.

Procedures to develop a task list include:

- Obtain interview input from the supervisors of and several experienced workers in the position being analyzed. Good interview questions are **open-ended** (e.g., "Describe what you do in a normal work shift starting with when you begin work until you complete your shift."). More detailed interviews can include questions about the time spent on specific tasks, position responsibilities, instances of interaction with other staff, and the importance, frequency, and difficulty of performing specific tasks.
- Use available written information. Examples include position descriptions that provide a summary and an overview of tasks, existing task lists, and training materials used to teach new staff about their jobs.
- Use a simple questionnaire that asks, "What do you and others in your position do as part of your job?"
- Observe staff members as they work in their positions; compare what they actually do to the tasks they identified when questioned about their position responsibilities.
- If practical, work in the position(s) for which a task list is being developed.

Typically, the best approach to generate input for a task list is to use all of these procedures. After input and analysis of information from these sources, one can develop an extensive list of tasks, and a validation process can finalize the list. This will likely involve (1) condensing/combining similar tasks, (2) clarifying other tasks to ensure accuracy, and (3) clearly identifying factors such as work shift or production volume that impact task responsibilities.

A format for a task list is shown in Figure 6.3.

Once developed, the scope of training requirements for a specific position is known. New trainees must be taught how to correctly perform each task in their new position. The definition of correct performance is addressed in the task breakdown.

Step: One element in a task. For example, to prepare sandwiches (a task), a cook must know how to portion ingredients required by standard recipes using proper portion control tools (one step in the task).

Open-ended (question): A question that allows the respondent to elaborate on his or her response (e.g., What do you like about your job?).

POSITION: _____

STAFF WORKING IN THIS POSITION MUST BE ABLE TO PERFORM THE FOLLOWING TASKS:

 1.
 2.
 3.
 4.
 5.
 6.
 7.
 8.
 9.
10.
11.
12.
13.
14.
15.

Notes:

Date of last review: _____

Task list approved by: _____

FIGURE 6.3: Task List

Develop a Task Breakdown

A task breakdown indicates how each task identified in the task list should be performed. It recognizes that each task requires a series of steps for completion. For example, one task for a dishwasher may be "to properly operate a dishwashing machine." The task involves several steps, including loading the machine, monitoring its operation, and adding additional detergent, wetting agents, and/or other chemicals.

Benefits of task breakdowns include:

- They indicate the correct way to perform a task to best ensure that performance standards are attained.
- Trainees benefit from written instructions. A trainer can review a task breakdown with a trainee, who can then demonstrate it using the task breakdown

as a guide. Another benefit is that trainees can practice each step and then compare procedures used with those noted in the task breakdown.

Even uncomplicated task steps can be done more than one way. For example, a room service attendant could push or pull a food cart as it is rolled from a hotel elevator. Which way is the best (safest)? Why? Written communication in a task breakdown is more precise than spoken words. Properly done, there is less chance that information will be misinterpreted when it is written.

How are task breakdowns written? A simple answer is, "Use the same basic process that yielded the task list." Experienced staff can be interviewed, available information (e.g., existing task breakdowns and/or existing training documents) can be studied, and/or employees can be asked to write, in sequence, the steps needed to perform a task. They can also be observed, and brainstorming sessions can be used.

Writing a task breakdown does not need to be complicated or time consuming and, properly done, can be cost effective. Consider a simple process such as when the manager or trainer:

- Watches an experienced staff member perform a task.
- Records each activity (step) in sequence.
- Asks the experienced staff member to review the information to confirm its accuracy.
- Shares the task analysis information with other experienced staff members and their supervisors.
- Makes modifications, if necessary, to yield the agreed-upon work method.
- Reviews the task worksheet with the staff member's supervisor and the employee.
- Validates the agreed-upon task breakdown by observing an experienced person performing the task using the identified procedures.

Figure 6.4 illustrates the format for a task breakdown worksheet.

Consider Performance Standards

Quality: The essential characteristics consistently required for a product or service to meet the appropriate standard(s); a product or service attains necessary quality standards when the product or service is suitable for its intended purpose.

Performance standards specify required **quality** and quantity outputs for each task. For example, the proper quality of a dessert prepared in a hotel's bakery is that expected when the applicable standard recipe is followed. The quantity of work output expected of a front desk agent in a hotel considers the number of guests to be checked in during a shift. Quality requirements cannot be sacrificed as quantity requirements are attained.

It is important that proper performance be clearly defined. Then staff members will know what is expected of them, and managers will know when performance is acceptable. The goal of training must be to teach a trainee how to correctly perform a task, and the definition of correct refers to both quality and quantity dimensions.

POSITION: _____

TASK: _____

DATE OF OBSERVATION: _____

EMPLOYEE NAME: _____

OBSERVER: _____

TASK STEP	WHAT IS DONE	TOOLS/EQUIPMENT	COMMENTS

GENERAL COMMENTS:

FIGURE 6.4: Task Breakdown Worksheet

Performance standards for a task should be reasonable (challenging but achievable). Staff should be trained in procedures specified by task breakdowns, and they must be given the tools and equipment needed to attain the performance standards.

Performance standards must also be specific so that they can be measured. Which of the following standards is better stated: "The front desk agent should be able to check in guests as quickly as possible" or "The front desk agent should be able to check in guests using the procedures specified in the task breakdown?" The latter standard is best because it can be objectively measured.

Write a Position Description

You have learned that a position description summarizes a position and lists the major tasks that constitute it. Some persons think about position descriptions during recruitment because they are used to provide applicants with an overview of a position. However, a position description also serves other purposes. First, it summarizes the breadth of training requirements. A new staff member must learn everything required to perform the job as summarized in the position description. From the perspective of the trainer, it provides an overview of what the training must address and accomplish. Position descriptions also help with supervision, because staff members should normally perform only those tasks noted in them. As well, they can be used for performance evaluation activities that consider the extent to which staff adequately perform the tasks in the position.

STEP 3: DEFINE TRAINING OBJECTIVES

Training objectives are used for two purposes:

■ *To help the trainer connect the purpose(s) of the training program with its content.* Specific reasons for training become clear when training needs are

A Position Analysis Is Comprehensive

When the position analysis process is correctly completed, tasks in each position (task list), how each task should be done (task breakdown), and quantitative and/or qualitative ways to determine if tasks are being done correctly (performance standards) will be known. As well, position descriptions will provide a handy way to reference and review the outputs of the position analysis process for managers, trainers, and staff.

Human Resources MANAGEMENT ISSUES   (6.3)

"**T**his just isn't practical," Ralph said to Lorine. "We're too busy to do extra paperwork, to talk to our staff, and to observe them for such a silly purpose."

Ralph was referring to his department head's request that supervisors help develop new position descriptions. (The current ones had not been revised for many years.) The recommended approach was to ask employees in selected positions and their supervisors to list tasks normally performed as part of the job. Two supervisors and two employees would then review the list and develop a final document. "I wish I knew what was going on around here," said Ralph. "When are we supposed to get our work done?"

"You're right on this one, Ralph," said Lorine. "I'm not sure what's going on."

QUESTIONS

1. What is the communication problem that appears to cause Ralph and Lorine to feel as they do?
2. If you were Ralph's and Lorine's department manager, how would you solicit their cooperation in revising position descriptions?
3. What process suggestions can you make to ensure that the position description revision task is practical?

---

defined (Step 1 in Figure 6.1), and when the content of the training program is known after position analysis (Step 2 in Figure 6.1) is undertaken.

- *To help evaluate training* (Step 9 in Figure 6.1)

After training objectives are developed, training plans can be created to provide an overview of the entire program. They are essential to ensure that the property's limited time, financial, and other resources are best used to develop and deliver training focused on achieving planned objectives.

Training objectives specify what trainees should know and be able to do when they have successfully completed the training. Those who plan training programs must know what the training is to accomplish, and training objectives help planners to consistently do this. You have learned that effective training is performance-based and must help trainees learn essential tasks. Competent staff are those who have been trained and are able to contribute to the achievement of desired results.

Training objectives are critical to training evaluation, and they should describe the expected results of the training rather than the training process itself. Consider the following objectives:

As a result of satisfactory completion of the training session, the trainee will:

Objective 1: Study the process to properly operate a dishwashing machine.

Objective 2: Properly operate a dishwashing machine.

The first objective is not performance-based because it emphasizes the training process ("study"). The performance expected if the training is successful is described in objective 2 ("properly operate a dishwashing machine"). The skills taught in training can be evaluated, because the trainer can compare how the trainee operates a dishwashing machine with the procedures that were taught during the training.

Figure 6.5 illustrates the importance of training objectives.

Figure 6.5 indicates that the knowledge and skills required for effective work performance drive training objectives. They, in turn, drive the content of the training program, which also impacts the training process that is implemented and the tactics that are used for training evaluation. Figure 6.5 also suggests that training evaluation can address the extent to which content was mastered and the usefulness of the training process.

To be useful, objectives must be reasonable (attainable) and measurable. Objectives are *not* reasonable when they are too difficult or too easy to attain. For example, the following objective for a supervisory training program is not likely to be attained:

> As a result of successful training, there will be a zero turnover rate except for natural attrition beginning with staff members employed after 1/1/2xxx.

By contrast, an objective stating that "The turnover rate for the Hilo Restaurant will be reduced by 20 percent within 12 months of training," may be reasonable.

Training objectives should incorporate an element of stretch. Assume that the Anytown Hotel is currently receiving numerous guest complaints each month. Reducing the complaint rate to zero immediately after training is likely to be overly optimistic. By contrast, the objective of reducing the complaint rate by one per month after a six-month period required for process revision and implementation

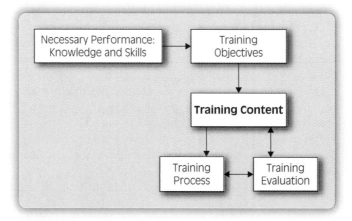

FIGURE 6.5: Training Objectives Are Important

Human Resources Management:
CURRENT EVENTS 6.1

WHAT ABOUT ONLINE TRAINING?

Costs are an important consideration in determining whether and to what extent training programs can be offered. Those who train are not available to do other work, and those who are being trained may have responsibilities that cannot be deferred for training at a specified time.

Online training (also called e-learning) provides a self-paced alternative to traditional face-to-face training. Courses can be available on the Internet for use by trainees at any time from their work, home, or elsewhere. Programs are self-paced, and trainees can learn what is relevant and skip unnecessary or already known information. Feedback is possible because employees can e-mail questions to and receive responses from the responsible trainer.

WHAT ABOUT COMPUTER ACCESS?

Some employees have access to computers with Internet connections at their workstations; others have computers at home; many employees, however, may not. Some properties can make training computers available in a spare office or, for example, even at a dedicated desk in an occupied office area.

E-learning can also be used to pretest employees for placement in on-site training programs and provide background content information to expedite traditional training.

may not be appropriate for the opposite reason: no or very little significant change in staff performance may be necessary to attain that objective. A better approach is when managers can assess common reasons for the complaints (Step 1 in the training process described in Figure 6.1). Then revised processes resulting from position analysis (Step 2 in Figure 6.1) can be developed to drive training content. Training objectives relating to the trainees' ability to master the revised process to reduce complaints can be developed, and the extent of reduction will be a measure of training effectiveness.

The concern that training objectives be measurable relates to their role in training evaluation. How can the effectiveness of a training program whose success would be measured by objectives such as the following be evaluated:

- Trainees will <u>realize</u> the importance of effective guest service.
- Trainees will <u>understand</u> the need to use a first-in, first-out (FIFO) inventory rotation system.
- Trainees will <u>recognize</u> the need to safely operate kitchen equipment.

Contrast these statements with objectives pertaining to the same topics that are measurable:

- Trainees will demonstrate a six-step method to manage guest complaints.
- Trainees will identify poor inventory rotation practices as they review a store-room with incorrectly arranged items.
- Trainees will operate kitchen equipment in a way that incorporates the manufacturers' safe operating instructions in the operating manual.

Training objectives typically use an action verb to tell what the trainee must demonstrate or apply after training. Examples of acceptable verbs include: *operate, calculate, explain,* and *assemble.* By contrast, verbs that are unacceptable because they cannot be measured include *know, appreciate, believe,* and *understand.*

STEP 4: DEVELOP TRAINING PLANS

Training plan: A description of the structure (overview) and sequence of the entire training program.

Training plans organize the training content, and they provide an overview of the structure and sequence of the entire training program. They show how individual training lessons should be sequenced to best allow trainees to learn required knowledge and skills.

Several factors should be considered to determine the sequence for subject matter in the training plan:

- Begin with an introduction explaining why the training is important and how it will benefit the trainees.
- Provide an overview of training content.
- Plan training lessons to progress from simple to complex. Simple information at the beginning of the training will allow trainees to feel comfortable more quickly in the learning situation. It will also give them the confidence needed to master the program.
- Build on the trainees' experiences. Combine unfamiliar information with familiar content to allow trainees to build on their experience.
- Present basic information before more detailed concepts are discussed.
- Progress from general to specific.
- Consider the need for nice-to-know and need-to-know information. Basics should be presented before other information, and it is generally best to address the whys before the hows.
- Use a logical order. What information is prerequisite to other information as knowledge is developed or as skills are attained?

Figure 6.6 illustrates a worksheet for a training plan.

Training plans allow trainers to (1) plan the dates and times for each training lesson, (2) consider the topic (lesson number and subject), (3) state the training location, (4) indicate the instructor(s) responsible for the training, and (5) determine the trainees for whom specific training lessons are applicable.

TRAINING TOPIC:						
DATE	TIME	TRAINING LESSON		LOCATION	INSTRUCTOR(S)	TRAINEES
		LESSON NO.	SUBJECT			

FIGURE 6.6: Worksheet for Training Plan

Assume a trainer is planning a training program for a new counter attendant in a hospital's dietary department who must learn how to correctly perform all tasks in the position. Perhaps some tasks can be taught in one training session. By contrast, several (or more) training sessions may be needed to teach just one other task. The training plan allows planners to think about what must be taught (training lessons) and the sequence and duration of each training lesson.

When a training plan is developed to teach all tasks to a new staff member, training dates and times must only consider the availability of the trainer and the employee. If the training concerns an issue impacting more than one employee, other tactics may be necessary. For example, each session might be planned for two (or more) alternate dates and times to accommodate all affected personnel. The training location could be the same for every session, or it could accommodate group training in a congregate setting and individual training in workstations. The trainees might include all staff members for some sessions and only selected staff members for other sessions.

STEP 5: DEVELOP TRAINING LESSONS

Training lesson: The information to be presented in a single session of the training plan. Each lesson contains one or more specific training objectives and indicates the content and methodology(ies) required to enable trainees to master the content.

A **training lesson** provides all of the information needed to present a single session that is part of a broader training plan. In effect, it is a turnkey module that tells the why, what, and how of a specific training session:

- Why? the objective(s) of the training session
- What? the content of the training session
- How? the method(s) used to present the training

A training lesson may be needed to teach new staff members how to perform a single task (e.g., how to operate a meat slicer), or it can be used to teach experienced staff new steps in a single task (e.g., steps in a hotel reservations task that are being revised to reduce costs and/or to increase quality).

Figure 6.7 reviews steps that can be used to develop training lessons.

Let's assume a training lesson on managing guest complaints has been developed and is shown in Figure 6.8.

Let's see how the steps identified in Figure 6.7 were used to develop the training lesson:

- *Step 1: Develop lesson objective(s).* A training objective is stated: "As a result of successfully completing this lesson, trainees will be able to effectively manage guest complaints using a six-step service recovery process."
- *Step 2: Determine topics that represent the required knowledge/skills to attain the objective(s).* The trainer determines that a video will provide most of the subject matter necessary to attain the objective.
- *Step 3: Consider topic sequence.* The trainer uses an organized topic sequence that begins with an introduction, continues with the video, and then uses a

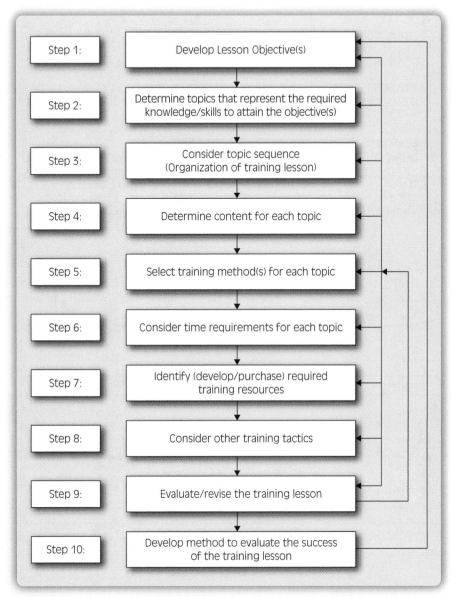

FIGURE 6.7: Steps to Develop a Training Lesson

PowerPoint presentation to review the video's specific learning points. There will also be trainee discussion, a role-play exercise, and a review and evaluation.

■ *Step 4: Determine content for each topic.* In this session, there is only one topic (managing guests' complaints). A review of off-the-shelf training resources reinforces the decision that the video will be effective.

TRAINING PLAN: Customer Service for Hilotown Restaurant Service Staff

TRAINING TOPIC: Service Recovery

TRAINING OBJECTIVE: As a result of successfully completing this lesson, trainees will be able to effectively manage guest complaints using a six-step service recovery process.

LESSON DURATION:	50 MINUTES	TRAINING LOCATION:	CONFERENCE ROOM	
TIME	**ACTIVITY/METHOD**		**MATERIALS**	**COMMENTS**
2 minutes	Introduction: Ask trainees for examples of customer complaints		None	Assure that examples come from several departments
8 minutes	Show video, "Customer Service Recovery Tactics"		Disc player, monitor, and video (from ACME Production Company)	Assure that video playback equipment is available and operative
5 minutes	Show PowerPoint overheads that review the video's six-step recovery process		Laptop computer, LCD projector, disc containing PowerPoint overheads	Assure laptop computer and projector are available and operative
5 minutes	Lead trainee discussion about a complaint noted in the session introduction and how it could be addressed using information in the video		Flipchart and pens	Relate discussion to video; note differences between the video and real world
15 minutes	Conduct role-play exercise and follow-up discussion service			Review role-play exercise procedures
5 minutes	Review six-step service recovery method			
10 minutes	Administer 10-question true/false review		Laptop, LCD projector, and overheads (two questions per overhead)	Show review on screen

FIGURE 6.8: Sample Training Lesson

- *Step 5: Select training method(s) for each topic.* A short (50-minute) lecture, video, PowerPoint overheads, trainee discussion, and a role-play exercise will be used.
- *Step 6: Consider time requirements for each topic.* The trainer knows that 30 minutes will be needed for the introduction, role-play, review, and evaluation. The video is eight minutes long. Five minutes is then allocated for video review and trainee discussion. The 43 minutes of formal contact time fit well into a planned 50-minute session.
- *Step 7: Identify (develop/purchase) required training resources.* The video and several PowerPoint overheads will be required.
- *Step 8: Consider other training tactics.* The trainer originally planned to facilitate the role-play after the video. Instead, he or she will facilitate trainee discussions before the exercise.
- *Step 9: Evaluate/revise the training lesson.* This should be done before the session is first conducted. Experience with previous training sessions, including this specific topic if it has previously been taught, help to plan an effective presentation.
- *Step 10: Develop a method to evaluate the success of the training session.* The trainer will use a 10-question true/false test.

Figure 6.7 also indicates the cyclical nature of training lesson development: evaluation/revision (Step 9) can lead to changes in any or all of the earlier steps in development. As well, the after-lesson evaluation in Step 10 helps the trainer to assess the extent to which the lesson objectives (Step 1) were attained.

Trainers can use a wide range of resources to develop training content including:

- Manufacturers' operating manuals for equipment
- Standard operating procedure manuals
- Task breakdowns for positions
- Applicable books and magazines including electronic editions
- Industry best practices
- Training resources from professional associations, such as the Education Foundation of the National Restaurant Association and the Education Institute of the American Hotel & Lodging Association
- Materials available from suppliers
- Ideas from other hospitality organizations
- Notes taken by the trainer at other training sessions
- The trainer's own experience

Training handbook: A hard-copy or electronic manual (file) that contains the training plan and associated training lessons for a complete training program. The program can be comprehensive (e.g., to prepare a new staff member for a position) or more specific (e.g., to present training information on an ad hoc topic such as sanitation or customer service).

STEP 6: DEVELOP TRAINING HANDBOOK (FILE)

The task of developing training programs requires time and creativity. The process is cost effective when the training plans, lessons, and applicable resource materials are used for more than one training experience. A **training handbook** is a hard-copy or

Human Resources Management:
CURRENT EVENTS 6.2

TRAINING AND RETURN ON INVESTMENT

It's easy to say, "Training must be worth more than it costs." However, it is not always easy to determine the cost of training or to quantify its benefits. Increasingly, and for good reason, hospitality managers must justify training by confirming that money spent for it cannot be better used for other purposes.

Hopefully, training objectives can assist with return on investment (ROI) assessment. Suggestive selling to increase check averages in the restaurant, upselling at the front desk to increase hotel room rates, and supervisory training to increase entry-level employee retention rates are examples of activities that can be assessed by studying pre- and post-training data. Costs for trainers and trainees' time and for materials can also be assessed, and a comparison of benefits can yield ROI conclusions.

Some training efforts such as those addressing how to clean a guest room and how to prepare food items can be evaluated (by, respectively, inspector's scores and adherence to standard recipes). However, these programs are more difficult to assess with an ROI emphasis: While training costs can be calculated, how does one quantify the training benefits?

In today's competitive hospitality industry, a hunch that training is good can be helpful. However, whenever possible, more objective measurements are needed.

electronic manual (file) containing the training plan and associated training lessons for a complete program. A wise trainer maintains this information in an organized fashion that allows, with revision as necessary, easy replication of training. It benefits managers because the time and money spent to develop training tools need not be replicated. After materials are initially developed, time can be spent on delivering rather than on planning the training activities. A training handbook or file also benefits the trainees, because they will have access to quality training programs that have been carefully planned rather than just thrown together.

A handbook (file) used to train a new person for all tasks in a position may include:

- An introduction
- A current position description
- A copy of the position's task list
- Copies of all task breakdowns
- Training lessons for each task breakdown including evaluation processes
- Training lessons for generic subject matter such as guest service and safety basics

Human Resources Management:
CURRENT EVENTS 6.3

THE PORTABLE TRAINER!

It wasn't too many years ago that training videos (films) were very large (and heavy) reel-to-reel videotapes about the size of a large deep-dish pizza. These were replaced by 35mm slides that fit into circular carousels about the size of a pie plate. Alternatively, trainers used transparency overheads that fit into notebook folders; a sufficient quantity for a full-day program might require space about the size of a small telephone book.

Today's trainers use laptop or notebook computers that are a must-have for other purposes as well. PowerPoint overheads can be transferred to the computer's hard drive or can be placed on a compact disc (CD). These CDs can also be used for training videos, and the World Wide Web allows trainees to view other training resources on the computer screen (for individualized training) or on a larger screen (for group training).

What's next in the technology of training? Futurists can best answer this question, but hospitality managers and trainers will likely have an increasing number of ways to deliver high-quality training content in the future.

STEP 7: PREPARE TRAINEES

The need to focus on the trainees is an obvious step that is often overlooked and/or done incorrectly. Providing training materials and activities will not necessarily yield more knowledgeable and skilled staff members. Instead, this goal can only be attained when the trainees want to learn.

Implementing training programs is easier when trainees have provided input into their development. This can occur when staff members provide suggestions about process revisions, and as task lists and task breakdowns are developed.

Additional ways to motivate trainees to benefit from training include:

- *Tell trainees what to expect.* The who, what, when, and where of training should be provided, specific questions should be addressed, and opportunities for group discussions about the training should be provided.
- *Explain why the training is needed.* Whenever possible, state this in terms of what's in it for the trainees, rather than how it will benefit the property.
- *Provide time for the training.* Effective training cannot be rushed, and it cannot be done during peak business times or whenever time is available. Dedicated time must be considered as schedules for trainers and trainees are developed.

- *Address trainees' concerns.* For example, persons with language or reading problems and those wanting to know about the relationship, if any, between training and advancement opportunities have concerns to be addressed before the training begins.
- *Emphasize the importance of training.* This factor is easy to accomplish in a property that supports training.
- *Explain that training will be directly related to the trainee's work.* Coupled with a discussion about how trainees will directly benefit from the training, this will provide a powerful motivator for training acceptance.
- *Stress that the training will be enjoyable and worthwhile.* This tactic should be easy to implement when the trainees have had positive experiences with past training efforts.
- *Tell the trainees how they will be evaluated.* New staff will be looking for assurance that their employment decision was a good one. Experienced staff will know about the track record of their employer relative to the importance of training and the benefits derived from it.

After trainees are prepared for training, the program can be conducted. This topic, along with training evaluation, is addressed in Chapter 8.

Human Resources Terms

The following terms were defined in this chapter:

Training	Task
Cost effective	Body language
Performance-based	Jargon
Competent	Position analysis
Feedback	Task list
Attitude	Task breakdown
Morale	Performance standards
Value-added	Position description
Turnover	Step (in task)
Employer of choice	Open-ended (question)
Off-the-shelf	Quality
Hire date	Training plan
Warm-body syndrome	Training lesson
Professional development programs	Training handbook

FOR YOUR CONSIDERATION

1. List some training activities in which you have participated that were beneficial to you. Why did you enjoy them? How did they help you to learn? What training principles noted in this chapter were incorporated in these activities?

2. List some training experiences in which you have participated that you did not enjoy. Why did you not like them? How did they hinder your learning experience? What training principles noted in this chapter did they violate?

3. If possible, interview a hospitality manager or supervisor and determine the following:

    a. What are the benefits of training?

    b. What are the most significant obstacles to training in the operation?

    c. How, if at all, could training for entry-level employees be improved in the operation?

    d. If the operation is part of a multiunit company, what, if any, training resources are provided by the company? How helpful are these resources? What types of training are mandated by the company? How much discretion does a unit manager have in determining content for training in the unit?

4. Select a common operating problem, such as excessive dish breakage in a restaurant or hotel dining room, low inspector's scores for guest room bath areas, or guest complaints about slow check-in times at the front desk. Then:

    a. Indicate the steps you would use to develop a task breakdown that addressed the problem.

    b. Explain how you would develop a training lesson for the topic.

CASE STUDY: HUMAN RESOURCES MANAGEMENT IN ACTION

Leilani has been a successful manager in quick-service restaurants for 10 years. She recently became an area manager for Good Food, a newer company with 35 units, and she reports to one of two regional managers. She accepted the position because of lessened travel requirements and the professional challenges presented by an opportunity to help grow this young organization.

The Good Food organization markets to nutrition-conscious guests and offers a variety of fresh vegetable and fruit salads, soups, and sandwiches. It is a tough market because, as many restaurant owners and managers know, the public's expressed interest in nutrition doesn't always translate to dining-out decisions.

Leilani has been with the company about three months, and she is impressed with the amount of operating and production support provided by headquarters. There are detailed standard recipes, food purchase specifications, nutritional information for interested guests, and even a nutrition training program that is mandatory for all staff.

In contrast, Leilani quickly noticed that many of the operating problems encountered by other restaurants also affected her units. Examples included high employee turnover that placed a continuing management emphasis on recruiting staff, cost control issues, and some opportunities for employee theft of products and money.

Her boss is aware of these concerns because they apply to units throughout his region. He explained that the company's owners also knew about the problems but considered them to be part of the business, and top management was currently more concerned about expanding the business than addressing these issues.

"Well, should we just go with the flow and ignore the problems, should we campaign for change in the organization's emphasis, or should we just dictate policies and procedures to control cost and theft problems?" Leilani asked. "Also, won't we increase our turnover rate even more if we create a more dictatorial atmosphere?"

"I'm also concerned about these issues, Leilani, and I have another option," replied the regional manager. "There is another area manager who shares your concerns. We all know the correct procedures that should be used, and a major problem is that they are not being used. What is needed, in part, is a training program for our supervisors to help them learn how to teach our staff to do things correctly. Perhaps the three of us can team up and address these problems. Let's assume I can talk headquarters into funding a pilot program to train our supervisors," he continued. "I know they will want proof that the expenditure of these funds is cost effective, and as professionals we want that as well."

"I came here because I wanted to confront challenges in a small and growing organization," said Leilani. "This is really a challenge. Let's do it, and I hope we're up to the task."

Dimension: Supervision

1. What tactics should Leilani use with her unit managers and supervisors to reinforce the renewed emphasis on training at the units?
2. How, if at all, should Leilani utilize input from her unit managers, supervisors, and staff to develop and implement training programs?
3. What, if any, types of rewards/incentives can Leilani and her unit managers use to encourage staff to maximize their participation in the training?

Dimension: Planning for Training

Assume that the regional manager, Leilani, and the other area manager initially meet to determine how to begin the training effort and to determine who should do what and when.

1. Develop a list of the most important initial decisions that must be made, suggest tasks that should be undertaken, and propose a list of intended

accomplishments for the first six months. (Recall that these three managers must also run the business.)

2. What, if any, identified tasks might be delegated to unit managers?

Dimension: Strategy

Assume that the planning team decides that the project will go more smoothly (and additional funding will be forthcoming) if a project yielding a quick and easy success is implemented.

1. Plan a simple project addressing an issue that can be developed and implemented quickly, such as reducing food cost by portion control, improved inventory management, or implementing more effective procedures for product receiving.
2. Outline the steps that you would use to develop and implement a training program that addresses this simple task. Also, describe how you might provide some quantitative ROI data to help justify the worth of training.

INTERNET ACTIVITIES

1. Numerous organizations offer off-the-shelf training resources. Enter "hospitality training" into your favorite search engine, review several sites, and answer the following questions:
   a. How, if at all, would you evaluate the worth of the training resources being advertised related to their cost?
   b. Do the materials offered seem to address real-world and practical training concerns?
   c. What factors would you consider as you evaluated resources from alternative suppliers?
2. Many hospitality training consultants advertise on the Internet. Type the phrase "hospitality training consultants" into your favorite search engine, and view some sites. Answer the following questions:
   a. What common themes are noted on the Web sites?
   b. How do the consultants differentiate their companies from competitors?
   c. What primary types of services are offered?
   d. How helpful are the testimonials, suggestions, and general information provided?
   e. What factors would be most important if you were considering use of an external training consultant?
   f. How helpful would review of the Web sites be in retaining a training consultant?
3. Many professional hospitality associations provide helpful training resources. Check out the Web sites for the following organizations to review the types

of training materials, resources, and information that the industry makes available:

- The Educational Institute, American Hotel & Lodging Foundation: *www.ei-ahla.org*
- National Restaurant Association Educational Foundation: *www.nraef.org*
- Club Managers Association of America: *www.cmaa.org*
- National Association of College & University Foodservices: *www.nacufs.org*
- Dietary Managers Association: *www.dmaonline.org*
- National Automatic Merchandisers Association: *www.vending.org*
- American Dietetics Association: *www.eatright.org*

Comment on the following statement: Because these training materials are developed by and for those working in the hospitality industry, topics and content will be timely and relevant.

CHAPTER SEVEN

Delivering and Evaluating Training Programs

CHAPTER OUTLINE

CHECKLIST OF CHAPTER LEARNING OBJECTIVES

As a result of satisfactory completion of this chapter, readers will be able to:

1. Provide an overview of the individual on-job training process.

2. Explain steps that are important in the four-step individual (on-job) training method:

   Preparation
   Presentation

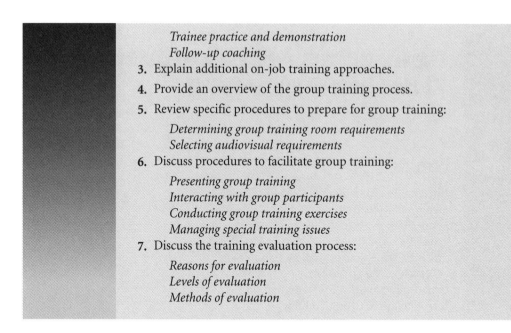

Trainee practice and demonstration
Follow-up coaching
3. Explain additional on-job training approaches.
4. Provide an overview of the group training process.
5. Review specific procedures to prepare for group training:

Determining group training room requirements
Selecting audiovisual requirements
6. Discuss procedures to facilitate group training:

Presenting group training
Interacting with group participants
Conducting group training exercises
Managing special training issues
7. Discuss the training evaluation process:

Reasons for evaluation
Levels of evaluation
Methods of evaluation

Introduction to Individual On-Job Training

1. Provide an overview of the individual on-job training process.

Figure 7.1 (previously shown in Chapter 6) indicates our progress in learning about training. Chapter 6 presented basic information applicable to the first seven steps. This chapter begins with a detailed discussion of the two basic

Impact on Human Resources Management

In Chapter 6 you learned about the importance of effective training. Its advantages were discussed in terms of the good things that can occur when training is done correctly and the bad things that typically arise when training is done improperly. It does no good to carefully plan the training process (Chapter 6) if the concern for effective training is not carried through when it is delivered. In addition, all resources, including time, money, and creative energies of managers, are in limited supply. It is, therefore, important to use these limited resources wisely. Training evaluation that occurs before, during, and after training is absolutely critical to ensure that the expenditure of training resources represent their best use. Revisions to training identified as part of the evaluation process allow the operation to continue on its journey of improvement. It also helps ensure that staff members at all organizational levels are fulfilling their work responsibilities in the best way possible.

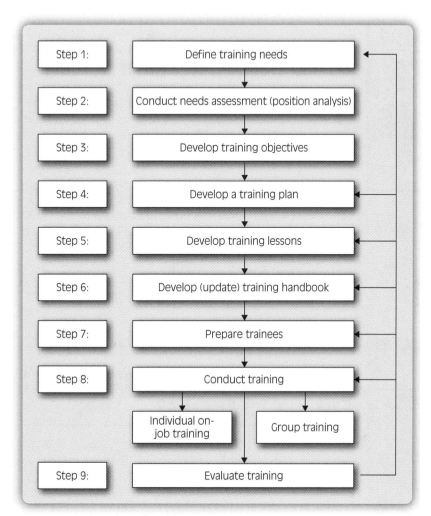

Step 1:	Define training needs
Step 2:	Conduct needs assessment (position analysis)
Step 3:	Develop training objectives
Step 4:	Develop a training plan
Step 5:	Develop training lessons
Step 6:	Develop (update) training handbook
Step 7:	Prepare trainees
Step 8:	Conduct training
	Individual on-job training / Group training
Step 9:	Evaluate training

FIGURE 7.1: Overview of Training Process

methods that can be used to conduct training (individual and group), and it concludes with a discussion of the final step in training: evaluation.

On-job training is commonly used in tourism and hospitality organizations. With this method, the trainer teaches job skills and knowledge to one trainee, primarily at the work station. Theoretically, it is the best type of training because it incorporates many of the learning and training principles explained in Chapter 6.

In practice, however, on-job training is frequently not done well. As suggested by other commonly used names (e.g., tag-along training, shadow training, and buddy system training), some supervisors erroneously believe that trainees can learn simply by watching and helping a more-experienced peer. Unfortunately, this approach ignores all or most of the important planning steps. Trainers who have not learned

On-job training: An individualized (one-on-one) training approach in which a knowledgeable and skilled trainer teaches a less-experienced staff member how to perform tasks required for a position.

On-Job Training: Not All or Nothing

The primary purposes of on-job training are to provide staff members with necessary knowledge and skills. The method is useful for new staff members who must learn all tasks, and for their experienced peers who must acquire new knowledge or skills to perform an existing task in a different way or new tasks resulting from work revisions.

On-job training can be supplemented by group training, and this tactic is especially useful when an operating problem affecting several staff members in a position must be addressed. Assume all front desk clerks or hospital cooks must learn how to operate a new piece of equipment. Because demonstration is likely to be an important tactic in this training, an individualized training method to address some tasks can be followed by a group training method for other tasks.

Is On-Job Training Best Because It Is Easy, Fast, and Inexpensive?

Some supervisors who prefer on-job training do so for the wrong reasons. They believe it to be easy, fast, and inexpensive because, "All you have to do is allow a trainee to follow along with an experienced staff member who can teach the trainee everything he or she needs to know to do the job."

This perception of on-job training is incorrect. The need to define training requirements; conduct a position analysis; develop training objectives, training plans, and training lessons; and retain materials in a training handbook is just as important for individualized training as for group training. Trainees must be prepared for the training, and this involves much more than a tag-along training tactic.

On-job training can be easy. The steps involved in its planning and delivery are not complicated. However, the process does take time, and a commitment of financial resources is required to effectively plan and deliver it.

how to train, who must do so as an add-on to their existing responsibilities, and who have been taught from equally unskilled trainers are not likely to be effective.

There are several advantages to on-job training:

- *It incorporates basic adult learning principles.* Training should focus on those being trained. Trainers should consider the trainees' backgrounds, and training should be organized and, when possible, informal. Trainees should be allowed to practice; their individual attention spans and learning speeds should be considered; and appropriate training tactics should be used.
- *It provides maximum realism.* Training must focus on real problems, and these are encountered in the workplace.
- *It provides immediate feedback.* On-job training allows a trainee to demonstrate (practice) what has been learned as soon as he or she has been taught. As the trainer observes this trial performance, he or she can recognize proper performance (the training has been successful) or address improper performance. In both instances, correct performance can be encouraged.
- *It can be used to train new and experienced staff.* On-job training can teach new staff members all of the tasks they must perform and experienced staff about revised work methods for just one or a few specific tasks.
- *It is frequently delivered by peers who regularly perform the task.* Trainees will not be intimidated by a higher-level manager or by an outside person such as a trainer from the human resources department. The trainer can be a role model and, in the process, teamwork can be encouraged, and a corporate culture that encourages cooperation and mutual assistance can be fostered.
- *It is well accepted by trainees.* This is an easy-to-understand point because it focuses on what's best for the trainee.

Group training is most effective when trainees can ask questions and receive immediate feedback and encouragement from the trainer.
Courtesy Purestock

Done correctly, there are few, if any, disadvantages to on-job training. Practiced the way it is in some tourism and hospitality organizations, however, several potential disadvantages can be cited:

■ *Experienced staff members who have not learned how to train can make numerous errors while talking about and demonstrating proper performance.*

■ *Training can be unorganized.* Effective training should present a step-by-step approach. This is difficult when a trainee follows (shadows) an experienced peer and, instead, learns tasks out of the sequence in which they should be done. Consider a cook trainee who should sequentially learn each step in a standard recipe. Instead, a disorganized approach may be used when the experienced staff member (trainer) performs one or two steps in the recipe, and is then interrupted to do other things before resuming preparation.

■ *It can ignore the correct way to perform a task.* When task breakdowns are not available or used, the trainer may teach the trainee how he or she does the work. This may be a modification of how the trainer learned the task from another trainer (who, in turn, modified the task from how he or she learned it!). This evolution of task performance can hinder attainment of quality and quantity standards.

■ *It can create inappropriate work attitudes.* Experienced staff members who know how and want to do their jobs correctly but do not know how to train can become frustrated with training responsibilities. This problem is compounded when the trainer must perform other required work while training.

Is On-Job Training the Least Expensive Method?

This question, or its corollary, "What will this training cost?", is frequently considered when training is planned. This question is not, however, always the best one to address. For example, the least expensive training alternative is to do *no* training. Unfortunately, some poorly run organizations use this approach, at least with some staff members.

A better question relates to "Is the training cost-effective?" This can only be answered by studying factors specific to the training situation. However, most training professionals agree that on-job training is best to teach physical skills such as operating a piece of equipment and the performance of a task such as following a standard recipe. By contrast, group training is likely to be the best approach when several staff members must learn basic knowledge such as principles of guest relations or the basics of a new benefits package.

Improperly planned and delivered training will not be cost effective because the desired result (a staff member who can perform tasks meeting performance standards) is not likely to be attained. It will be even less effective if it results in frustrated trainers and trainees who have not received the organizational support they require. This, in turn, can yield high employee turnover rates and/or disgruntled employees.

Steps in On-Job Training

2. **Explain steps that are important in the four-step individual (on-job) training method:**

   Preparation

   Presentation

   Trainee practice and demonstration

   Follow-up coaching

As noted in Figure 7.2, there are four steps in the individual on-job training method.

As you'll note in Figure 7.2, the first step in on-job training involves **preparation** activities, and the second step is the actual presentation of the training. The third step allows practice and demonstration by the trainee, and a final step involves various **coaching** and related activities that are the trainer's responsibility. In this section, we will explain important aspects of each of these steps.

STEP 1: PREPARATION

The following principles are useful when preparing for on-job training. Each will have already been addressed if the earlier steps in the training process noted in Chapter 6 were implemented.

■ *State training objectives.* Training objectives for the entire training program must be available in the training plan and for each segment of the training in training lessons. Assume that a training lesson addresses a single step in a task: how to prepare one dessert of several on a menu. The objective for that specific training session will be available in the applicable lesson in the training

Preparation: The first step in individualized (on-job) training, preparation involves all activities that must be done prior to the delivery of training.

Coaching: A training and supervisory tactic that involves informal on-job conversations and demonstrations designed to encourage proper behavior and to discourage improper behavior.

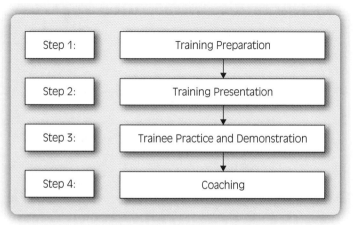

FIGURE 7.2: Steps in Individual On-Job Training Method

handbook. In this example, the trainer will know that the training objective is to "Prepare baked fruit pies according to the applicable standard recipes."

▪ *Use/revise applicable task breakdown.* A task breakdown explains how a task should be performed. The trainer who will teach a vending commissary cook how to prepare a baked dessert item should review the applicable task breakdown and recipe in the training handbook. While doing so, he or she can duplicate a copy of both for the trainee's use during the training.

▪ *Consider the training schedule.* The training plan should indicate how long the training activity will require, as well as where in the overall training sequence that dessert preparation training should occur. Experience may suggest that training for one bakery recipe normally takes 25 minutes. This can occur any time after workplace safety and equipment operation has been taught, so the trainer has flexibility in determining the training schedule. The best time to conduct training is when production volume is low, when employees who are normally in the area are working elsewhere or on a break, and when the trainer has adequate time to facilitate the training.

▪ *Select training location.* When practical, training should occur at the actual work station where the task will be performed. Training in dessert preparation is planned for the bake shop area.

▪ *Assemble training materials/equipment.* The training lesson and supporting standard recipe should be in the training handbook. These files will indicate

The training location for this new Uniformed Services Attendant is the entire hotel as he applies what he has learned to assisting guests.
Courtesy
PhotoDisc/Getty Images

needed materials and equipment. The trainer may also duplicate a copy of the standard recipe for the trainee's use; ensure that all equipment is available; and confirm that all tools, supplies, and ingredients are assembled.

- *Set up work station.* The trainer should ensure that the work station is relatively free of anything that might detract from the training.
- *Prepare the trainee.* A new staff member should know the purpose of initial training: to provide the knowledge and skills required to perform all tasks required for the position. Experienced staff receiving on-job training should understand that the training purpose is to provide the knowledge and skills needed to perform a task in a different way, or to learn a new task that was not part of the original task list. Trainees should be told how their training (in the training lesson) relates to their overall training experience (in the training plan).
- *Determine what the trainee already knows.* Assume a specific item of equipment must be operated. If the trainee claims to have this skill, he or she can demonstrate it. If successfully done, no further training is necessary. If the trainee cannot correctly operate the equipment, training will be needed. The trainer can maximize available training time on activities where training is most needed. When the trainee knows that part of the training has been mastered, he or she will know that the remaining training requirements are achievable.

Figure 7.3 reviews activities that are important when preparing individual training programs.

STEP 1: PREPARATION

The Trainer Should:

- [ ] 1. Develop a schedule that considers the time allocated for a specific training lesson and the sequence in the training plan when it should be taught.
- [ ] 2. Use a task breakdown to identify how a task should be done.
- [ ] 3. Have all necessary equipment, tools, and materials ready for the training session.
- [ ] 4. Select and properly arrange the appropriate training location.
- [ ] 5. Know *precisely* how to begin the training process.
- [ ] 6. Identify the tasks that the trainee must learn.
- [ ] 7. Put the trainee at ease.
- [ ] 8. Find out what the trainee already knows about the task.
- [ ] 9. Explain what the trainee should expect to learn in the session.
- [ ] 10. Set a good example for the trainee.
- [ ] 11. Explain what's in it for the trainee.

FIGURE 7.3: Checklist for On-Job Training Preparation

STEP 2: PRESENTATION

Preparation activities already completed will make this step much easier. Completion of Steps 1 to 7 in the training process (see Figure 7.1) provides a solid foundation of planning tools that can be implemented. In addition to the training lesson (Step 5 in Figure 7.1), task breakdowns completed during position analysis (Step 2 in Figure 7.1) will be helpful as the training is presented.

To review appropriate training presentation procedures, let's consider how a trainer might train a new staff member to conduct a physical inventory in a restaurant storeroom. A copy of the applicable position description is provided to confirm that the inventory task is integral to the trainee's position, and the importance of the task is explained.

The training lesson suggests that the training should occur in the storeroom, and begins with an overview of how the task should be performed. Then applicable activities are demonstrated. For example, the trainer shows the trainee how the storage area is organized and reviews how the inventory worksheet is completed. Procedures about how to count (e.g., whether **broken cases** are counted) are reviewed.

The training lesson used is well-developed, so the task is divided into separate, teachable steps. The trainer explains the first step in the task, answers questions posed by the trainee, and then allows the trainee to repeat, practice, and/or demonstrate the step. If necessary, the sequence of steps can be repeated so the trainee can learn all of the steps in the task.

As the presentation process evolves, the trainer follows several principles:

Broken case: A shipping container such as a case that contains less than the complete number of issue units (e.g., cans or bottles).

Closed-ended question: A question that can be answered with a "yes" or "no" response. Example: Do you like your job?

■ Speak in simple terms and do not use jargon.
■ When possible, present easier tasks before more complex activities. For example, the trainer teaches how to conduct a physical count before analysis of data from computer printouts is considered.
■ Explain and demonstrate tasks slowly and clearly.
■ Use a questioning process to help assure trainee comprehension. The trainer does not use a **closed-ended question:** "Do you understand what I am doing?" Instead, an open-ended question is used: "Why do you think it is important to count full cases before opened cases?"
■ Emphasize the task breakdown as the training evolves. The trainer suggests that the trainee follow along using the task breakdown provided at the beginning of the training session.
■ Provide clear and well-thought-out instructions for each task. The trainer indicates why each step is necessary and why it should be done in a specific sequence.
■ Ask questions to help ensure that the trainee understands and to suggest when additional information, practice, or demonstration can be helpful.

Figure 7.4 provides a review of important training points that are helpful when on-job training is presented.

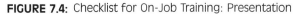

STEP 2: PRESENTATION

The Trainer Should:

- [ ] 1. Explain tasks and steps.
- [ ] 2. Demonstrate tasks and steps.
- [ ] 3. Assure that the trainee understands each task.
- [ ] 4. Encourage the trainee to ask questions.
- [ ] 5. Respond appropriately to questions.
- [ ] 6. Check for understanding by asking open-ended questions.
- [ ] 7. Provide information about and demonstrate only one task or step at a time.
- [ ] 8. Follow an orderly sequence using the training lesson as a guide.
- [ ] 9. Maintain a patient and appropriate pace throughout the training session.
- [ ] 10. Provide only the amount of information or instruction that can be mastered during one session.
- [ ] 11. Assure that the training session is interesting.
- [ ] 12. Assure that all instruction is clear, concise, complete, and accurate.
- [ ] 13. Provide an applicable task breakdown.

FIGURE 7.4: Checklist for On-Job Training: Presentation

STEP 3: TRAINEE PRACTICE AND DEMONSTRATION

As indicated in Figure 7.2, the third step in on-job training allows the trainee to practice and demonstrate what has been taught. During this step, several principles become important:

- *The trainee should be asked to repeat or explain key points.*
- *The trainee should be allowed to demonstrate and/or practice the task.* If practical, he or she should practice each step in the task a sufficient number of times to learn its basics before training continues. This allows the trainer to confirm that the trainee can perform the task and that the trainee understands what successful performance of the task involves. Typically, steps are taught by the trainer and practiced or demonstrated by the trainee in the proper sequence.
- *The trainer can use tactics to coach the trainee to reinforce positive performance* (e.g., "Joe, you did that task flawlessly") *and to correct improper performance* (e.g., "Andrew, you shouldn't have to look for the next item to be counted in the inventory because it is listed on the inventory sheet according to its storeroom location").
- *Trainers should recognize that, especially when the task and/or steps are difficult, initial progress may be slow.* Then the trainee will require more repetition to build speed and to more consistently and correctly perform the task or step.

IT'S THE LAW!

Numerous legal issues could be addressed in on-job training for persons in selected positions. Should front desk staff loudly announce the room number of a check-in guest, or should a housekeeper let a guest who says he "lost his key" into a guest room? Of course not, and these staff members must be taught about these safety concerns during training. Should food and beverage servers indicate that there is no monosodium glutamate (MSG) in menu items if they don't know for certain whether there is (this ingredient can be very harmful to some people)? Can a server indicate that a steak is "USDA Prime" when it is not? Of course not, and on-job training should address these and related concerns that, if not addressed, can lead to lawsuits.

Franchisees sign agreements with franchisors about what they will and will not do. Many of these organizations require owners and/or managers to attend management training programs when properties become affiliated with the organizations. They may also require that entry-level employees in some positions complete guest relations programs.

Staff members in many positions perform their responsibilities within the restraints of legal considerations all the time. Bar managers must know about safety codes relating to occupancy levels in the lounge; preparation staff must know about health and safety requirements applicable to spraying pesticides in the kitchen; and housekeepers must know what they should and should not do if they suspect the use of controlled substances in guest rooms.

Employees of contract management companies may work in outlets on military bases. They have access to information such as troop movements that is not to be shared with anyone. Vending route drivers must obey traffic laws, and staff members in many organizations must comply with Occupational Safety Health Act requirements. Persons in these and in numerous other situations must comply with the law at all times, and this is more likely to occur when they acquire needed knowledge in training.

Sandwich method (performance appraisal): A tactic that involves praising an employee, suggesting an improvement tactic, and thanking the staff member for improvements made.

- *Trainers must realize that some trainees learn faster than others.* Within reason, training can be presented at the pace judged best for the individual trainee. The time allowed for trainee demonstration can also be varied.
- *Correct performance should be acknowledged before addressing performance problems.* Some trainers refer to this as the **sandwich method** of appraisal. Just as a sandwich has two slices of bread with a filling between them, the sandwich method uses an introductory phrase (e.g., "Phyllis, you have mastered almost all parts of this task"), followed by problem identification (e.g., "All you need to do is ensure that the scale is set to zero before weighing the products"), and finally a concluding phrase (e.g., "I'm glad you are learning how to conduct the physical inventory count, and you will do it well.").

STEP 3: PRACTICE AND DEMONSTRATION

The Trainer Should:

☐ 1. Request that the trainee perform the step after it is presented.
☐ 2. Ask the trainee to explain the how's and why's of each task or step.
☐ 3. Correct all improper (substandard) performance.
☐ 4. Assure that the trainee understands each step by asking open-ended questions.
☐ 5. Complement the trainee when he or she correctly performs a task or step.
☐ 6. Point out errors made during practice and demonstration to help the trainee learn from mistakes.
☐ 7. Allow the trainee time to practice and build confidence and speed.

FIGURE 7.5: Checklist for On-Job Training: Practice and Demonstration

- *Trainees should be praised for proper performance.* Everyone likes to be thanked for a job well done, to be told how important and special they are, and to receive immediate input about their performance. Trainers should frequently reward trainees for success by noting it and by thanking the trainees for it.

Figure 7.5 reviews some tactics that are helpful to implement the practice and demonstration step in on-job training.

STEP 4: COACHING

The coaching step includes activities to help ensure that the training will be effective; that is, that performance-based training objectives are attained. Useful coaching procedures include:

- At the end of the training session, the trainee should be asked to perform, in sequence, each step in the task or step.
- The trainer should encourage questions.
- The trainer should provide ongoing reinforcement about a trainee's positive attitude and when the trainee improves his or her skills and knowledge.
- Close supervision immediately after training, and occasional supervision after a task is mastered, can help ensure that the trainee consistently performs the task correctly.
- Trainers should request that the trainee always perform the task correctly. *Note:* The trainer may ask the trainee about suggestions for other ways to perform tasks after the staff member has gained experience on the job.
- Trainees should be asked to retain copies of training materials provided during the session for later referral, if warranted.

Figure 7.6 reviews principles for effective coaching during on-job training.

STEP 4: COACHING

The Trainer Should:

- [ ] 1. Encourage the trainee to seek assistance.
- [ ] 2. Tell the trainee who should be contacted if assistance is needed.
- [ ] 3. Check the trainee's performance frequently but unobtrusively.
- [ ] 4. Reinforce proper performance. Let the trainee know how he or she was doing.
- [ ] 5. Help the trainee to correct mistakes, if any.
- [ ] 6. Assure that mistakes, if any, are not repeated.
- [ ] 7. Ask the trainee about suggestions for better ways to do the task.
- [ ] 8. Encourage the trainee to improve on previous standards.
- [ ] 9. Compliment the trainee for successful demonstration.

FIGURE 7.6: Checklist for On-Job Training: Coaching

This employee is trying to do an excellent job, but coaching may still be needed to ensure that standards are consistently attained. *Courtesy Digital Vision*

Other Individual Training Methods

3. **Explain additional on-job training approaches.**

The four-step training approach is the most frequently used individual training method, but other individualized training processes can be used alone or with another method, including the following:

Distance education: An individual training method in which a staff member enrolls in a for-credit or not-for-credit program offered by a post-secondary educational facility or a professional association. Training can occur in a traditional manner, including use of hard-copy resources and examinations, or by more contemporary electronic education and training media.

- *Self-study.* Trainees can enroll in **distance education** programs offered by a post-secondary educational institution or a professional association. Self-study in a broader sense also occurs when interested staff members, perhaps following the advice of a supervisor or mentor, enroll in a college course, read a recommended book, or view videos in the human resources department's library.
- *Structured work experiences.* A staff member may be assigned a specific project under the guidance of a mentor or more-experienced staff member to both learn and to assist the employer (e.g., when a hotel designs a new menu, plans a very special catered event, or revises procedures for guest room cleaning).
- **Cross-training.** This training method includes general activities that allow staff to learn tasks in another position. Some staff members may be assigned fast-track status and, in this capacity, they may learn and perform numerous tasks in different positions. This may be done at a staff member's request

Human Resources Management: CURRENT EVENTS 7.1

Many observers believe that computers will increasingly be used for hospitality training. Benefits include the advantages of individualized learning and opportunities to provide quality training in small organizations without training departments or in multiunit organizations. Properties with high turnover and with seasonal staffing needs might also benefit from providing e-courses.

E-learning trainees use a computer rather than attending training sessions or reading correspondence course manuals. Tests and pre- and post-course evaluations help assess learning, and these tests can be electronically tabulated, with results made available to managers. Courses can be customized to deliver specific information for individual employees, who can participate in the courses on a 24/7 basis. Content can be changed quickly, and updates can be put in place almost immediately.

Today's generation of new staff members frequently are familiar with computers and use them for many purposes. Now, learning how to better perform their tourism and hospitality industry–related jobs may be one of these purposes.

Performance Appraisal and Job Enrichment

One opportunity for using job enrichment as a training tactic occurs during the performance appraisal process. A staff member who is currently performing all tasks in his or her present position might agree to learn a new task in a position at a higher organizational level. This assignment would be agreed upon during the performance appraisal session. The extent to which the employee can perform the new task by the next performance appraisal would be part of the second evaluation. In turn, additional job enrichment assignments and compensation increases could be based on that performance.

Cross-training: A training tactic that allows employees to learn tasks in another position.

Underemployed (job status): The condition that arises when a staff member is capable of working in a position with greater responsibilities than the position he or she currently occupies.

(e.g., to add variety if one is **underemployed**) or to help someone gain knowledge and skills that will be helpful when he or she assumes another position.

- **Job enrichment.** Job enrichment occurs when a trainee learns tasks that are traditionally performed at a higher organizational level. This is sometimes called vertical job expansion. As with other methods of individualized instruction, job enrichment can benefit both the staff member (trainee) and the organization. It can be used to make a job more challenging and rewarding by adding more employee control and responsibility. It is also useful when a manager must take on additional responsibilities and, to do so, must *delegate* some duties.

- **Job enlargement.** This training opportunity occurs when additional tasks that are part of a position at one organizational level are added to another position at the same level. This is sometimes called horizontal job expansion. Assume that the position of cook is at the same organizational level as the position of baker. Job enrichment could occur as the cook learns baking tasks and as the baker learns cooking tasks.

More About Job Enrichment and Job Enlargement

You have just learned that job enrichment and job enlargement tactics can be used for training. However, they are really multidimensional tools that can be used to address organizational issues such as managing positions with nonchallenging tasks in efforts to reduce turnover and reducing positions by combining tasks. Effective managers consider and use these alternatives as an integral part of their position analysis efforts (see Chapter 6), and as part of their ongoing training activities.

Human Resources MANAGEMENT ISSUES (7.1)

"I know a trainer must be patient," said Bernice, "but I can't get my own work done while I'm training Lovi-Ann." Bernice was talking to her supervisor in the coin room of the vending company about her experiences with a new staff member.

"Tell me what's going on, Bernice," said the supervisor. "You've trained lots of people before with no problem. What's happening this time?"

"Well," said Bernice, "it's as if there was a perfect storm of factors working against me. First, I haven't trained anyone in the past six months, and you know my duties have expanded during that time. Second, we've had lots of problems with some of our coin-counting equipment, and it's difficult to teach equipment operation when the equipment doesn't operate. Also, we're short two employees since Wilma left and Rita went on sick-leave. I haven't been feeling well, and I can't locate some of the training materials I've used in the past, and Lovi-Ann wants to do such a good job that she is slow to admit that she can do something before we can move on to the next step. Also, remember that we've gotten some new equipment and have changed some operating procedures recently."

"There are some problems," responded Bernice's supervisor. "I'd like to help you, but I'm just swamped with other things. Let's just get through this training issue, and then we'll have time to improve the training experience for you and the next trainee."

QUESTIONS

1. What is the real problem here, and who might be causing the most trouble?
2. What types of training resources would best help Bernice as she attempts to train Lovi-Ann?
3. What, if anything, can Bernice's supervisor do to provide more time for Bernice to conduct training?
4. What short-term tactics can help provide Bernice with more time to train? How, over the longer term, can Bernice learn how to be a more effective trainer?

■ **Job rotation.** This training method involves the temporary assignment of persons to different tasks to provide work variety or experience. Like other individualized work methods, job rotation benefits the staff member and helps create backup expertise within the organization.

Introduction to Group Training

4. Provide an overview of the group training process.

Group training is used to teach the same job-related information to more than one trainee at the same time, and it can be done at or away from the worksite. Advantages include:

Job enrichment:
This individual training method involves adding tasks to a position that are traditionally performed at a higher organizational level; also called vertical job expansion.

Job enlargement:
This individual training method occurs when additional tasks that are part of a position at the same organizational level are added to another position; also called horizontal job expansion.

Job rotation: The temporary assignment of persons to different positions or tasks to provide work variety or experience while creating backup expertise within the organization.

Group training: A training method that involves presenting the same job-related information to more than one trainee at the same time.

■ It can be time- and cost-effective when more than one staff member must receive the same information (e.g., when several dietary assistants must learn how to complete a new dietary intake form).

■ A large amount of information can be provided in a relatively short amount of time.

Disadvantages of group training typically relate to the difficulty of or inability to incorporate the individual differences of trainees into the training. Group training does not typically allow the trainer to focus on a specific trainee's knowledge and experience, speed of learning, or desire to receive immediate and individualized feedback.

Fortunately, the advantages of both individual and group training can often be incorporated into one training program. This occurs when all new staff members learn general information about the tourism or hospitality organization in a group orientation program. This can be followed up with individualized training to enable each trainee to learn specific tasks required for the position.

Two popular group training methods are used in tourism and hospitality organizations:

■ **Lecture.** The trainer talks and may use audiovisual equipment or **handouts** to facilitate the session. Question-and-answer components may also be included. This method provides much information quickly, but it does not typically allow active trainee participation.

■ **Demonstration.** The trainer physically shows trainees how to perform position tasks. Trainees can hear and see how something is done, often in the actual work environment. A potential disadvantage is that, without immediate and frequent repetition, trainees may forget all but the basics of the information

Trainers Should Use a Variety of Training Methods

Effective trainers consider the best way to deliver required content as they develop training lessons for individualized (on-job) and group training programs. For example, sessions in an individualized training program could include demonstration, review of handout materials, a question-and-answer session, the viewing of a video, and an on-job project. A training lesson for group training might involve all of these tactics along with class discussions, exercises including role-plays and case studies, and **breakout** group activities.

Effective trainers are aware of alternative training delivery methods, know when they are best used, and vary the tactics used to deliver individualized and group training programs.

Lecture (group training): A spoken presentation or speech made by a trainer to instruct a group of trainees.

Handouts: Hard-copy information applicable to the training topic that is given to trainees to help them learn a training concept.

presented. The best group training methods often include some (but relatively little) lecture supplemented with other activities, such as demonstrations, question-and-answer sessions, *discussions*, role-plays, case study analysis, and project assignments. *Note*: Role-play and case study activities are discussed later in this chapter.

Other combinations of group training methods are possible. The challenge is for the trainer to consider the best way to deliver training content while maintaining the trainees' interest in the session.

Preparing for Group Training

Demonstration (group training): A training method in which the trainer shows trainees how to perform all or part of a task.

Breakout (group training): A group training method in which all trainees are divided into small groups to complete selected training exercises. Groups may use a separate room or space within a single training room to conduct their activity.

Full-service hotel: A lodging operation offering food and beverage services, including à la carte dining and banquet operations and, frequently, room service.

Limited-service hotel: A lodging property that offers no or limited food and beverage service. Many limited-service hotels offer a continental or other cold breakfast selection.

5. **Review specific procedures to prepare for group training:**
   Determining group training room requirements
   Selecting audiovisual requirements

Experienced trainers know that the best training content does not automatically yield the best training program. Consider problems that can occur if the planning process does not address the training environment or the audiovisual tools needed to facilitate the training.

TRAINING ROOM REQUIREMENTS

Training rooms should be clean, well-ventilated, free from noisy distractions, and provide controlled room temperature. Meeting facilities such as conference centers and lodging properties with significant meeting business consider these environmental factors as meeting spaces are planned. Unfortunately, in many tourism and hospitality organizations, dedicated space for meetings of any type, including training, is not available. Instead, trainers must use multipurpose space such as meeting rooms or staff dining areas, and sometimes must creatively find space in dining room or other public access areas. *Note*: Nearby lodging operations including **full-service** and **limited-service hotels** may have meeting space available at no or little cost, especially if food and beverage services for refreshment breaks and breakfasts or lunches are purchased.

Proper table and chair arrangements help facilitate training. Figure 7.7 illustrates popular training room set-ups. Front-of-room areas must allow space for all of the trainer's materials and equipment. This can include a table, **lectern, flip chart(s),** laptop computer, and **digital projector** (if **PowerPoint overheads** will be used). Other equipment needed can include a television monitor, videocassette recorder (VCR) or digital video disc (DVD) player (frequently on a mobile cart), screen (unless wall- or ceiling-mounted), **overhead transparency projector,** and other items necessary for demonstrations, handouts, or other needs. Trainers

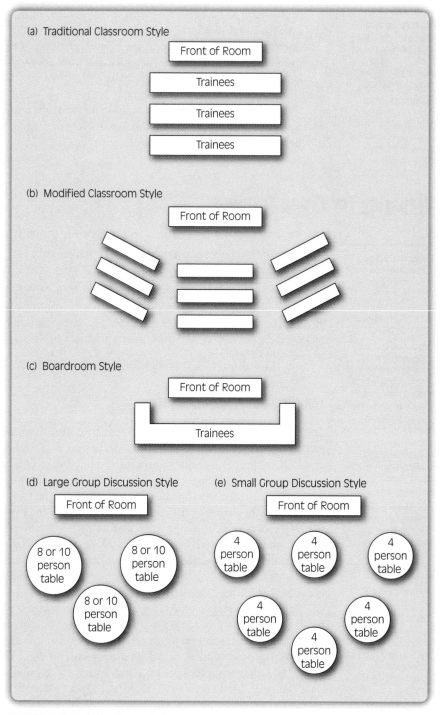

FIGURE 7.7: Training Room Set-ups

Lectern: A floor stand or tabletop unit, usually with a slanted top, used to hold the trainer's teaching materials.

Flip chart: A pad of large paper sheets placed on a tripod or other stand that allows a trainer to write helpful training information.

Digital projector: A machine that converts image data from a computer or video source and projects it onto a screen for viewing.

PowerPoint overheads: Electronic overheads that are displayed on a screen with a digital projector using a disc or from a computer's hard drive.

Overhead transparency projector: A machine that projects light under clear plastic-type sheets containing images and projects the images onto a screen for viewing.

Brainstorming (group training): A method of group problem solving or alternative generation in which all group members suggest possible ideas.

also appreciate ice water or another beverage, so tabletop space for this purpose is also required.

Each of the room set-ups illustrated in Figure 7.7 is useful for a specific purpose. The traditional classroom style favors interaction between the trainer and the individual trainees. (Trainees should ideally be able to relocate their chairs for small-group activities.) The modified classroom style allows trainers to walk between trainee tables, and interactive trainee exercises are possible if chairs are relocated. The boardroom style encourages all trainees to interact with their peers and with the trainer. The large- and small-group discussion room styles allow, respectively, large or small groups of trainees to participate in interactive exercises. *Note:* In ideal training room set-ups such as in facilities with dedicated meeting space, a traditional classroom style can be used for lecture and large-group discussion, and one or more breakout rooms will be available for small-group discussions.

AUDIOVISUAL REQUIREMENTS

Effective trainers use a variety of supplemental media to emphasize training points and to maintain the trainees' attention. Among the most popular audiovisual tools are flip charts, hard-copy overhead transparencies, videos, and PowerPoint overheads.

Many trainers use flip charts to illustrate training points. If they are used, trainers should:

- Assure that the charts are in full view of all trainees.
- Not talk to the flip chart; maintain eye contact with trainees.
- Assure that there is an ample supply of flip chart pages before the session begins.

Sometimes, especially in interactive sessions such as **brainstorming** with trainees, trainers use all of the space on a flip chart and must continue on a separate page. Trainers should consider where completed pages will be placed and how, if at all, they will be adhered to a wall to be in full view of all trainees.

Handouts

Handouts can supplement and enhance training. Perhaps a handout contains a brief outline of the training or an exercise to be completed after applicable discussion. Alternatively, the trainer may wish to circulate a worksheet to be completed as a sequence of training points is addressed.

The best use of handouts occurs as the trainer:

- Assures that each handout enhances the opportunities for learning in a way that is more appropriate than other alternatives.

- Proofreads (more than once) to assure that there are no word processing or other errors.
- Assures that multiple handouts are in proper sequence.
- Confirms that handouts are brief, well-organized, and relevant to the training.
- Confirms that handout information corresponds to training points.
- Allows space for trainees to take notes, if desired.

Trainers should consider when handouts should be circulated (e.g., before or at the beginning of the training session, or when they are discussed).

Videos

Trainers teaching relatively generic topics have an increasingly large variety of off-the-shelf videos available to them. Those employed by large tourism and hospitality organizations may additionally have customized videos. Before using these tools, trainers should be certain that a video is the most appropriate way to deliver training content. Off-the-shelf videos rarely explain a training concept exactly as the trainer desires. Some revision in training content is required or, alternatively, time is needed before and/or after the video is shown to explain differences between the training and video content.

Timing of the video activity is another concern. A video may be so short that its excellent quality is marginalized by the effort required to obtain and set up the equipment. (*Note*: This is especially so when, for example, video equipment must be rented.) Alternatively, longer-than-desired videos require the trainer to judge whether time should be taken from other training or whether only part of the video should be shown. The latter problem becomes more significant when a video must be stopped and restarted to eliminate unnecessary material.

Trainers should preview videos to determine the differences, if any, between their content and that desired for training. Further, if discussion materials supplement an off-the-shelf video, they may need revision to fit the trainer's objectives. Trainers should decide whether to show the video uninterrupted or to make training points as the video is shown.

Video equipment must be set up before the training begins, and the trainer must know how to use it. If the video must be cued to a starting point, this should also be done before the training begins. *Note*: New technology provides increased alternatives to show videos and, especially for less tech-savvy trainers, the possibility of equipment set-up problems also increases. For example, VCR and DVD players have traditionally been connected to television monitors, and it is relatively straight-forward to do so. Today, equipment set-ups that connect VCR or DVD players to digital projectors used to display PowerPoint overheads on screens eliminate the need for television monitors. Many trainers also use their laptop computers to play DVDs directly through a digital projector and require no other video playback equipment. As always, wise trainers know how to use the video equipment, and they ensure that the system is working properly before the training begins.

PowerPoint Overheads

PowerPoint overheads are increasingly used today. Technology makes them easy to develop, and they can have significant visual impact. Their basic purposes are the same as those of overhead transparencies: to supplement, emphasize, and facilitate lecture or discussion points. Many tactics applicable to developing overhead transparencies are also useful for PowerPoints. These include limiting the number of words, using a font style and size that is easy to read, and including appropriate and interesting graphics. Unfortunately, some trainers incorporate design features into their PowerPoints that are annoying and can even distract from training presentations. Examples include word or phrase dropdown features, animated graphics, and computer-generated noises. There are literally thousands of Internet Web sites providing information about PowerPoint development and presentation techniques.[1]

Savvy trainers who use PowerPoints allow appropriate time to connect their computer to the LED projector, and they understand that details are important. Hospitality operations that generate significant meeting business typically have audiovisual technicians to set up the equipment and to manage the technical difficulties that can occur. Unfortunately, trainers in other organizations do not typically have technical expertise available. The best suggestion is to allow ample time for

Training room set-up and presentation style can be varied depending on available resources and training goals to create an ideal training program.
Courtesy Digital Vision

equipment set-up and have a backup plan such as the availability of hard-copy over-head transparencies.

Trainers often provide hard-copy handouts of their PowerPoint overheads on formats that include two or three images per page, with additional space available for trainees to record notes. This provides an organized way for trainees to take notes, minimizes the number of notes that need to be taken, and provides convenient resources for trainees' use after the training is completed.

Facilitating Group Training Sessions

6. **Discuss procedures to facilitate group training:**
   Presenting group training
   Interacting with group participants
   Conducting group training exercises
   Managing special training issues

Effective trainers must be good communicators. This is important when an on-job training method is used, but it is especially critical for group training. Trainers have fewer opportunities to solicit feedback and to determine whether training content is understood.

TRAINER PRESENTATION SKILLS

Many group trainers are excellent public speakers who can keep their trainees' attention. One does not need to be a professional speaker to be an effective group trainer. What is required is a planned, organized, and practiced approach to training delivery that avoids common public speaking mistakes. Trainers who have this foundation of public speaking skills will likely deliver an effective training session.

Let's discuss the three steps identified in Figure 7.8.

Step 1 indicates that the training should begin with an *introduction*:

Ice breaker (training): A brief exercise facilitated at the beginning of a training session that allows trainees to meet each other, provides a transition from the job to the training environment, and generates enthusiasm about the training.

- Use a warm and genuine introduction. If necessary, the trainer should introduce him or herself and allow the trainees to introduce themselves. The introduction should focus on what's in it from the perspective of the trainees.
- The training session can be previewed. Training goals can be noted, and trainees can be informed about training tactics.
- Establish training requirements, including those about restroom and coffee breaks, cell phone usage, trainee participation, and related issues.
- If applicable, use an **ice breaker** to help trainees transition into the session.
- Indicate whether questions should be asked when they arise during the session or, alternatively, whether they should be held for discussion at its end.
- Gain the trainees' attention. Ask for trainee anecdotes or tell one's own stories about situations related to the training topic.

A Note About Public Speaking

Numerous surveys over many years have queried the general public about their greatest fears. Surprisingly (at least to professional trainers!), a fear of public speaking is near the top of the list of many survey respondents. While fears about public speaking might be greatest when one addresses an audience of strangers, it can also be a concern to some trainers who interact with trainees with whom the trainer works every day.

Trainers who are competent in the subject matter, who have properly prepared for the session, and who recognize that the goal of training is to improve on-job performance (not to impress the trainees!) will likely have reduced public speaking anxieties. Over time, they will be able to speak to large or small groups without stress, and public speaking activities will become an enjoyable part of their experience.

Effective public speaking begins with a well-planned training lesson that identifies the main and subpoints to be addressed. Chapter 6 explained the role of a training lesson in organizing training sessions, identifying the need for handouts or other supplements, and specifying allowable time for the entire session and for the training points within it. Figure 7.8 shows the three basic steps in presenting a group training session.

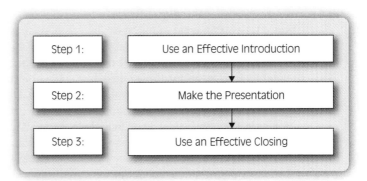

FIGURE 7.8: Three Steps to a Successful Group Training Session

A note about humor: many trainers begin a training session by telling a humorous story. This can gain the trainees' attention, transition them from the workplace to the training, and provide a subconscious message that the training will be enjoyable. However, inappropriate humor can hinder the training, and many topics that were socially acceptable in the past are totally inappropriate today. In a workplace that is becoming more culturally diverse, it is increasingly difficult to anticipate how a humorous story will be viewed by all of the trainees.

Step 2 in Figure 7.8 also addresses *training delivery*:

- Limit the number of training points. This is easy when an effectively developed training lesson provides the presentation outline.
- Discuss topics in the same sequence as they are noted in the introduction.
- Use transitions between main points (e.g., "Now that you know how to assemble the equipment, let's learn how to safely operate it.").
- Conclude each main point with a summary (e.g., "To this point, you have learned that the equipment must be operated according to the manufacturer's instructions. Now let's learn how to use it for some specialty items.").
- Manage questions effectively. Suggestions include repeating the question, providing a response, or, alternatively, asking other trainees to provide a suggested response.
- Be aware of nonverbal communication. Body language can frequently tell the trainees more than the trainer can say. Facial expressions can suggest that the trainer is frustrated with the trainees' inability to learn, or pacing back and forth may suggest that the trainer is bored.
- Use an outline to stay organized. A well-developed training lesson is, in part, an outline of the training points.

Experienced trainers keep trainees tuned in to the session by providing methods for their active involvement and by asking open-ended questions of all trainees (not just of those who volunteer). They speak at the appropriate volume and pace. Trainers should avoid slang terms and jargon that hinder communication effectiveness. This is frequently a challenge because of the diverse group of employees in many organizations. Effective trainers pronounce words correctly, change voice tones, and avoid public speaking errors such as the frequent use of stalling expressions (e.g., "you know," "let's see," "ahhhhh," and "like, you know").

Step 3 in Figure 7.8 indicates the need for an *effective closing*. Summarize main points and refer to something noted during the introduction: "When we began the training, I indicated that you would learn how to safely operate the equipment." It should also involve a call to action about what the trainees should do: "Now that you've learned how to safely operate the equipment, please do so all the time. The right way is the safe way, and there should be no compromise in this standard."

Group training will not automatically be effective if the trainer is a good public speaker, but training cannot be effective if the trainer is not a good communicator. Fortunately, this skill can be enhanced through experience and when the trainer has an interest in improving communication skills.

INTERACTING WITH GROUP PARTICIPANTS

A lecture-only presentation is often an ineffective way to facilitate a group training session. Trainers must attempt to get the trainees involved in their own learning process. One effective way is to ask questions and lead discussions.

Human Resources Management:
CURRENT EVENTS 7.2

On-job training may be the best approach to teach new employees the skills required to perform physical tasks in the workplace. However, a 2002 study by the American Society for Training and Development (ASTD) found that more than 70 percent of organizations consider classroom training the best choice.* Reasons for classroom instruction preferences included allowing employees to concentrate on learning, taking them away from the workplace, and access to experienced and knowledgeable trainers. Trainees could also interact with others and learn from those with diverse backgrounds. Opportunities to interact with capable instructors and interested peers is seen as the best way for trainees to acquire the competencies needed to move ahead in their careers and help their companies move forward.

*Reported in "Training for Today's Business Needs: An AMA White Paper." Retrieved from *www.amanet.org* on May 27, 2006.

Some trainers discuss a training point, ask for questions, and facilitate a discussion stemming from the questions before continuing to the next point. Others ask questions more frequently throughout the training session. Effective trainers do not lecture extensively, read from lecture notes, stray from an organized sequence of training points, or move on when they sense trainees do not understand concepts being presented.

What should trainers do if it appears that only one or a few trainees do not understand the material? When redundancy is not necessary for the majority of trainees, it is generally best to continue the training. Then the trainer can initiate a discussion with applicable trainees about troublesome concepts outside of the training session.

Basic principles can help trainers guide discussions:

- *Have an attitude of openness.* Trainers should not be defensive and have to sell a training point. They should solicit questions, consider discussion feedback, and use it as a benchmark for assessing comprehension. Trainees who note, "When I tried that, it didn't work," are providing excellent comments to direct the trainer's responses and improve the training.
- *Treat trainees as professionals (not subordinates).* Successful tourism and hospitality organizations promote teamwork, and this is as important during training as at any other time.
- *Ask clear and direct questions.* The question, "Does everyone understand?" will not be as helpful as an open-ended question such as, "Why is it important to consider a guest's concern when addressing complaints?"

- *Invite participants to make comments.* Some trainees like to dominate the training. Others may be passive but able to contribute when requested to do so. A question such as "Sally, what do you think about this technique?" can be very helpful to generate new opinions and information.
- *Allow only one person to talk at a time.* This rule is needed to show respect and is important to control the training environment. Comments such as "It's important that everyone has a chance to express an opinion," or the question, "I'd like to learn what you think about this. Who wants to be first?" can often be helpful.
- *Listen carefully; show respect for all ideas.* Trainers should listen to the remarks of everyone to understand what is being said. The common mistake of formulating a response while tuning out additional points must be avoided.
- *Encourage more than one response.* Effective trainers make trainees feel at ease and subtly encourage responses, including questions and comments from everyone.
- *Don't be afraid of silence.* If there is no response to a question, ask another one or use it to guide the next interaction: "Since there's no response, I'd like to repeat what I'm asking in another way."
- *Keep the discussion focused.* Using a training lesson is an excellent way to do this. Trainee discussions can be more difficult to guide, but an effective trainer knows when to steer the discussion back to the applicable topic: "That's an interesting idea, John. It would be great to discuss that, but we should focus on inventory management right now to ensure that we'll have time to cover everything."

Experienced trainers know that more rather than less time than planned is often needed to fully address a training concept. To compensate, they work hard to stay on point. They also evaluate training sessions as they evolve to make time adjustments so they can focus on the most important training points.

THREE TYPES OF TRAINEES

Trainers are likely to encounter three very different types of trainees in group sessions, and each must be managed differently. Some trainees are passive and much less responsive than their peers. To include them, trainers can:

- Repeat questions
- Restate questions
- Provide examples of training points; ask trainees for additional examples
- Break a training point into more specific elements, and ask a passive trainee how an element relates to a larger concept
- Directly question a passive trainee about the topic

Other trainees wish to dominate the session or discussion. Tactics to manage them include:

- Don't call on them.
- Don't make eye contact with them.
- When they speak, wait for a moment, thank them for their input, do not make a comment about that input, and immediately call on another trainee.
- Ask them to take notes during future training sessions.

Sometimes a trainee may become disruptive during a session, and his or her actions cannot be left unnoticed. Then it is appropriate to:

- Ask the trainee to please make positive contributions.
- Request that all conversations relate to the discussion.
- Remain enthusiastic and friendly, and continue with the training.

During the next training break, the trainer should talk with the disruptive trainee, note the problem(s), and personally request that the behavior cease. *Note:* The trainer should express concern about the trainee's behavior rather than about the trainee personally.

CONDUCTING GROUP TRAINING EXERCISES

Creative trainers can utilize role-play, case study, and brainstorming exercises that allow trainees to more fully participate in and benefit from the training.

Role-Play Exercises

Role-plays are group training exercises in which trainees pretend to be persons in situations addressed by the training who apply information presented in the training. Sometimes called dialog training, a role-play exercise can be very useful because it allows trainees to practice what they have learned in a risk-free situation.

Consider a training session that addresses how to handle guest complaints or how to discuss an unacceptable budget variance with a unit manager. The appropriate techniques could be explained, a question-and-answer discussion could evolve, and a role-play could be initiated.

Trainees might be broken into three-person teams. One trainee could pretend to be the trained staff member applying the principles just taught. A second trainee could role-play the individual with whom the trainee is interacting. The third trainee could be an observer. The trainee using proper tactics could respond to comments made by the second trainee, and the trainee observer could note how the situation was managed. At the conclusion of the role-play, the trainees could switch roles until each practiced and demonstrated the skills. Final components of the role-play exercise could be a report back to the convened group and a reinforcement and summary by the trainer.

Principles to help trainers manage role-plays include:

- Provide a complete orientation.
- Explain the purpose: to allow trainees to apply training principles in a risk-free situation.
- Stress the need for objective feedback. Trainees critiquing their peers should focus on training points.
- Allow participants to develop role-play situations.
- Permit participants to develop factors for evaluation. Assume that the trainer presented five tactics to manage guest complaints. Each trainee team could determine how to assess the extent to which each of the tactics was addressed.
- Allow time for each trainee to consider the strategies to be used when interacting with other trainees in the role-play.

Case Study Exercises

A case study allows trainees to study a real-world situation and to use what was learned in training to address the case study problem(s). Two examples of training content that could be supplemented with a case study are:

- An organization with high staff turnover rates could be described to determine what might be causing the problem.
- A budget and income statement could be shown. Follow-up analysis could allow trainees to determine where financial variances exist and to suggest what might be causing them.

Prepared case studies are available from numerous sources. One of the best is contemporary textbooks that address topics covered by the training. Alternatively, trainers can write short (several paragraphs) case studies that focus directly on specific training session topics.

To best manage case studies, trainers should:

- Assure that cases are realistic
- Incorporate training concepts
- Allow trainees time to study the case
- Serve as a facilitator when leading case discussion
- Summarize each case's learning points

Some trainers separate trainees into teams, with each team addressing the same or a different case. Each team reads and prepares a response to the case study and reports its findings and recommendations to the convened group of trainees. A follow-up discussion is then facilitated by the trainer. When one case study is discussed by different teams, the learning objective typically emphasizes the largest possible number of perspectives. When trainee teams consider different cases, the learning objective may consider a wider range of situations to be addressed by using the training points covered in the session.

Brainstorming

Brainstorming is a method of group problem solving or alternative generation in which all group members suggest possible ideas. A typical use of this tactic is in a work setting where groups of affected staff members nominate suggested ideas to address a problem or to suggest alternative courses of action.

In today's increasingly diverse workforce, staff members with widely different backgrounds and experiences bring a broad range of perspectives to a decision-making process. Creative trainers can use this diversity to improve training. Training exercises can allow trainees to brainstorm how a training point could be applied in a work situation, alternative solutions to case study or role-play exercise issues, or about the development and/or conduct of out-of-session projects.

Trainers who use brainstorming exercises should develop ground rules that include:

- The encouragement of creative ideas
- A request that alternatives generated during a brainstorming session not be evaluated until all alternatives are expressed
- The opportunity to piggyback on ideas (i.e., to allow one idea to suggest a variation of another)
- The provision of necessary time for trainees to study the ideas presented, and to then continue the brainstorming session, if possible
- The opportunity for the trainer and trainees to organize or categorize ideas and to evaluate them when the brainstorming session is completed

Trainers and trainees will likely find that brainstorming tactics used during training can be useful opportunities for generating ideas for process improvement when the staff members return to the work environment.

MANAGING SPECIAL TRAINING ISSUES

A wide range of important training issues should be considered because, regardless of how minor they appear, they can dramatically impact training outcomes:

- *Be aware of personal mannerisms that can be annoying or distracting.* A trainer's body language can distract trainees. Some trainers may not be aware of these expressions and actions and could easily correct them if they were. One suggestion is that trainers can make a presentation to professional colleagues and solicit objective feedback, or they can arrange for a videotaping of a training session to learn something that might otherwise be overlooked.
- *Schedule training so applicable procedures can be implemented on a timely basis.* Hopefully, trainees will become enthused about their training and will want to immediately begin applying the knowledge and skills they have learned. This may not be possible if, for example, necessary equipment has not been installed, or when one phase of an initiative must be implemented before a

follow-up phase. Then it might be useful to delay training and/or to provide introductory training followed by detailed training when content can be implemented on a timely basis.

■ *Effectively manage trainees who don't want to be trained.* Tactics include making a direct request (e.g., "Joe, we're looking for input from everyone after this discussion, so you'll need to be prepared for it"). It may also be useful to take a short training break so the trainer can personally speak with an inattentive trainee. There may be other times when many trainees appear unresponsive. Then it becomes necessary to reconsider the training approach and to implement efforts to reduce concerns.

■ *Don't attempt to accomplish too much.* Allow sufficient time for practice (skill training) and discussion (group training). Realize that training often takes longer than the planned time.

■ *Listen to trainees.* Be alert for trainee overload and side conversations, blank stares, and a preoccupation with nontraining activities. Remember also that the trainees' body language can speak to the trainer.

■ *Be flexible.* Change the training schedule when necessary. Be alert to the need to change training content, training location, or to use alternative training delivery formats to make the training more beneficial.

■ *When applicable, field-test (pilot) the training.* Assume that new technology will be used to manage inventory data. Should that technology be installed in the quickest manner possible, and should all affected staff members be trained accordingly? Alternatively, is a phased implementation of the new technology with staggered training most appropriate?

■ *Use humor appropriately.* It is difficult to prejudge one person's perspective of humor relative to many training topics, especially in a large group training session.

■ *Keep the training on track of its stated objectives.* This is easily done when training plans and lessons have been carefully developed and are consistently used. The trainer's role is to facilitate training by pacing it according to a realistic schedule. *Note:* A trainer's experience with a specific session will be useful input to its revision.

■ *Don't reinvent the wheel; if cost-effective materials are available, use them.* A corollary to this principle is also important: don't rewrite training materials that have been developed in previous sessions. The use of an organized training handbook (file) can be a great way to ensure that materials can easily be located when needed.

■ *Rehearse before training.* Just as trainees must practice to learn a task, trainers should also practice to gain experience with their presentation. Be aware of appearance and hygiene.

■ *Don't develop a trainer's ego.* Remember that the objective of training is to improve the trainees' performance, not to impress trainees with the trainer's knowledge, skills, or experience.

■ *Keep training sessions as short as practical.* Experienced trainers know that several short training sessions are better than one relatively long one.

Human Resources MANAGEMENT ISSUES   (7.2)

"We really do try hard to keep our staff members updated with new information so they can be on the cutting edge of their jobs," said Rodger. "However, it's difficult to do this when you're the director of human resources for a relatively small contract management company that wants to think and act like a large competitor, but just doesn't have the resources to do it." Rodger was speaking with Francine, his counterpart at a relatively large lodging organization as they met at a hospitality conference focusing on training.

"I know what you mean, Rodger," said Francine. "I supervise four staff members in my department who spend most of their time on training activities. Even with that commitment of resources, it's hard to do all that we want to do to assure that our company can meet its goals and help our staff to attain their professional development objectives."

"I guess the bigger a company becomes, then, the more challenges it has, and a large company is not necessarily any further ahead than a smaller organization even if it has more resources available," said Rodger. "No organization has all of the time, money, and human resources that it would like to have, and each of us must do what we can, given what we have to best meet our needs. However, can you give me some advice about several concerns I'm now confronting as we think about the best ways to plan group training programs for experienced staff?"

"Well, Rodger, you know how valuable free advice is! I'd be glad to help. What are your questions?"

How should Francine respond to the following questions posed by Rodger?

QUESTIONS

1. We want to develop a supervisory program for entry-level employees who have recently been promoted to a supervisory provision. How should we categorize and organize the basic supervisory principles to be taught, and where do we find training programs to address these concepts?
2. How can I educate my supervisors and managers who are group trainers that just lecturing to trainees is not likely to be an effective training tactic?
3. Many of our staff members have been turned off by previous group training methods. How can we get them excited about new training efforts that involve more interactive training activities?
4. Based on your experience, what are the most significant mistakes that group trainers make as they present their training programs? (I want to assure that these topics are discussed in a train-the-trainer program being planned.)

- *Recognize the importance of the training environment.* Experienced trainers know that the environment of the meeting room is often more detrimental to training effectiveness than is the training content or its delivery.
- *Have backup contingencies for problems.* Some problems such as inoperative audiovisual equipment and out-of-place training materials can be anticipated. Others such as building emergencies or trainee health problems will have generated fewer planning considerations. However, should these instances occur, trainees are likely to look to the trainer for the appropriate reactions.
- *Respect the trainees' knowledge and experience.* Wise trainers recognize that adult trainees bring a wide variety of personal experiences, attitudes, core values, and preconceptions to their training experience. They recognize and use them to deliver the best possible training.
- *Link training to assessment and performance.* Hopefully, training will show a cause-and-effect relationship. Training will cause behavior change, and this will yield a result (effect) that is beneficial to the trainees and the organization.
- *Have fun!* Trainees cannot learn if they do not enjoy their training. What is pleasurable to one trainee may not be for another. Using a variety of training tactics that involve active trainee participation is preferable to less interactive approaches.

Training Evaluation

7. **Discuss the training evaluation process:**

   Reasons for evaluation

   Levels of evaluation

   Methods of evaluation

Figure 7.1 notes that evaluation is the final step in the training process. Evaluation can suggest the need to repeat the entire planning process from Step 1 when training needs were identified or, alternatively, to refocus efforts on interim planning steps. Consider a training program to improve supervisory skills to reduce turnover. Assume the initial definition of training needs (Step 1) led to a training program that was planned and implemented (Steps 2 to 8) to address improvements in how supervisors interacted with employees. Also assume that post-training evaluation indicated that the turnover rate was not reduced. Instead, further analysis revealed that the problem (Step 1) was really selection and orientation of staff members. In this example, trainers may need to plan and implement an entirely different training program to properly address turnover.

In a more common situation, post-training evaluation may indicate that the program was less than successful. It did focus on the correct problems (Steps 1 and 2), but the training plans and/or lessons, or the way trainees were prepared and the training was conducted, contributed to the disappointing results. Figure 7.1 notes that only selected steps rather than the entire training process may need revision to improve training results.

REASONS TO EVALUATE TRAINING

Time, money, and labor are increasingly in limited supply. Managers must determine whether their commitment of resources to planning and implementing training procedures is a better use than are alternatives. This is one reason that the evaluation of training efforts is important. More specific reasons to evaluate training include to:

- *Assess the extent to which training achieved planned results.* Training objectives have a two-fold purpose: (1) to identify competencies to be addressed in training, and (2) to provide a benchmark against which training can be evaluated.
- *Identify strengths and weaknesses of training.* Few training programs are 100 percent effective or ineffective. Some training lessons are better than others, some training activities are more useful than their counterparts, and some trainers may be more effective than their peers. Successful evaluation can identify aspects of the training that should be continued and elements that may require revision.
- *Determine the success of individual trainees.* Trainees who are successful (i.e., who achieve planned results on the job) will not require remedial training. However, training for others may need revision and/or repetition. Assessment of individual trainees is relatively easy when an individualized, on-job training method is used, but it is more difficult with a group training process.
- *Gather information to help justify future programs.* As noted previously, limited resources require their effective use. When the success of a training activity is quantified, objective information becomes available to help justify future training efforts. Alternatively, managers can determine whether resources are better invested in other ways to improve the organization.
- *Establish a database for future decisions.* Assume that a training program for dishwashers has been successful, and staff members can wash serviceware and operate equipment according to standards. If there is a need (desire) for faster output (clean dishes), then increased speed may need to come from an increased use of technology rather than from improved dishwasher skills.
- *Determine trainees who are eligible for future training.* Some organizations provide educational or training activities in formalized career development programs that require prerequisite training. Other companies have formal or informal fast-track programs in which selected trainees who have successfully completed training programs are eligible for additional training opportunities. This training, in turn, leads to increased promotional considerations as vacancies occur. In both of these and related instances, managers must know whether and to what extent individual trainees successfully completed the training.

■ *Assess the costs and benefits of training.* This reason for training evaluation has already been suggested. The expenditure of any resource must generate a return greater than the cost of resources allocated for it. Some benefits of training, including improved morale and increased interest in attaining quality goals, are difficult to quantify. Other benefits, including improved guest service skills and reduced operating costs for a specified task, may be easier to quantify, and both could be assessed by training evaluation.

■ *Reinforce major points for trainees.* Some training evaluation methods, including objective tests and performance appraisal interviews, allow the evaluators to reinforce the most important training points. For example, questions on a written assessment likely address the most important training concepts. If they are self-graded or reviewed by the trainer, reinforcement of these important points becomes possible. Likewise, if performance appraisal interviews address training concepts, additional opportunity for reinforcement arises.

■ *Assess trainees' reactions to training.* Trainers who are interested in improving training programs want to gain the trainees' perspectives about the programs. Anonymous input gained before, during, and after training can be helpful in this assessment.

■ *Assess trainers' reactions to training.* "There's always a better way," is an old saying that applies to training as well as to other management tactics. Trainers who have used a training lesson, for example, may well have ideas about ways to improve it in the future.

LEVELS OF TRAINING EVALUATION

Many managers think about training evaluation in the context of an after-training assessment used to determine its effectiveness. While training should be evaluated at its completion (and, perhaps, many months after its completion as well), evaluation can also be helpful before training even begins and while it is conducted.

Human Resources Management:
CURRENT EVENTS 7.3

There is nothing more current than today's news. To view an excellent source of daily news of interest to human resources professionals, check out the Web site for Workforce Management (*www.workforce.com*). Although the site is not specific to the tourism and hospitality industry, you can type "hospitality training" into the site's search box, and numerous current news features and articles will appear.

All training evaluation methods must meet at least five assessment criteria. The methods must be:

- *Valid.* They must measure what they are supposed to measure. Assume that a training objective focuses on the ability of trainees to successfully complete an inventory count using methods taught during training. Trainee demonstration of scanning equipment operation and proper use of inventory counting procedures suggests that the training was successful (at least at the time of the demonstration). In contrast, a training assessment that queried trainees about issues such as "Did you like the training?" and "Did the trainer seem enthusiastic?" would not allow trainers to determine whether training objectives were attained.
- *Reliable.* Training evaluation methods are **reliable** when they consistently provide the same results. Training activities that are implemented in the same way by the same trainers using the same training resources and procedures to employees in the same position may be consistent. Will the results will be the same or similar each time the training is replicated? Trainers do not know unless the same evaluation methods are used.
- *Objective.* Objective evaluation methods provide quantitative (measurable) training assessments. Acquisition of knowledge can be objectively measured by performance on a well-designed test. Efficiency in a skill might be best assessed by observing the trainee's acceptable performance of the task after training. Then acceptable performance can be defined as procedures that are in concert with those taught during training.
- *Practical.* A training evaluation method is practical when the time and effort required for the assessment is worth its results. Knowledge assessments that require trainees to memorize mundane facts and skill demonstrations that are benchmarked against staff with extensive experience and efficiency in performing the task are not practical.
- *Simple.* An evaluation method is simple when it is easily applied by the trainer, easily understood by the trainees, and when results are easy to assess and analyze by those evaluating the training.

Let's look at before, during, and after training methods that incorporate these assessment concerns.

Evaluation Before Training

Assume that a trainee participated in a food safety training session and completed a knowledge assessment at its conclusion. Assume further that the trainee missed only two questions out of the twenty that were asked. Most trainers would help the trainee to learn the concepts addressed in the two missed questions. However, many trainers would likely conclude that the training was successful because the participant scored 90 percent (18 questions correct divided by 20 questions total). In fact, the training could really have been a waste of the organization's resources and the trainee's time if the trainee already knew the concepts addressed by the 18 questions that were answered correctly before the session began. In actuality, the after-training evaluation really measured what the trainee knew when the training was completed rather than what he or she learned from the training session.

To address this concern, some trainers use a **pretest/post-test** evaluation. A trainer can identify key concepts to be addressed during the training. These concepts are addressed in a pretest administered before the training begins. This same measurement tool is administered at the conclusion of training. The improvement in scores between the pre- and post-test represents a measure of training effectiveness.

Other advantages of pretest/post-test evaluation include:

▪ Provides trainees with an overview (preview) of the training
▪ Helps trainees to identify some of the most important concepts to be addressed in training
▪ Presents an opportunity for trainers to preview the lesson and suggest priority learning points before training begins

As is true with other training evaluation methods, it may help to administer the post-training assessment several months (or even longer) after training is completed. This tactic can help determine the extent to which training information has been retained and applied in the workplace.

Another pretraining evaluation tactic involves an exercise that requests trainees to answer the following concern: "If this training is ideal, I will learn the following from it." This exercise can be part of an introductory session that previews subject matter. Trainees might be asked to retain their responses to this ideal training exercise until the end of training. Then they could undertake a post-training assessment to note their perceptions about the extent to which the training was ideal. Figure 7.9 illustrates a self-evaluation form that could be used.

Evaluation During Training

Effective trainers indicate in an introductory session that they will ask for feedback during the session. As this feedback is solicited, trainers can obtain a first-half reality check to yield information helpful to improve the remainder of the training. Trainers facilitating group sessions can ask trainees to write anonymous responses to questions such as:

▪ I wish you would stop doing (saying). . .
▪ I hope we continue to. . .
▪ I don't understand. . .
▪ I hope you will begin to. . .
▪ A concept that I wish you would discuss further is. . .
▪ A concept that I really want to learn more about that has yet to be discussed is. . .

The major point is to learn how to maximize use of the remaining training time. Then revisions to training content and/or delivery methods can better assure attainment of training objectives.

Pretest/Post-test evaluation: A method used to evaluate training that involves administering the same test to trainees before (pretest) and after (post-test) the training. Positive differences in post-test scores provide an objective measure of training effectiveness.

**TRAINING
TOPIC:** _____

**NAME OF TRAINEE
(OPTIONAL):** _____

TO BE COMPLETED BEFORE TRAINING	TO BE COMPLETED AFTER TRAINING

If this Training Program is Ideally Effective, I Will Learn the Following:

To What Extent did you Learn What You Wanted to Learn (Check One)?

	NOT ALL	SOMEWHAT	VERY MUCH
1. _____	☐	☐	☐
2. _____	☐	☐	☐
3. _____	☐	☐	☐
4. _____	☐	☐	☐
5. _____	☐	☐	☐

COMMENTS:

FIGURE 7.9: Training Self-Assessment Form

Evaluation After Training

After-training evaluation can help assess whether training achieved its planned results. It may also identify how training sessions might be improved and assess the trainees' success. Numerous evaluation methods can be used. Experienced trainers often employ more than one method and analyze the combined results to yield a comprehensive assessment of training results.

TRAINING EVALUATION METHODS

Several training evaluation methods are commonly used. Hopefully, more than one tactic will be used. Each can provide anecdotal information that, in total, can suggest training outcomes.

Common assessment methods include:

■ *Objective tests.* These can be written, oral, and/or skill-based, and can be traditional written exams, oral assessments (utilizing open-ended questions), and/or after-training demonstrations. Written and oral assessments are typically used to assess after-training knowledge, and skill-based assessments address physical (skill) proficiencies. Written exams can be multiple-choice, true/false, fill-in-the-blank, matching, short-answer, or essay. Multiple-choice and true/false questions are most used in tourism and hospitality organizations because they

What About Anonymity of Trainee Evaluations?

Input from any training evaluation method is not useful unless it is truthful. It is generally easier to obtain anonymous input from group trainees than from those participating in individualized training. An obvious reason is that trainees perceive that "There is safety in numbers."

The best evaluations are provided by unidentified trainees who do not fear on-job retaliation (especially if they are supervised by the trainer), and those who believe the request for input is genuine and that the results will be used. Tourism and hospitality organizations with a culture of respect for employees and a history of utilizing their input for improvements will likely obtain useful feedback. By contrast, organizations that suffer from adversarial relationships between supervisors and staff will have great difficulty in obtaining useful information by any evaluation method.

Given these issues, should names of any evaluators be requested? The answer is "probably not," unless there is a unique and specific reason to do so. A compromise is that some trainers request anonymous input and then seek out trainees to provide more detailed one-on-one input. Mentors in some organizations receive trainee input and summarize this information in reports to human resources or other applicable staff members.

Objective tests: Assessment tools such as multiple-choice and true/false instruments that have only one correct answer and, therefore, a reduced need for trainers to interpret the trainees' responses.

Manage by walking around: A management and supervision technique that involves a manager's presence in the workplace to determine if there are challenges that require corrective action, to praise staff for a job well-done, and to learn how and where one's management expertise, knowledge, and skills can best be utilized.

Critical incident: Any situation that identifies behaviors that contribute to success or failure on the job.

are **objective tests.** There is only one correct answer, little or no interpretation is needed, and minimal time is required for trainees to complete the exam and for trainers to score it. (Lengthy exams can be computer-scored using optical scan [op-scan] sheets completed by the trainees.) Objective measurements should be written after training objectives and instructional materials are developed, and a separate assessment should be used for each performance objective in the training lesson.

■ *Observation of performance after training.* Managers, supervisors, and trainers can **manage by walking around** and, in the process, note whether knowledge and skills taught during training are being applied. Storeroom personnel can be observed as they receive incoming products, and procedures used can be compared to those presented during training. *Note*: When proper procedures are used, a "Great job!" compliment is always in order. By contrast, a coaching activity to remind staff members about incorrectly performed procedures may also be needed.

■ *Records of events (***critical incidents***).* Assume there has been a theft of food products from a storage area after training in appropriate accounting and control procedures has been presented. Subsequent investigation determines that the recommended procedures were not used. The training program would not be considered effective, and staff with responsibilities to double-check as part of the inventory control process must, at the least, be retrained. Alternatively, procedures may need to be revised and followed with updated training in revised procedures.

■ *Self-reports.* Figures 7.10 to 7.12 illustrate formats for a questioning process that could provide partial input for training evaluation.

Figure 7.10 illustrates a simple rating scale containing evaluation factors that trainees can rate (from very unacceptable to very acceptable). Figure 7.11 lists open-ended questions to which trainees can respond. Finally, Figure 7.12 illustrates the format for and questions that might be applicable to a group training session that involves numerous training lessons.

■ *Interviews with trainees and/or trainers.* The use of open-ended questions by trainers, managers, mentors, and/or human resources personnel may provide useful input about the training. As well, trainers can be questioned by their supervisor and/or human resources staff for the same purpose.

■ *Trainee surveys.* Trainees can be questioned immediately after training, months after training, and/or during performance evaluation sessions about their training perspectives. As well, general staff opinion surveys can, in part, address training issues.

■ *Third-party opinions.* Feedback from guests can help assess training that addressed aspects of products and service that affect them. The use of **mystery shoppers** in applicable types of hospitality operations is another example. Feedback can also be generated by comment cards, interviews, and/or follow-up surveys with guests.

■ *Analysis of operating data.* Training that addresses guest service and food costs should result in, respectively, increased guest service scores and lowered food

Mystery shopper: A person posing as a guest who observes and experiences an organization's products and services during a visit and who then reports findings to managers.

TRAINING TOPIC: _____			
EVALUATION FACTOR	**RATING FACTOR**		
TIME SPENT ON TOPIC	**VERY UNACCEPTABLE**	**NEUTRAL (NO COMMENT)**	**VERY ACCEPTABLE**
Applicable to job	☐	☐	☐
My interest in topic	☐	☐	☐
Organization of training	☐	☐	☐
Effectiveness of training	☐	☐	☐
Usefulness of training methods	☐	☐	☐
Comfort of training room	☐	☐	☐
My interest in future training sessions: _____			
COMMENTS:			

FIGURE 7.10: Trainee Evaluation Rating Scale

These hotel sales personnel are evaluating a training program at its conclusion. Trainee input is often an important part of an educational program's overall assessment. *Courtesy PhotoDisc, Inc.*

Training Topic: _____

1. The three most useful aspects of the training were:

   _____

   _____

   _____

2. The three least useful aspects of the training were:

   _____

   _____

   _____

3. I will apply the following information learned during the training on the job:

   _____

   _____

   _____

4. The best way(s) to improve the training is by:

   _____

   _____

   _____

5. What I liked about the program:

   _____

   _____

   _____

6. What I disliked about the program:

   _____

   _____

   _____

FIGURE 7.11: Open-Ended Training Evaluation Form

Summary Training Evaluation

Your response to this evaluation will assist us in evaluating different aspects of the program.

Please indicate the extent to which you agree or disagree with the following statements.

5 = STRONGLY AGREE   1 = STRONGLY DISAGREE   **(MARK ONE ANSWER ONLY)**

The training met my expectations.	5	4	3	2	1
The training challenged my thinking.	5	4	3	2	1
The training held my attention.	5	4	3	2	1
The training appropriately involved the participants.	5	4	3	2	1
The subject matter presented was useful and worthwhile to my career.	5	4	3	2	1
The training was well organized.	5	4	3	2	1
The training matched the description as it was announced.	5	4	3	2	1
The training presented information that was new to me.	5	4	3	2	1
As a result of the training, I am more confident of my knowledge and ability.	5	4	3	2	1
The training environment met my expectations.	5	4	3	2	1

COMMENTS:

FIGURE 7.12: Training Summary Evaluation Form

costs if components of these data can be separated to determine how they were influenced by training.

■ *Exit interviews.* Formal and informal conversations with employees who are leaving the organization can provide input that is helpful for training evaluation. Unlike their peers, most departing staff will likely have fewer concerns about providing candid and frank responses to queries about training, among other issues. Managers may learn, for example, that inadequate orientation and initial on-job training contributed to frustrations that resulted in turnover.

FOLLOW-UP DOCUMENTATION

Documentation is a final part of training evaluation. Training records to be maintained in the applicable staff member's personnel file include:

■ Name of trainee
■ Training dates
■ Training topics

- Notes, if any, regarding successful completion
- Other applicable information

This documentation is useful for planning professional development programs, for considering staff member promotions, and for input to interviews for

Human Resources MANAGEMENT ISSUES   (7.3)

"I just don't understand," said Rolando. "I agree with almost every suggestion made by the trainer in this workshop until now. However, all of these formal evaluation ideas seem like a waste of time. I work with the people I train every day. I can easily see if the training has been effective because the employees either do their assigned tasks correctly or they don't. What's the big deal?"

Rolando was talking to Jacelyn, a supervisor peer who worked at the Hilotown Family Restaurant. They were attending a one-day train-the-trainer workshop facilitated by a faculty member from the local college's hospitality management program.

"When she first started talking about training evaluation, I thought the same thing, Rolando," said Jacelyn. "But after the instructor made a few more comments and led the follow-up discussion, I began to see her perspectives about evaluation."

"Well," said Rolando, "it's pretty easy for her to give a simple example of how to do a cost/benefit assessment for reducing dish breakage in a restaurant. However, I'm trying to teach our staff members how to work safely and be hospitable to our guests. How can these benefits be quantified?"

"You're giving great examples to make your point," said Jacelyn. "However, there must be something you can do to determine the effectiveness of training. After all, you can't closely follow every employee every day. Our company does spend a lot of money on training. What would we do if you decided your training was effective, and our boss decided that the training for other people was not worthwhile? Do the limited funds go to others to improve training, to you because you say your training works, or to no department because no one can really justify the funds that are spent?"

QUESTIONS

1. What are your thoughts about Jacelyn's responses to Rolando's concern about training evaluation?
2. Do you think that training evaluation must be all or nothing; that is, must it totally determine the worth of training or else not be done at all?
3. What advice might you give to Rolando as he develops safety and hospitality training programs about what he should do before, during, and after training to provide some assessment of training results?
4. What simple and practical steps could Rolando take to help evaluate the effectiveness of training provided to his new employees to prepare them to work safely and be hospitable to guests?

performance evaluation purposes. Documentation of training is also helpful when trainers develop long- or short-term plans that address training and professional development opportunities for staff members. *Note*: Professional development programs are discussed in Chapter 11.

HUMAN RESOURCES TERMS

The following terms were defined in this chapter:

On-job training	Full-service hotel
Preparation (on-job training)	Limited-service hotel
Coaching	Lectern
Broken cases	Flip chart
Closed-ended question	PowerPoint overheads
Sandwich method (performance appraisal)	Digital projector
Distance education	Overhead transparencies projector
Cross-training	Brainstorming (group training)
Underemployed (job status)	Ice breaker (training)
Job enlargement	Valid (training evaluation measure)
Job enrichment	
Job rotation	Reliable (training evaluation method)
Group training	Pretest/post-test evaluation
Lecture method (group training)	Objective tests
Handouts	Manage by walking around
Demonstration (group training activity)	Critical incident
Breakout (group training activity)	Mystery shopper

FOR YOUR CONSIDERATION

1. Assume that you have been assigned to develop and implement a formalized and organized method of on-job training in your organization.
   a. What are the most important factors you would consider as you identified the experienced staff members who will receive train-the-trainer training?
   b. What training preparation tasks should be the responsibility of the staff member who will be conducting the training?
   c. What training preparation activities should a trainer normally expect to have available in a training handbook or other available resource?

2. Develop a checklist to evaluate the public speaking skills of a trainer who will facilitate a group training session.
3. Think about training sessions in which you have participated. Identify special training issues in addition to those discussed in the chapter that should be of concern to trainers.
4. Assume that you are developing a training lesson on the topic of this chapter. Develop 10 true/false and 10 multiple-choice questions that might be used to assess the trainees' knowledge at the completion of the training.
5. The chapter discusses the concept of managing by walking around. Assume that you are a supervisor of entry-level staff who just received training in food safety concerns. Develop a checklist of items that you might formally or informally attempt to observe while you are managing by walking around.

CASE STUDY: HUMAN RESOURCES MANAGEMENT IN ACTION*

Stacey was the foodservices manager at Global Bank's world headquarters in New York City. The bank employed about 2,000 staff members. Average lunch volume was about 800 meals, and daily lunch revenues were approximately $3,800 at the several foodservices venues. She was unhappy with daily customer counts and revenues, in part because they were lower than expectations based on business at similar accounts operated by her employer, C & L Contract Management Company.

After a series of meetings with her client's representative (the bank's assistant finance manager) and with input from frequent customers, she devised some creative marketing tactics. One involved use of the bank's intranet system to alert employees about daily specials and to allow them to use the system to place orders for pick-up. Another called for an assistant manager to serve in a catering director role and meet with bank employees in their offices to plan parties for special occasions such as birthdays and retirement parties. As well, an existing but inactive group of customer volunteers (the food advisory committee) was reactivated to provide advice, sample menu items, and serve as a general sounding board about the concerns of their employee peers. Other tactics that were nominated included:

- Customer appreciation events
- Frequency of purchase (reward) program
- Theme events
- Guest chef events
- Holiday sale events
- Reinvention of one self-service station to generate excitement

*This case study was contributed by Curtis Lease, District Manager, ARAMARK Business Services, Houston, Texas.

As Stacey looked over these ideas, she was pleased with the creativity they represented. As she looked at the list a little longer, she began to realize that the easiest part of her business turnaround task was to generate ideas to do so. The more difficult task would be to implement the ideas and keep them ongoing.

Training seemed to be a common element in each of the ideas. Some involved group training because all staff members needed to know about the renewed emphasis on customer service and about special concerns that would be generated from customer input. Other ideas involved individual training such as for administrative (secretarial) staff who would be sending and receiving e-mails on the intranet, and the assistant manager who would serve as the function planner. Interestingly, other ideas involved training the customer, really educating them about foodservices functions and the services that would be provided.

Stacey did not know which ideas were best, and she knew that not all of these changes could be made at the same time. As well, perhaps none of them could be implemented quickly. She had to be confident that the best tactics were chosen, that the processes designed were the most appropriate, and that affected staff knew exactly how their job responsibilities and tasks would be changed.

Stacey pondered her plans and thought to herself: "It's easy to decide that efforts to build the business are needed. It is even relatively simple to generate ideas to do so. However, I'm beginning to realize that a much more significant effort will be required to build our business."

Dimension: Strategic

1. Is it important that Stacey do what is necessary to ensure that quality and quantity standards can be attained before these new procedures are put in place? Why or why not?
2. What additional tactics might Stacey have used to generate input about improvement alternatives?
3. What, if any, planning assistance might Stacey request from her regional human resources department since the program is managed by a contract management company?
4. How should Stacey and her team evaluate the worth of the tactics that are implemented?

Dimension: Marketing

1. What long-term tactics can Stacey use to generate input about program improvement from potential customers? From her frequent customers?
2. What persons or groups of persons can assist Stacey in her efforts to tell the story about food services?
3. Should a separate public relations campaign be implemented to inform customers about the benefits of the foodservices program? Why or why not?
4. What process should Stacey and her team use to determine which lunch-building tactics should be implemented?

Dimension: Training

1. What procedures should be used to develop the new processes for using the company's intranet for communication with customers?
2. Assume the intranet communication system will be implemented. What specific techniques can be used to train those who will be working with it?
3. Assume the tactic of naming a catering director will be implemented. Outline the subject matter to be covered in a training lesson to update the assistant manager about his or her staff party planning responsibilities.
4. Who should be responsible for being the point person for interactions with the customer advisory committee? What are the main responsibilities for this task? Which, if any, involve knowledge or additional training?

INTERNET ACTIVITIES

1. To read numerous articles about hospitality training, go to: *www.hotel-online .com*. (Type "training" into the "Find It Fast" box on the Web site.)
2. To view a wide range of general management information about numerous aspects of training and development, go to: *www.managementhelp.org*. (Click on "Training and Development" in the list of management library topics.)
3. The American Management Association has a great Web site with information about training that is useful to human resources personnel in tourism and hospitality organizations. Go to: *www.amanet.org*. (Click on "Free Resources" and then go to "Training Zones.")
4. To view the Web site for one organization that is developing an e-course for the hospitality industry, go to: *www.lexingtoninteractive.com*. There you can read about benefits of e-learning, read about custom course development possibilities, and review information about courses that are available.

ENDNOTE

1. To view applicable Web sites, use your favorite search engine and type in "How to use PowerPoints to train." Review some of these sites to learn basics about developing PowerPoints and recommendations about procedures to use when facilitating training with them.

CHAPTER EIGHT

Compensation Programs

CHAPTER OUTLINE

Compensation Management
Legal Aspects of Compensation Management
  Federal Legislation
  State Legislation
  Local Legislation
Direct Financial Compensation
  Salaries
  Wages
  Incentives and Bonuses
  Tips
Indirect Financial Compensation
  Mandatory Benefits
  Voluntary Benefits
  Other Voluntary Benefits
Nonfinancial Compensation
Human Resources Terms
For Your Consideration
Case Study: Human Resources Management in Action
Internet Activities

CHECKLIST OF CHAPTER LEARNING OBJECTIVES

As a result of satisfactory completion of this chapter, readers will be able to:

1. Describe the differences between extrinsic and intrinsic rewards as they relate to employee compensation programs.

2. Explain how compensation programs are affected by federal, state, and local laws.

3. List and describe the most common forms of direct financial compensation.

4. List and describe the most common forms of indirect financial compensation.

5. List and describe some of the most common forms of nonfinancial compensation.

Impact on Human Resources Management

Despite arguments to the contrary, pay is not the central issue responsible for attract-ing and retaining most employees. Pay is only one of a variety of factors that impact an employee's willingness to work. Worker pay is, however, critically important to employees and employers alike, because it affects so many other business issues.

In general, workers who feel they are unfairly paid will, if possible, seek jobs they believe more equitably reward their efforts. Alternatively, employers who pay their employees significantly more than other employers may find their operating costs are too high to allow them to stay competitive and achieve the profits they need to stay in business. Unfortunately for HR managers, elusive concepts such as fair, equitable, and competitive defy unanimous agreement. As a result, the chal-lenge faced by HR managers is to design and manage compensation systems that are simultaneously perceived as reasonable by both employees and employers. The best of HR managers actually go one step further and use their compensation programs as an essential tool for attracting and retaining excellent workers, as well as maxi-mizing profits for their employers.

It is important to realize that people rarely are attracted to, or leave, a job for money alone. Instead, they are attracted or leave for career advancement, new chal-lenges, lack of appreciation by the company, inability to have an impact, coworker con-flict, job insecurity, family matters, and a variety of other factors. This is not to imply that pay is unimportant to workers at all levels; it is critically important. Employee demands for higher wages, shorter working hours, better benefits, and the like are important in and of themselves. Viewed more deeply, they are an expression of far more general strivings for self-worth, responsibility, power, and even calls for justice.

As is true in many other HR areas, managers designing compensation systems must understand the law. When creating effective compensation systems, however, more is at stake than ensuring the system's legality. Managing compensation systems well involves two main issues: controlling costs and leveraging pay (getting the most bang for the buck). This can be done by establishing a compensation and benefits system that tracks costs, helps ensure pay equity, is understood by all employees, and recognizes the fundamental, long-term wisdom of justly balancing the financial interests of both employees and employers.

Compensation Management

1. Describe the differences between extrinsic and intrinsic rewards as they relate to employee compensation programs.

The majority of hospitality workers like their jobs and enjoy the rewards they receive from working in the industry. For most of these workers, however, a critically

Compensation: The amount of money and other items of value (e.g., benefits, bonuses, perks) given in exchange for work performed.

Compensation package: The sum total of the money and other valuable items given in exchange for work performed.

important part of their job satisfaction relates to the **compensation** they receive for doing their jobs.

While some hospitality workers consider their jobs to be fun, few people have the luxury of working just for the fun of it. In most cases, workers seek to evaluate the entire **compensation package** offered by their employer when they assess the amount they are paid for their work, and when they consider whether that payment is adequate, or fair. It is important that managers ensure that employees know about their hourly pay, but it is just as important that employees be informed about their entire compensation package (including items such as meals, travel discounts, benefits, bonuses, perks, and the like).

Most employees, naturally, would like their compensation package to be as large as possible. Interestingly, however, it is rarely in the best interest of employers to make compensation packages as small as possible. The reason for this is twofold. First, employers who advertise positions offering a below-average compensation package tend to attract workers with lesser skills. This is so because more highly skilled workers seek higher-paying positions and employers. Second, those employers who seek to minimize the amount paid to their employees tend to lose the best of their workers to other organizations that are willing to pay more. Consequently, when less-skilled workers are attracted to an organization, and when the best of an organization's workers ultimately seek employment elsewhere, customer service levels inevitably are below average, resulting in below-average company profits. The optimum compensation program attracts very high-quality workers, provides for excellent customer service levels, and, by doing so, allows the company to maximize profitability.

In most cases, when discussing their compensation, employees will point out their salaries, wage paid per hour, or tips received during their average shift. When HR managers discuss their own operations' compensation programs, they talk about much more than the amount of money paid to their workers, because experienced HR managers know a comprehensive compensation program consists of important **extrinsic rewards** as well as **intrinsic rewards.**

Extrinsic rewards: Financial, as well as nonfinancial, compensation granted to a worker by others (usually the employer).

Intrinsic rewards: Self-initiated compensation (e.g., pride in one's work, a sense of professional accomplishment, or enjoying being part of a work team).

For most employees, both extrinsic and intrinsic rewards are important. As a result, HR managers must consider both types when developing their operation's total compensation program. Figure 8.1 lists some of the most common extrinsic and intrinsic rewards utilized in the hospitality industry.

It is important to recognize that not all employees react in the same manner to rewards offered by employers. For some workers, intrinsic rewards are critically important. For others, financial rewards may be most important, and for still others, status and the nonfinancial extrinsic rewards may be what they like most about the compensation they receive. All employees do exchange work for rewards. Probably the most important (or at least the most talked about!) reward is money or pay. While not all employees earn the same amount of money, nearly all employees view the amount they are paid as a real indication of their value in the eyes of management. Therefore, an employee who discovers that a coworker makes as little as 5 or 10 cents more per hour than he or she does can become upset. For many workers, the amount of money they make significantly enhances or detracts from their own feelings of status and self-worth. Thus, an equitable compensation program that considers pay, as well as all other employee rewards, is critical.

EXTRINSIC REWARDS	INTRINSIC REWARDS
FINANCIAL	
Salaries	Participation in job design
Hourly pay	Participation in decision making
Cost-of-Living Adjustments (COLAs)	Greater job freedom
Tips	More interesting work
Commissions	Opportunities for personal growth
Bonuses	More job security
Merit pay	Empowerment
Incentive pay	
Profit sharing	
Paid leave	
Mandatory benefits	
Voluntary benefits	
NONFINANCIAL	
Preferred office space or work station	
Preferred personal computer or kitchen tools	
Preferred meal privileges	
Designated parking place	
Business cards	
Special dress codes	
Secretary	
Impressive titles	
Travel/meal discounts	

FIGURE 8.1: Extrinsic and Intrinsic Employee Rewards

Compensation management:
The process of administrating an organization's extrinsic and intrinsic reward system.

The goal of any effective **compensation management** program should be to attract, motivate, and retain competent employees. To achieve this goal, the program must be perceived by employees as essentially fair and equitable.

It is important to remember that fairness in pay can only be considered in the context of organizational profitability. Organizations that can pay employees less, but still deliver a quality product, will, in the short run, be more profitable than competitors who pay their employees more. This is so because profits are simply computed as revenue minus expenses, and, in the hospitality industry, employee compensation is one of any operation's largest expenses. Experienced HR managers know, however, that an employer whose compensation program is not perceived as fair by employees will not, in the long run, attract and retain the best and most talented workers. Outstanding employees who have the ability to do better financially for themselves and their families will seek employers who do pay fairly. This is not to imply that those employers who pay the most money in direct salaries and wages will attract the best workers. In fact, those HR managers who can clearly show employees the inherent fairness of their company's *complete* compensation program will, in the long run, attract and retain the best workforce. This is so because compensation directly affects employee motivation, and motivation affects employees' view of compensation. Highly motivated workers tend to view their company's compensation programs as fair, while those who are less motivated often find fault with the manner in which they are compensated.

Managing compensation is, to a great degree, the management of employee expectations and perceptions. To do this well, HR managers must devise an effective compensation system. To be useful, such a system typically includes:

1. *Categorizing of jobs.* Not all employees do the same work, and the result is that employee pay differences do exist. It is also true that most employees will readily accept this rationale as the reason for pay variations. It is easy for most employees to understand, for example, that a tray line supervisor in a hospital's dietary department would make more money per hour than a tray line server working in the same facility.

   In a similar manner, employees will undoubtedly understand that a fine-dining operation's executive chef would be paid more than that operation's sous chef. When employees understand real differences in job responsibilities, they can better understand the reasons for differences in pay.

   HR managers can add flexibility and enhance employees' understanding of their compensation programs by creating several categories within the same job, each of which may have its own **pay range.** For example, desk agents in a hotel may be classified as trainee, intermediate, senior, and so on to designate different experience or skill levels. Each classification would, under this system, have its own pay range. Employees can also routinely be made aware of the skills or experience needed to advance to higher levels and of any opportunities offered by the employer to help them become trained or eligible for these higher positions.

2. *Comparison of employee pay to the local labor market.* Assume that three different hotels offer their employees identical nonwage compensation packages. In such a scenario, would $7.50 be a fair hourly wage to be paid to each hotel's laundry workers? The answer, to some degree, will depend on exactly where the hotels are located. Hourly wages paid for laundry workers in New York City will be higher than those paid to similar workers in rural Midwest U.S. communities.

   International hotel companies operating in Punta Cana in the Dominican Republic, for example, would likely pay yet another rate. Between the extremes will lie a variety of prevailing **local wage rates,** each based on the individual community and labor market in which the operation is located.

   HR managers can stay abreast of local wage rates by conducting periodic **salary surveys.**

Pay range: The lower and upper limit of hourly wages or salary paid for a specific job. For example, the pay range for an entry-level room attendant in a hotel may be between $7.50 and $8.50 per hour to start.

Local wage rate: The prevailing pay range for distinct job categories in a specific community or labor market.

Salary survey: A comprehensive review of local wage rates and pay ranges paid for one or more individual job categories (e.g., the average local wage rate, or range, paid to hotel bartenders, room attendants, or groundskeepers).

You can easily conduct your own salary surveys by talking to your counterparts working at other hospitality operations in your area. They will usually be happy to share such information, because they want to have the benefit of your data just as much as you desire access to their numbers. In addition, managers may be able to purchase commercial salary surveys in some locations.

Salary surveys can tell you a lot. First, they provide a way to establish pay ranges for various jobs. Second, they can tell how your wages or salaries compare with the labor market. Third, surveys can give you an idea of how many job categories should be established for each job group.

Managers need not follow the local market conditions by matching the wage rates found in a salary survey. For example, an HR manager may pay more aggressively for some jobs than others, based on a view of how many qualified workers are available, how critical it is to fill the jobs, and the amount of position turnover they are expecting.

3. *Management of internal pay equity.* Most HR managers agree that managing internal pay equity is more important than ensuring external equity. This is so because employees are much more likely to know the hourly pay or salary of the persons they work with than the amount paid to a person in another operation. Also, many employees realize that it is difficult to compare, for example, the pay at two different restaurants, because each may offer differing benefit packages that help explain the pay differences.

Employees typically feel that they can make comparisons about coworkers within their own operation. Also, employees will have a better foundation for pay comparisons because they have a better idea of what their coworkers actually do on the job and how well they do it. All of these factors create a much higher potential for morale problems and turnover if pay rates are not seen as equitable.

Some managers control this internal equity issue by mandating that employees not discuss their pay with other employees. While this approach may sometimes be effective, its legality is questionable, and it will not likely prevent employees from covert discussions. In fact, some employees may believe that a "no discussion of pay" policy implies that there are pay system inequities, and managers are trying to cover it up.

Internal equity is best achieved by paying people within the pay range established for their jobs and by paying for identifiable measures such as job performance, full- vs. part-time status, shifts worked, assignments completed, or other objective factors. For example, a hotel may elect to pay a desk agent working the 11 P.M. to 7 A.M. shift more per hour than a coworker doing identical work on the 7 A.M. to 3 P.M. shift. In this example, the shift worked, rather than the tasks completed, justifies the pay differential between the two employees.

4. *Linkage of pay to job performance.* Most managers and employees agree that workers who perform their jobs better should receive greater pay and larger

pay increases than their peers who do not. At the same time, they may not believe that their own companies do a good job of rewarding superior effort.

In Chapter 9, you will learn more about how HR managers evaluate employee contributions to their operations' effectiveness. You'll learn that a quality performance evaluation system is an effective tool for achieving many goals, including improving employee skills and identifying employee efforts worthy of additional pay and responsibility.

Merit pay system:
A compensation program that links increases in pay to measurable job performance. Under such a system, those workers who perform better receive proportionally larger percentage pay increases.

Measurable employee effort and other factors, such as difficulty level of the work, shift assignments, and current pay, should play an important role in helping HR managers develop a **merit pay system** that effectively helps them determine appropriate employee pay rates.

The hospitality industry is unique in that many jobs have their own built-in individual merit pay plans. For example, servers and bartenders working in tipped positions often find that the money they earn from tips is directly tied to the quality of service they provide. This same principle of closely associating effort with pay is an important one and is a key component in any effective compensation program.

Some hospitality managers feel that pay should not be closely tied to individual performance. They reason that linking individual pay with performance erodes teamwork. It does take more than one individual to effectively perform work tasks in most hospitality operations. However, because paychecks are not issued to groups rather than individuals, most employees believe that they should be paid according to their own best individual efforts. An evaluation of that effort should include an assessment of each worker's contributions to their team's success. Such an open and objective assessment is typically viewed by employees as a much fairer system than one where the assessment is based primarily on membership in a specific group (whose members were not likely chosen by the employee).

5. *Maintenance of open communications.* While some HR managers find it uncomfortable to talk to employees about pay, it is a topic that every employee talks or thinks about on an ongoing basis. The amount of pay-related communication that is appropriate will vary between operations. Many companies do not effectively communicate the mechanics of compensation plans in the organization.

For example, unit managers typically must inform employees about their pay, but they may be reluctant to say too much for fear that they will have to justify some perceived pay inequity that they may not fully understand or even agree with. When managers say nothing, this often requires employees to rely on the rumor mill, an information source that is well noted for its inaccuracy and exaggeration.

Discussing employee pay is always a delicate situation. What is most critical for all employees (including HR managers!) to understand is how their pay or pay increase was determined, why it is that amount, and what, if anything, the employee can do to earn more.

IT'S THE LAW!

Managing the compensation for tipped employees is a challenge in nearly all segments of the hospitality industry. Legally, tipped employees are those who customarily and regularly receive more than $30 per month in tips. Tips actually received by tipped employees may be counted as wages for purposes of the FLSA (Fair Labor Standards Act, see Chapter 2), but the employer must pay not less than $2.13 per hour in direct wages. If an employer elects to use the tip credit provision, the employer must (1) inform each tipped employee about the tip credit allowance (including the amount to be credited) before the credit is utilized; (2) be able to show that the employee receives at least the minimum wage when direct wages and the tip credit allowance are combined; and (3) allow tipped employees to retain all tips, unless they participate in a valid tip-pooling arrangement.

If an employee's tips combined with the employer's direct wages do not equal the federal minimum hourly wage, then the employer must make up the difference. If an employee is employed concurrently in both a tipped and a nontipped job, the tip credit is available only for the hours spent in the tipped job.

Current law forbids any arrangement between the employer and the tipped employee, where any part of the tip received becomes the property of the employer. A tip is the sole property of the tipped employee. Where an employer does not strictly observe the tip credit provisions issued by the FLSA, no tip credit may be claimed, and employees are entitled to receive the full cash minimum wage, plus all of the tips they have received.

Many hotels and restaurants charge guests a compulsory service charge. A service charge (e.g., 15 percent of the guest's total bill) is *not* a tip but, instead, is part of the employer's gross receipts. Where service charges are imposed and the employee receives no tips, the employer must pay the entire minimum wage and overtime required by the FLSA.

The requirement that an employee must retain all tips does not preclude tip-splitting or -pooling arrangements among employees who customarily and regularly receive tips, such as servers, bellhops, counter personnel (who serve customers), bussers, and bartenders. Tipped employees cannot, however, be forced to share their tips with employees who have not customarily and regularly participated in tip-pooling arrangements, such as dishwashers, cooks, chefs, and janitors. Only those tips that are in excess of tips used for the tip credit may be taken for a tip pool.

Where tips are charged on a credit card, and the employer pays the credit card company a percentage on each sale, the employer may pay the employee the tip, minus that percentage, but the charge on the tip may not reduce the employee's wage below the required minimum wage. The tip amounts due from payment cards must be paid no later than the employee's regular payday, and cannot be held while the employer is awaiting reimbursement from the payment card company.

Legal Aspects of Compensation Management

2. **Explain how compensation programs are affected by federal, state, and local laws.**

Generally, employers may establish wages and salaries as they wish, but they also must comply with federal, state, and local laws that directly affect compensation programs. For example, you learned in Chapter 2 that the Equal Pay Act (1963) requires that equal pay must be given to men and women for equal work, if the jobs they perform require equal skill, effort, and responsibility, and if they are performed under similar working conditions. In addition to equal pay for equal work, numerous other federal, state, and local laws regulate how much an employer must pay employees. In the hospitality industry, these laws have a broad impact.

FEDERAL LEGISLATION

By the end of the 1800s, the industrial age was spurring the growth of factories known as sweatshops that employed women, children, and recent immigrants who had no choice but to accept inferior wages and harsh working conditions. Social activists pushed for laws at the state level to pay all workers, regardless of social status or gender, a wage that would allow them to maintain an adequate standard of living.

Minimum wage: The least amount of wages that employees covered by the FLSA or state law may be paid by their employers.

In 1912, Massachusetts became the first state to enact a law mandating a **minimum wage** (interestingly, in 2006, it also became the first state to mandate health insurance for all of its citizens). By 1938, twenty-five states had enacted minimum wage laws. Some states established commissions to determine the minimum wage based on what was perceived to be a fair wage for employees. Eventually, however, a U.S. Supreme Court decision held that state laws regulating wages were unconstitutional. According to the courts, these laws violated the rights of employers and employees to freely negotiate and form contracts over appropriate wages. Other state courts, following the precedent set by the Federal Supreme Court, ruled that their own state statutes were also unconstitutional. President Franklin D. Roosevelt responded by attempting to enact federal legislation granting the president the authority to mandate a minimum wage as part of the federal government's right to regulate interstate commerce. The Supreme Court ruled President Roosevelt's first attempt at such legislation to be unconstitutional, but the Court upheld his second attempt, the 1938 Fair Labor Standards Act (FLSA), as constitutional.

The FLSA, among other provisions, established child labor standards and set the nationwide minimum wage to be paid to covered employees. It also defined the wage rates that must be paid for working overtime.

Some, but not many, hospitality operations may be too small to be covered under the FLSA. HR managers should check with their local offices of the Wage and Hour Division, listed in most telephone directories under "U.S. Government, Department of Labor, Wage and Hour Division."

The minimum wage is established and periodically revised by Congress. Its most recent revision occurred in 2007. HR managers would do well to continually monitor the actions of Congress with regard to changes in the minimum wage, because nearly all hospitality employees are covered by the minimum wage, with some exceptions. For example, the FLSA allows an employer to pay an employee who is younger than 20 years of age a training wage, which is below the standard minimum, for the first 90 consecutive calendar days of employment. Also, tipped employees can be paid a rate below the minimum wage if the reported tips plus the wages received from their employer equals or exceeds the minimum hourly rate.

The FLSA does not limit the number of hours in a day or days in a week that an employee over the age of 16 may work. It does allow employers to require employees to work more than 40 hours per week. However, under the FLSA, covered employees must be paid at least one and one-half times their regular rates of pay for all hours worked in excess of 40 in a workweek. Some employees are exempt from the overtime provision of the FLSA. These include salaried professional, administrative, or executive employees.

To enforce federal wage and hour laws, the Wage and Hour Division of the Federal Department of Labor has investigators stationed throughout the country. If they encounter violations, they recommend changes in employment practices to bring the employer into compliance, and they may require the payment of any back wages due to employees. Employers who willfully or repeatedly violate the minimum wage or overtime pay requirements of the FLSA are subject to civil penalties of up to $1,000 per violation. Employees may also choose to bring a lawsuit against their employer for back pay as well as other costs, including attorney's fees and court costs.

STATE LEGISLATION

Many states continue to maintain their own minimum wage laws. In those states, employees are covered by the law that is most favorable to them (in other words, whichever wage [state or federal] that provides the highest compensation). The differences in state employment laws can be significant, and HR managers must be aware of those that relate to the state(s) in which they do business. To illustrate this fact, consider the very specific differences contained in the sample wage and hour laws, of selected states, detailed in Figure 8.2. Clearly, individual states have a great deal of latitude in enacting their own wage and overtime laws.

The actual hourly minimum wage rates for the individual states vary widely and change often. For an up-to-date listing of the minimum wage in each state, go to: *www.dol.gov/esa/minwage/america.htm.*

LOCAL LEGISLATION

In addition to wage and hour legislation passed at the federal and state levels, some wage and hour laws have been passed at the city or county level. In many

ALASKA: Workers employed as school bus drivers receive at least two times the Alaska minimum wage.

ARKANSAS: Employers of workers who receive board, lodging, apparel, or other items as part of the worker's employment may be entitled to an allowance for such board, lodging, apparel, or other items, not to exceed 30 cents per hour, credited against the minimum wage.

INDIANA: An employer must pay a base wage for tipped employees (any employee who receives more than $30 per month in tips), and the employer must pay the difference between the base wage and federal minimum wage if applicable.

MICHIGAN: Workers younger than age 18 are entitled to a 30-minute meal break after five hours of work. Michigan law does not require a meal break for workers older than age 18.

NEW HAMPSHIRE: An employer cannot require a worker to work more than five hours without a 30-minute meal break. An employee who reports to work at the employer's request is entitled to be paid a minimum of two hours' wages.

OREGON: State law prohibits employers from taking a credit against minimum wage for tips. Employees are entitled to 30-minute meal periods for work shifts six hours or longer, and 10-minute work breaks during each four-hour work shift.

VERMONT: State minimum wage is increased annually by law.

WEST VIRGINIA: Minors 14 or 15 years of age must receive work permits before working. The permit is forwarded to the Division of Labor, which ensures that minors are not working in hazardous or unsuitable conditions.

WASHINGTON: No employer may employ a minor without a work permit from the state along with permission from the minor's parent or guardian and school.

FIGURE 8.2: State-Enacted Wage and Hour Legislation

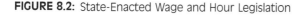

Living wage: The minimum hourly wage necessary for a person to achieve some subjectively defined standard of living. In the context of developed countries such as the United States, this standard is generally considered to require that a person working 40 hours per week, with no additional income, should be able to afford a specified quality or quantity of housing, food, utilities, transportation, and health care.

cases, this local legislation takes the form of **living-wage** laws that, in most cases, can directly affect hospitality businesses.

The first living-wage law was passed in Baltimore in 1994. The ordinance there stipulated that businesses holding service contracts with the city pay a minimum of $6.10 per hour, rising to $7.70 as of July 1998, and thereafter moving in step with inflation. A single mother working full time at $7.70 per hour would (at that time) have been able to live with her child above the federally defined poverty line. Within four years of the Baltimore ordinance, living-wage laws passed in New York, Los Angeles, Chicago, Boston, Milwaukee, Jersey City, Durham, Portland, Oregon, and eight other cities. Today, more than 120 cities and counties have enacted such measures.

The living-wage ordinance in Los Angeles goes further than mandating wages alone. Passed in 1997, the ordinance was only the country's third living-wage law, but it was the first to include a provision for healthcare benefits. It applies to certain businesses in four categories: (1) those that have service contracts with the city, (2) lease land from the city, (3) require city operating permits, or (4) receive city financial assistance. Restaurants, hotels, and bars operate with city permits, so they are covered by the ordinance. The law mandates that workers at these businesses be paid $7.72 per hour if the company provides health benefits, or $8.97 per hour if no health coverage is provided.

Emeryville, California, provides another example of why local wage laws must be understood by HR managers. In that city, a ballot initiative allowed 194 citizens to cast the deciding votes in setting minimum wages for the city's hotels. The 2005 Emeryville law mandates a minimum wage of $9 per hour and an average wage of at least $11 per hour for employees at hotels with more than 50 rooms. Interestingly, employers operating in the tourist zones in Santa Monica and Berkeley, California, must pay a higher minimum wage rate than employers in other parts of these cities. In Santa Fe, New Mexico, employers with 25 or more employees (including most hotels) must pay a minimum wage of $9.50.

Human Resources MANAGEMENT ISSUES   (8.1)

Sharon Alexander operated The Texas Saloon, an upscale steakhouse restaurant that also served beer and wine. Sharon's average menu item sold for $20. Employees were allowed to eat one meal during their shift. For those who voluntarily elected to eat this meal, Sharon would deduct 25 cents per hour ($2 per eight-hour shift) from the federal minimum wage rate she paid her entry-level dishwashers, which reflected the reasonable cost of the meal.

Sharon relied on the Fair Labor Standards Act (FLSA) Section 3(m), which states that employers can consider, as wages, "reasonable costs . . . to the employer of furnishing such employees with board, lodging, or other facilities if such board, lodging, or other facilities are customarily furnished by such employer to his employees." Sharon interpreted this regulation to mean that she could pay the entry-level dishwashers a rate that, when added to the 25-cent per hour meal deduction, equaled the federal minimum wage.

One day, Sharon was contacted by her state Department of Employment, which charged that she was in violation of the state minimum wage law. That law stated that "total voluntary deductions for meals and uniforms may not decrease an employee's wages below the federal minimum wage on an hourly basis." Sharon maintained that, because she was in compliance with the federal law, she was allowed to take the meal credit against the wages paid to her entry-level dishwashers.

QUESTIONS

1. Is Sharon in compliance with all of the compensation-related laws that affect her?
2. Do federal wage laws take precedent over state wage laws?
3. Do state wage laws take precedent over federal law? Explain your answer.

Rules about tip recording and reporting are complex, and it is the responsibility of HR managers to explain these rules fully to tipped employees. *Courtesy PhotoDisc/Getty Images*

Specific wage rates to be paid by employers are adjusted often by local governmental entities, but the examples cited here demonstrate the importance of hospitality managers understanding the local wage and hour legislation that affects their operations, and in making their own opinions well-known when such legislation is under consideration in their communities.

As a final word on the legal aspects of compensation, it is important to note that employers may (voluntarily) commit themselves to the legal responsibility to pay workers a specific amount. Thus, for example, when an employer agrees, in writing, to pay one of its executives $100,000 per year, it is legally obligated to do so. In a similar manner, an organization that agrees to specific wage rates in a union contract must pay those rates to employees covered by the contract.

Direct Financial Compensation

3. **List and describe the most common forms of direct financial compensation.**

In many cases, when employees consider compensation, they are concerned with direct financial payments they receive. Although it may take a variety of forms, direct financial compensation for hospitality employees typically consists of one or more of the following:

- Salaries
- Wages

■ Incentives and bonuses
■ Tips

SALARIES

Salary: Pay calculated on a weekly, monthly, or annual basis rather than at an hourly rate.

Exempt (employee): An employee who is not subject to the minimum wage or overtime provisions of the Fair Labor Standards (FLSA).

Nonexempt (employee): An employee who is subject to the minimum wage or overtime provisions of the Fair Labor Standards (FLSA).

In the hospitality industry, managers and some higher-level supervisors are typically paid a fixed **salary** rather than an hourly rate.

The advantage to employees of a salary system is the consistency of their pay. An advantage to employers is that such employees are not subject to the overtime provisions of the FLSA. To illustrate, Jack Lester works as a salaried dining room supervisor. He regularly works between 45 and 65 hours per week, but Jack's employer is not required to pay him overtime for the hours in excess of 40 that he works weekly.

The FLSA requires that most employees in the United States be paid at least the federal minimum wage for all hours worked, as well as overtime pay at one and one-half times the regular rate of pay for all hours worked over 40 in a workweek. Section 13(a)(1) of the FLSA, however, provides an exclusion from both minimum wage and overtime pay for employees employed as verifiable executive, administrative, professional, and outside sales employees. Such employees are termed **exempt** employees (to distinguish them from **nonexempt** employees).

To qualify for exempt status, employees must meet certain tests regarding their job duties and be paid a minimum salary ($23,660 annually at the time of this text's production).

Job titles do not determine exempt status. Therefore, Jack Lester's title (dining room supervisor) does not determine his exempt status. Rather, his specific job duties and salary must meet all of the requirements of the Department of Labor's regulations to qualify for exempt status. In the hospitality industry, most exempt jobs fall into either executive, administrative, or (in the case of some hotel sales and marketing positions) outside sales classifications.

In general, to qualify for the executive employee exemption, all of the following tests must be met:

■ The employee must be compensated with a salary of not less than $455 per week.
■ The employee's primary duty must be managing the operation or managing a customarily recognized department or subdivision of the operation.
■ The employee must customarily and regularly direct the work of at least two or more other full-time employees or their equivalent.
■ The employee must have the authority to hire or fire other employees, or the employee's suggestions and recommendations as to the hiring, firing, advancement, promotion, or any other change of status of other employees must be given significant weight.

To qualify for the administrative employee exemption, all of the following tests must be met:

- The employee must be compensated with a salary of not less than $455 per week.
- The employee's primary duty must be the performance of office or nonmanual work directly related to the management or general business operations of the employer or the employer's customers.
- The employee's primary duty includes the exercise of discretion and independent judgment with respect to matters of significance.

To qualify for the outside sales employee exemption, all of the following tests must be met:

- The employee's primary duty must be making sales (as defined by the FLSA) or obtaining orders or contracts for services or for the use of facilities, for which a payment will be paid by the client or customer.
- The employee must be customarily and regularly engaged away from the employer's place or places of business.

The exemptions provided by FLSA Section 13(a)(1) apply only to white-collar employees who meet the salary and duties tests described in their regulations. The exemptions do not apply to manual laborers or other blue-collar workers who perform work involving repetitive operations with their hands, physical skill, and energy. FLSA-covered, nonmanagement employees in production, maintenance, construction, and similar hospitality-related occupations such as cooks, bakers, carpenters, electricians, mechanics, plumbers, craftspeople, engineers, or general construction workers and laborers are entitled to minimum wage and overtime premium pay under the FLSA. They are not exempt under the Part 541 regulations no matter how highly they are paid.

There has been some confusion in the hospitality industry regarding when employers may legally deduct pay from salaried (exempt) employees. Generally speaking, exempt employees must receive their full salary for any workweek in which they perform any work, without regard to the number of days or hours worked. However, the following conditions allow employers to deduct wages in daily increments from exempt employees:

- Absence for one or more full days for reasons other than illness or disability
- Absence for one or more full days for illness or disability provided the deduction is made in accordance with a policy that provides compensation for time lost due to illness (e.g., sick leave)
- To offset amounts received for jury duty, witness fees, or military pay
- Per diem (per day) payment in the initial and last weeks of employment
- Good-faith penalties for violation of major safety regulations
- Good-faith unpaid disciplinary suspensions for one or more full days for violation of workplace conduct policies

Several widely publicized lawsuits have been filed against companies in the hospitality industry that violated salary provisions of the FLSA. As a result, it is important that HR managers understand the federal provisions related to salary payments. They must also remember that, when the state laws regarding salary payments differ from the FLSA, an employer must comply with the standard that is most protective (beneficial) to the salaried employee. For example, in California employers must take into consideration several critical differences when classifying employees. To cite one such difference, the salary threshold in California required to reach exempt employee status requires that employees must earn a monthly salary of no less than two times the state minimum wage, or $2,340 per month (vs. the current $1,966 per month federal minimum). HR managers can find links to their own state labor departments at: *www.dol.gov/esa/contacts/state_of.htm.*

WAGES

Hourly wages: Money paid or received for work performed during a one-hour period.

Piecework wages: Money paid or received for completing a certain amount (one piece) of work.

In the hospitality industry, wages paid to workers typically take the form of **hourly wages** or **piecework wages.**

Interestingly, the definition of *wages* can vary greatly, depending on the way the word is used. *Wages* is a term used in a variety of contexts, and thus HR managers must realize, for example, that a taxing authority, such as a state government, may view the term *wages* as including:

- All remuneration paid for personal service, including salaries, bonuses, and commissions, paid to all workers of all ranks, including officers of a corporation
- The cash value of any remuneration paid in any medium other than cash
- All tip income
- Monies paid for time lost due to sickness or accident
- Expense allowances
- Dismissal (termination payouts)
- Money paid to workers for such items as board, lodging, union dues, employee payments to pension or benefit funds, social security tax, and premiums on group insurance policies

For purposes of this chapter, *wages* will refer only to those monies paid directly to workers based on the number of hours worked (hourly wage) or the amount of work completed (piecework wage).

While most hospitality workers, such as cooks, front desk agents, clerical staff, and others, are paid an hourly wage in keeping with their position and the area in which their jobs are located, some hotel managers use a piecework wage system when compensating hotel room attendants. The disadvantages to such a piecework payment system, based on the number of rooms workers are assigned to clean, can be numerous and significant. Consider Sara and Jenny, two employees working at the same 700-room convention hotel. Sara is a front office agent and is paid an hourly wage. Jenny works as a room attendant and is paid a flat piecework wage for successfully cleaning each assigned room. In Sara's case, the wages she earns will be based on her skill and ability as well as local employment conditions. In contrast, Jenny's wages will be based in large measure on factors beyond her control such as:

- The number of guests staying in the hotel (and thus the number of rooms to be cleaned)
- The day, month, or season of the year
- The total number of room attendants employed by the hotel
- The total number of room attendants scheduled to work each day by the hotel's housekeeping supervisor

The piecework wage systems used in hotel housekeeping departments are very different from those used in manufacturing industries, where workers are typically guaranteed a standard wage rate for achieving a preestablished standard output. When the worker output exceeds this standard, the employee earns a predetermined amount for each piece produced. In these systems, workers who, for example, complete an hour's worth of quality work in 50 minutes obtain a bonus percentage (e.g., 50 percent) of the labor saved.

It should be easy for most HR managers to understand that, while a true piecework wage system may be intended to minimize the time it takes for room attendants to do their jobs, in addition to other disadvantages, such a system as currently applied in hospitality also encourages employees to hurry through their work and, as a result, speed rather than room cleanliness is rewarded.

Required room amenities such as bedding components mandated by hotel chains are increasing. HR managers who are interested in fair compensation programs should be careful about implementing a payment system that places selected employees (room attendants) in a compensation program that is difficult to defend. This is especially so when they (the managers) would likely be displeased if the program could be applied to them.

INCENTIVES AND BONUSES

Performance-based pay: A compensation system that rewards workers for their on-job accomplishments rather than for time spent on the job.

In addition to salaries and wages, many hospitality organizations that are committed to developing compensation systems designed around **performance-based pay** include **incentives** and **bonuses** in their overall programs.

Incentive: Motivational plan provided to employees based on their work efforts.

Incentive or bonus programs may be designed to reward individuals, work teams, departments, or entire operations. Incentive and bonus programs are becoming increasingly common in the hospitality industry, because managers believe that they increase their workers' quality and quantity outputs. From a motivational perspective, tying compensation to specific job accomplishments will typically focus employee efforts on those tasks that lead directly to increased financial rewards. When designed carefully, performance-based pay components can increase worker income and lead directly to improvements in guest service and product quality levels.

Bonus: Financial reward paid to employees for achieving predetermined performance goals.

Some managers believe that employee bonuses and incentives should be avoided because they are costly. In fact, the opposite is often true. As a cost-saving device, performance-based bonuses and other incentive rewards avoid the fixed expenses of annual and permanent employee pay increases. Bonuses and other financial incentives do not typically become a permanent part of the employee's base (regular) compensation. Therefore, employee pay increases are not computed based on the value of the incentives, and the result can be significant labor cost savings.

Despite the many advantages of including some performance-based components in an operation's compensation system, there can be potentially negative effects. Consider two college students, each of whom has been assigned to read a book with information related to a course in which they are enrolled. One student is told that reading the book will result in extra points being added to the final grade. The other student is given no such assurance. Which student is more likely to read the book? This example also illustrates that, despite potentially positive results, with this type of grading system, students may choose to do important work only when it leads directly to a payoff. In a hospitality environment, the result may be employees who perform only tasks that lead directly to additional financial compensation, while they ignore other important job components that are not directly tied to performance pay. When incentives are tied to specific aspects of job performance, some workers may avoid performing unmeasured, and thus unrewarded, activities in favor of measured and rewarded activities.

TIPS

Tip: A gift of money given directly to someone for performing a service or task. Also known as a *gratuity*.

In the hospitality industry, **tips** (and the practice of tipping) are perhaps the most unmistakable example of a performance-based compensation system.

As a form of employee compensation, tips are often controversial. Tips are given to employees by customers and, therefore, if the business did not exist, neither would the employee's tips. As a result of this somewhat unique situation, the laws regarding tips and how they may (or may not) be considered as employer payments to employees are constantly being examined at the federal, state, and local levels.

The subject of tips is directly addressed in federal compensation-related legislation. The FLSA defines a tipped employee as one whose monthly tips exceed the minimum established by the Wage and Hour Division of the Department of Labor. Currently, tips received by these employees may be counted (credited) as wages for up to 50 percent of the minimum wage. The Wage and Hour Division also determines the minimum cash wage that employers must actually pay to tipped employees. If an employee's hourly tip earnings (averaged weekly) added to this hourly wage do not equal the minimum wage, then the employer is responsible for paying the difference between the minimum wage and the **tip credit** amount.

Tip credit: The amount of tips employers are allowed to count (credit) toward the wage payments they make to employees.

The value of the tip credit to hospitality employers is significant. Consider the case of Lawson Odde, who is employed in a state with a minimum wage of $8 per hour.

Under the law, his employer is allowed to consider Lawson's tips as part of his wages. Therefore, his employer is required to pay Lawson only $4 per hour, and take a tip credit for the other 50 percent of the wages needed to comply with the law.

HR managers should remember that the Department of Labor will also allow employers whose employees are tipped on a credit (or debit) card to reduce the payment card tips by an amount equal to the handling charges levied by the payment card company. Like the minimum wage and the requirements for overtime pay, state and local laws regarding tipped employees and allowable tip credits can also vary. It is very important that HR managers remember that, because tips are given to employees (and not to employers), the law carefully regulates the influence that employers have over these funds. In fact, if an employer takes control of the tips an employee receives, that employer will not be allowed to utilize the tip credit provisions of the FLSA.

In some hospitality operations, employees routinely share tips. Consider, for example, the table busser whose job includes refilling water glasses at a fine-dining establishment. If a guest leaves a tip on the table, the size of that tip would have

Human Resources Management: CURRENT EVENTS 8.1

CALCULATING OVERTIME PAY FOR TIPPED EMPLOYEES

Tipped employees are generally subject to the overtime provisions of the FLSA. The computation of the overtime rate for tipped employees when the employer claims a tax credit can be confusing. Consider, for example, a state in which the minimum wage is $8 per hour, and the applicable overtime provision dictates payment of one and one-half the normal hourly rate for hours worked in excess of 40 per week. To determine the overtime rate of pay, use the following three-step method:

1. Multiply the prevailing minimum wage rate by 1.5.
2. Compute the allowable tip credit against the standard hourly rate.
3. Subtract the number in step 2 from the result in step 1.

Thus, if the minimum wage were $8 per hour, and the allowable tip credit were 50 percent, the overtime rate to be paid would be computed as:

1. $8.00 $\times$ 1.5 = $12.00
2. $8.00 $\times$ .50 = $4.00
3. $12.00 $-$ $4.00 = $8.00 overtime rate

Tip-pooling: An arrangement in which service providers share their tips with each other on a predetermined basis.

Service charge: An amount added to a guest's bill in exchange for services provided.

been influenced by the attentiveness of the busser assigned to that table, as well as the server who waited on the guests.

Generally speaking, when a tip is given directly to an employee, management has no control over what that employee will ultimately do with it. An exception to this principle is a legitimate **tip-pooling** arrangement. The FLSA does not prohibit tip pooling, but HR managers must approach this area with extreme caution.

As you have learned, a tip is given to an employee, not to the employer. As such, a tip is different from a **service charge** that is collected from the guest by the employer and distributed in the manner judged best by the employer.

Human Resources MANAGEMENT ISSUES   (8.2)

Stephen was hired as a busser by the Sportsman's Fishing Club. This private club served its members lunch and dinner, as well as alcoholic beverages. Stephen's duties were to clear tables, replenish water glasses, and reset tables for the servers when members finished their meals. Stephen's employer paid a wage rate below the minimum wage, because they utilized the tip credit portion of the FLSA minimum wage law.

When he was hired, Stephen read the tip-pooling policy in place at the club, signed a document stating that he understood it, and voluntarily agreed to participate in it. The policy stated that "All food and beverage tips are to be combined at the end of each meal period, and then distributed, with bussers receiving 20 percent of all tip income."

John Granberry, an attorney, was a club member and a guest who enjoyed dining in Stephen's assigned section because Stephen was attentive and quick to respond to every member's needs. Mr. Granberry tipped well, and the dining room staff was aware that Mr. Granberry always requested to be seated in Stephen's section.

One day, after Mr. Granberry had finished his meal and had added a generous tip to his member charge slip, he stopped Stephen in the club lobby and gave him a $20 bill, with the words, "This is just for you. Keep up the good work." A club bartender observed the exchange. Stephen did not place Mr. Granberry's tip into the tip pool. When confronted by his supervisor, Stephen stated that Mr. Granberry's $20 gratuity was clearly meant for him alone. Stephen's supervisor demanded that Stephen contribute the tip to the pool, but Stephen refused.

QUESTIONS

1. Is Stephen obligated to place Mr. Granberry's tip into the tip pool?
2. If Stephen continues to refuse to relinquish the tip, what steps, if any, should his employer take?
3. Do you feel Stephen should be allowed to voluntarily withdraw from the tip-pool arrangement and still maintain his current employment?

Not surprisingly, tip pooling is a complex area, because the logistics of providing hospitality services is sometimes complex. When a server clears a table, resets it, serves guests by him- or herself, and then again clears the table, the question of who should benefit from customers' tips is straightforward. When, however, a hostess seats a guest, a busser—who has previously set the table—provides water and bread, a bartender provides drinks, and a server delivers drinks and food to the table, the question of who deserves a portion of the tip can become perplexing. Employers are legally allowed to assist employees in developing a tip-pooling arrangement that is fair: one that is based on the specific duties of each service position. This participation should be documented in the employee's personnel file.

By law, employees in a tip-pooling arrangement cannot be required to share tips with their peers who do not customarily receive tips, including those in positions such as janitor, dishwasher, and cook. Even well-constructed, voluntary tip-pooling arrangements can be a source of employee conflict. In addition, state laws vary, so it is a good idea to check with your state trade association or Wage and Hour Division regulator to determine the regulations applicable in a specific operation.

Indirect Financial Compensation

4. List and describe the most common forms of indirect financial compensation.

Benefits (employee): Indirect financial compensation offered to attract and keep employees or to comply with legal mandates.

Mandatory benefits (employee): Indirect financial compensation that must, by law, be offered to employees.

Voluntary benefits (employee): Indirect financial compensation a company chooses, on its own, to offer its workers in an effort to attract and keep the best possible employees.

While many employees tend to focus primarily on the amount of direct financial compensation paid as salary or wages, HR managers know that the cost of employee **benefits** will account for 20 to 40 percent of the total amount their operations actually spend on employee compensation.

In most countries, an employer's compensation program must include more than just the salaries or wages owed to employees. As a result, employers must provide their workers with more than just money. In the United States, federal, state, and local legislators have passed laws that require employers to provide their workers a variety of **mandatory benefits**. In addition, many companies seek to enhance their ability to attract and retain the best possible workforce by providing additional **voluntary benefits**.

MANDATORY BENEFITS

The amount of money employers are actually required by law to spend on employee benefits is significant. Most experts estimate that government-mandated benefits such as social security, workers' compensation, and unemployment insurance represent approximately 10 percent of an employer's total payroll cost.

At the federal level, the government's mandatory social security program is an insurance program funded through a dedicated payroll tax. It is formally known as the Federal Old-Age and Survivors Insurance Trust Fund and the Federal Disability Insurance Trust Fund program (OASDI), in reference to its three components (OA for old-age retirement, S for survivors' (widow/widower) income, DI for disability income). When initially signed into law by President Franklin D. Roosevelt in 1935, the term *social security* covered unemployment insurance as well. The term now is used to mean only benefits paid out for retirement, disability, or death. In this program, an employer's contributions are matched by a mandatory, equal contribution from the employee.

At the state level, workers' compensation now provides medical and disability benefits for work-related injuries and illnesses. In addition, all states mandate an employer's participation in a workers' unemployment insurance program. Unemployment insurance specifics vary by state, but all essentially provide some money for a temporary period of time, if employees lose their job due to no fault of their own. Under this insurance program, the employer pays the insurance premiums, while the employee is the recipient of any payments.

Many employers voluntarily offer pension plans for employees. While the offering of such plans is, in fact, voluntary, the 1974 Employee Retirement Income Security Act (ERISA) governs the activities of employers who offer pension plans. If employers offer pensions, the plan must comply with a wide range of reporting and disclosure requirements.

Similarly, many employers voluntarily offer their employees the opportunity to participate in a group health insurance program. The Consolidated Omnibus Budget Reconciliation Act of 1985 (COBRA) mandates requirements for the continuation of healthcare benefits in the event of an employee's job loss or a business closing. These provisions cover group health plans of employers with 20 or more employees. Essentially, COBRA gives workers who were covered by health insurance, but who are no longer employed, the ability to maintain their insurance coverage under the employer's health plan at their own expense for a limited period of time (currently 18 months).

VOLUNTARY BENEFITS

When hospitality organizations design their overall compensation programs, a crucial area of concern relates to the voluntary benefits they should provide. All employers must provide those benefits required by law. Today's workers, however, expect more than just a salary or hourly wage and mandatory benefits; they seek additional considerations that will enrich their lives and assist them financially. Employers understand that their employees desire these benefits. Each organization must determine what it feels is the best set of benefits to offer. In many cases, the answer to this question is determined by the type of worker employed, the profitability of the company, and the operational philosophy of the employer.

In many cases, employees are allowed to choose from a variety of voluntarily offered benefits based on their own life needs. These popular cafeteria-style benefit programs recognize that, for example, the benefits sought by a single mother working full time may be vastly different from those desired by a semiretired employee working only a few hours per week. In this case, it is not likely that an unvarying benefit package would be best for either employee.

Employers offer a variety of benefits voluntarily, and one of the most popular voluntarily offered employee benefits is health insurance, because virtually all employees (and their families) have health-related needs. Health insurance plans typically cost organizations 8 to 10 percent or even more of their total payroll dollars. Yet, as costly as these plans are, employees often take them for granted. Properly promoted, however, healthcare plans can make a significant difference in the quality of employees an organization attracts and retains.

A variety of health insurance programs can be offered by employers, including:

Medical insurance. This is the most costly item in this category, equaling 7 to 8 percent of the typical organization's payroll. In most cases, companies pay a percentage of the cost of such programs (from 25 to 75 percent of the premium charged) and pass the remaining premium costs on to employees.

Prescription drug plans. These plans allow employees to purchase prescription drugs through a network of pharmacies at a reduced rate. In the typical prescription drug plan, employees pay $30 to $50 for a brand-name prescription and $10 to $20 for a generic prescription. The balance of the prescription's cost is picked up by the insurer.

Dental plans. A typical dental plan has a fixed, but modest deductible (e.g., $50 to $100 per visit) and an annual maximum amount that will be provided to the insured person (typically $1,000 to $2,000 per year). Routine dental care is usually fully covered, while 50 percent of the cost of major treatment (e.g., bridges and crowns) is covered. Some programs also provide partial funding for orthodontics treatments.

Vision care plans. These popular plans are offered by many companies as part of their overall health insurance program. Vision plans subsidize the cost of eyeglasses or contact lenses and eye exams. The premiums required to obtain programs of this type are relatively low.

In addition to health-related insurance, many employers offer their employees life and accident insurance policies as well. In the most common case, life insurance equal to two or three times the employee's annual pay and **AD&D insurance** equal to two times the employee's annual pay are provided. Supplemental life insurance plans are also offered by many companies. These plans allow employees to purchase additional life insurance coverage through **payroll deduction** at little or no cost to the employer.

An additional and popular income protection plan is a short-term disability, or pay continuance, program. Typically, these plans offer income continuance that provides the employee with full pay for the first month of disability, and then provides a benefit that ranges from 50 to 75 percent of the employee's pay for up to

AD&D insurance: Short for Accidental Death and Disability, a form of life and income replacement insurance.

Payroll deduction: A payment method in which the employer deducts money from an individual employee's paycheck and submits it directly to a program (e.g., insurance, savings, or retirement) in which the employee participates. These deductions may be made from an employee's after-tax or pretax wages.

All hospitality employees have healthcare needs that can be cost effectively addressed through employer-sponsored group health insurance policies.
Courtesy Corbis Digital Stock

three more months of disability. At some companies, long-term disability policies that continue the employee's pay beyond that provided by the short-term disability policy are also offered.

OTHER VOLUNTARY BENEFITS

While health, disability, and life insurance are the most widely offered voluntary employee benefits, others that are offered by many hospitality organizations include:

- *Paid time-off.* Companies spend approximately 10 percent of payroll on paid time-off plans. This is usually money well-spent by the organization, because paid time-off is highly valued, especially with today's time pressures on employees and their families. Paid time-off typically takes one of three forms:
  - *Holidays.* The paid holidays that virtually every company provides are New Year's Day, Memorial Day, Independence Day (July 4), Labor Day, Thanksgiving Day, and Christmas Day. In the hospitality industry, most businesses are open on these days. Then employers may offer employees additional wages to work on these days.
  - *Vacation days.* Paid vacation granted to, usually, only full-time employees, often varies with years of service. Typically, employees are granted 10 days of vacation per year upon hire, with the number of days granted increasing as the number of years worked increases.

- *Sick pay.* Sick or personal days are paid time-off for employee illness. Most companies also allow employees to use these days for the illness of a family member.
- *Retirement programs.* Retirement plans typically cost organizations about 3 to 5 percent of payroll. These are most often offered as either a pension plan or a *401(k) plan.* Pension plans are typically funded only by the company. They have lost their popularity recently because they are highly regulated and, therefore, difficult to administer. Currently, fewer than 8 percent of small companies (under 1,000 employees) and about 20 percent of large organizations offer pension plans.

  401(k) retirement plans, however, are very popular. Today, many companies offer employees the opportunity to contribute their own pretax money to a 401(k). These plans have several advantages over pensions, including the fact that they are portable: if employees leave the company, they can take the full value of the 401(k) account with them. Furthermore, employees can typically choose where to invest their funds from among several investment options. These programs are relatively easy for companies to administer. Some hospitality companies match a portion of their employees' retirement contributions.

- *Employee Assistance Plans (EAP).* These programs provide counseling for employees encountering a variety of life issues related to:
  - Alcohol
  - Drugs
  - Health
  - Legal
  - Financial
  - Housing
  - Mental health
  - Child care
  - Elder care
  - Grief
  - Spousal/child/parent abuse
  - Career planning
  - Retirement

- *Health Care Reimbursement Accounts (HCRA) and Dependent Care Reimbursement Accounts (DCRA).* These programs allow certain medical expenses, deductibles, and child care costs for employees and their families to be paid by employees on a pretax basis.
- *Hospitality-specific benefits.* By the very nature of their businesses, some hospitality companies can offer their employees benefits such as reduced-cost meal programs, hotel stays, or travel. Discounted dining, guest rooms, and transportation offered at greatly reduced employee rates are very popular employee benefits and can usually be offered by employers at a relatively low cost.

401(k) (retirement) plan: A retirement plan that allows employees in private companies to make contributions of pretax dollars to a company pool that is then invested for them in stocks, bonds, or money market accounts.

Human Resources Management:
CURRENT EVENTS 8.2

WHEN IS PAYDAY?

The Fair Labor Standards Act (FLSA) places many obligations on employers, including overtime, minimum wage, and child labor requirements. However, the law does not specify exactly when the wages must be paid. It simply states that "every employer shall pay to each of his employees . . . who in any workweek is engaged in commerce or in the production of goods for commerce . . . not less than the minimum wage."

However, courts generally have read the FLSA to require the prompt payment of wages due. For example, in *Rogers v. City of Troy*, 148 F.3d 52 (2d Cir. 1998), the court considered whether a city could change its pay period. In allowing the city to make the adjustment, it pointed out that although the FLSA does not assert when wages must be paid, the courts have interpreted the statute to require that wages be paid in a timely (prompt) manner.

Most states have stepped in to fill the void left by the FLSA. In fact, almost every state has passed legislation specifying minimums for how frequently (usually biweekly or monthly) wage payments must be made to employees. Because state laws vary, HR managers should consult the Wage and Hour Division of their State Department of Labor for detailed information on when wages they owe to their workers must be paid.

Nonfinancial Compensation

5. **List and describe some of the most common forms of nonfinancial compensation.**

Earlier in this chapter, you learned that intrinsic rewards can be powerful employee motivators. In addition to mandatory and voluntary benefits and other financial incentives, many companies complete their compensation programs by including intrinsic rewards designed to enhance workers' positive feelings about themselves and their jobs. While these rewards may not include direct financial payments to employees, they are certainly an integral part of a company's overall compensation program. Some of the most common and effective of the intrinsic motivators used in the hospitality industry provide employees with:

- Increased participation in decision making
- Greater job freedom

- More responsibility
- Flexible work hours
- Opportunities for personal growth
- Diversity of tasks

Perhaps the most critical part of an effective intrinsic compensation package is provided simply by giving employees more responsibility in their work assignments. Effective HR managers determine their employees' suggestions about changes that can yield efficiency, productivity, customer service, or other improvements, and then determine if it is possible to make these changes. Other examples of simple tactics that HR managers can undertake to make their employees' work more meaningful include:

- Simple thank-you notes that show appreciation for good work. A personal note can be an excellent and much-appreciated reward.
- Staff or employee meetings outside of the operation (possibly a nice restaurant or park).
- Birthday programs where a gift is delivered to employees during the week of their birthday.

Many hospitality managers encourage away-from-work employee activities to build team spirit and to enhance the social aspects of the workplace. *Courtesy Image 100 Ltd.*

- Employee outings arranged by employees and designed to increase camaraderie. Outings of these types can include picnics, visits to skating rinks or bowling lanes, golfing, or another activity desired by employees.
- Paid time-off certificates to reward perfect attendance.
- Baseball caps, hats, shirts, jackets, and the like, embossed with the company name or logo.

Regardless of the components of the specific compensation program you institute, the employees must know exactly how and why that system was developed. Failing to keep employees informed about how the program was created and, when it changes, the reason for the changes, will likely yield employee dissatisfaction and conflict. Many experienced HR managers believe that an organization's ability to communicate the rationale behind its compensation programs is just as important as the quality of the programs. Organizations that maximize the effectiveness of their overall compensation programs often find that clear communication of the program's processes and objectives helps them to achieve employee recruitment and retention goals established for the programs.

Human Resources Terms

The following terms were defined in this chapter:

Compensation	Piecework wages
Compensation package	Performance-based pay
Extrinsic rewards	Incentive
Intrinsic rewards	Bonus
Compensation management	Tip
Pay range	Tip credit
Local wage rate	Tip-pooling
Salary survey	Service charge
Merit pay system	Benefits (employee)
Minimum wage	Mandatory benefits (employee)
Living wage	Voluntary benefits (employee)
Salary	AD&D insurance
Exempt (employee)	Payroll deduction
Nonexempt (employee)	401(k) (retirement) plan
Hourly wages	

FOR YOUR CONSIDERATION

1. In this chapter you learned about different forms of direct, indirect, and non-financial compensation. Consider your own career. Which of these types of compensation is most important to you? Do you believe the same form(s) of compensation would be most important to those you will directly manage? Explain your answer.

2. Insurance benefits have traditionally been offered to employees and their immediate families. Today's employees, however, often define *family* in a much different manner than did previous generations of workers. The increase in openness of same-sex living arrangements has resulted in more employees seeking insurance benefits for their domestic (live-in) partners, regardless of their marriage status or their partner's gender. Some companies now offer insurance benefits to domestic partners, but others do not. Do you think companies should offer benefits to domestic partners? Why or not?

3. Finding affordable, quality day care is a challenge for many hospitality employees. In some cases, progressive hospitality employers have done a good job of securing reduced-cost services of this type, or even providing on-site day care for no- or low-cost to their employees. Assume you were an HR manager in such a progressive facility. How would you respond to a group of older employees who questioned the company's use of significant compensation resources directed at a targeted category of workers (those with young children)?

CASE STUDY: HUMAN RESOURCES MANAGEMENT IN ACTION

"Look," said Adrian, "I really like it here. It's great. But the Downtown Inn is paying three dollars more per hour. I have a family. I have to take it for them."

"It" was a banquet manager's job that had been offered to Adrian, a young and talented banquet manager at the Uptown Inn. Adrian was meeting with LeeAnn Krenshaw, his boss and the director of banquet services at the hotel where he had worked for two years.

"Are you sure the tips will be the same?" asked LeeAnn.

"They said their service charge was 20 percent, same as ours," replied Adrian.

LeeAnn thought about the situation before she approached Tim Thatcher, the hotel's HR director. She told Tim about Adrian's pending resignation.

"That's really unfortunate," replied Tim. "Adrian is a great worker, and we really don't have anyone on staff ready to move up to his position. Do you have any active applicants for the job?"

"No, but I do know the banquet supervisor at another local property," replied LeeAnn. "She's good, and makes about the same money there as Adrian does here."

"Do you think she would want to work here?" asked Tim.

"If the money was right, I think she would," replied LeeAnn.

"How much do you think it would take to make her consider the move?" asked Tim.

"Well, she wouldn't likely move for the exact same pay," replied LeeAnn. "She'll want a raise to move. I think it would need to be in the three-dollar range or so per hour to make it worthwhile for her."

Dimension: Employee Perspective:

Review the scenario described in the case study, and then address the following questions:

1. Why (in addition to money) do you think Adrian seems prepared to accept the job offer from the Downtown Inn?
2. Assume you are Adrian. What, if anything, could your current employer do to convince you to stay?
3. As a tipped hotel employee, Adrian's income could vary based on the tip-pooling policy in place at the Downtown Inn. Identify at least three additional areas in which the compensation program at the prospective employer might vary significantly from the Uptown Inn's program.

Dimension: Company Perspective

Review the conversation described in the case:

1. What, in addition to a pay increase, do you believe is the primary cause of workers seeking alternative employment opportunities?
2. What are the specific real, and potential, disadvantages to your organization of losing an employee such as Adrian?
3. Assume Adrian is one of several talented banquet managers on the hotel's staff. Also assume LeeAnn's colleague Sara is hired at a pay rate $3 per hour higher than the average pay of these employees. What are the likely outcomes that would occur if and when Sara's pay becomes common knowledge in the food and beverage department?

Dimension: Compensation Program Assessment

1. If you were Tim, would you advise LeeAnn to pursue Sara as a potential employee? Why or why not?
2. Assume you are LeeAnn. What specific problems within your departmental compensation program does this situation illustrate?
3. Assume you are the general manager of this hotel. Who on your management team is responsible for ensuring that your property does not lose talented employees such as Adrian to your direct competitors? Explain your answer.

INTERNET ACTIVITIES

1. For most HR managers, the U.S. Department of Labor can be a significant source of up-to-date information about employer responsibilities at the federal and state levels. To access their site, and to see an example of how to use the site effectively, go to: *www.dol.gov.*
   a. Select "Search."
   b. Enter "State Minimum Wage."
   c. Select "Minimum Wage Laws in the States" from the search results.
   d. Select the state where you live or go to school.
   e. Identify the minimum wage rate for workers in your state.

2. The Internet offers a tremendous amount of specific information to HR managers. The Human Resource (HR) site is one such example. To access the site, go to *www.hr.com.*
   When you arrive, click on:
   a. Areas of Interest
   b. Choose "Benefits" (or "Compensation")
   Read the information presented about the subject area you selected, and then answer the following questions:
   a. The information on sites such as *www.hr.com* is quite valuable. How do you believe such sites fund their cost of operation?
   b. What are the potential hazards of utilizing a site such as HR.com?

3. The Internet is also a good source of creative ideas that can be used by all HR managers to enhance their own compensation programs. To see an example of a site that offers a wide range of specific compensation-related information, and specifically, to view information about employee incentives, go to: *www.authoria.com.*
   When you arrive:
   a. Select "Solutions."
   b. Select "Incentives."
   c. Select "Watch the Demo."
   When you have reviewed the incentive demo, answer the following questions:
   a. How critical do you think incentives are to the effectiveness of an operation's total compensation program?
   b. Do you think hospitality managers currently use incentives to their maximum potential? Defend your answer.

CHAPTER NINE

Performance Management and Appraisal

CHAPTER **OUTLINE**

Performance Management
Overview of Performance Appraisal
Common Performance Appraisal Methods
Other Performance Appraisal Methods and Issues

Progressive Discipline
Documented Oral Warning
Written Warning
Suspension
Dismissal

Behavior Improvement Tactics
Reinforcement of Acceptable Good Behavior
Elimination of Unacceptable Behavior

Employee Separation
Voluntary Separation
Involuntary Separation
Exit Interviews

Legal Considerations of Performance Management and Appraisal
Title VII of the Civil Rights Act
The Equal Pay Act
Americans with Disabilities Act
Age Discrimination in Employment Act

Human Resources Terms
For Your Consideration
Case Study: Human Resources Management in Action
Internet Activities

CHECKLIST **OF CHAPTER LEARNING OBJECTIVES**

As a result of satisfactory completion of this chapter, readers will be able to:

1. Identify the benefits of a formal performance appraisal program.

2. Explain the rationale for each of the four steps in a progressive disciplinary program:

   Documented oral warning
   Written warning
   Suspension
   Dismissal

3. Describe the role of employee improvement tactics as an integral part of the performance management process.

4. Differentiate between a voluntary and a nonvoluntary employee separation, and explain the function of the exit interview.

5. Identify major legal issues related to performance management and appraisal.

Impact on Human Resources Management

In previous chapters, you learned how hospitality managers recruit, select, orient, and train their employees to help ensure they have the best possible staff. However, these are continual, not static, processes because jobs continually evolve as guests' needs and desires change and new work methods are implemented. Employees and their job performance may also change.

Hospitality managers' activities to improve their employees' job performance must be ongoing and, fortunately, they are typically successful. Sometimes, however, problems with the quality and/or quantity of work outputs arise. In other cases, an employee's work may be acceptable, but difficulties arise about compliance with workplace rules and procedures. Managers must fairly evaluate the quality of their employees' efforts and, if necessary, correct and improve performance.

Most staff members want to do a good job, but concerned and enlightened managers can often help them to do better. Knowing how to objectively evaluate and improve worker performance and, if necessary, to properly terminate employees, are important aspects of an HR manager's job. Actions taken are important because laws related to how and why employees are disciplined and/or terminated are complex. Violation of these laws may cause managers to spend an inordinant amount of time defending their actions, can create substantial financial hardship if fines or penalties are levied, and, if widely publicized, can result in significant adverse publicity.

Performance Management

1. Identify the benefits of a formal performance appraisal program.

Effective hospitality managers provide ongoing performance feedback to their employees. This process is integral to maximizing the effectiveness of an operation's workforce. Documenting performance appraisal efforts may be a human resources responsibility, but those who directly supervise the worker and have firsthand knowledge of the performance often can best perform the evaluation, and they are best able to help employees improve their performance levels.

Performance management and **performance appraisals,** when properly implemented, can help employees do their best.

Performance appraisal is not a new concept, but performance management has only recently become integral to human resources management. As shown in Figure 9.1, performance management is ongoing and includes:

- *Planning* work and setting expectations
- *Monitoring* performance continually

Performance management: A systematic process by which managers help employees to improve their ability to achieve goals.

Appraisal (employee): An objective and comprehensive rating or evaluation of employees.

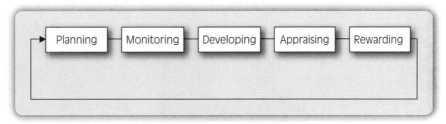

FIGURE 9.1: The Performance Management Process

- *Developing* employee skills
- *Appraising* performance periodically in an objective manner
- *Rewarding* good performance

The distinguishing characteristic of an effective performance management program is its focus on achieving results. It addresses the effectiveness of employees, work processes, and output quality. To illustrate, consider a skilled foodservice employee who chops cabbage quickly and produces a high-quality product. Traditional performance appraisal systems might rate the employee highly because of his or her hard work and efficiency. A performance management system, however, would involve the worker in an objective assessment of effectiveness. Perhaps the cabbage chopping process should be mechanized (new equipment should be purchased) or prechopped cabbage should be used. Then the employee's knowledge and skills might be better utilized. A properly designed performance management system emphasizes goal attainment over employee effort (output).

Traditional performance appraisal systems frequently emphasized employees' negative characteristics. While performance management systems identify and correct employee weaknesses, they also recognize, reinforce, and reward employees' strengths.

Performance appraisal is the employee evaluation component of a performance management process. An effective process yields clear employee goals and an objective rating of goal attainment.

OVERVIEW OF PERFORMANCE APPRAISAL

The most successful performance appraisal programs typically combine four critical characteristics. HR managers should use them as they develop procedures for those who conduct appraisal sessions.

- *Performance goals set by supervisors and employees.* Goals can be short- or long-term and address numerous issues. They should be specific and quantifiable where possible (e.g., completion of a specific task within a defined time at an established quality level). Employees may require additional training or other support to meet their goals. As workplace changes occur, goals should be reviewed and modified, if needed, with employee input.

Quality perfor-
mance appraisal
systems should
be designed to
recognize and
reward employ-
ees' strengths as
well as identify
and correct
weaknesses.
*Courtesy Digital
Vision*

- *Regular, informal feedback from supervisors.* Annual formal appraisals do not allow employees to assess progress toward goal attainment. More frequent input is needed, which occurs as supervisors work closely with employees and provide them with ongoing coaching.
- *A formal method to address performance or disciplinary problems.* Methods used to correct inadequate job performance should be known, fair, and applied equally to all employees. From a legal perspective, this means using a formal method that details, in writing, the procedures and policies to be consistently followed by all managers. Performance problems should be identified as they occur, and a course of action for improvement should be agreed upon. Written procedures should require that managers document the problem and the agreed-upon resolution plan and schedule.
- *Regular and formal appraisal.* Formal reviews that accurately document each staff member's performance should be conducted regularly. In addition to pinpointing improvement concerns, appraisals should identify specific steps for employees to enhance their long-term position with the organization.

Each of these performance appraisal characteristics may appear obvious, but busy supervisors may not receive training in the methods required by the hospitality organization. In large properties, human resources specialists typically work with department heads, managers, and supervisors to develop property-wide procedures. In small organizations, the general manager and other personnel with human resources duties must ensure that these characteristics are incorporated into the performance appraisal system.

A properly implemented formal performance appraisal system yields many benefits:

- *Recognition of outstanding performance.* In the best appraisal systems, employees learn about those areas in which they excel, which increases their morale and helps reduce turnover. Unless a termination decision has been made, managers should praise desired employee behaviors. Every employee likely has laudable personal work characteristics, such as attendance, punctuality, neatness, adherence to dress code, friendliness, or other traits. Emphasize these because positive reinforcement of employee strengths often makes it easier to achieve improvements in other areas.

- *Identification of necessary improvements.* When an employee knows and can excel in a position, it becomes more enjoyable. Few employees want a job that they do not understand, nor one in which their performance is poor. Some employees may not know about needed improvements. When an unbiased supervisor conducts a regularly scheduled appraisal, employees will learn how their performance can be improved, and both the employee and the operation will benefit.

- *Clarification of work standards.* Well-designed performance appraisal systems emphasize how well employees have attained goals. Sometimes, this is simple. For example, a room attendant's guest room cleaning times can be assessed. In other cases, performance is more difficult to measure. While most hospitality managers agree that helpfulness is an important characteristic of a good hotel concierge, an objective evaluation of this trait is more complex than a timed measurement of task completion. Regardless of measurement difficulty, if friendliness will be evaluated, an employee should understand its importance, how the trait should be displayed, and the expected end results of its display. Guest comments, management observation, and shopper's services can provide input for the appraisal. If a friendliness concept is not communicated clearly, it is questionable whether managers can evaluate its occurrence. Performance appraisal provides the opportunity and responsibility for HR managers to clearly define and communicate job expectations.

- *Opportunity to analyze and redesign jobs.* An effective performance appraisal program can identify the need for job redesign. Consider a situation in which a better way to perform an inventory count is volunteered by an employee who is responding to concerns that his or her performance of this task is below standards. If a specific job should be, but has not been, redesigned, applicable benefits are lost.

- *Identification of specific training and development needs.* A performance appraisal system that identifies deficiencies, but does not address them, is deficient because it creates frustration. Specific steps that an employee and the operation

Performance Management and Performance Appraisal Systems

Performance management systems can help managers deal with changes affecting their employees. Globalization, quality initiatives, changing franchise brand standards, variable product market forms of foods and beverages, telecommuting, and the increased importance of teamwork are some factors changing the world of work in the hospitality industry. Recurring performance appraisal sessions are opportunities for regular examination about how these and other important factors affect employee performance. Professional, respectful, and two-way conversations during appraisal sessions are important and can yield mutual benefits.

should take to improve the employee's skill levels are needed. Opportunities to discuss professional development activities can be part of this dialogue.

- *Determine professional development activities.* Information discussed in a performance appraisal session establishes a foundation to help plan the employee's career. If career goals are known, beneficial educational or training activities can be considered, agreed upon, and used as a benchmark for subsequent performance appraisal. For example, an agreement might be made that an employee will complete an Internet-based course offered by a community college, and the hospitality organization will reimburse the employee if the course is successfully completed. This can be a factor in a subsequent appraisal session, because the manager and the employee agreed that successful completion would be a priority.

- *Validation of screening and selection processes.* In Chapter 4, you learned about the importance of proper employee selection. Performance appraisal sessions allow managers to evaluate the effectiveness of these procedures. If employees consistently do not meet expectations, screening and selection tactics may be reasons. Well-managed appraisal systems help managers to pinpoint potential shortcomings.

- *Opportunity for employee feedback and suggestions.* The best managers use appraisal sessions to learn about issues that affect guest satisfaction from the employees who actually interact with them. Remember that employees at all levels of the organization serve either **internal customers** or **external customers.** Most employees are eager to share beliefs about how their jobs could be improved and how service to guests can be enhanced.

- *Objective method to identify candidates for pay increases and promotion.* Performance appraisal systems commonly yield decisions about which employees will receive compensation increases and promotions. It is a workplace reality that scarce organizational resources must be allocated rationally, and properly designed appraisal systems help with this task.

Customers (internal): Employees of the hospitality operation.

Customers (external): Guests served by the hospitality operation.

Performance Appraisal Systems Must Be Consistent

Basic procedures should be used to evaluate the performance of all employees at the same organizational level regardless of their functional department. HR managers can develop policies and procedures that address concerns such as:

- Specific goals of the appraisal process
- Mechanics of the system
- Frequency of appraisal
- The process, if any, by which appraisal comments are provided to employees before the formal session
- Suggested length of time for the appraisal session
- Disposition of appraisal information (e.g., a copy provided to the employee and included in the staff member's permanent personnel file)

Those responsible for conducting appraisal sessions will likely require training. HR managers should design and implement this training for all new supervisors and managers with appraisal responsibility. Training updates may also become necessary as policies and procedures change, and as new laws and regulations impact the performance appraisal process.

What is the role of human resources personnel in the performance appraisal process? Figure 9.2 addresses this question:

As noted in Figure 9.2, human resources personnel have three primary roles in performance appraisal: (1) advocate for effective appraisal, (2) coordinate process planning and implementation, and (3) determine legal requirements. In efforts to coordinate the planning process, they should evaluate alternative processes. Should an in-house-developed system or an externally purchased system be used? Human resources personnel can assist with the selection decision by providing specialized input and interacting with legal counsel.

After the performance appraisal system is established, the human resources role continues as applicable policies, procedures, evaluation forms, and other documents are developed. Implementation involves communication with affected personnel. Those who will conduct performance appraisals must be trained, and employees must learn about the system. Follow-up tasks, including process evaluation, revision, if necessary, and management of specific ad hoc issues, are required. Also, because appraisal information will become part of the employees' personnel records, information must be collected and managed.

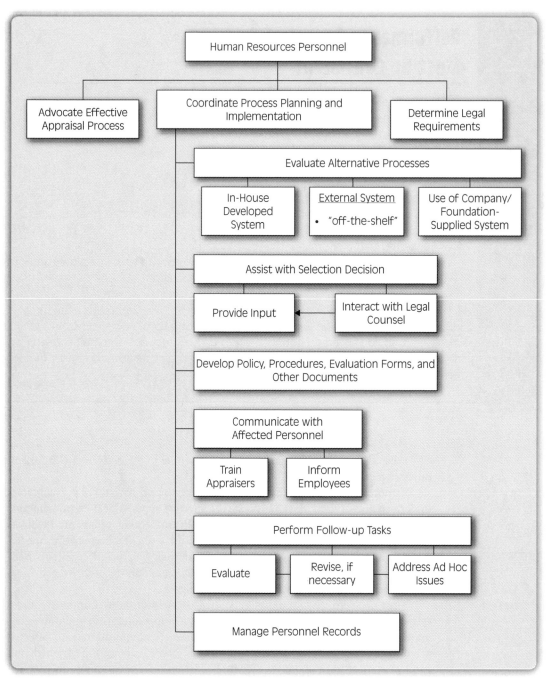

FIGURE 9.2: Human Resources Role in Performance Appraisal Process

What About the Money?

Wage and salary increases are often based on performance and thus are discussed during performance review sessions. When should this financial discussion occur? Industry observers make three suggestions. Some say that financial discussions should occur at the beginning of the performance appraisal session. Then employees can focus their attention on the discussion that follows. Others believe that approach is out of sequence, because the compensation decision will (should) have been based on performance, so the appraisal review should precede information about wage/salary adjustments. A third view is to discuss compensation matters in a separate interview/discussion that can occur before or after the performance appraisal session.

There are pros and cons to each of these alternatives. However, the timing of wage and salary change notification is important, and it exemplifies the types of issues that must be considered as performance appraisal procedures are determined.

This brief description of steps in the process of developing and implementing a performance appraisal system suggests that it is complex (many steps are required), and it must be centralized to apply to all personnel. Human resources employees in many organizations are in the best position to assume this coordinating responsibility.

COMMON PERFORMANCE APPRAISAL METHODS

Hospitality organizations can use several approaches and methods for performance appraisal, and HR managers have an obvious role in their selection. Three philosophically different approaches involve absolute standards, relative standards, and targeted outcomes, detailed as follows.

Absolute Standards

Absolute standard (performance appraisal method): Measuring an employee's performance against an established standard.

When an **absolute standard appraisal** method is used, employee performance is compared to an established standard independent of any other employee.

Examples of absolute standard evaluation methods include:

Critical incident. Critical incidents are those specific behaviors essential (critical) to doing a job successfully. With this approach, behavioral traits that employees exhibit on the job (the critical incidents) are documented in writing. For example, an observation about Tonya, a bartender, might be: "Tonya showed poise, maturity, and patience with an agitated guest after she could no longer serve him alcoholic beverages. She calmed him down, and he ordered coffee."

Note that the incident report focuses on Tonya's behaviors and their results, rather than on Tonya's personal traits. One advantage of this method is that, during a formal appraisal session, the discussion can address specific positive and negative critical incidents to help support an objective evaluation of the employee's performance. A disadvantage is that frequent documentation can be time consuming.

Checklist appraisal. As shown in Figure 9.3, yes or no responses are used to address behavioral factors applicable to the successful completion of tasks identified in a job description. While the checklist can be modified to apply to specific positions, this can become a disadvantage if individualized checklists must be prepared for multiple job categories and positions.

Continuum appraisal. This approach uses a scale to measure employee performance relative to specific factors. The point on the scale that best represents the employee's performance is selected. Figure 9.4 shows a sample of continuum appraisal questions that address two factors: work quantity and dependability. Note that each performance factor is carefully defined to maximize consistency among those conducting the appraisals.

The number of alternative rating choices in a continuum appraisal system usually ranges between four and eight. In Figure 9.4, each of the five rating response categories, like all continuum scales, represents an ordinal (rank or sequence) level of measurement. While the categories represent an inherent order (e.g., more to less, stronger to weaker, or very unsatisfactory to highly satisfactory), the categories do not indicate the magnitude (size of differences) between each level. While the system lacks the depth of analysis found in, for example, a critical incident appraisal system, an advantage is ease of administration. This approach, along with the checklist appraisal system just described, can be used to compare the observed performance of individuals.

	YES	NO
1. Laundry supervisor's instructions consistently followed	_____	_____
2. Quantity of work performed consistently acceptable	_____	_____
3. Quality of work performed consistently acceptable	_____	_____
4. Work area consistently kept clean	_____	_____
5. Dryer maintenance (lint filters cleaned) consistently performed	_____	_____
6. Responds willingly to special linen and terry cleaning requests	_____	_____

FIGURE 9.3: Partial Laundry Worker Checklist Evaluation

PERFORMANCE FACTOR: Quantity of work (the volume of work done in a normal workday)

PERFORMANCE RATING (check one):

Consistently unsatisfactory	Occasionally unsatisfactory	Consistently satisfactory	Sometimes excellent	Consistently excellent
_____	_____	_____	_____	_____

PERFORMANCE FACTOR: Dependability (following directions and company policies without supervision).

PERFORMANCE RATING (check one):

Requires constant supervision	Requires occasional supervision	Usually can be counted on to perform	Requires very little supervision	Requires minimum supervision
_____	_____	_____	_____	_____

FIGURE 9.4: Sample Continuum Appraisal Questions

Forced-choice appraisal. This appraisal method is a special checklist in which the evaluator must choose between two (or more) alternative statements that describe two (or more) opposing choices. Alternative statements may be favorable or unfavorable, and the appraiser selects the statement that is most descriptive of the employee being evaluated. An example of this approach follows:

Which of the following tasks is best performed by the employee?:

☐ Those involving detailed guest-service interaction

☐ Those involving detailed non-guest-service duties

Because there is no right answer associated with questions of this type, these appraisal systems can only be properly scored by professionals who are very familiar with the device's specific design and intent.

Relative standard (performance appraisal): Measuring one employee's performance against another employee's performance.

Relative Standards

When HR managers use a **relative standard** of performance appraisal, they compare one employee's actions to those of another employee.

The two most common approaches to this appraisal alternative are group order ranking and individual ranking.

Group order ranking. Group order ranking requires the evaluator to place the employee into a specific classification, such as the top 10 percent or lower 50 percent. This approach is often used when evaluating employees for possible promotion.

Assume that Julia is the dining room supervisor at a restaurant and that she supervises 20 servers. She must rank (compare to each other) all 20 employees. For example, if the system asks Julia to identify her top 10 percent of employees, she must identify only her top two employees (10 percent of 20 employees = 2 employees).

One advantage of this appraisal system is that raters cannot inflate evaluations, so everyone is rated above average, nor can they rate nearly all employees as average (outcomes that are not unusual with the continuum appraisal systems described earlier).

A disadvantage, especially with small groups of employees, is that some individual or individuals must always be rated in the below-average group, regardless of their actual talent level. A second disadvantage is that a supervisor with clearly inferior workers will still generate groups of best and worst staff members (although the best employees may simply be the best of the worst!). Conversely, a supervisor with a group of outstanding employees must still rank some of them in a below-average group.

Individual order. This ranking method requires supervisors to rank employees in order, from highest to lowest. Only one employee can be rated as best, and ties are typically unacceptable. This system tends to work best with smaller groups of workers. However, because this system also represents an ordinal level of measurement, the rank achieved does not indicate the magnitude (size) of differences between the ranks. For example, if 10 employees are ranked, there is no real rationale for believing that the difference between the first- and second-ranked employees is equal to the difference between the ninth- and tenth-ranked workers. The system is simple, but it is a subjective, not objective, system.

Targeted Outcomes

A third approach to employee evaluation involves the identification of **targeted (achieved) outcomes.** Employees are evaluated based on how well they accomplished a specific set of objectives deemed critical to successful job completion. For example, restaurant managers might be evaluated primarily on whether they did (or did not) achieve preestablished food and/or labor cost percentages and net operating income targets.

Targeted outcome (performance appraisal): Measuring the extent to which specified goals were achieved.

Among increasingly popular targeted outcome appraisal systems are those utilizing rating scales designed to award employees for the exhibiting specific behaviors. Behaviorally Anchored Rating Scales (**BARS**) and Behavioral Observation Scales (**BOS**) both seek to rate employees along a continuum; however, the

BARS: Short for Behaviorally Anchored Rating Scales, an appraisal system in which employees are evaluated based on their display of definitive, observable, and measurable behaviors.

BOS: Short for Behavioral Observation Scale, a type of appraisal system in which judgments about employee performance are related to a series of statements describing specific examples of observable behaviors.

Management by objectives: A plan developed by an employee and his or her supervisor that defines specific goals, tactics to achieve them, and corrective actions, if needed.

Peer evaluation: An appraisal system that utilizes the opinions of coworkers to evaluate an employee's performance.

Upward assessments (appraisal system): An appraisal system that utilizes input from those staff members who are directly supervised by the staff member being evaluated.

360-degree appraisal (performance appraisal system): A method of performance appraisal that utilizes input from supervisors, peers, subordinates, and even guests and others to provide a comprehensive evaluation of a staff member's performance.

points on the continuum represent examples of actual behaviors on a specific job, rather than general descriptions or traits.

Management (hopefully in conjunction and consultation with employees) should set and communicate the employee's targets or goals, whether they are of a financial, attitudinal, or behavioral nature. An inherent advantage of this approach is that those employees who know their goals and who participate in establishing them will more likely work diligently to achieve them. *Note*: Goal setting and goal achievement measurements and rewards are not new concepts. **Management by objectives (MBO),** the concept of using identifiable objectives to measure performance and to assign employee rewards, is decades old.

Essentially, a targeted outcome appraisal system requires four components:

- Identification of potential performance targets
- Employee input in final target selection
- A defined time period for target completion or achievement
- Performance feedback (appraisal)

Properly managed, targeted outcome appraisal systems can be successfully implemented at all levels of a hospitality operation.

OTHER PERFORMANCE APPRAISAL METHODS AND ISSUES

Several other methods can be used for performance appraisal or, more typically, can be used in conjunction with other approaches. While performance appraisal is primarily a managerial task, employees can play a valuable role in their own performance evaluations. While many employees believe their input would be helpful, few managers seriously consider self-evaluation information. This is often a mistake because valuable information can be lost. Consider a current or previous job you have held, and then think about the self-appraisal questions in Figure 9.5. How much would a manager learn about your work performance if you could address such questions?

Guests can provide additional information helpful for performance appraisal. Consider, for example, comments that guests might make on guest comment cards or in surveys in response to questions designed to solicit this input. In addition, some hospitality organizations utilize **peer evaluation** information to generate the perspectives of those at the same organizational level and **upward assessments** that involve feedback from one's subordinates. These methods can be combined with a traditional appraisal approach involving the perspectives of one's own supervisor with a **360-degree appraisal** method.

Some industry observers forecast the role of employee teams to increase in importance in the future. As this occurs, teams may be involved in determining work responsibilities and schedules, performance standards, and even play an increased role in compensation and team peer evaluations. Team members might

- What skills and knowledge do you possess that our work team would find difficult to replace?
- What have you done, on your own, in the past six months to maintain your job knowledge?
- What have you done in the past six months to fine-tune your work skills?
- Identify specific instances when, in the past six months, you have gone beyond what persons in your position are expected to do to directly benefit our company and our goals?
- In one sentence, how would you describe the main reason you contribute to our team's long-term success?
- Describe some instances when you have gone beyond what you are expected to do to help team members accomplish their goals.
- What specific traits make you better than average at what you are assigned to do?

FIGURE 9.5: Sample Employee Self-Evaluation Questions

use factors such as initiative, creativity, teamwork, communication skills, and collegiality to evaluate their peers.

HR managers may purchase performance appraisal tools from companies that specialize in their development, or they may create their own assessment devices internally. A primary consideration in their use remains the same: to adopt a system that is fair to the employees, that benefits the organization, and that meets applicable legal requirements.

Any tool used for performance appraisal must be reliable and valid. In this context, **reliability** and **validity** have very specific meanings.

Reliability (measurement tool): The ability of a measuring tool to yield consistent results.

Reliability refers to the degree to which a measurement tool delivers consistent and dependable measurements. A performance appraisal instrument is reliable if it consistently measures the employee trait being evaluated. Assume you are preparing a recipe for a dessert, and exactly one tablespoon of flour is needed. A reliable measuring device (a one-tablespoon measure), if properly used, will consistently (reliably) measure exactly one tablespoon of flour. Contrast that situation with the use of a one-cup measuring device, in which you must guess the amount to put into the cup to yield one tablespoon. A reliable measurement device is available in the first example, but not in the second case.

Validity (measurement tool): The ability of a measuring tool to evaluate what it is supposed to evaluate.

Reliable appraisal tools must also possess validity. Validity is the ability of a measuring tool to evaluate (measure) what it is actually supposed to evaluate. Even with use of a reliable measuring device, the cook could accurately and dependably measure the wrong thing. Consider the previous example: assume a one-tablespoon measure was used to measure salt instead of flour. While the measuring device was reliable, it would consistently measure the wrong ingredient if salt, not flour, were added to the recipe. In this case, the recipe results would not be good, despite the reliability (but not validity) of the measuring device.

To better understand the validity concept in performance appraisal, assume that a supervisor is evaluating a front desk agent relative to the employee's speed when guests are being checked out of the hotel. On a personal level, this employee appears not to care for the supervisor very much, and thus rarely engages the supervisor in general conversation (e.g., "How are you today?", "How was your weekend?", and other general comments of that nature).

If the supervisor can ignore this less than friendly (to the supervisor) trait, and focus solely on evaluating the speed of the employee when checking out guests, that measurement will be valid. If, however, the supervisor (because of the employee's lack of sociable conversation) subconsciously deflates the speed of check-out score, then the supervisor is most likely assessing friendliness to him or her, rather than speed, and thus the speed of check-out score would not be valid.

Reliability and validity can be complex concepts. Some companies use sophisticated procedures to calculate the reliability and validity scores of the performance

Halo effect: The tendency to let the positive assessment of one individual trait influence the evaluation of other, nonrelated traits.

Pitchfork effect: The tendency to let the negative assessment of one individual trait influence the evaluation of other, nonrelated traits.

1. Basing evaluation scores on the employee's most recent behavior rather than evaluating the entire performance period
   For example, rating a usually outstanding employee negatively based on a recent argument.
2. Allowing irrelevant or non-job-related factors to influence the evaluation
   For example, evaluating physical appearance or disabilities, race, social standing, participation in employee assistance programs, or use of excused time-off instead of actual performance.
3. Failing to include unfavorable comments on the evaluation, even when justified
   For example, not wishing to offend an employee by not discussing undesirable traits, such as poor personal grooming or consistent display of a negative attitude.
4. Rating all subordinates at about the same point on a ranking scale, usually in the middle
   For example, the tendency of supervisors, because they want to be liked by all employees, to avoid strong negative (or even positive) statements about their employees.
5. Judging all employees too leniently or too harshly
   For example, the tendency of some supervisors, wanting to enhance their own credibility, to unfairly criticize (or praise) the performance of those they are evaluating.
6. Permitting personal feelings to bias the evaluation process
   For example, the tendency of some supervisors to rate employees they like very highly, while rating employees they dislike much lower.
7. Allowing one very good (or very bad) trait to affect all of the other ratings of the employee (the **halo effect** and the **pitchfork effect**).
   For example, rating an employee with one exceptional (or unfavorable) trait as equally exceptional (or unfavorable) in all other measured criteria.

FIGURE 9.6: Threats to Fair Performance Appraisals

appraisal devices they use, but others do not. Those using the results of unreliable and/or invalid assessment devices to make decisions about employee promotion, discipline, and/or termination risk significant legal liability.

Human resources managers should know about additional challenges related to the legitimate measurement of employee performance. Some evaluation actions, if taken, can threaten and even invalidate the results. Figure 9.6 presents seven significant threats to legitimate appraisal and specific examples of their occurrence.

Progressive Discipline

2. **Explain the rationale for each of the four steps in a progressive disciplinary program:**

   Documented oral warning

   Written warning

   Suspension

   Dismissal

Discipline (management action): Any effort designed to influence an employee's behavior.

Disciplined (workforce description): The situation in which employees conduct themselves according to accepted rules and standards of conduct.

Discipline (positive): Any action designed to encourage proper behavior.

Discipline (negative): Any action designed to correct undesirable employee behavior.

Progressive discipline: A program designed to modify employee behavior through a series of increasingly severe punishments for unacceptable behavior.

To many, **discipline** implies reaction to an employee's improper behavior. While this is necessary, a broader view considers discipline to be any effort to influence an employee's behavior. Managers should reinforce desired behavior and discourage undesirable actions. The term **disciplined,** as used in the military (e.g., a disciplined squad or platoon is one in which soldiers follow orders and perform in a way that enhances the ability of the unit to achieve its objectives), is appropriate to the hospitality industry. Disciplined staff members follow the established set of rules and regulations, and thus a disciplined workforce is to be highly desired.

Positive discipline is used to encourage desired behavior, while **negative discipline** is used to discourage improper behavior. Both human resources and supervisory personnel should be concerned about the proper use of a property's discipline efforts.

Managers use direct instruction, written directions, employee manuals, role modeling, and, often, organizational tradition to relay their expectations about employee behavior. Most employees will carefully adhere to behavioral standards when they know what is expected of them.

Unintended mistakes and occasional errors do occur, and coaching activities can typically correct these actions. However, intentional and repetitive noncompliance with standards should result in preestablished consequences that are identified in a **progressive discipline** program.

The consequences of noncompliance with appropriate behavior should follow the "hot stove principle" explained by Douglas McGregor, the well-known management theorist. He points out that, when one touches a hot stove, the consequence is immediate: a burn, and there is no doubt about what caused the pain.

The typical reaction is not to be upset with the stove. Instead, a rational reaction is to question why it was touched and to avoid the clearly foreseen consequences of touching it again.

Humans have emotions and cannot typically remain neutral and consistent like a stove. However, a consistently applied progressive discipline program lets employees know, in advance, the consequences of unacceptable behavior, which become more serious as the behavior is repeated. For this approach to be effective, the subordinate must view the consequences of repeated behavior to be undesirable. If they are not, behavior is unlikely to change.

Figure 9.7 reviews the human resources role in the progressive discipline process. Similar to that required to develop and maintain the performance appraisal process (Figure 9.2), human resources managers typically perform coordination, communication, and administration responsibilities.

As you review Figure 9.7, note the role of human resources personnel in advocating for an effective progressive discipline process and determining the basic legal requirements to be incorporated into it. Coordinating efforts include soliciting input from top-level property leaders, managers, and supervisors, and, hopefully, the employees themselves. Proposed procedures must be developed, reviewed, and revised, and input from legal counsel is required as a final step before process adoption. Then, policies, procedures, and necessary documents must be developed and used in communication efforts with affected personnel. Follow-up tasks, including evaluation, revision, if necessary, and the possibility of addressing unanticipated issues, if any, are possible tasks. Finally, information from the progressive discipline process must be managed as it is entered and maintained in personnel records.

A commonly used four-step progressive discipline program includes documented oral warning, written warning, suspension, and dismissal. Coaching to correct behavior may precede the documented oral warning, especially if a one-time occurrence does not create significant difficulties (e.g., an initial violation of a policy regarding use of solid-toed shoes in the kitchen).

DOCUMENTED ORAL WARNING

Documented oral warning: The first step in a progressive discipline process: a written record is made of an oral reprimand given to an employee.

Reprimand: A formal criticism or censure by a person with authority to do so.

The first step (mildest) in this form of employee discipline is the **documented oral warning.**

The written record of an oral warning should include the employee action that preceded the warning, the date of the incident and of the oral warning, and the name of the supervisor issuing the **reprimand.** Figure 9.8 illustrates the format for an oral reprimand record.

Some managers believe that initial discipline activity should not become part of the employee's permanent personal file but instead should be maintained in a separate manager's file. Other managers document the issuance of an oral warning,

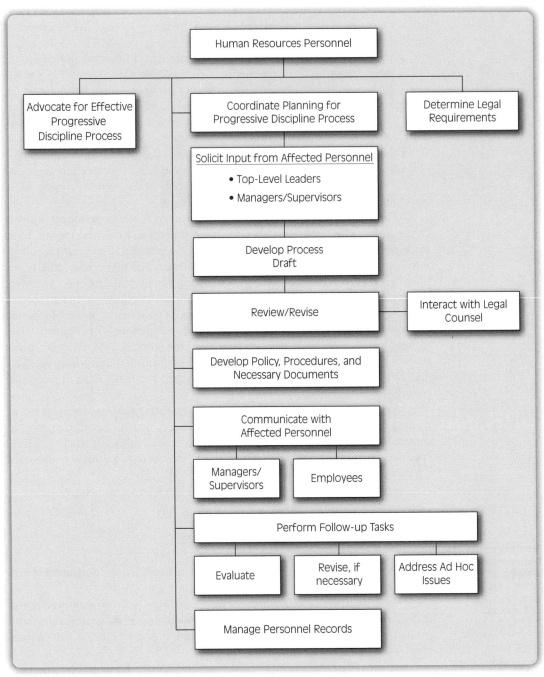

FIGURE 9.7: Human Resources Role in Progressive Discipline Process

DISCUSSION RECORD

Name of Employee: _____

Discussion Date: _____ Time: _____

Incident Date: _____

Incident Description: _____

_____

_____

_____

Follow-up action(s): _____

_____

_____

Employee's Signature: _____ Date: _____

Supervisor's Signature: _____ Date: _____

Note: A copy of this discussion record will be included in the personnel file and is available for the employee upon request.

FIGURE 9.8: Oral Reprimand Record

but do not include the actual reprimand in the employee's permanent file. The property's progressive discipline program should explain the disposition of this documented record so all employees receive identical treatment.

To illustrate this initial progressive discipline step, assume that Sam, a new cook in a hospital, has been late twice in the last week and has been coached about the problem by Ajay, his supervisor. When the problem next occurs, Ajay meets privately with Sam to explain why punctuality is important. Ajay should then allow Sam to respond. Ajay may discover that Sam did not understand some aspect of the expected behavior, or learn that a legitimate reason existed for the late arrival.

Ajay and Sam should mutually develop and agree upon an appropriate solution, and Ajay should tell Sam about the consequences of further late arrivals. An oral reprimand record can be completed and signed by Ajay and Sam to finalize the oral warning process. Hopefully, this will resolve the problem. If not, the next step in the progressive disciplinary process is necessary.

Written warning: The second step in a progressive discipline process that alerts an employee that further inappropriate behavior will lead to suspension.

WRITTEN WARNING

A **written warning** is a document that becomes part of an employee's permanent file.

The content of a written warning is similar to that of the oral written warning (see Figure 9.8). It should include the employee's name, date of the incident, the name of the supervisor issuing the written warning, and the plan to prevent further occurrences. It also typically permits the employee to provide his or her own version of the incident. Signatures of the supervisor and the affected employee will be required.

Human Resources MANAGEMENT ISSUES (9.1)

"Let me see if I understand," said Allisha, the Food and Beverage Director at Foxwoods Country Club, as she reviewed the employee file of Lani Meier, a dining room server. "Lani has worked here for five years with no write-ups. Now, in the two weeks since you have become her supervisor, Lani is at stage three of our progressive discipline process, and your recommendation is suspension."

"She did it to herself, Allisha," replied Michelle, a former dining room server and Lani's new boss. "Lani never liked me. I think she is jealous of me, but I played it straight up. Every write-up I give is legitimate. She needs to be suspended or fired, because I don't think she'll ever change."

Allisha reviewed the file one more time. Lani's first written oral warning, dated 10 days ago, was for returning from her unpaid lunch period 10 minutes late. Lani stated that she had gone to the bank and was caught at a train crossing returning to work, which delayed her timely return.

The written warning followed two days later, when Lani was reprimanded for being out of uniform. In fact, in the written report, Lani admitted that she was working without a nametag, but that she was on her way to the locker room to put it on when a club member asked her some questions. While Lani was responding to the member, Michelle noticed she was "working while out of uniform," verified that Lani had already punched in, and, as a result, wrote her up.

The suspension that Michelle was now proposing was the result of an incident yesterday when, as required by the employee handbook, Lani failed to notify her supervisor four hours before her shift began that she would not be at work as assigned on the schedule.

Interestingly, Allisha had talked to Lani earlier in the day, and Lani mentioned she had taken her son to the emergency room on the previous morning. She was scheduled to work at 7 A.M. and had left a voice mail on Michele's office phone at 5 A.M. That was two hours later, Michele now pointed out, than the time allowed by the employee manual, and so it justified the suspension.

QUESTIONS

1. Do you think Allisha should support Michelle's recommendation that Lani be suspended? Why or why not?
2. Do you believe Michele is following a progressive disciplinary process? Why or why not?
3. What do you think is happening in this situation? How would you address it if you were Allisha?

The written warning step must be done correctly to protect the organization if the employee later challenges the legitimacy (legality) of the progressive disciplinary process. The employee behavior leading to this step should relate to that exhibited in the first step. Managers should remember that the courts view the term *progressive* as generally meaning "related to the same."

Returning to the example of Ajay and Sam, assume that Sam neglected to properly label and date a pan of food before placing it in the cooler, and that this action resulted in loss of the product. It would not be appropriate to issue a written warning to Sam for this behavior, because it does not relate to his late arrival behavior. Because this is a first offense, an oral written warning may be necessary. Is an incident one in a series or the beginning of a new series of incidents? This sometimes difficult question must be answered to determine the appropriate management action.

It is a good rule to praise in public and to reprimand in private. However, many progressive discipline processes require an observer to be present at the second and later steps in the process. Co-managers, supervisors, or others can monitor the discussion and serve as an eyewitness.

SUSPENSION

Suspension: The third step in a progressive discipline process: a period off from work resulting from ongoing inappropriate behavior.

Suspension is the third step in the progressive discipline process, and it should only be undertaken when the previous steps have not resolved the problem. A suspension may be for any period deemed appropriate by management. Suspensions, however, should be applied consistently: if one employee is suspended for a specific period for a particular behavior, then all other employees suspended for the same behavior should be suspended for the same length of time.

An action to suspend an employee must be documented, and the information should be placed in the employee's permanent file. Some employees may refuse to sign the document. Despite an employee's view that an unsigned document will somehow invalidate it, this refusal carries virtually no meaning if the employee had the opportunity to sign it. If an employee refuses to sign a discipline report, then the observer should sign the document and note the employee's refusal to do so.

An employee's suspension, with or without pay, is a serious step. It should signal that the employee's behavior is clearly not acceptable and that he or she is in danger of losing the job. If the employee's behavior is not corrected at this step, dismissal is likely.

DISMISSAL

Dismissal: An employer-initiated separation of employment.

Dismissal is the final step in the progressive discipline process and should only be implemented for serious infractions. Unfortunately, in some cases, this step may be management's only alternative. Later in this chapter, you'll learn more about the specific issues related to employer-initiated dismissals. In the context of a progressive disciplinary program, dismissal represents not only a final step in the process, but also a failure on the part of both the employee and the employer.

From an employee's perspective, dismissal means that even after repeated warnings, the organization's behavioral norms were not met. From the employer's perspective, dismissal means that the manager was unable to persuade the employee to modify his or her behavior sufficiently to maintain the job.

Effective progressive discipline programs modify and improve employee behavior. Too often, however, the focus is on the past, rather than the future. During counseling sessions that should occur at each stage in the discipline process, managers should carefully explain the predictable consequences of continued negative behavior. They should convey this information as a factual statement rather than as a threat.

Behavior Improvement Tactics

3. **Describe the role of employee improvement tactics as an integral part of the performance management process.**

Discipline was defined earlier to involve efforts to reinforce acceptable behavior and to eliminate unacceptable behavior. These are the topics of this section.

REINFORCEMENT OF ACCEPTABLE GOOD BEHAVIOR

When managers encourage employees to perform in specific ways and the employees can do so, the desired behavior is reinforced, and it will occur more frequently. Even when the employee cannot perform a task, enthusiastic encouragement can cause performance improvement.

Most staff members, like all people, respond to praise and encouragement. It feeds their self-esteem and ego, and pushes them to achieve more and to try harder. However, many managers focus on poor performance and ignore the employee's internal and fundamental motivators. Recognizing the efforts (not just the results) can elevate a manager to a position of greater leadership.

Here are examples of specific tactics to reinforce positive behavior:

■ *Saying more than "thank you" or "good job."* The best managers encourage specific behaviors. For instance, assume you are a hotel manager, and Carol, your director of sales, has just completed a phone conversation with a difficult customer: You could say:

"Carol, I heard your conversation, and I really liked how you handled it. You kept calm and focused on resolving the complaint, and you paraphrased the client to show you were listening to the concerns."

Note that Carol will be encouraged with specific mention of actions that you want to affirm and see repeated.

■ *Doing it on the fly.* The best managers do not wait to encourage employees until it is less hectic. Encouragement only takes an extra moment, and busy, chaotic times are when employees typically most need encouragement. When managers only praise employees during formal performance reviews, the employees may feel cheated the rest of the year.

- *Telling them directly.* Managers may tell those around them how much they appreciate an employee, but they sometimes feel uncomfortable telling that employee directly. Employees will not get inflated egos or expect a raise if they are complimented. The more likely case is that they will be thrilled when their effort is noticed, and they will work even harder to justify their manager's continued appreciation.
- *Meaning what is said.* A manager's tone of voice, eye contact, and body language can enhance or detract from a message. Managers must be sincere, make eye contact, and take the time to stop and look at the employee when conversing. Insincere praise is worse than no praise at all!
- *Putting it in writing.* Encouraging words need not be typed and formal. A short, handwritten note is fast and easy. A complimentary note from one's boss can be shared proudly with family members and friends. A written compliment is a source of pride to nearly every employee and demonstrates the power of recognition.

ELIMINATION OF UNACCEPTABLE BEHAVIOR

When employees exhibit unwanted behavior, it is usually because they don't know the desired behavior, know it but do not know how to perform it, or know it and do not want to perform it.

In the first case, behavior improvement may involve careful explanation about the performance standard. In the second case, skills training is likely required (see Chapter 6). In the third case, a progressive discipline process is likely the appropriate response, and **counseling** is an important tactic in the process.

Counseling (employee): A process to assist employees in overcoming performance problems.

Effective employee counseling assists workers in making their own good decisions from among available choices. To plan counseling to overcome employee performance problems, the manager requires a list of concerns about the employee's performance, including times, dates, and other information about unsatisfactory behavior. Time when uninterrupted conversation with the employee is possible should be arranged. The employee should receive sufficient notice about the meeting and subject matter to prepare for it.

During the counseling session, focus on the behavior, not the person or his or her attitudes. For example, managers should not say: "Sam, you are totally irresponsible. You arrive late nearly every day!" Rather, the comment could be: "Sam, you have been arriving at work late nearly every day, and this causes a problem for our operation. What is the reason for your lateness?"

Listening to the employee helps him or her feel valued and understood. Employees should be encouraged to talk and to explore and explain their behavior. Hopefully, options can be considered, and a realistic solution to the performance problem will be proposed. Then clear objectives can be developed, specific action plans can be identified, and the manager will commit to supporting the employee's improvement efforts.

In some cases, undesirable employee performance may result from forces beyond his or her control. Financial difficulties, marital traumas, family emergencies, death of parent, spouse or child, substance abuse, and legal issues are examples of factors that can negatively affect performance. Despite management admonitions that employees must leave their personal problems at home, employees cannot always do so. Notwithstanding the desire of caring managers to want to help in these and related situations, comments should be limited to the employee's performance. Some off-job factors affecting employees may be the result of poor lifestyle choices, whereas others will be caused by circumstances the employees legimately could not control. In all cases, when external factors are the prime reasons for unsatisfactory performance, the best course of action is to refer the employee to an effective internal or external employee assistance program (EAP; see Chapter 10).

Employee Separation

4. **Differentiate between a voluntary and a nonvoluntary employee separation, and explain the function of the exit interview.**

Turnover: The replacement of one employee by another.

Despite the costs and disruption that occur when an employee leaves a job, in some segments of the hospitality industry, **turnover**, as measured by the business's turnover rate, is exceptionally high.

The inevitable result of turnover is an increase in managerial time and other real financial costs. In a 2006 survey of more than 400 HR managers, 15 percent said that the cost to replace the average employee was about equal to the employee's annual wage; 42 percent said that the cost was equal to two times the worker's annual salary; 26 percent said three times; and 17 percent said four or more times the annual wage! All managers agree that costs associated with employees who do not remain with the organization are high, and they should be avoided when it is possible to do so. Then HR managers will not need to continually recruit new staff members and move them through the expensive and time-consuming orientation and training processes.

Some turnover is inevitable and is good for a business, because new staff members with diverse attitudes and ideas can be recruited. However, excessive turnover rates are detrimental to an operation's ability to maintain quality standards and costs and, sometimes, to remain financially viable.

Employee separations can be viewed as voluntary or involuntary, and both types are discussed in the information that follows.

VOLUNTARY SEPARATION

Voluntary (separation): An employee-initiated termination of employment.

Voluntary employment separations are inevitable. Employees graduate from school, retire, move away, and, for numerous other reasons, elect to resign from a job.

While these employee-initiated separations are often inconvenient, they rarely cause significant replacement issues. In the best-case scenario, the employee will

Human Resources Managers and Counseling Sessions

It is unlikely that many supervisors promoted to their positions after successful performance in entry-level jobs will be able to conduct effective counseling sessions without training in how to conduct them. Communication and counseling skills can be addressed in a basic supervisory training program. These can be enjoyable sessions, when, for example, role-play and dialog training activities allow the new supervisors to practice basic skills taught during these sessions.

Many hospitality industry observers believe that numerous problems are caused by managers, not by those whom they supervise. Human resources managers must assume their responsibility to help supervisors become successful, and training to assist them in interacting with their staff members is, perhaps, their most important training responsibility.

Human Resources Management:
CURRENT EVENTS 9.1

IT'S NONE OF YOUR BUSINESS, OR IS IT?

Despite an interest in maintaining their focus on employees' work performance, many HR managers are asked for advice about the personal lives of their staff members. Some managers readily provide it; others feel it is best to keep an arm's-length distance from non-work-related issues.

In her extremely popular book, *Nickel and Dimed; On (Not) Getting By in America*, essayist and cultural critic Barbara Ehrenreich researched the lives of low-wage-earning employees. In 1999 and 2000, Ehrenreich worked as a waitress in Key West, Florida, as a cleaning woman and a nursing home aide in Portland, Maine, and in a Wal-Mart in Minneapolis, Minnesota. Her book details what she did and what she saw in the lives of her fellow workers.

Despite your agreement or disagreement with her conclusions, her book should be required reading for those who are not aware of the challenges faced by many of the working poor. *Note:* In 2008, the take-home pay for a full-time federal minimum wage worker supporting one child was less than the federal poverty level. Experienced HR managers know that utility shutoffs, jail time for relatives, personal or family member substance abuse problems, transportation crises, immigration issues, and the stress of past-due rent are just some of the harsh realities of life for many workers. An appreciation of the issues they face is helpful to HR managers who want to assist these workers to navigate real challenges in their personal and professional lives.

inform managers about the pending departure in enough time that a replacement can be recruited and trained.

INVOLUNTARY SEPARATION

Involuntary (separation): An employer-initiated termination of employment.

Involuntary employment separations are frequently caused by poor employee performance. However, management may also have failed to properly select, orient, train, and direct the work of these employees.

Involuntary employee separations affect more than just immediate employee replacement and training costs. In most states, employees who are involuntarily separated qualify for unemployment compensation payments. While there are exceptions (e.g., for employees dismissed for theft, assault, or other illegal activities), significant increases in payments to employees who are involuntarily

- What is your primary reason for leaving?
- Did anything specific make you decide to leave?
- What did you like best about working here?
- What did you like least about working here?
- Were your job duties the same as you anticipated when you were hired? (If not, how were they different?)
- Did you receive enough training?
- Did you receive enough feedback about your performance from your supervisor?
- Did this job help you advance in your long-term career goals?
- Are there any current employees you feel would perform well in your job?
- Do you have any tips to help us find your replacement?
- What would you do to improve our operation?
- Were the pay, benefits, and other incentives in our operation fairly administered?
- What was the quality of your supervision?
- Based on your experience with us, what does it take to succeed at this company?
- Did any company policies or procedures (or any other problem) make your job unusually difficult?
- Would you be leaving this job if your pay was higher?
- Would you consider working for our company in the future (or at another location)?
- Would you recommend working for this company to your family and friends?
- What does your new job offer that this job does not?
- Can this company do anything to encourage you to stay?
- Did anyone in this company discriminate against you, harass you, or cause you to feel hostility in your working conditions?
- Is there anything you would like the owners (managers) of this operation to know about their business that they may not currently know?

FIGURE 9.9: Sample Exit Interview Questions

separated will result in an increase in the amount the employer must pay into the state's unemployment compensation accounts.

We have examined employment separation from the perspectives of employees who leave the organization for good reason and those who are asked to leave. A third case, however, is the employee who leaves voluntarily but does so involuntarily! In other words, the employee decides to leave the job, but the reason relates to the job.

Consider Stella, a good employee who likes her job, but who is leaving for another job doing the same work at the same rate of pay. She feels her manager does not appreciate her, and recognition of a job well-done is important to her (as it is to many employees). Because Stella does not receive the recognition she seeks, she will leave the organization. Often, the motivations of employees like Stella remain unknown. In other cases, exit interviews can help uncover reasons for the involuntary/voluntary separation of employees.

EXIT INTERVIEWS

Exit interview: A meeting between a representative of the organization and a departing employee.

Exit interviews are typically utilized when an employee voluntarily resigns. Then HR managers ask questions while taking notes, or request that the employee complete a questionnaire or a short survey.

Exit interviews can yield vital workplace information and, sometimes, can prevent the loss of employees who really want to remain at the job, but feel they cannot. Figure 9.9 lists examples of questions that may be asked of separating employees during a well-planned exit interview.

No organization wants to lose good employees. Well-designed exit interviews are an effective tool in helping HR managers reduce the loss of their good employees by identifying and eliminating, wherever possible, those factors that cause these employees to resign.
Courtesy Image 100 Ltd.

IT'S THE LAW!

In many cases, employers justify the nonvoluntary separation of their employees based on the at-will employment doctrine discussed in Chapter 4. In most cases, at-will employment laws allow employers great latitude to terminate employees with or without cause. There are at least five exceptions to these statutes, however, and if evidence of any one of these exceptions is documented in the appraisal process or elsewhere, it is likely that the affected employee could win a wrongful termination lawsuit.

Contractual relationship. Employees may not be terminated at will if there is a contractual relationship. A contractual relationship exists when employers and employees have a legal agreement regarding how employee issues are handled. Under such contracts, discharge may occur only if it is based on just cause.

Implied contractual relationship. An implied contract is any verbal or written statement made by members of the organization that suggests organizational guarantees or promises about continued employment. These statements are most often found in employee handbooks that have not been carefully reviewed to ensure there is, in fact, no implied contractual relationship.

Public policy violation. An employee cannot be terminated for refusing to obey an order from an employer that is considered an illegal activity (e.g., being asked to bribe a public food safety inspector to receive a higher kitchen inspection score). Furthermore, employees cannot be terminated for exercising their individual legal rights, such as agreeing to serve on jury duty or filing a complaint against an employer with a governmental entity, even if that complaint ultimately is dismissed because it was unfounded.

Statutory considerations. Employees may not be terminated if doing so would result in a direct violation of a federal or state statute. For example, an employer may not terminate an employee for reasons that would violate either the Civil Rights or Age Discrimination Acts. Thus, an employer who terminates a female employee in preference of a male employee is in violation of a federal mandate that such gender-based employment decisions are not permitted.

Breach of good faith. While it is difficult for employees to prove breach of **good faith** on the part of an employer, the courts have determined that the at-will employment concept does not allow employers total freedom to terminate. For example, if the national director of sales for a large hotel company secures a contract with a very large organization, the employer may not, to avoid paying the legitimately earned, but significant-sized, bonus due to the salesperson, terminate that person's employment. In such a case, the courts would take the position that the employee worked on the sale in good faith (expecting to earn the commission), and the employer cannot use the at-will employment doctrine to avoid paying the commissions because doing so would not be acting in good faith.

Legal Considerations of Performance Management and Appraisal

5. **Identify major legal issues related to performance management and appraisal.**

Good faith: The honest intent to act without taking an unfair advantage over another person.

As you have learned, employers have great latitude in how they design and administer their performance management and appraisal systems. They are not, however, free to terminate employees in violation of the laws specifically enacted to ensure fairness in these systems. While the laws vary greatly based on the country in which the business operates (as well as local laws), in the United States, several laws directly affect performance appraisal and termination systems.

TITLE VII OF THE CIVIL RIGHTS ACT

Title VII of the Civil Rights Act (1964) specifically prohibits employers from using non-job-related factors for employee evaluation, promotion, or termination. While most of today's hospitality employers are too sophisticated to formally and blatantly utilize individual characteristics such as race, religion, or gender when evaluating or terminating employees, equally sophisticated HR managers responsible for administering the process should be alert for the following signals that an informal discrimination system is in place:

Protected class: A group of workers with a characteristic specifically identified by an employment-related law or ordinance as protected.

- The underrepresentation of workers in specific **protected classes** in highly desired jobs
- Variations in performance appraisal scores based on a worker's membership in a protected class
- Variations in employee pay based on a worker's membership in a protected class
- Variations in employee promotions based on a worker's membership in a protected class

For example, under the Civil Rights Act of 1964, the characteristics of age, color, disability, national origin, race, religion, and sex designate protected classes of workers. Employees in protected classes cannot be treated differently from other employees, discriminated against, fired, or laid off because of their protected class status.

THE EQUAL PAY ACT

The Equal Pay Act (1963) requires equal pay for men and women doing equal work, if the jobs performed require equal skill, effort, and responsibility, and if they are performed under similar working conditions. Surprisingly, some hospitality managers perceive some jobs to be best suited for men, while they believe other jobs are best suited for women. Women working in these operations are often

Human Resources MANAGEMENT ISSUES   (9.2)

"**W**e need to reduce payroll during the holidays, when our business drops off," said Penny, the Landmark Restaurant's manager.

Mark, the kitchen manager, was discussing staffing in his department.

"Well," he said, "the two people I could lay off are Nita and Nate. They both are in the pre-prep area, and when it gets slow, I really only need one of them."

"Which one will you keep?" asked Penny.

"They both are equally good," replied Mark, "but Nate has a wife and family to support, and Nita lives at home with her folks. She'll be okay with the layoff; Nate would have more problems getting by."

QUESTIONS

1. Do you think Mark's proposed decision is a violation of either the Civil Rights Act or the Equal Pay Act (or both)? Why?
2. Do you believe Penny should allow Mark to go forward with his layoff plan? Why or why not?
3. As an HR manager what would you advise Penny to tell Mark?

evaluated in a way that disallows them from qualifying for the higher-paying jobs considered best suited for men. In nearly all cases, this approach to employment is a clear violation of the Civil Rights Act and is typically accompanied by compensation and performance appraisal systems that violate the Equal Pay Act. Enlightened HR managers should be constantly aware of signs that might indicate the existence of hidden gender-based bias in their operations.

AMERICANS WITH DISABILITIES ACT

The Americans with Disabilities Act (ADA) affects the hiring of workers in this protected class, and it also directly affects the manner in which managers evaluate workers with disabilities. The Act prohibits managers from considering disability when evaluating worker performance. For example, a worker possessing limited hearing ability who is hired for a job in which hearing level is immaterial may not be evaluated lower than his or her coworkers, based solely on the employee's hearing limitation.

An employer can, however, hold employees with disabilities to the same standards of performance as other employees without disabilities for performing essential job functions with or without reasonable accommodation (see Chapter 2). More complex, however, are issues related to employee evaluations that consider employee behaviors that, in fact, may be disability-based, but are unacceptable. Assume a manager first learns during an appraisal review that an employee believes his disability is the cause of his poor performance or misconduct. Must the manager excuse the poor performance? The answer is "no." As long as managers treat these employees in exactly the same manner as they would any other employee who performed poorly or violated conduct rules, they are not in violation of the ADA, even if the employee has a disability.

If a performance appraisal system uncovers a previously undisclosed disability, however, management action may be required. Assume that Shondra cleans floors and bathrooms for a restaurant. She did not disclose any disability when she was hired. During her appraisal review, however, her supervisor discusses performance problems. Shondra states that she has a learning disability and does not always understand instructions. She asks that instructions be given to her both orally and in writing so she can review them carefully. Her manager may legally address her current poor performance through the regular appraisal process, but the manager

Human Resources Management:
CURRENT EVENTS 9.2

While the ADA's noncoverage of employees engaging in illegal drug use is clear, the Act's impact on those disabled by alcoholism is less straightforward. Assume that a manager sees a bartender stealing and consuming alcohol while on the job. Assume also that the bartender is covered under the ADA because of alcoholism. In this situation, the manager suspends the bartender and later decides to terminate the employee. The employee claims he or she cannot be terminated because of an alcoholism-related disability, and an employee may not be terminated for a previously disclosed, and covered, disability.

The bartender in this example may be technically correct, but should still lose the job because the employer has, in fact, acted legally. While a current illegal user of drugs is not protected by the ADA, a person who currently uses alcohol is not automatically denied protection. An alcoholic is a person with a disability and is protected by the ADA if he or she is qualified (as is true in this case) to perform the essential functions of the job. In fact, an employer may even be required to provide a reasonable accommodation to an alcoholic. However, an employer can discipline, discharge, or deny employment to an alcoholic whose use of alcohol adversely affects job performance or conduct. An employer also may require that employees do not work under the influence of alcohol. Furthermore, ADA-covered employees are not immune from workplace rules. If drinking on the job is prohibited, then all employees are affected, and unfortunately for the bartender in this scenario, employees who steal are not permitted to do so under the guise of ADA provisions!

must now consider providing a reasonable accommodation to enable Shondra to meet performance standards in the future. Before providing an accommodation, the manager may require Shondra to provide medical documentation to establish that she, in fact, has a disability and needs a reasonable accommodation.

Here's a final example of how the ADA should be considered when evaluating and terminating (if necessary) a disabled employee: assume that Nestor, a hotel's swimming pool attendant, is observed by several other employees and his manager to be smoking marijuana in the employee locker room. When he originally applied for his job, Nestor disclosed that he was recovering from a drug addiction, so he was covered by ADA provisions. However, Nestor may be terminated because any person currently engaging in the illegal use of drugs is specifically excluded from the definition of a "qualified individual with a disability" protected by the ADA. Nestor's employer can take action against him based on his confirmed illegal drug use. In fact, under the circumstances in this example, *failure* to terminate Nestor for illegal drug use could, because of the nature of his job, subject the employer to charges of negligent retention (see Chapter 4) if an accident that Nestor should have prevented resulted in serious injury or death to a guest.

AGE DISCRIMINATION IN EMPLOYMENT ACT

The Age Discrimination in Employment Act (ADEA) prohibits organizations with 20 or more employees from treating workers aged 40 and older differently (including in the areas of appraisal and performance management) from other workers based on their age. While most hospitality managers understand that age discrimination is illegal, they should carefully monitor their own operations for telltale signs that age discrimination may be occurring.

The EEOC is responsible for ADEA enforcement. The following situations indicate activities that could lead the EEOC to conclude that age discrimination is present in a hospitality operation:

- The boss wanted younger-looking, more attractive females (or males) for front-of-house positions, so older workers were not hired.
- The boss selected workers for advanced training based on his view of which employees would be with the company for a long time and were, therefore, worth the significant investment required. As a result, older workers closer to retirement age were not selected for the training.
- Money was tight, so the boss fired older, higher paid workers to keep younger workers who are paid less.
- The boss intentionally gave older workers lower employee evaluation scores, and then used the record of these employees' allegedly poor performance to justify terminating them.
- The boss turned down an older, more experienced worker for a promotion and, instead, hired someone from the outside who was younger because he said the company "needs new blood."

Managers assigned to evaluating older workers must be careful to focus only on job performance, and not on negative stereotypes that illegally discriminate against them. *Courtesy PhotoDisc/Getty Images*

In these cases, it is possible (and probable!) that bosses engaging in such activities are practicing illegal age discrimination and should be prohibited from doing so by their supervisors.

HUMAN RESOURCES TERMS

The following terms were defined in this chapter:

Performance management

Appraisal (employee)

Customer (internal)

Customer (external)

Absolute standard (performance appraisal method)

Relative standard (performance appraisal method)

Targeted outcome (performance appraisal method)

BARS

BOS

Management by objectives

Peer evaluation

Upward assessment (performance appraisal method)

360-degree appraisal
   (performance appraisal
   method)
Reliability
Validity
Halo effect
Pitchfork effect
Discipline (management action)
Disciplined (workforce
   description)
Progressive discipline
Oral warning (documented)

Reprimand
Warning (written)
Suspension
Dismissal
Counseling (employee)
Turnover
Separation (voluntary)
Separation (involuntary)
Exit interview
Good faith
Protected class

FOR YOUR CONSIDERATION

1. Some managers maintain that employee rating and appraisal systems must include the evaluation of subjective employee characteristics such as personality, attitude, appearance, demeanor, friendliness, and social behavior. Other managers maintain that these characteristics most often do not reflect a worker's ability to successfully perform a job. In addition, they point out that an overreliance on subjective factors can undermine employee morale and lead to perceptions of unfairness. What role do you believe subjective factors should play in evaluating hospitality employees? Explain and defend your answer.

2. Some forms of undesirable employee behavior are so serious that they warrant immediate termination, despite the existence of a progressive disciplinary program. Examples could include on-the-job fighting or intoxication. Consider the case of theft by an employee. Should such behavior result in the use of progressive discipline, or should it always result in immediate termination? Would the item or dollar amount taken by the employee affect your decision? Why or why not?

3. When being evaluated by their bosses, most employees say they prefer a system that treats each employee in exactly the same manner. Interestingly, however, these same employees believe bosses should consider the individual circumstances of an incident when evaluating objectionable behavior. As an employee, which system would you prefer your boss use? Explain your answer.

CASE STUDY: HUMAN RESOURCES MANAGEMENT IN ACTION

"The problem, I'm afraid, may just be her age," Lisa Oliver, the executive housekeeper, said to Ashley Austin, the hotel's general manager.

"What do you mean?" asked Ashley.

"Well, Paula Cooper has worked as a housekeeper in this hotel for more than twenty-five years and has always done an excellent job. Recently, she has had trouble cleaning her rooms in the time allowed. Some room attendants are complaining because, after they finish their own rooms, they must help Paula. They think it's unfair to make them do her job."

"She tries hard," continued Lisa, "but as you know, room cleaning is a tough, physically demanding job. With our chain's new bedding standards, even lots of the younger room attendants are challenged. In Paula's case, she knows what to do, but she cannot do it as fast as she used to. The room inspectors find her work acceptable; it's the quantity that is the problem. She almost never meets the 30-minute-per-room standard anymore. I just wonder how long we can keep her."

Dimension: Performance Appraisals

Review the conversation described in the case:

1. What do you believe is the most likely cause of Paula's substandard work performance?
2. Assume you are the hotel's general manager. Do you believe your executive housekeeper is evaluating Paula's work performance any differently than that of other room attendants based on her age? Why or why not?
3. What would you, as the hotel's general manager, advise Lisa to do about Paula? Explain the intended goal of each recommended step.

Dimension: Responsibility to the Team

Review the conversation described in the case:

1. What obligation does Lisa have to be fair to the other employees in her department? Justify your answer.
2. Is the fact that Paula now works slower than her peers inherently unfair to the other employees? Explain your position.
3. Many hotels and restaurants utilize a work system that essentially requires all team members to complete the tasks assigned to its members (e.g., cleaning up at the end of a shift, cleaning all guest rooms, and preparing all menu items) before any person leaves work. Other managers allow individual team members who complete their work ahead of their teammates to leave when they are finished. Identify at least one advantage and one disadvantage of each approach.

Dimension: Responsibility to the Individual

1. Should Paula's length of employment affect the manner in which her current work performance is evaluated? Explain your position.
2. Assume you operate a business in which there are some jobs that most younger workers can do more easily than older workers. Should your employee compensation programs reflect such differences? Would such an approach be fair? Explain.

3. Identify at least two legal issues inherent in the human resource dilemma identified in this case.

INTERNET ACTIVITIES

1. The Internet is a good source of information and products related to employee evaluation systems. To see an example, go to: http://www.360degreeassessment. info/products/stperf.html
   a. Click on "Products."
   b. Click on "Total Performance."
   c. Click on "Video Tour."

   Review the characteristics of this employee performance tool. Identify the specific features it offers that were topic areas in this chapter. Which features might you add to address your interests in the hospitality industry?

2. In the hospitality industry, many managers with responsibility for evaluating staff members may have limited or even no previous experience doing so. Some professional appraisal training companies offer assistance to such managers and supervisors. To view one such company's offering, go to: *www.performance-appraisal.com/training.htm.*
   a. Review the topics covered in the company's "Performance Appraisal" seminar offering.
   b. Review the cost(s) per participant.
   c. Review the other training session information supplied by Archer North.

   Would you likely choose to utilize the services of such a company? Why or why not?

3. Many hospitality managers lament that they simply cannot get their employees to consistently exhibit the behaviors they seek. Some companies specialize in helping managers modify employee behavior in positive ways. To view one such company, go to: *www.gbehavior.com.*
   a. Click on "Behavior Modification."
   b. Scroll down to review this company's "SMART" performance objectives.

   Based on the "SMART" performance objectives, would you hire such a company to assist your own operation? What factors might cause you to do so?

CHAPTER TEN

Employee Health and Safety

CHAPTER OUTLINE

CHECKLIST OF CHAPTER LEARNING OBJECTIVES

As a result of satisfactory completion of this chapter, readers will be able to:

1. Explain the roles of the two most important federal agencies responsible for ensuring employees are safe at work and are protected from those who would illegally harass them.

2. Explain the advantages enjoyed by employers who provide healthy worksites for their employees.

3. Describe the differences and similarities between employee assistance programs and employee wellness programs.

4. Review the legal and moral responsibilities employers have to ensure a safe and secure worksite for their employees.

5. List and describe specific steps employers can take to help prevent workplace violence.

Impact on Human Resources Management

A common theme throughout this text is the vital importance of individual employees to the success of any hospitality business. In fact, most managers would agree that their employees are the most important asset, and their protection must receive the highest priority. Effective hospitality managers carefully enact programs designed to help ensure the long-term care and protection of physical assets, such as their buildings, equipment, and cash. In a similar manner, it makes sense for these managers to just as carefully design and implement those programs that will help ensure the safety and protection of their workers.

While it is certainly good business for managers to ensure the health and safety of workers, it is also a legal requirement that they do so. The hospitality industry includes job positions that, if not properly structured, may be quite dangerous or threatening. Legislation has been enacted to guide managers in addressing these concerns. It is the responsibility of HR managers to prevent employees from working in unhealthy or threatening environments, because healthy workers are more productive than those who are not. In addition, from an ethical perspective, employers should want to ensure the safety of their workers simply because it is the right thing to do.

Despite the best efforts of concerned employers to make their worksites safe and secure, good workers can still encounter personal difficulties that negatively affect their performance. Those organizations with designated employee assistance programs find they can help minimize the effects of the personal difficulties faced by employees and, in many cases, can assist these workers in completely overcoming their challenges. Those employers who have implemented employee wellness programs also often find that performance-affecting challenges faced by their employees can be prevented, minimized, or even eliminated, before they cause a significant negative impact at work.

Despite their best programs and planning, HR managers can encounter unavoidable as well as avoidable situations that directly threaten employee safety and security. While unavoidable crises of these types may not be preventable, they can be managed. Experienced HR managers know that well-planned and frequently practiced emergency response programs, as well as crisis management preplanning, can make the difference in successfully surviving an unavoidable catastrophic event.

Unavoidable crises are unfortunate, but even more unfortunate are those crises that, with proper preplanning, could have been prevented. Experienced HR managers know that security programs designed to eliminate threatening and violent behavior at work are important—and critical to the protection and productivity of their employees.

Legal Aspects of Employee Protection

1. Explain the roles of the two most important federal agencies responsible for ensuring employees are safe at work and are protected from those who would illegally harass them.

Most HR managers and the organizations for which they work for would agree that they have a moral obligation to ensure that their workplaces are free from unnecessary hazards and that conditions in the workplace are safe for employees' physical and mental health. Regardless of whether they agree about moral responsibility, they all must recognize their legal responsibilities to ensure healthful working conditions. In the United States, the federal government has enacted two pieces of legislation that directly influence what hospitality organizations must do to ensure an appropriately safe and secure workplace. In this chapter, you will learn about both of these laws.

Before examining those two pieces of legislation in detail, it is important for hospitality managers to remember that most members of society must work to maintain the lifestyle they desire for themselves and their families. Because that is so, it is not surprising that society maintains its legitimate interest in requiring employers to take reasonable steps designed to ensure worker safety. While some business owners and managers might find legislation related to worker safety time consuming or cumbersome to implement, it is certainly in the best interest of all businesses to minimize on-job accidents, especially when reasonable management action could prevent worker accidents, or even worker deaths.

OSHA: Short for the Occupational Safety and Health Administration, the agency responsible for enforcing the Occupational Safety and Health Act.

Despite the importance to society (as well as businesses!) of protecting its members who must work, the first legislation specifically designed to address workplace safety was not enacted until 1970. In that year, Congress passed the Occupational Safety and Health Act, and in doing so created the Occupational Safety and Health Administration (**OSHA**).

OCCUPATIONAL SAFETY AND HEALTH ACT

The passage of the Occupational Safety and Health Act dramatically changed the way HR managers in hospitality, and other industries, viewed their role in ensuring that the physical working conditions in their operations met subscribed standards. Just as the Civil Rights Act of 1964 significantly altered the manner in which employees were to be selected and treated while at work, passage of the Occupational Safety and Health Act ultimately altered the physical conditions under which workers would do their jobs.

History and Enforcement

Concerned about worker safety and health, the U.S. Congress passed the Occupational Safety and Health Act in 1970. It heralded a new era in the history of public efforts to protect workers from harm on the job. The Act established, for the first time, a nationwide, federal program to protect almost the entire workforce from job-related death, injury, and illness.

Then Secretary of Labor James Hodgson, who had helped draft the law, termed it "the most significant legislative achievement" for workers in a decade. Hodgson's first step in putting the law into action was to establish, within the Labor Department, a special agency (the Occupational Safety and Health Administration: OSHA) to administer the Act.

As initially created, OSHA's stated mission was to prevent work-related injuries, illnesses, and deaths. OSHA's current role is to ensure the safety and health of America's workers by setting and enforcing standards; providing training, outreach, and education; establishing partnerships; and encouraging continual improvement in workplace safety and health.

The work of OSHA has been a tremendous success. Since the enforcement agency created by this law began its work, occupational deaths have been cut by 62 percent, and injuries have declined by 42 percent. This fact is even more impressive when you consider that, during the same period, U.S. employment has doubled from 58 million workers at 3.5 million worksites to more than 115 million workers at 7.2 million sites.

The safety and health standards administered by OSHA are quite complex. They include standards related to noise levels, air quality, physical protection equipment, and even the proper size for ladders, to name but a few. Regardless of one's view of the detail with which OSHA involves itself, hospitality managers are responsible for knowing, and following, the Act's provisions. From a practical perspective, HR managers will most often interact with OSHA in the areas of enforcement and record keeping.

The top priority for enforcing violations of the Act are reports of imminent dangers, or accidents about to happen; second are fatalities or accidents serious enough to send three or more workers to the hospital. The third priority is employee-initiated complaints. Referrals from other government agencies are the fourth priority. Fifth are targeted inspections that focus on specific employers and industries that report high injury and illness rates.

Compliance and Recordkeeping Requirements

The Occupational Safety and Health Act applies to nearly all hospitality employers. It requires employers to keep detailed records regarding employee illness and accidents related to work, as well as the calculation of on-job accident rates.

OSHA monitors workplace safety with a large staff of inspectors called compliance officers. Compliance officers visit workplaces during regular business hours and perform unannounced inspections to ensure that employers are operating in compliance with all OSHA health and safety regulations. In addition, the officers are required to investigate any complaints of unsafe business practices. Managers can accompany OSHA compliance officers during an inspection, and they should do so for two reasons: (1) the manager may be able to answer questions or clarify

IT'S THE LAW!

OSHA penalties can range from $0 (for nonserious violations) to $70,000 (for repeat and willful violations). In most cases, penalties may be discounted if an employer has a small number of employees, has demonstrated good faith, or has few or no previous violations. In the hospitality industry, some of the most commonly cited safety violations and penalties relate to an employee's "right to know" about potential threats to their safety.

Early in 1984, OSHA put in place the Federal Hazard Communication Standard that has come to be known as the "right-to-know" law. Originally, the law affected primarily chemical manufacturing facilities. However, in 1985, the courts decided that these regulations should apply to all facilities. The "right-to-know" law is designed to protect workers from potentially hazardous chemicals. The requirements and regulations concerning "right-to-know" include three major areas:

1. Locating, inventorying, and tracking potentially hazardous chemicals
   - Information about what chemicals are used, where they are stored, and how much is used all falls into this category.

2. Identifying, labeling, and providing information about potentially hazardous chemicals
   - All chemicals (and areas where chemicals are used) within a facility must be identified and labeled.
   - Labels must show what health, fire, and reactive hazards are associated with each chemical, as well as what protective equipment must be used to handle the chemical.
   - In addition, definitive information about the chemical must be provided to employees, based on the Material Safety Data Sheets (MSDSs) provided by manufacturers that provide detailed information about the specific chemical, its use, and any potential danger.

3. Training and educating employees
   - Employees must be educated about:
     a. Employees' rights under the legislation
     b. What hazardous chemicals are used by the facility (especially those the employee might come in contact with)
     c. How the chemicals will be labeled
   - The general uses of, protective clothing required, and accident-response procedures associated with the chemical must be communicated.

procedures for the compliance officer; and (2) the manager should know what transpired during the inspection. Afterward, the manager should discuss the results of the inspection with the compliance officer and request a copy of any inspection reports filed. Generally, inspections are not announced, although the compliance officer must state a specific reason for the inspection.

Human Resources MANAGEMENT ISSUES (10.1)

Carlos Magana was a Spanish-speaking custodian working in a healthcare facility's kitchen. Bert LaColle was the new food and beverage director. Mr. LaColle instructed Mr. Magana to clean the grout between the red quarry kitchen tile with a powerful cleaner that Mr. LaColle had purchased from a chemical cleaning supply vendor. Mr. LaColle, who did not speak Spanish, demonstrated to Mr. Magana how he should pour the chemical directly from the bottle onto the grout, and then brush the grout with a wire brush until it was white.

Because the cleaner was so strong, and because Mr. Magana did not wear protective gloves, his hands were seriously irritated by the chemicals in the cleaner. In an effort to lessen the irritation to his hands, Mr. Magana decided to dilute the chemical. He added water to the bottle of cleaner, not realizing that the addition of water would cause toxic fumes. Mr. Magana inhaled the fumes while he continued cleaning, and later, because of that, suffered serious lung damage.

Mr. LaColle was subsequently contacted by OSHA, which cited and heavily fined the facility for a safety (MSDS) violation. Mr. LaColle maintained that MSDS statements, including the one for the cleaner in question, were, in fact, available for inspection by employees.

QUESTIONS

1. Assume MSDSs were, in fact, available to the facility's employees. Do you think the facility fulfilled its obligation to provide a safe working environment for Mr. Magana?
2. Do you believe the facility has an obligation to provide safety information to Mr. Magana in his primary language (Spanish)?
3. Based on your knowledge of HR management, if you were Mr. LaColle, what specific steps would you take to avoid future OSHA violations of this type?

The Occupational Safety and Health Act requires the Secretary of Labor to produce regulations that ensure employers keep records of occupational deaths, injuries, and illnesses. Recording or reporting a work-related injury, illness, or fatality does not mean that the employer or employee was at fault, that an OSHA rule has been violated, or that the employee is eligible for workers' compensation or other benefits. Instead, the records are used for a variety of purposes.

Injury and illness statistics are used by OSHA to help direct its programs and measure its own performance. Inspectors use the data during inspections to help direct their efforts to the hazards that are hurting workers. The records are also used by employers and employees to implement safety and health programs at individual workplaces. Analysis of the data is a widely recognized method for

OSHA enforces employees' right to know if chemicals used on the job pose any dangers to health or safety. *Courtesy PhotoDisc/Getty Images*

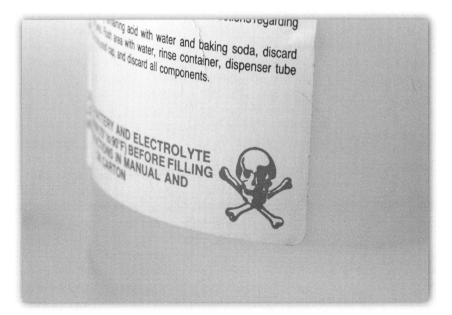

discovering workplace safety and health problems and for tracking progress in solving them. The records employers submit to OSHA also provide the base data for the Annual Survey of Occupational Injuries and Illnesses, the country's primary source of occupational injury and illness data.

Currently, the major areas of OSHA-mandated record keeping related to the hospitality industry include:

- *Log and summary of all recordable injuries and illnesses.* All OSHA-recordable injuries and illnesses that occur in the workplace or during the course of an employee's duties must be entered in a log (OSHA form 300 or its equivalent) within six working days after the employer is notified that a recordable injury or illness has occurred. A summary of the reported accidents or illnesses (OSHA form 300A) must be signed by a responsible company official, and posted each year, in regular work areas from February 1 through March 1. If no recordable injuries or illnesses were reported during the previous year, zeros must be written in the required spaces, and the blank form still must be posted.
- *Personal protective equipment (assessment and training).* The Personal Protective Equipment (PPE) Standard specifically addresses an employer's responsibility to identify any potential threat to an employee's eyes, face, head, and extremities and to allow for the necessary clothing or gear required to protect

employees from harm. If potential hazards, such as chemical or radiological hazards, or mechanical irritants are identified, issues related to those substances must be assessed. The assessment must be written, certified by a responsible official, and be work area and job specific. Employers must train employees on the use of any needed PPE. The facility's policy on PPE and training must be documented in the employer's records and retained for at least five years.

- *Control of hazardous energy (lock out/tag out).* The Lock Out/Tag Out Standard applies to activities related to servicing and/or maintenance of machines and equipment. It is intended to protect employees from the unexpected movement or start-up of machines and equipment. OSHA requires that employers develop a written plan that identifies specific equipment and activities that would require lock out or tag out of the equipment when broken or under repair, and include an employee training element about them. The program must include specific lock out/tag out procedures for each affected piece of equipment. Employees must be trained on the company's Lock Out/Tag Out policy and procedures, and the record of this training must be documented and maintained in the employer's files for at least five years.

- *Hazard communication standards.* The Hazard Communication Standard is intended to address the issue of potentially hazardous chemicals in the workplace and informing employees of the specific hazards and protective measures that must be undertaken when using, handling, and/or storing these products. Some recordkeeping requirements include (1) developing and maintaining a written hazard communication program, including lists of hazardous chemicals in the workplace; (2) providing employees with access to MSDSs; (3) employee training (including documentation) about the hazards of the chemicals they are or may be exposed to and protective measures that must be undertaken; and (4) labeling of chemical containers in the workplace.

- *Emergency action plans and fire prevention plans.* Any facility that employs more than 10 people must develop a written Emergency Action and Fire Prevention Plan. Facilities that employ fewer than 10 people do not have to develop a written plan, but they are required to orally communicate emergency action procedures to each employee.

Additional examples of recordkeeping requirements that may or may not directly apply to a specific hospitality organization include those related to the respiratory protection of workers, asbestos exposure, hepatitis B, and bloodborne pathogens. HR managers can remain current about recordkeeping requirements by regularly logging into the OSHA Web site *(www.osha.gov).*

CIVIL RIGHTS ACT OF 1964 RE: HARASSMENT

In Chapter 2, you learned that Title VII of the Civil Rights Act of 1964 outlaws discrimination in employment on the basis of race, color, religion, sex, or national origin. It is also important to recall that, in 1972, the passage of the Equal Employment Opportunity Act, a revision to the Civil Rights Act of 1964, resulted in the formation of the Equal Employment Opportunity Commission (EEOC).

In 1980, the Equal Employment Opportunities Commission (EEOC) issued regulations defining sexual harassment and stating that it was a form of sexual discrimination prohibited by the Civil Rights Act of 1964. In 1986, the U.S. Supreme Court first ruled that sexual harassment was a form of job discrimination—and held it to be illegal. Today, there is greater understanding among managers that the Civil Rights Act prohibits sexual (and other types of) harassment at work, even when the harassment occurs within the same gender. In addition, most states have their own fair employment practices laws that prohibit harassment based on a variety of factors, and, as a result, many state harassment laws are even stricter than the federal law.

Employees can face a variety of harassment forms. These include:

- *Bullying*. Harassment that can occur on the playground, in the workforce, or any other place. Usually, physical and psychological harassing behavior is perpetrated against an individual, by one or more persons.
- *Psychological harassment*. This is humiliating or abusive behavior that lowers a person's self-esteem or causes them torment. This can take the form of verbal comments, actions, or gestures.
- *Racial harassment*. The targeting of an individual because of his or her race or ethnicity. The harassments include words, deeds, and actions that are specifically designed to make the target feel degraded due to his or her race, origin, or ethnicity.
- *Religious harassment*. Verbal, psychological, or physical harassment used against targets because they choose to practice a specific religion.
- *Stalking*. The unauthorized following and surveillance of an individual, to the extent that the person's privacy is unacceptably intruded upon, and the victim fears for his or her safety. In the workplace, those who know, but do not necessarily work with, the victim most commonly exhibit this form of harassment.
- *Sexual harassment*. This harassment can happen anywhere but is most common in the workplace (and schools). It involves unwelcome words, deeds, actions, gestures, symbols, or behaviors of a sexual nature that make the target feel uncomfortable. Gender and sexual orientation harassment fall into this form of harassment.

In U.S. legal terms, sexual harassment is any unwelcome sexual advance or conduct on the job that creates an intimidating, hostile, or offensive working environment. Such environments are unsafe for employees both physically and mentally. In real-life terms, harassing behavior ranges from repeated offensive or belittling jokes to outright physical assault. In the hospitality industry, workers can be subject to extreme forms of harassment by coworkers and customers. Workers can be required to follow company policies regarding harassment, but employers can also be held directly responsible for the acts of customers and vendors who are not subject to the company's disciplinary procedures. These types of individuals are, however, subject to laws against assault. Therefore, the effective management of a **zero-tolerance** sexual (and other forms of) harassment policy should be implemented, should apply to all individuals with whom employees come into contact, and should be designed to help ensure the safety and security of all employees. Because they are so important, zero-tolerance programs will be examined in detail in this chapter.

Zero tolerance: A policy that permits no amount of leniency regarding harassing behavior.

Employee Health

2. **Explain the advantages enjoyed by employers who provide healthy worksites for their employees.**

Unhealthy workplaces should be a concern to all HR managers employed in the hospitality industry. If worker productivity is reduced because workers cannot function properly at their jobs due to constant headaches, watering eyes, nausea, or fear of exposure to elements that can cause long-term health problems, then the entire industry and its guests will suffer. Consequently, maintaining a healthy work environment benefits the hospitality organization, its workers, and its customers.

WORKSITE HEALTH

Although the specifics of exactly what constitutes a healthy work environment will vary based on the specific hospitality business under examination, in general, HR managers concerned about the health of their workers should directly address the following issues:

1. *Provide sufficient quantities of fresh air.* In the hospitality industry, air-quality concerns in work areas can be significant. Ventilation hoods in cooking and other food production areas should provide workers with enough fresh air to do their jobs comfortably. In most cases, the cost of providing an increased number of air exchanges per hour (to reduce heat levels) is minimal.
2. *Provide a smoke-free environment.* Smoking has long been banned in food production areas. In dining room areas and bars, secondhand smoke is the major threat to worker safety. Most worker safety experts firmly oppose the position of any manager who forces employees to work in tobacco smoke-filled environments. While the issue of smoking in restaurants, bars, and hotels evokes strong reactions from many in the industry, the reality is that, in the future, few businesses will likely be able to maintain environments in which customers (and thus the workers who serve them) will be involuntarily exposed to air they believe to be unhealthy.

Carpal tunnel syndrome: Nerve damage resulting in a burning, tingling, or itching numbness in the palm of the hand and the fingers, especially the thumb and the index and middle fingers.

3. *Keep air ducts clean and dry.* Water and grease in air ducts is a fertile breeding ground for mold and fungi. The regular cleaning of air and grease filters can prevent air-quality problems such as mold and mildew before they start.

4. *Maintain effective equipment inspection programs.* The frequent and thorough inspection of restaurant equipment, especially those pieces using gas as their energy source (e.g., hot water heaters, boilers, ovens, ranges, broilers, and the like), can help detect gas or carbon monoxide leaks before they endanger staff or guests.

5. *Monitor repetitive movement injuries.* Whenever workers must do repetitive tasks, they risk the potential for headaches, swollen feet, back pain, or nerve damage. The most frequent site of repetitive movement injury is the wrist (**carpal tunnel syndrome**). Properly designed work areas can help minimize or eliminate repetitive stress injuries of this type.

6. *Monitor stress levels.* Stress can be caused by a variety of factors, and an in-depth discussion of stress, various means of reducing it, and the many methods of

Human Resources Management:
CURRENT EVENTS 10.1

WOULD YOU PREFER A NONSMOKING OR A NONSMOKING ROOM?

Industry observers were surprised but not shocked when Westin Hotels & Resorts in the United States, Canada, and the Caribbean went 100 percent smoke-free in January 2006.

The hotel industry really took notice, however, when Marriott International Inc. announced that, effective September 2006, all 2,300 of its U.S. and Canadian properties—representing 400,000 guest rooms—would be 100 percent smoke-free. All hotel common areas such as restaurants, lounges, meeting rooms, public space, and employee work areas were also designated as smoke-free.

"Creating a smoke-free environment demonstrates a new level of service and care for our guests and associates," stated J. W. Marriott Jr., Marriott International's chairman and chief executive officer. "Our family of brands is united on this important health issue, and we anticipate very positive customer feedback."

When the major quick-service restaurant chains (e.g., Wendy's, Taco Bell, and McDonald's) implemented smoke-free dining room policies years ago, detractors predicted financial disaster. It didn't happen; nor is it likely that history will record a decrease in Marriott revenues directly tied to their nonsmoking hotel status, even though their guests can now choose only between nonsmoking and nonsmoking rooms. Look for all hospitality chains to announce similar bans within the coming years.

channeling stress in a positive direction is beyond the scope of this text. HR managers should be aware, however, that in the fast-paced hospitality industry, stress can be job-related or it can be brought to the job. Employees often arrive at work concerned about personal matters such as troubling family issues, personal economic problems, and even their individual personality characteristics (e.g., prone or not prone to have high stress levels). When the stress levels at work are excessive, absenteeism, burnout, and turnover typically increase.

7. *Make lifesaving equipment and training readily accessible.* Sudden cardiac arrest (SCA), which claims the lives of 220,000 people each year, can strike any workplace, and at anytime, without warning. But experts know that early access to cardiopulmonary resuscitation (CPR) and an **automated external defibrillator (AED)** can save many of these lives. Because so many people spend the majority of their day in the workplace, the American Red Cross advocates training all workers in CPR and AED use.

8. *Pay attention to workers' complaints.* Dates, events, and employee concerns should be recorded to detect any potential patterns that would indicate continued threats to employee safety.

Automated external defibrillator (AED): A portable electronic device that can audibly prompt and deliver an electric shock that, in many cases, can increase survival rates of those suffering cardiac arrest.

Employee Assistance Programs (EAPs)

3. Describe the differences and similarities between employee assistance programs and employee wellness programs.

Even if hospitality employers work hard to provide healthy worksites, employees will occasionally have personal problems. Whether the problem relates to job stress or to marital, relationship, legal, financial, or health issues, the common feature of such issues is simply this: eventually, the issue will be reflected at the workplace in terms of lowered productivity levels and increased absenteeism or turnover.

To help employees address problem areas in their lives, more companies are implementing employee assistance programs (EAPs). As you learned in Chapter 3, an EAP relates to a variety of employer-initiated efforts to assist their employees with family concerns, legal issues, financial matters, and health maintenance.

In the United States, large companies such as DuPont, Standard Oil, and Kodak implemented the earliest EAPs in the 1940s, as they recognized that some of their employees were experiencing difficulty dealing with alcohol-related issues and addictions. Formal programs were held on the employer's worksite to educate workers about the dangers of alcohol and to help those who were addicted to overcome their dependence on alcohol. The identifiable goal of these programs benefited both employee and employer, because they were aimed at getting the employee back to work, in a productive manner, as quickly as possible. In the hospitality industry, because many worker positions involve the service and, in the case of some sales and management positions, the consumption of alcohol, the need for and benefits of programs of this type are self-evident.

To illustrate the importance of EAPs, consider the case of Mike Edgar. Mike is in the maintenance department at the hotel where you are the HR manager. Mike is a talented worker and has performed very well during his 15 years of employment with the property. He is respected by his fellow employees, his department head, and the hotel's other managers. In addition, he has been selected as employee of the month several times during his tenure with the property. Most recently, however, Mike's performance has not been so good. He has been late three times in the past five weeks and, just yesterday, called in sick to work only 15 minutes before the beginning of his scheduled shift. The rumor in the hotel is that Mike is having significant marital problems and that his wife and children are now living in a town several hours away.

Mike's boss approaches you to discuss the disciplinary action to be taken against Mike. Certainly, your hotel has every right to discipline Mike for his performance shortcomings. Ultimately terminating Mike, however, will likely result in the implementation of a new employee search, involving significant expenditure of time and money, and an extended period of training to bring the new employee up to Mike's level of experience and productivity. In this case, you would likely want to help Mike through this difficult period, and retain a quality employee. Effective EAPs are designed and implemented for cases such as Mike's.

Today, more hospitality employers are implementing EAPs to address nontraditional areas of employee assistance, including adoption counseling, legal assistance, and bereavement counseling, as well as mental health and substance abuse counseling. Such programs can be very cost-effective if an operation's employees view them positively. For employees, the biggest concern about utilizing their employer-provided EAP relates to confidentiality. Simply put, employees must be assured that, if they voluntarily enroll in an EAP, their participation will be kept strictly confidential. In quality EAPs, the administrators of the programs ensure that the confidentiality of its participants will be scrupulously maintained.

EMPLOYEE WELLNESS PROGRAMS

Despite the proven effectiveness of EAPs, some progressive companies have taken the position that it is best to help employees eliminate those lifestyle factors that typically lead to personal problems, and thus prevent these difficulties before they begin. To do so, more employers are implementing employee **wellness programs.**

Wellness programs (employee): An employer-sponsored initiative designed to promote the good health of employees.

Typical examples of employer-initiated wellness programs include the topics of quitting smoking, nutrition and weight management, high blood pressure control, weight loss, self-defense, exercise, and stress management. In many cases, employers who provide these programs find that their employees stay healthier and that the business's health insurance carriers offer discounts for implementation of these programs. In addition, some companies have found that employee participation in wellness programs increases when the employee's family members participate because the rules allow them to do so. Thus, for example, employees who are interested in participating in a company-sponsored weight loss program may be more inclined to attend sessions regularly if their spouse (or significant other) is also allowed to join in.

Employee Safety and Security

4. Review the legal and moral responsibilities employers have to ensure a safe and secure worksite for their employees.

In most English-language thesauruses, you would find the words **safety** and **security** listed as synonyms. In the context that we will examine these terms, each will designate a distinct concept related to HR management.

Safety: Freedom from the conditions that cause personal harm.

Security: Freedom from fear and anxiety related to personal harm.

From the perspective of an HR manager working in hospitality, **safety** can be considered a condition that minimizes the risk of harm to workers, while **security** relates to employees' feelings of fear and anxiety. Thus, an individual employee at work might be very safe, but still not feel secure. Alternatively, employees might feel they are quite secure, while they are, in reality, quite unsafe.

HR managers should seek to ensure that their employees are as safe as possible at work, and as a result, that these same employees feel a high degree of security. Managers can do so by implementing well-designed programs that enhance worker safety and security. For example, employers could implement fire safety programs designed to minimize the fire-related risk of harm to employees. Figure 10.1 details

Vandalism
Fire/arson
Bomb threats
Robbery
Looting
Severe storms, including:
- Hurricanes
- Tornadoes
- Floods
- Snow
- Ice

Accident/injury
Drug overdose
Medical emergency
Rescue breathing/cardiopulmonary resuscitation (CPR)
Death/suicide of guest or employee
Civil disturbance
Terrorist attack
Foodborne illnesses

FIGURE 10.1: Potential Crisis Situations in the Hospitality Workplace

Crisis: A situation that has the potential to negatively affect the health, safety, or security of employees.

additional types of **crises** for which HR managers may consider designing specialized employee safety and/or security programs.

While it is not realistic to believe that employees can be insulated from all potential threats to their safety or security, effective HR managers should take steps to help minimize these threats. From a moral perspective, employers certainly have a responsibility to provide workers with a worksite that is as free from threatening conditions as it can reasonably be. From a legal perspective, the Occupational Safety and Health Act of 1970 (PL 91-596) requires that employers address safe and healthful working conditions. Specifically, the law requires employers to provide their employees with a place of employment that is:

> "free from recognizable hazards that are causing or are likely to cause death or serious physical harm to employees," as well as "the exposures at which no worker will suffer diminished health, functional capacity, or life expectancy as a result of his or her work experience."

EMPLOYEE SAFETY PROGRAMS

Because the safety and security needs of different hospitality organizations vary so widely, it is difficult to provide one all-purpose step-by-step list of activities that should be implemented to minimize the chances of employee accidents or injury. From a legal perspective, a hospitality operation's basic obligation is to act responsibly in the face of threats. One way to analyze and respond to those responsibilities is illustrated by the four-step, simplified system presented in Figure 10.2.

Step 1: Recognition of the safety threat. Safety programs generally start with the recognition of a need; that is, a realization that a threat to people (or property) exists. Some of the most common threats to employee safety in the hospitality industry include those related to natural disasters, coworkers, guests (in dining rooms, bars, lounges, guest rooms, and the like), the worksite, and even the employees themselves.

STEP 1	Recognition of the safety threat
STEP 2	Program development in response to the threat
STEP 3	Program implementation
STEP 4	Program evaluation

FIGURE 10.2: Four-Step, Simplified Safety Management System

The overwhelming majority of guests pose no threat to employees, but effective HR managers still train employees in the proper response to those guests who do pose a threat.
Courtesy PhotoDisc/Getty Images

Step 2: Program development in response to the threat. Once a threat to safety or security has been identified, HR managers can develop an appropriate response to address it. The proper response to an identified threat may take the form of any one or more of the following:

1. Employee training for threat prevention
2. Increased surveillance and/or patrol of facilities (for external threats)
3. Systematic inspections
4. Modification of physical facilities to reduce the threat
5. Establishment of standard procedures

Step 3: Program implementation. When a hospitality operation has identified a threat and designed a safety and security program that directly addresses the threat, it must put the program into action. A large hospitality facility may have a safety and security department. Its head would ordinarily report to the general manager of the facility. Staff members in the department would be responsible for routine duties, such as patrolling the facility for unauthorized people or suspicious activity, performing inspections, assisting the police with crime reports, and serving as a liaison with insurance carriers.

In a smaller facility, a property safety committee can play a valuable role in the identification and correction of safety and security problem areas. Ideally, a safety committee should consist of members from each of an operation's departments. For example, a restaurant might have members from the preproduction, production, and clean-up areas in the back of the house, and bartenders, servers, and hosts in the front of the house. A hotel's safety committee might have one or more members from housekeeping, laundry, maintenance, food and beverage, front desk, guest services, and the administrative offices. In the smallest of hospitality facilities, the operations manager would assume the primary responsibility for ensuring the implementation of appropriate safety-related training.

Step 4: Program evaluation. If a safety program is not working (i.e., if it is not reducing or eliminating the threats to people or property you have identified), then the program must be reviewed for modification. Legally, if it was necessaary, you will be in a much stronger position to defend your safety-related activities if you can document not only that you have a safety program, but also that the program is effective. There are a variety of ways to measure your safety program's effectiveness. Some tangible measurements managers may utilize include:

- Number of facility inspections performed
- Inspection or quality scores
- Number of safety-related incidents reported
- Dollar amount of losses sustained
- Number of insurance claims filed
- Number of lawsuits filed
- Number of serious or minor accidents
- Number of lost workdays by employees
- Number of employees disabled
- Number of drills or training exercises properly performed

The important point for HR managers to remember is that a safety-related program can be said to have been successfully implemented only after an appropriate evaluation component has been developed. Unless you know a program has made a measurable difference, you may easily be lured into a false sense of confidence about the program's effectiveness in reducing safety threats.

CRISIS MANAGEMENT PROGRAMS

Just as the safety needs of hospitality organizations vary widely, so too will their crisis management needs. For example, a hotel would more likely face challenges associated with evacuating employees and guests during a weather-related crisis than would the manager of a take-out restaurant. Geographic location is also a factor in crisis preparations. Hospitality managers in the Midwest, for example, do not have to worry about preparing for a typhoon, but they would have to be ready for snow and ice storms that can be just as disruptive and threatening.

Planning for such contingencies is an activity that affects all managers, not just those with HR responsibilities. Because guests, as well as facilities, are typically affected in a crisis, hospitality managers in all functional areas should develop plans to deal with the potential for calamities they cannot prevent. As previously pointed out, in many small hospitality operations, the general manager may be responsible for a crisis response and for anticipating and managing the ways it will directly affect the employees.

Recall that, earlier in this chapter, a crisis was defined as a situation with the potential to negatively affect someone's health, safety, or security. Even though some types of crises cannot be prevented by management (e.g., floods, severe weather storms, robberies, and the like), effective HR managers still seek to manage crises to the greatest possible degree. Essentially, precrisis management consists of two distinct activities. These are:

■ Precrisis planning
■ Emergency plan practice

Precrisis Planning

It is too late to prepare for a crisis when your operation is experiencing one. If you are unprepared, and as a result, respond poorly, you may not only increase the severity of the crisis, but you may also be held legally responsible by guests or employees for your lack of planning. To prepare effectively for a crisis, HR managers should develop and practice **emergency plans.** An emergency plan identifies a likely crisis situation and then details how the operation will respond to it. After it is developed, an emergency plan must be practiced, so all employees will know what they should do during the crisis and when they should do it.

Emergency plan: The specific actions to be taken by managers and staff in response to a crisis.

Managers cannot prevent every type of crisis from affecting their operations, but they can plan what to do in the event of such emergencies. *Courtesy Digital Vision*

No one can prepare for every crisis that could occur in a hospitality facility, but it is the responsibility of managers to be prepared for all of those situations that can be readily foreseen.

Experienced managers know that many crises will actually require similar responses. For example, training employees in the proper procedures for handling general medical emergencies will prepare them for responding to slips and falls, employee accidents, guest injuries, and other threats to safety that could require medical attention. Similarly, preparing a facility **evacuation plan** will be helpful not only in case of a fire, but also during a weather-related disaster or power outage.

Evacuation plan: The specific actions to be taken by managers and staff when vacating a building in response to a crisis.

By developing responses to a relatively small number of circumstances, you and your staff will be well equipped to address a wide variety of potential crises, because all crises have some characteristics in common, including:

- Urgent danger
- Halt in normal operations
- Human suffering
- Financial loss

It is important to commit emergency plans to writing. This is crucial for two reasons: (1) a written plan will clarify precisely what is expected of management, as well as employees, in times of crisis; and (2) if the operation is involved in a lawsuit, the written emergency plan can serve as evidence to support its defense. A judge or jury would readily acknowledge that an operation's emergency plan was in place, indicating a level of reasonable care.

An effective emergency plan need not be complicated. In fact, it is best if it is not. A crisis is a stressful time, during which confusion is a real threat. Thus, any planned response to an emergency should be clear and simple, regardless of the number of steps required. In its simplest form, a written emergency plan should address:

- The nature of the crisis
- Who is to be informed when the crisis occurs
- What each employee is to do in response to the crisis
- When they are to take the required action

When emergency plans have been finalized, each manager and affected employee should be given copies or have immediate access. Subsequently, it is important to review and practice the emergency plans regularly.

Emergency Plan Practice

Once your emergency plan has been developed, the next step is to practice the procedures you have included in it. Obviously, it is not possible to create, for example, an actual snowstorm in order to practice your staff's response to it, but you can still practice your response. Practicing an emergency plan may include verbal plan review or an actual emergency plan run-through. The question of which emergency plans to practice (and how often) will vary by the individual operation's needs. Management can, however, write and follow an emergency plan practice schedule. The objective in developing a schedule for practicing emergency plans should be to emphasize the most likely and serious threats and to allow each staff member with responsibilities during the crisis to fully understand his or her role.

Crises affect employees both in the short and long run. Experiencing a crisis, especially one that entails injury or loss of life, can be very stressful. Negative effects on employees can include anxiety, depression, nightmares, flashbacks, and even physical effects such as insomnia, loss of appetite, and headaches. Collectively, these and related symptoms are known as **post-traumatic stress disorder (PTSD)**. Increasingly, employers have been called on to recognize and respond to the post-traumatic stress disorder symptoms of employees following their exposure to a crisis.

> **Post-traumatic stress disorder (PTSD):** A severe reaction to an event that caused a threat to an individual's physical or emotional health.

Employee Security Programs

> 5. **List and describe specific steps employers can take to help prevent workplace violence.**

It would be nice to believe that groups of employees, all united toward achieving the same goals, would be able to work with a high degree of peace, harmony, and security. Unfortunately, sometimes that simply is not the case. Although hospitality workplaces are generally peaceful, HR managers must ensure, to the greatest degree possible, that they stay that way.

As you have seen, employers should take a variety of steps to help ensure that their employees enjoy a high degree of safety while at work. These workers deserve management's best efforts to ensure their security as well. In most cases, these security-related efforts will take the form of protecting workers from harassment of all types, as well as from physical aggression, cruelty, and bodily harm.

ZERO-TOLERANCE HARASSMENT PROGRAMS

If employees are to enjoy security (freedom from fear and anxiety) at work, it follows that they must work in a harassment-free environment. While most media attention tends to focus on sexual harassment (see Chapter 2), it is one of an HR manager's most important jobs to eliminate all forms of harassment (e.g., racial, gender, sexual orientation, religion, and the like) from the workplace. Because there is more established case law about how the courts view sexual harassment, and because of its common presence in the hospitality industry, the major focus of this section is on preventing sexual harassment.

The U.S. Supreme Court first ruled that unwelcome sexual conduct creating a hostile and offensive work environment violates Title VII of the Civil Rights Act in *Meritor Savings Bank, FSB v. Vinson* (1986). Since then, the Equal Employment Opportunity Commission (EEOC) and the courts have expanded the hostile and offensive work environment analysis to prohibit harassment based on race, color, sex, religion, national origin, age, and disability. The EEOC is the federal agency that enforces Title VII of the Civil Rights Act. The regulations issued by the EEOC on sexual harassment provide that

> [a]n employer should take all steps necessary to prevent sexual harassment from occurring, such as affirmatively raising the subject, expressing strong disapproval, developing appropriate sanctions, informing employees of their right to raise and how to raise the issue of harassment under Title VII, and developing methods to sensitize all concerned. (Source: EEOC).

Hostile work environment (sexual harassment): A workplace infused with intimidation, ridicule, and insult that is severe or pervasive enough to create a seriously uncomfortable or abusive working environment with conduct severe enough to create a work environment that a reasonable person would find intimidating (hostile).

Quid pro quo (sexual harassment): *Quid pro quo* literally means "something for something." Harassment that occurs when a supervisor behaves in a way or demands actions from an employee that forces the employee to decide between giving in to sexual demands or losing her or his job, losing job benefits or promotion, or otherwise suffering negative consequences.

The EEOC expects employers to affirmatively act to prevent all types of harassment. HR managers need to understand that the *Meritor Savings Bank* case ruling by the Supreme Court also addressed different standards for determining liability in cases of **hostile environment** and **quid pro quo** sexual harassment.

From a legal perspective, if harassment is established under the *quid pro quo* version, the employer automatically is liable and will be held accountable for whether or not steps were taken to correct the situation. In contrast, an employer's liability in a hostile work environment case must be established by showing not only that the harassment occurred, but also that the employer did not take appropriate action to stop it.

Sexual (and other forms of) harassment policies and the training procedures required to fully comply with the law can be quite complex (for a detailed discussion, see Stephen Barth, *Hospitality Law: Managing Legal Issues in the Hospitality Industry*, 3rd edition. New York: John Wiley, 2008) and should be thoroughly reviewed by legal counsel prior to their implementation.

For general guidelines in preventing harassment of all types, all HR managers should understand:

- *What is, and isn't, a hostile work environment.* A hostile work environment can exist even if no employees have yet complained. HR managers and supervisors have a legal duty to stop anything that could generate charges of harassment.
- *The company policy.* The company's harassment policy should be as familiar to supervisors as their own work schedules. Sometimes, supervisors know there is a policy but have little idea of what it entails. If the operation is sued, and supervisors cannot display a good understanding of the company policy, then it will likely be viewed by the courts as not having been enforced.
- *The impact on unions.* If you are unionized, how supervisors deal with harassment can have a lot to do with how well management gets along with the union and the number of grievances filed. If you are not unionized, failure to address harassment creates a workplace that can be ripe for union organization.

■ *The effect of speech.* Just about everyone who works has heard coworkers or customers use language that could be considered inappropriate, hostile, sexist, racist, ethnically charged, crude, gross, insensitive, age-based, or derogatory. HR managers need to know and inform their supervisors about the specific types of language that will likely lead to charges of harassment in their own operation.

■ *Proper investigations.* Properly conducted harassment investigations are essential to limiting an operation's legal liability. It should be clear who will investigate claims, what should be done if the supervisor is the target of the investigation, at what point legal counsel should be involved, and whether, when applicable, the supervisor can continue to oversee the complaining employee during the investigation.

■ *Personal liability.* When a harassment case results in a lawsuit, the operation will be sued, but in most cases, so will the supervisor and/or HR manager. If you are the individual in charge of the operation, this can be the case even though you weren't the harasser, did not know about the situation, and the employee allegedly being harassed did not report directly to you.

Earlier in this chapter, you learned about the concept of zero-tolerance (harassment) policies. A legitimate question for workers who will be disciplined or fired if they violate their company's zero-tolerance policy is:

"When, exactly, does the language used or action displayed constitute harassment?"

This question can be difficult to answer, because not all employees would find the same behavior offensive. For example, some culinary employees (male and female) might find that hearing coworkers swearing while working the entrée station in the kitchen during a busy Saturday night rush is very offensive and thus potentially harassing, whereas others may not find it to be so.

Reasonable person (standard): The typical, or average, person (and their behavior and beliefs) placed in a specific environmental setting.

The courts have addressed this question and have instituted a **reasonable person** standard. Thus, in determining whether conduct is considered hostile environment harassment, the courts, as well as the EEOC, typically evaluate the objectionable conduct from the standpoint of a "reasonable person" under similar circumstances. Under this standard, complaining employees must establish not only that they personally perceived their work environment to be hostile, but also that a reasonable person would have perceived it to be hostile as well.

Interestingly, a few courts have adopted a "reasonable woman" standard to use instead of the reasonable person standard for sexual harassment cases. In *Ellison v. Brady* (1991), the U.S. Ninth Circuit Court concluded that offensive conduct must be evaluated from the perspective of a reasonable person of the same gender as the victim. That court rejected the reasonable person standard, because it does not take into consideration the different perspectives of men and women.

Human Resources Management:
CURRENT EVENTS 10.2

RIGHTS OF THE ACCUSED?

Everyone would agree that harassment, of any type, has no place in a work environment. Managers should understand, however, that a charge of sexual harassment is not synonymous with an incident of sexual harassment any more than being accused of a crime means the accused is automatically guilty of it. Because of perceived abuses by some who have charged harassment, and the response of some employers, the state and federal courts are increasingly defining the rights of the accused in sexual harassment cases. The rights of accused individuals vary by state. In Ohio, for example, state law requires that the accused have the right:

1. *To be free from discrimination.* For example, an employer cannot punish the accused more harshly than someone outside of the accused's protected class. In other words, if the accused is a 60-year-old manager and the business's owner has condoned the same or similar behavior by his own young son, then the owner must treat the 60-year-old manager in the same way. Similarly, for example, blacks may not be treated differently from whites when assessing whether harassment occurred or how it will be dealt with.
2. *To a thorough investigation.* An employer cannot conduct a "Kangaroo Court" (i.e., a mock or unauthorized justice proceeding) without risking a jury second-guessing what the employer might have found if it had looked at all of the facts. This is so because it is simply naïve to believe that there have never been unfounded charges of harassment.
3. *To a good-faith basis for believing that the allegations are true before taking adverse employment action.* This is especially true if the employee can point to a "just cause" employment contract. In Ohio, the employer's policies and conduct can create such a contract.
4. *To be free from defamation.* An employer should not share information about an investigation with anyone other than those who have a need to know the results.

Certainly, the rights of the accused in harassment cases are still in their infancy and have a long way to go before they are fully developed by case law. For now, employers have a clearer duty to protect employees from harassment, which carries far greater penalties if it is breached, than to protect the rights of the accused. Therefore, employers are well advised, in cases that are not clear-cut, to continue to err on the side of protecting the victim in a harassment case. Increasingly, however, employers will be legally required to keep the rights of the accused in mind as well, especially as the number of same-gender harassment cases wind their way through the court systems.

In all cases, a company will be held liable for a hostile work environment created by its workers if it knew (or should have known) that the harassment was occurring and it did not take reasonable action to stop it. Thus, a swift and appropriate resolution of harassment complaints is the best way to ensure a secure work environment and to protect your company from liability. For example, in *Tutman v. WBBM-TV* (2000), the Seventh Circuit Court held that the employer in the case was not liable for a racially hostile work environment because it took "prompt and

Human Resources MANAGEMENT ISSUES   (10.2)

"**Y**ou've got to be kidding me!" said Jodi Waldo.

"It's no joke," replied Bob Zollars, the Regional VP of HR for Richland Hotels.

Jodi and Zollars were discussing the lawsuit that had just been filed by Ann Roberts, a former employee at the hotel, which Jodi managed for Richland. The lawsuit, claiming sexual harassment and constructive discharge, named as defendants Select Hotels, the hotel's franchise company; Richland Hotels, which owned Jodi's property as well as 10 others; and Jodi Waldo, the hotel's general manager. Jodi had just discovered she was named personally in the suit.

"Essentially," said Zollars, "the lawsuit maintains that you should have known about the harassment Ann claims she encountered and that you should have stopped it."

"But I didn't know anything about her claims." replied Jodi. "How can she try to sue me?"

"She isn't *trying* to sue you," replied Zollars. "She already is suing you—and our company too. What you and I need to discuss now is whether you want to utilize our company attorneys for your defense or hire your own lawyer?"

QUESTIONS

1. Some HR managers are surprised to hear that they can be held personally liable for their actions at work, even when those actions are taken as the result of direct instructions from their boss or when events occur of which they are simply unaware. Assume you are Jodi Waldo. What factors would you consider before electing to utilize your own attorney to address the charges leveled in this lawsuit?

2. Consider the "constructive discharge" charge filed by Ann Roberts. Should there be written records of the incidents leading to her allegation, as well as management's response? What would it mean if such records do not exist?

3. Assume you are Bill Zollars. Would your primary concern in this situation be the liability exposure of this hotel's general manager, that of your company, or the future of your own career? Explain.

appropriate" action to remedy the harassment, including reporting the incidents to supervisors, conducting an immediate investigation, and taking appropriate disciplinary actions.

Managers should use zero-tolerance harassment policies to take action even for offensive conduct that does not meet the legal standard of a harassing environment. The reason is that even mild forms of harassment that go unchecked can disrupt an operation through decreased morale and productivity and increased employee turnover.

For example, HR managers can take disciplinary action against employees who occasionally use obscene language or tell off-color jokes, even if that conduct would not generally constitute illegal harassment unless the employees engaged in it on an ongoing basis. Utilizing this approach goes well beyond the legal standard for harassment, and it emphasizes the expectation, at all times, of respectful and professional behavior in the workplace. When implemented, such policies should apply to customers, guests, and on-site vendors as well.

Before concluding our examination of zero-tolerance harassment policies, it is important to note that use of such policies is not devoid of its own legal issues. In fact, their use can create unique litigation issues of their own. If, for example, you are taking disciplinary actions against the perpetrators of harassment, the question of appropriate punishment is often legitimate. In fact, the term *zero tolerance* could make it more difficult to defend a case on appeal, because a third party (judge or jury) could conclude, however mistakenly and inappropriately, that you did not consider a penalty appropriate for the particular harassment offense.

Consider a female who had worked for a company for 10 years, had a stellar record, and who admitted to telling a single off-color joke to a longtime friend and coworker (but within earshot of other employees). If that employee were reported and treated (under the zero-tolerance policy) in exactly the same manner as a supervisor in the same operation who was found to have traded choice work assignments for sexual favors, one might argue that the policy would have resulted in a punishment that did not fit the crime.

There are other possible consequences. The term *zero tolerance* might appear to eliminate any flexibility you have in dealing with highly complex and difficult situations, even when that is not the policy's intent. Consider the case of two coworkers who date for several years, then break up, with the immediate result that one of these workers charges the other with harassment because of pestering designed to continue the dating relationship.

Lastly, another potentially undesirable side effect is that, in some cases, the appearance of inflexibility can actually discourage employees from reporting incidents because they do not want to get their coworker fired; they simply want the behavior stopped. This may discourage generally collegial coworkers from reporting the actual occurrence of harassing behavior. As a result, some companies have changed wording in their harassment policies from:

> To ensure a quality workplace, this company has a policy of "zero" (no) tolerance of any objectionable harassing behavior.

To wording such as:

> To ensure a quality workplace, this company simply will not tolerate harassing behavior; as a result, all reports of harassing incidents will be taken seriously and dealt with appropriately.

PREVENTING WORKPLACE VIOLENCE

Workplace violence: Any act in which a person is abused, threatened, intimidated, or assaulted in his or her place of employment.

While harassment, in the belief of many, is most often considered verbal abuse at work, HR managers must increasingly concern themselves with **workplace violence,** a concept that includes harassment, physical assault, and even homicide.

Just as some managers think of harassment as a verbal attack, some managers think of violence only in terms of a physical assault. However, workplace violence is a much broader problem. It occurs any time a worker is abused, threatened, intimidated, or assaulted in his or her place of employment. Workplace violence includes:

Implicit (threat): A threatening act that is implied rather than expressly stated. For example, the statement: "I'd watch my back if I were you!" said in a menacing voice by one employee to another.

Explicit (threat): A threatening act that is fully and clearly expressed or demonstrated, leaving nothing merely implied. For example, the statement: "If I see you in my work area again, I'll personally throw you out of it!" said in a menacing voice by one employee to another.

- *Threatening behavior.* Includes actions such as shaking fists, destroying property, or throwing objects.
- *Verbal threats.* These can include **implicit threats** or **explicit threats** made in person or left on answering machines or as cell phone messages.
- *Written threats.* These can consist of everything from Post-It notes, to e-mails, to long letters.
- *Harassing activities.* These can include a wide range of behaviors that demean, embarrass, humiliate, annoy, alarm, or verbally abuse a person and that are known or would reasonably be expected to be unwelcome (including sexual harassment). This can include words, gestures, intimidation, bullying, or other inappropriate activities.
- *Verbal abuse.* This includes swearing, insults, or condescending language.
- *Physical attacks.* These can include hitting, shoving, pushing or kicking, rape, or homicide.

Spreading rumors, playing pranks, inflicting property damage, vandalism, sabotage, armed robbery, theft, physical assaults, psychological trauma, anger-related incidents, rape, arson, and murder are all examples of workplace violence.

Managers should understand that workplace violence is not limited to incidents that occur within a traditional workplace. Work-related violence can occur at off-site business-related functions such as conferences and trade shows, at social events related to work, and in clients' offices or away from work but resulting from work (e.g., a threatening telephone call from an employee to another employee's home or cell phone).

Angry employees pose serious threats to workers. The seriousness of the threats can be demonstrated by the fact that workplace homicide is the leading cause of death among female workers in the United States and is the second leading cause of death, at work, for men. For example, according to the Bureau of Labor Statistics'

(BLS) most recent detailed data, 856 employees were murdered on the job in 1997, and of those, 731 (85 percent) died during robberies. Among those killed during robberies, 46 percent worked in the retail trade, such as convenience stores, gas stations, and fast-food restaurants. Another 17 percent worked in the service industry, which includes taxi service, hotels, auto repair, and guard services. Of the remaining 15 percent of workplace homicides, 10 percent involved vindictive customers and coworkers, and 5 percent involved angry relatives and acquaintances. In addition, about 18,000 employees were nonfatally assaulted *every week* while on the job.

Every hospitality workplace must be protected from disgruntled workers and customers, but, as the events of 9/11 clearly demonstrated, workplaces must now be prepared to face the traditional internal workplace threats and the external threat of terrorism. Certainly, effective HR managers should take reasonable steps to protect their workers from violence. In the hospitality industry, these steps can include concrete activities such as the following:

- Install bulletproof glass and limited-access barriers for drive-thru windows (restaurants) and late-night-accessible front desk areas (hotels).
- Increase workplace security by installing video surveillance, alarm systems, and door detectors.
- Increase lighting in dimly lit areas such as parking lots and around trash dumpsters.
- Trim back bushes and shrubs that provide hiding places for would-be thieves and attackers.
- Locate drive-thru windows (restaurants) within the same building as the restaurant, rather than in the parking lot by themselves.
- Implement effective alcohol server training programs to prevent and discourage excessive alcohol consumption (bars and restaurants).
- Train room attendants to keep guest room doors open when cleaning occupied rooms (hotels).
- Minimize the amount of cash available to cashiers (all businesses).

Specific actions that can be taken to help deter workplace violence are important, but it is also important to understand that, in most cases, workplace violence is committed by a business's current and former employees. Because that is true, it is equally critical that HR managers in hospitality implement written workplace violence policies for current employees.

At the very least, an effective workplace violence policy will detail:

- What specific behaviors (e.g., swearing, intimidation, bullying, harassment, and the like) management considers inappropriate and unacceptable in the workplace
- What employees should do when incidents covered by the policy occur
- Who should be contacted when reporting workplace violence incidents (including a venue for reporting violent activity by one's immediate supervisor)
- That threats or assaults that require immediate attention should be reported to the property's security department (if applicable) or directly to the police at 911

While these points will cover the basic minimum of a workplace violence policy, the best workplace violence prevention policies will:

- Be developed by management and employee representatives.
- Apply to management, employees, customers, clients, independent contractors, and anyone who has a relationship with the operation.
- Define exactly what is meant by workplace violence in precise, concrete language.

Human Resources MANAGEMENT ISSUES   (10.3)

Charles Lapinski was the district manager for a franchised quick-service Mexican-style restaurant in a large city. On a Friday night at 11:30 P.M., just after the restaurant locked its front doors to the general public, three masked men entered the store through the unlocked back kitchen door. They demanded that the assistant manager on duty at the time turn over all of the restaurant's cash. Nervously, the 19-year-old assistant manager explained that all of the cash had been deposited in a safe in the manager's office and that he had no ability to open it.

Angry at their inability to rob the restaurant, the gunmen, one of whom was a former employee, shot two of the restaurant workers, including the assistant manager, as they fled the restaurant. The assistant manager later died from his wounds. The attempted robbery and shooting made that night's local television news.

A lawsuit filed by the assistant manager's parents charged that the restaurant lacked proper alarms and locks on the back door. In addition, they charged that the restaurant owners and the franchise company failed to provide any training to its staff regarding the proper response to an armed robbery. The lawsuit was reported in a front-page article in the local paper.

An investigative reporter from another television station in the city called the restaurant's general manager to request an on-air interview regarding the training the restaurant's employees receive related to robberies. The manager referred the call to Mr. Lapinski.

QUESTIONS

1. What issues do you think the courts and a jury would likely consider as they evaluate the legitimacy of the parents' lawsuit?
2. What is the likely outcome if Mr. Lapinski refuses to meet with the investigative reporter? What if Mr. Lapinski has not been properly trained to do so?
3. Assume you were the HR manager assigned to Mr. Lapinski's district; what would you advise him to do regarding this investigative reporter's request?

- Provide clear examples of unacceptable behavior.
- State in clear terms the operation's view toward workplace violence and its commitment to preventing workplace violence.
- Precisely state the consequences of making threats or committing violent acts.
- Encourage the reporting of all incidents of violence.
- Outline the confidential process by which employees can report incidents and to whom.
- Ensure that no reprisals will be made against those employees reporting workplace violence.
- Outline the procedures for investigating and resolving complaints.
- Describe how information about potential risks of violence will be communicated to employees.
- Commit to provide support services to victims of violence.
- Describe an active and effective Employee Assistance Program (EAP) to allow employees with personal problems to seek help.
- Demonstrate a commitment to monitor and regularly review the policy.
- Describe any regulatory or union-related requirements related to the policy (if applicable).

Unfortunately, no matter how carefully an operation is managed, or what attempts at prevention are made, workplace violence will continue to occur. When it does, hospitality managers must be prepared to deal with its effects and the aftermath of these crisis events.

HUMAN RESOURCES TERMS

The following terms were defined in this chapter:

OSHA

Zero tolerance

Carpal tunnel syndrome

Automated external defibrillator (AED)

Wellness programs (employee)

Safety

Security

Crisis

Emergency plan

Evacuation plan

Post-traumatic stress disorder (PTSD)

Hostile work environment (sexual harassment)

Quid pro quo (sexual harassment)

Reasonable person (standard)

Workplace violence

Implicit (threat)

Explicit (threat)

For Your Consideration

1. Some business owners believe that OSHA has too much power to dictate the manner in which employers operate their business. In your opinion, what limits, if any, should apply to OSHA's ability to dictate employee-related safety and security activities on the job? Defend your answer.

2. Assume you are a unit manager in a hospitality organization and that a talented young assistant manager reporting to you approached you and confessed that he was struggling with a substance abuse problem. The employee also states that he wants help from the company's EAP to overcome it.

   Assume also that, previously to this, your evaluation of the employee was that he was ready to assume responsibility for his own unit. Would the fact that the employee was seeking to enroll in your company's EAP affect your assessment of his readiness for promotion? Explain the reason for your answer.

3. Some companies have gone as far as refusing to employ (or continuing to employ) workers who these companies know engage in legal, but unhealthy activities (such as drinking or smoking) while off the job. To ensure that the employees do not engage in such behavior, the workers in such companies must agree to submit to random testing. Do you feel employers have a right to force employees to conform to prescribed off-the-job behaviors? Would your reaction change if the employer's health insurance company would provide, at significantly lower premiums to the employer and employee, enhanced employee coverage for those employers who implemented such lifestyle-monitoring programs?

4. Assume that a testing company approached you and indicated they had developed a test to predict, with a high degree of but not perfect accuracy, the likelihood that individuals you employ would be prone to commit an act of workplace violence. Assume also that the cost of implementing such an employee-testing program was quite reasonable. Would you purchase such a test for use in your operation? Would you terminate a current employee who tested poorly (i.e., tested as likely to commit an act of workplace violence)? Explain why or why not.

CASE STUDY: HUMAN RESOURCES MANAGEMENT IN ACTION

"If he touches me again, I'm going to deck him," said Angela Larson, a cocktail server at the Windmere Casino, as she walked into Peggy Richards office. "He's creepy."

"He" was Roger Sheets, corporate vice president of operations for Jennus Casino Management, the operator of the casino, as well as the immediate supervisor of Peggy Richards, the casino's general manager.

Angela was a very attractive, single mother of two who had worked at the casino for three years. Her coworkers considered her to be very friendly, and her attendance was excellent.

Tom Delaney, the casino's HR manager, had brought Angela to Peggy's office. The day before, Angela had approached Tom regarding Roger's last visit to the casino. Tom had called Peggy to give her a heads-up about the meeting's purpose. According to Angela, this was not the first time Roger had gotten close or brushed up against Angela while talking to her on the casino floor.

But during Roger's last visit to the casino, he had put his hand on Angela's back while he asked her about her future career goals and indicated that, if she really wanted to advance, he would be glad to discuss her future career goals, over dinner, away from the casino. This he said as, according to Angela, his hand trailed a good bit lower than her back.

"When I first met Roger, he seemed really nice, and we had really friendly conversations about me, my kids, and my ex. But now, well, I can handle the normal flirting of customers," said Angela to Peggy. "I'm pretty touchy-feely myself. You know, patting a customer's arm when I deliver a drink—that kind of thing. I know most of my customers are harmless, and I can deal with the ones who aren't, but this is different. Ms. Richards, you know I really need this job, and I think Roger was implying that if I didn't have dinner with him, well, I don't know for sure. But I do know he needs to keep his hands off my backside!

"I talked to a lawyer friend, who I'm dating now," Angela continued, "and he said it's definitely sexual harassment, and that I needed to report it. My lawyer friend said the company needs to fire him or I should sue, and I'd win. A lot of money. So I'm officially reporting him."

Dimension: Employee Protection

Review the scenario described in the case study, and then address the following questions:

1. What evidence is there, in this case, of a hostile work environment?
2. What evidence is there, in this case, of *quid pro quo* harassment?
3. Discuss the specific advantages and disadvantages to Angela Larson if she initiates an EEOC sexual harassment charge (or lawsuit) in this case.

Dimension: Management Response

Review the conversation described in the case, and assume that the Windmere Casino has a zero-tolerance harassment policy:

1. What are the most important rights of Angela Larson that must be protected?
2. What are the most important rights of Roger Sheets that must be protected?
3. If you were Peggy Richards, how would you advise Tom Delaney to proceed?

Dimension: Company Protection

Assume that you are the CEO of Jennus Casino Management, and Roger Sheets was hired by and reports to you. In your best-case scenario:

1. What would you like to see Peggy Richards and her HR director do next?

2. Assume that, when approached, Roger Sheets denies that the conversations and actions reported by Angela Larson ever took place. Would you instruct your corporate attorneys to defend, at company expense, him and your corporation in any forthcoming legal action brought by Angela Larson?

3. What specific steps would you instruct your corporate-level HR director to take to minimize the chances that a problem such as this would occur again?

INTERNET ACTIVITIES

1. Healthy worksites are not only important to employees, but they also often directly affect the safety of guests. In the hospitality industry, one of the most devastating events that can affect a foodservice operation is a foodborne illness outbreak, and specifically, one caused by either *E. coli* bacteria or a Norovirus. Even if your area of hospitality specialization is not food production, you should understand the sources of foodborne illnesses and how to prevent them. The National Restaurant Association provides free information about how to do just that. To access some of their food safety-related information, go to: *www.restaurant.org/food safety/how_to_pathogens.cfm*.

   a. Select "E. coli" and read the information presented there.

   b. Select "Norwalk (noro) Virus" and read the information presented there.

   After you have read the information presented about the subject areas you selected, answer the following questions:

   a. What similarities exist between how each of these threats can be controlled?

   b. How could you, as an HR manager, evaluate your own operation's efforts to prevent a foodborne illness caused by either *E. coli* bacteria or a Norovirus?

   c. What, specifically, would you do if you found out that your operation's efforts at prevention in this area were deficient?

2. The recordkeeping requirements of OSHA do change. Some organizations create and sell resources to help HR managers stay abreast of such changes. To view one such resource, go to: *www.ailancorp.com*

   a. Select "Products."

   b. Then scroll down to "OSHA Log" sc.

Then read that section as well as the other benefits listed.

    a. Would you buy such a product if you were responsible for HR management in your organization?

    b. What factors would influence your decision to do so?

3. From food safety issues to employee violence, hospitality managers face increasing challenges related to guest and worker safety. To view one of the sites that continually identifies the best workplace safety-related training information for those in the hospitality industry, go to: *www.hospitalitylawyer.com.*

    a. Select "Safety and Security Marketplace" from the Solution Store.

    b. Review the publication, "Adams Fact Book 2005."

    Alcoholic beverages and their service result in significant safety and security risks for many hospitality operations. Visit the Adams Fact Book Web site, review the book's table of contents, and then answer the following questions:

    a. How extensive is the book's coverage about alcoholic beverages and their service?

    b. What is the cost of this resource?

    c. Describe the type of hospitality manager or hospitality operation(s) for whom such a resource would be valuable.

PART **FOUR**

Special Human Resources Concerns

CHAPTER ELEVEN

Role of Human Resources in Strategic Planning and Organizational Change

CHAPTER **OUTLINE**

CHECKLIST **OF CHAPTER LEARNING OBJECTIVES**

As a result of satisfactory completion of this chapter, readers will be able to:

1. Identify factors that influence organizational change, and discuss how they impact the role of human resources in managing it.

2. Explain the role of the human resources function in strategic planning.

3. Review the continuum of organizational change, and the role of the human resources function to manage change along it.

4. Explain basic issues that create organization-wide resistance to change, and explore human resources aspects of these issues.

Impact on Human Resources Management

Hospitality organizations, like their peers in other industries, are in an almost continuous state of change. Some change is gradual; other change is more dynamic. In effective organizations, much change results from purposeful management planning, but even the most resourceful and insightful managers cannot anticipate all change that will be necessary, or they cannot provide well-thought-out and proactive ways to adapt to it. Numerous external—and internal—organizational factors create change. Managers must know what these factors are, must recognize how they can impact their organization, and must be able to effectively deal with them.

An organized strategic planning process can be used to anticipate and prepare for change. Because employees will be affected by changes that are made, they should be considered, and their input should be encouraged and utilized whenever it is possible to do so. Those who manage human resources have numerous responsibilities as this planning process evolves, and these HR managers are a significant influence on the extent to which strategic planning efforts are successful.

Some changes are gradual, and may be implemented by no more than simple revisions to affected policies and/or operating procedures. At the other end of the change continuum, some types of change affect the entire organization, including every department, each manager, and all other employees. Along this continuum from gradual to dynamic change are a wide variety of other pressures for altering the status quo that are evolving all the time. This chapter explores the continuum of change, with a special emphasis on the role of human resources personnel in the management of change.

Many persons at all organizational levels resist change, in part because of the uncertainty and perceived risks that are associated with it. In this chapter, we'll review why top-level managers in organizations sometimes desire to maintain the existing situation (the status quo) and tactics they use to resist change. While not all change is good, some is. It is the challenge of human resources and other managers to determine which pressures for change are important, what types of changes will be useful, and how planning for that change will be undertaken.

When managers say, "Change affects organizations," what they are really saying is that "Change affects people." The organization consists of the staff members at all organizational levels who work to fulfill its mission. Change clearly affects the organization's human resources. Staff members will react to every change in a way that, hopefully, improves the organization. A focus on the role of human resources in the change management process is the general topic of this chapter. It is an important one, because how the organization is managed in times of change dramatically influences its future. The discipline of human resources would be much simpler if one only needed to review or revise a policy or explain a procedure to make things happen. In fact, human resources managers must often provide creative input to their organizational peers as they think outside the box to help plan for the future. It is their ability to consistently do so that sets them apart from their counterparts, who view their primary role as implementing rather than influencing change.

Organizational Change Is Constant

1. Identify factors that influence organizational change, and discuss how they impact the role of human resources in managing it.

Hospitality organizations are dynamic; they cannot stay the same, because, if they do so, they essentially go backward. Line operating supervisors and managers are confronted by internally directed changes of all types. Many are driven by an evolution in guests' preferences. For example, restaurant managers modify a menu, and hotel managers change a guest room's décor to modernize it. Entry-level employees are affected when, in the first case, cooks must learn to prepare new menu items and, in the second instance, as housekeeping personnel alter guest room makeup procedures.

Organizational
change: The process
by which an
organization moves
away from what it is
currently doing
toward some
desirable future
status.

Organizational change is ongoing, and it must be effectively managed to the extent possible. Human resources managers in large organizations are members of their property's executive committee, and they participate with their top-level peers in decision making that impacts their entire organization. For example, department heads on the committee work with their subordinate managers and supervisors to implement plans within their areas of responsibility. By contrast, managers with human resources functions in smaller organizations must make decisions, and they must then directly manage the activities of the affected staff members who must implement these changes that enable the organization to remain viable.

External organizational factors originally discussed in Chapter 1 (see Figure 1.3) can influence the need for a hospitality organization to plan for and implement changes.

Let's review these external influences:

- *Legislation.* Labor-related and other laws and regulations impact what a hospitality organization must and cannot do. Sometimes a regulation results in change that directly affects only some of an operation's employees or one or more specific procedures. For example, if the Internal Revenue Service (IRS) modifies how tipped employees are to report their income, then payroll procedures must be modified to comply with IRS guidelines. In this case, only selected employees (those receiving tips) are affected.

    In other cases, changes in legislation or regulations affect all employees. For example, the Hazard Communication Standard, required by the Occupational Safety and Health Administration (OSHA) and implemented to help ensure a safe work environment, resulted in mandated policy and procedural changes that affected all managers and employees. For an even more dramatic example, consider that the Americans with Disabilities Act (ADA) mandated significant changes about selection procedures for job applicants (future employees), the need to make reasonable revisions in work procedures to accommodate employees covered by the Act (current employees), and even changes in requirements related to an operation's physical facilities.

■ *Competition.* Some hospitality operators react to their competitors in a (seemingly) never-ending effort to stay one step ahead to enhance the perceived value of their products or services and attract additional guests. Others try to lead the pack by being early innovators. Still other organizations consider the competition, but try to develop (or improve) core business strategies to distinguish their business in the minds of the marketplace. Regardless of the strategy, all hospitality operators must consider their competitors and, in doing so, they may initiate change in response to actions taken by the competition. For a specific industry example, consider the 99-cent value menu introduced by Wendy's restaurants. Its competitors were quick to respond (by necessity!), and each introduced its own version of a value menu to appeal to the value-conscious customer.

Niche marketing: The activity of offering specific products and services to subsegments of a market in efforts to attract large numbers of this subsegment to the operation.

■ *Consumer preferences.* **Niche marketing** has been used to create opportunities for hotels, restaurants, and other commercial hospitality operations to meet the needs of ever-smaller groups of potential guests. What do narrow (or broad) markets of guests want? As this question is addressed, internal changes will be necessary. Then, after changes are implemented, the question can be asked repeatedly, with the result of never-ending changes that will impact the organization's staff members.

One of the most successful examples of niche marketing in the hospitality industry can be seen in the "W" brand of Starwood Hotels (*www.whotels .com*). W hotels are specifically designed to attract a younger, highly affluent business traveler.

■ *Demographic issues.* The size, age, and skills of the local labor force impact employee recruitment and selection decisions. Income levels in the area affect employees' compensation levels and the ability and interests of potential guests in the community to visit a hospitality operation.

■ *Global issues.* Rising oil prices, which dramatically increase product costs including their transportation, and political and terrorism concerns, which can have a significant influence on the sometimes fragile hospitality industry, are examples of factors that decision makers must consider.

■ *Ethical concerns.* Ethical considerations impact how employers treat their employees, provide products and services to guests, and conduct business with suppliers. Ethics and corporate social responsibility concerns also influence the extent to which the organization feels compelled to be a contributing community citizen. This, in turn, can impact the management decision-making process in many ways.

■ *Economy.* The financial health of the country (which is often affected by global issues), the state, and the community within which the hospitality operation is located influences the interest of businesspeople and tourists to travel and of persons living in the community who consider eating out or preparing meals at home. Interest rates affect the cost of borrowing money and of conducting business in general. Inflation (rising costs) mandate the need for careful cost analysis, which often leads to revised work procedures.

- *Employee unions.* Collective bargaining efforts that create stronger or weaker management and employee obligations to each other can significantly impact the discretion of managers.

The external influences just cited can impact hospitality organizations, including their human resources function and culture, in dramatic ways. They do so by influencing what employers do and how they do it. Employers must react to these influences and implement the changes driven by them.

The judgment and experience of managers, including those with human resources responsibilities, will drive the planning process. The plans that are generated must then be implemented, and tools will be required to do so. For example, **strategies** and **tactics** often create the need to develop or revise policies and procedures to identify work processes needed in response to desired (or required) organizational changes. As well, job descriptions and specifications may need to be changed to reflect the organization's updated human resources requirements.

Strategy: A general method or plan developed in efforts to attain a long-range goal.

Tactic: A specific action step used to help attain a short-term objective.

All Managers Are Part of the Change Management Team

Managers at all organizational levels are decision makers, but their level of decision-making authority and responsibility differs. Human resources managers in large organizations will likely be involved in broad and long-term concerns relating to, for example, approaches to anticipate and/or to adjust to external and internal organizational influences. Their input can be very helpful in answering questions such as: "How will this new legislation impact our hiring practices?" "How should we train all of our employees about new guest service skills?" "Should we outsource some activities in response to reduced revenues caused by decreased occupancy rates?" "What should our coming-in and fallback positions be during the next round of union bargaining?" Managers in smaller organizations without human resources specialists will need to address these types of concerns along with numerous other day-to-day operating issues that are within their job responsibilities.

Middle-level managers and supervisors in most hospitality organizations are less involved with these issues and related big-picture concerns and are more likely to be concerned about shorter-term issues applicable to their own departmental responsibilities. Often, their decision-making concerns relate to how the decisions made by higher-level managers are to be implemented. Examples include rearranging work tasks in a specific position to meet legislative (ADA) requirements, planning the delivery of specific new guest services in response to competitive threats, developing work schedules for departmental staff when labor hours must be adjusted, and ensuring that collective bargaining agreements are followed during interactions with their staff.

Successful hospitality operations attempt to proactively manage significant changes that can be anticipated with strategic planning procedures. This process, with an emphasis on the role of the human resources function, is discussed in the next section.

Human Resources and Strategic Planning

2. Explain the role of the human resources function in strategic planning.

Strategic planning: A systematic method of developing long-term plans to attain business objectives by anticipating and adapting to expected changes.

Many significant changes that confront hospitality organizations can be anticipated and, to the extent practical, should be addressed using **strategic planning** procedures. Details of applicable procedures are beyond the scope of this book, but an overview with an emphasis on the role of the human resources function is desirable, because the people dimension of planning is of obvious importance in the development and success of any plans.

CLOSE LOOK AT STRATEGIC PLANNING PROCESS

A wide variety of procedures can be used to develop strategic plans, and numerous industry consultants and consulting firms offer their services to facilitate the process for those hospitality organizations desiring assistance. For the purposes of this discussion, consider the steps noted in Figure 11.1. It summarizes activities in a basic strategic planning process and highlights the role of human resources personnel in each activity.

The sequence of steps noted in Figure 11.1 suggests a road map that can be used for strategic planning to consider appropriate dynamic change, with an emphasis on the human resources implementations of each step. Let's see what it suggests:

■ *Step 1: Consider the organization's mission.* The mission of the hospitality operation (what it intends to do and how it intends to do it) should drive the entire planning process. Ownership of the mission is improved as employees at all organizational levels provide input as the mission is developed and revised. Managers should routinely publicize and support the development process and the end result: a philosophy that will guide organizational decision makers to keep the operation on the proper course. Note the role of human resources managers to, as integral members of the top-level team, assist with the mission's development, facilitate the feedback process, and disseminate information about the mission to all staff members, including an emphasis on the mission during orientation sessions for new employees.

GENERAL STEPS IN PLANNING PROCESS

Step No.	Activity	Human Resources Role
1	Consider the organization's mission	Human resources managers are part of the top-level team with responsibility for development of the mission. They provide input and may plan and deliver programs to train other managers about how to facilitate team input into discussions about the organization's mission. They may represent the property's top leaders in staff meetings to discuss the mission and its planning and revision process. Revisions to and discussions about the mission in new employee orientation sessions may be required.
2	Scan the environment	Human resources managers keep current with industry trends and how, if at all, they relate to current and future personnel needs. They share insights with other organization leaders and suggest procedures to keep current with trends and the potential organizational changes that these trends may suggest.
3	Analyze the situation	Human resources personnel participate in the situation analysis process and contribute their perspectives to the analysis. *Note:* Their input is critical because of the human resources implications of many situation variables that are typically identified.
4	Determine long-term goals	Human resources perspectives are useful because they provide input about current staff and future needs and about the organization's workforce (especially those in key positions). They make suggestions about revisions, if needed, to the organizational structure, and suggest professional development opportunities to update staff about human resources issues that are critical as priority goals are identified. In effect, human resources personnel provide important advice about broad personnel-related aspects of proposed goals.
5	Establish strategies	Human resources managers can assist in establishing strategies by helping to develop necessary planning programs. They can also facilitate the recruitment and selection of new staff and/or retraining of existing staff in efforts to ensure that the necessary human resources are in place to implement preferred strategies.
6	Identify interim objectives	Human resources personnel can review current staffing plans (are required staff available?) and recent employee appraisal results (are current staff able?) to move toward attainment of short-term objectives. They can help implement benchmarking and/or data-gathering procedures needed to assess "where we are" and to measure movement toward specific objectives.

FIGURE 11.1: Human Resources Role in Strategic Planning

GENERAL STEPS IN PLANNING PROCESS		
Step No.	Activity	Human Resources Role
7	Assign responsibilities and timelines	Employee appraisal factors or methods may be needed to address and maintain plan responsibilities and timelines. For example, if specific staff members are responsible for a tactic required to implement a plan to attain an objective, then their efforts and successes should be evaluated. Then their performance can, in part, be measured by the extent to which required efforts were successful.
8	Communicate the plan	Company newsletters, information on the company's intranet, bulletin board displays, and even paycheck notices can inform employees about the status of long- and short-term plans. Some human resources personnel have property-wide responsibilities, and they typically have the best opportunity to publicize this information.
9	Monitor the plan; take corrective action as needed	If progress is delayed because of staff turnover, vacant positions, and/or the need for training/retraining, human resources tactics will be useful to address them.
10	Celebrate a successful plan	Compensation increases, if any, impact payroll procedures and records, which are maintained by human resources personnel. Human resources staff may, as well, plan property-wide celebration activities.
11	Repeat the planning process	Human resources managers in large organizations can provide specialized assistance where needed throughout the property. Those in smaller organizations must assume this responsibility, as well as all other aspects of the planning process.

FIGURE 11.1: (*Continued*)

■ *Step 2: Scan the environment.* Effective leaders, including those with human resources responsibilities, know what's going on in their industry, organization, and community. They use this information to consider the need and to plan for gradual and more dynamic change. They read print and electronic industry periodicals, are active in hospitality organizations, and participate in community organizations and events. They think about their organization and its future in the context of the societal, business, economic, political, and other changes that are occurring. Human resources managers focus their attention on potential guest, labor, and cost-related implications of these trends and share them with other property leaders. This ongoing process provides input to management concerns, including the need to plan for organizational change.

■ *Step 3: Analyze the situation.* **SWOT analysis** (strengths, weaknesses, opportunities, and threats) is a popular method used to address the current situation

SWOT
analysis: Strengths, Weaknesses, Opportunities, and Threats Analysis—a systematic approach to assess an organization's current environment as part of the strategic planning process.

confronting an organization. Planners consider the influences on the organization (recall the discussion in the previous section). They then identify (1) strengths and consider how to increase and more fully utilize them, (2) weaknesses and how to overcome them, (3) opportunities that might be best given the strengths and weaknesses that have been identified, and (4) threats, including the best way to overcome them. As noted in Figure 11.1, the input of human resources managers is critical at this time because of the role the organization's staff members play in each dimension of this analysis.

■ *Step 4: Determine long-term goals.* The results of the SWOT analysis (Step 3) help planners establish organizational goals that, first, must be in concert with the organization's mission (Step 1). Planners then consider how to use the organization's strengths to take advantage of opportunities while addressing (correcting) weaknesses in their efforts to manage threats. Human resources input is critical during these discussions to emphasize current staff abilities and needs and to advocate HR-related implications of the goals as they are identified and prioritized.

■ *Step 5: Establish strategies.* What must be done to attain the goals identified in Step 4? Strategies are developed to answer this question. A goal for a hotel may be to significantly increase the weekend occupancy rates by marketing to guests with demographic characteristics that differ significantly from week-night visitors. There are, hopefully, numerous ways to do this that can be evaluated. Those strategies judged best can be implemented with a long-range planning process that involves the next several steps.

■ *Step 6: Identify interim objectives.* Goals developed as part of long-range plans are meant to be attained within several (usually three to five) years. Interim objectives specify how much of the longer-term goal should be attained within a shorter time span (usually one year). If, for example, a long-term goal (see Step 4) is to attain an average weekend occupancy rate of 75 percent, then perhaps the rate can increase to 50 percent from its current 40 percent within 6 months (the time frame for the shorter-term plan). Figure 11.1 indicates that human resources personnel can assist with supportive tasks applicable to objectives that relate to ensuring that a full complement of properly trained staff will be available. They can also help benchmark existing work methods and assist in the development of data-gathering systems required to monitor progress toward objectives.

■ *Step 7: Assign responsibilities and timelines.* The interim objectives identified in Step 6 will not be accomplished unless persons are assigned to address them and are held accountable to do so. Often these tasks must be accomplished in addition to numerous other existing responsibilities. If not properly managed, this overload can create difficulties and stress for personnel and hinder the attainment of the objectives. A progress reporting method must be established to help indicate when, if at all, corrective actions are needed to revise the method(s) used to move toward the objective and to stay on track of attaining it.

■ *Step 8: Communicate the plan.* The organization's long-range plan should be communicated to staff members, as should progress in attaining it.

Hopefully, input from affected staff was solicited and utilized as plans were developed. To the extent this occurred, the organization's plans are "ours" (the employees) rather than "theirs" (those of the top leaders). Human resources personnel typically play an important role in property-wide communication, and their assistance in this step in the planning process is very important.

■ *Step 9: Monitor the plan; take corrective action as needed.* As suggested in Step 7, monitoring is not possible without the availability of current and applicable data. There is good news when plans are being implemented according to targeted schedules. When this is not occurring, corrective actions are required. *Note:* One corrective action—moving the schedule back to compensate for process slippage—should not be considered unless other tactics to maintain the plan's schedule have first been attempted. As seen in Figure 11.1, the assistance of human resources personnel in this step depends on the implementation challenges that require corrective action. *Note:* This step and the previous step (Step 8) can occur almost simultaneously, because communication is required to indicate progress, note implementation challenges, and facilitate corrective actions.

■ *Step 10: Celebrate a successful plan.* Some hospitality managers are quick to criticize and place blame when plans are not attained, but are slow to celebrate when they are. Management observers recognize that responsibility (accountability) cannot be delegated. At the same time, they realize that success is not possible without the effective performance of one's subordinates. A simple conclusion from these observations is that managers must be responsible (held accountable) if plans are not attained, and plans can only be successful because of the cooperation and assistance of the staff members who complete the work. Also, in some hospitality organizations, the end result of an employee's successful work performance is more work! (Special projects are assigned to high- not low-performing staff members.) Acknowledgments ranging from a simple "thank you" to a staff event to a compensation increase (bonus) are examples of how the attainment of plans can be celebrated.

■ *Step 11: Repeat the planning process.* The planning process just described should be part of a **rolling plan.** If, for example, a five-year planning horizon is used, each year planners should move one additional year into the planning horizon, so that there are always long-term (five-year) goals. It is likely that an organization will have several (or more) goals addressing different dimensions of the mission that consider the best ways to move toward it. Each department within the organization may also have a departmental mission statement, which broadly defines its own role in helping the organization to attain the broader mission. Each department, then, will have developed and implemented department plans that are "rolled up" to become the organization's plan. Human resources personnel should be available in large organizations to assist with department-level planning that has organization-wide or specific human resources planning needs. Managers in smaller organizations must assume responsibility for managing the human resources and all other aspects of their department's plan.

Rolling plan (long-range planning): A plan in which the final year in the planning cycle is moved ahead one year as plans for each year are implemented.

SUMMARY OF STRATEGIC PLANNING PROCESS

Figure 11.2 summarizes the relationship between and components of the organizational planning process that were detailed earlier. It emphasized the needs for basic planning tools, including mission statements, SWOT analysis results, and long-range plans, and it also suggested the role of business (action) plans that represent the tactical implementation phase of the planning process. Finally, it

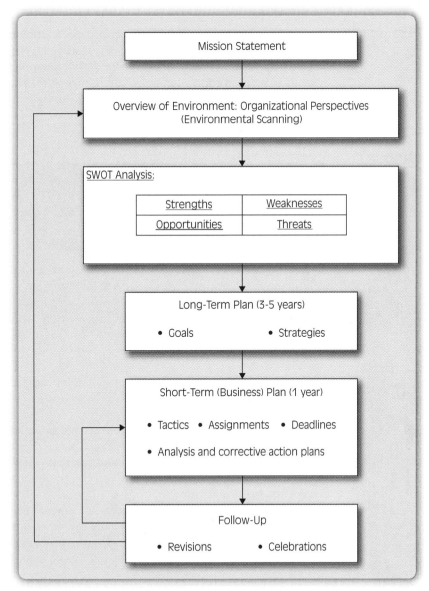

FIGURE 11.2: Summary: Elements in Organizational Planning Process

identified the need for follow-up activities—including, hopefully, celebrations—and it stressed the cyclical nature of the planning process: follow-up efforts may reveal short-term issues that need to be addressed and longer-term challenges that impact on the organization's long-term plans. The planning process to accommodate dynamic change is never-ending.

Our brief review of the planning process described suggests that the process is time consuming, if not complex. It involves organized thought, creative input, and generation of planning alternatives and implementation assistance from staff members at every organizational level. Because the plan is developed and implemented by the organization's staff members, its planning process involves human resources management concerns and perspectives at every step. Human resources managers are integral members of their organization's top-leadership team. In this capacity, they represent and should be able to communicate the abilities of existing staff to accomplish reasonable plans, and to suggest the need for additional, perhaps more specialized, personnel to help the organization move forward in its goal attainment efforts.

Human Resources Management:
CURRENT EVENTS 11.1

GLOBAL ISSUES AND CHALLENGES IN THE HOSPITALITY INDUSTRY: 2007

You have learned that hospitality managers must consider big-picture concerns confronting their industry to enable them to best consider how change is likely to affect their organization, and what they might do to take advantage of (or, at least not to be negatively affected by) it. Here is the list of the top ten issues confronting the lodging hospitality industry for 2007 as identified by the International Society of Hospitality Consultants (ISHC):

- *Labor and skills shortages.* Changing labor conditions include a shrinking labor force, lagging wage rates, industry reputation issues, and a de-emphasis on training and employee satisfaction.
- *Escalating construction cost.* Construction costs and those for furnishings, fixtures, and equipment (FF&E) were increased at a rate greater than twice that of the consumer price index. Costs for hotels currently being planned will be much greater because of costs for steel, diesel fuel (transportation of construction commodities), and concrete.
- *Keeping up with technology.* Complex operating environments, which require systems to interact with each other, maintaining an awareness about potential efficiencies, historic preferences that de-emphasize investments in systems, and lack of access to expert technical support create problems for operators.

- *Changing demographics impact travel trends.* Increased retirement travel of "baby boomers," the impact of globalization of business travel, and an increase in experiential travel are examples.
- *The impact of profits as higher expenses are countered by the need to increase wages.* It is difficult to sustain profitability as operating and capital costs increase and as labor, benefits, and energy expenses continue to climb.
- *Consumer confusion about brands.* Ongoing proliferation of new brands makes it increasingly difficult for consumers to understand differences despite extensive promotion and advertising messages.
- *Changes in distribution.* The sale of guest rooms through Internet sites and online research about room alternatives makes it difficult but necessary for organizations to keep up with dynamic changes in how guest rooms are sold.
- *The impact of travel restrictions on travel.* Increased restrictions on international travel, even between the United States and Canada, and the possibility of increased travel document control by countries including China, India, and in South America, may reduce international travel.
- *Growth of new markets.* While the number of visitors in all regions of the world are forecasted to increase, historic travel destinations such as Europe and the Americas will see declines, while those in East Asia and the Pacific will increase.
- *Availability of capital.* Investors' concerns about risk may be increasing and, if so, the availability of funds available for development and construction may be lessened.

"Top Ten Global Issues in the Hospitality Industry for 2007." Retrieved 11/29/2006, from: *www.hotel-online.com/News/PR2006_4th/NOV06_ishc.html*. Readers interested in further information about these issues will find a detailed discussion at this site.

Continuum of Change

3. **Review the continuum of organizational change and the role of the human resources function to manage change along it.**

Change is inevitable in modern organizations, and its pace is increasing. Today, managers of successful hospitality operations spend a significant amount of time and effort addressing the challenges of change.

TWO BASIC TYPES OF CHANGE

Successful hospitality managers undertake ongoing efforts to determine the products and services their guests need and want, and how to meet these demands at a

Gradual change:
Organizational change that is simple and narrowly focused on a specific department or management function, and that has an incremental impact on the hospitality organization.

Dynamic change:
Organizational change that is complex and broadly focused and that impacts the entire hospitality organization as it creates a significant difference in its operation.

value to guests while optimizing costs as they do so. This effort creates evolving and **gradual change** in numerous aspects of the operation. Some observers view this as a "journey toward excellence." This journey never ends because the definition of excellence changes as guests' wants and needs evolve. Managers attempt to stay at the forefront of change to ensure that quality and quantity standards are consistently met while excessive costs are eliminated. They know this emphasis is necessary to provide value to their guests while attaining the organization's financial goals.

At the other end of the continuum of change are the types of changes brought about by significant, seemingly all-at-once pressures. These require a significant departure from how things are being done and often create radically revised work models. While some of these **dynamic changes** are purposeful and are brought about by the organization, others are created by external influences to which the organization must react. Hopefully, managers have anticipated at least some of the dynamic changes, and planning is in process to address them. However, other significant changes can occur with little planning and preparation time available. Consider, for example, a restaurant chain that experiences a well-publicized case of foodborne illness. Employees' schedules and assignments, production levels, and the attention of management will all be significantly affected by this unforeseen event.

Figure 11.3 shows examples of factors that influence change and typical organizational reactions to them along the continuum of change. A review of this figure can help you to see how typical reactions intensify as the factors prompting change become more significant and as change, in turn, moves from gradual to dynamic. After we review these types of changes, we will discuss the role of those with human resources responsibilities to assist in managing them.

Let's look at Figure 11.3 more closely. You've learned that, at its most basic level, gradual change occurs all the time. New staff members bring new ideas to the workplace, new products are introduced, and managers apply their knowledge and experience to address operating challenges in new, and sometimes better, ways. Let's look at the three examples of gradual change noted in the figure:

Data mining: The use of technology to analyze guest information in efforts to improve marketing-related decisions.

- *Food trends.* These can create the need for changes in the menus of restaurants, hotels, and other hospitality operations. The changes brought about by these trends may be more significant than they appear because of their impact on purchasing, receiving, storing, issuing, and food production, and they may also impact necessary equipment and work methods. However, effective planning typically minimizes their impact on the overall operation.

- *Lodging industry competition.* Historical amenities battles and contemporary bedding upgrades are examples of issues that can create challenges with hotel employee work schedules, capital costs, laundry procedures, and storage space, among others. These reactions can generally be efficiently planned and managed without significant concern to other departments within a lodging organization.

- *Faster/more accurate data collection.* **Data mining** in the marketing department and predictive information to help staff scheduling may create the

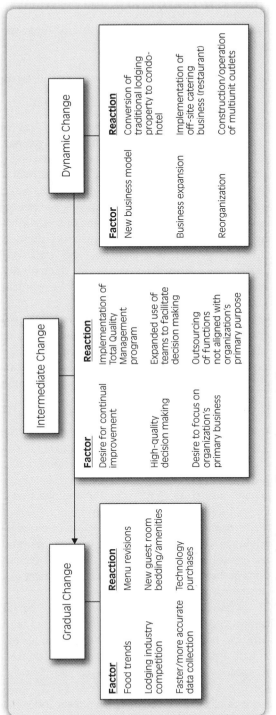

FIGURE 11.3: Examples of Gradual, Intermediate, and Dynamic Change

justification for technology purposes for almost any type of hospitality organization. The acquisition and use of these systems can help move the operation forward incrementally.

Figure 11.3 also identifies some intermediate examples of change that can have an increasing impact on the organization:

Total quality management (TQM): A management system (process) that focuses on identifying what guests want and need, and then consistently delivering these products and services while attaining expected performance standards.

Empower: The act of delegating necessary authority to staff members that allows them to make decisions that otherwise would be made by their managers.

- *Desire for continuous improvement.* One significant reaction to this factor could be implementation of a **total quality management** (TQM) program. These efforts can (1) identify exactly what guests need and (2) discover approaches to consistently deliver them in the most cost-effective manner. Significant planning that impacts the entire organization is required, and managers must **empower** their staff members to assist in identifying and meeting the guests' needs.
- *Higher-quality decision making.* Some organizations expand the discretion of employee teams and allow them to make decisions about work goals, employee scheduling, performance appraisal, and work methods among numerous other responsibilities. This model can dramatically change the function of managers and redirect their efforts from being in charge to becoming coordinators and facilitators.
- *Desire to focus on an organization's primary business.* The outsourcing of functions not critically aligned with the organization's primary purpose may be a useful strategy for a hospitality operation to return to its core business. However, as discussed in the next chapter, significant human resources challenges (among others) are generally created and must be successfully addressed as this alternative is implemented.

Now let's review the examples of dynamic change seen in Figure 11.3:

Condo-hotel: A lodging property that offers transient guest rooms that are owned by persons who place their rooms into the property's rental pool, and who then receive a portion of their room's rental revenues.

- *New business model.* Today, many traditional hotels are being converted to **condo-hotel** properties. As they do so, real estate, ownership, legal/contractual, and numerous other implications impact, at least, every top-level and mid-level staff member in the organization.
- *Business expansion.* The implementation of an off-site catering business by a traditional restaurant is an example of a dynamic change that will impact every management function and every department head. It will challenge the talents and creative energies of business owners to expand without affecting their traditional core business.
- *Reorganization.* Business construction and expansion from a single-unit operation to multiunit outlets requires careful consideration by the owner/managers. It also impacts the time and ability of the manager to operate the first unit, and it dramatically changes the organization and how it is managed.

As one might expect, there are significant differences in how these different types of changes are managed. Figure 11.4 reviews several of these differences.

Sometimes things change rapidly in the hospitality industry. Consider the condominium-hotel (condo-hotel) phenomenon of the mid 2000s: a developer typically builds or purchases and renovates an existing hotel and sells hotel rooms to individuals who then own and operate the property as a traditional hotel.

The primary purpose of a condo-hotel is to serve transient guests. Most unit owners place their units in the hotel's rental program when unoccupied and receive a share of rental proceeds in return. Most properties are upscale, full-service developments in popular vacation destinations, or in large cities where suburbanites frequent hotels for business or leisure purposes. Unit buyers must be convinced about ownership advantages, which can include low interest rates, the mortgage interest tax deduction, and property appreciation.

Condo-hotel HR managers face unique challenges. The nature of these properties requires that:

1. All line-level employees are in regular contact with the hotel's owners, so they require owner- rather than guest-service training.
2. Accounting activities are specialized and intensified. HR managers will be challenged to find (or develop) individuals capable of mastering the complexities of specific income statements for each unit owner and an overall property income statement.
3. Unit sales procedures must comply with numerous regulations. For example, salespersons cannot state that owners are likely to receive an excellent investment return, because this is contrary to Securities and Exchange Commission (SEC) regulations. Precisely what can (and cannot) be stated when selling a condo-hotel unit involves highly complex and still-evolving issues. The training of sales staff in a small hotel is often done by the property's general manager. In a larger property, a designated training department may have this responsibility. In either case, the SEC-related information that HR managers provide to sales staff must be current and understood completely by every salesperson.
4. Ownership interaction challenges must be addressed. For example, assume a front desk clerk is asked by the owner of Unit 300 (in a 600-unit property) to help ensure that his unit is rented "a bit more often" than it is now. The owner indicates that, if the unit is indeed rented more, he can make it "help the clerk." Ethics training initially provided by the HR department before the condo-hotel conversion would not prepare the employee for this situation.

Responsibility for room damages, violation of condo association rules by owners or guests, and the care of common spaces are a few examples of how the operation of condo-hotels vary from traditional properties. Each will require modifications in the approach that HR personnel use to prepare employees for the challenges they will face.

Some observers believe that HR managers in condo-hotels have more in common with their colleagues in club management than they do with hoteliers. The evolutionary nature of the hospitality industry continues to challenge HR managers who must assist employees in learning what is necessary to perform their jobs.

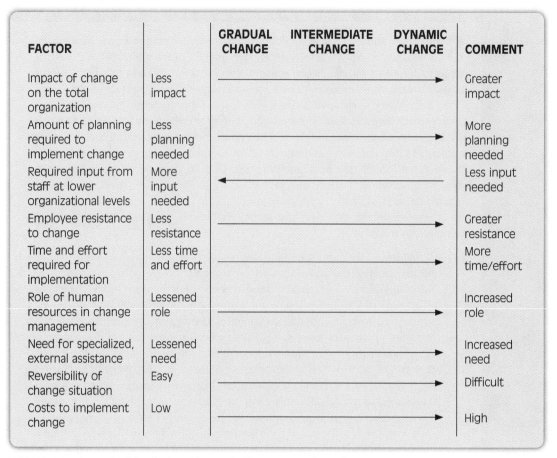

FIGURE 11.4: Impact of Gradual and Dynamic Change on Selected Factors

As noted in Figure 11.4, the impact on the total organization, the amount of planning required, the level of employee resistance, and the amount of time and effort needed for implementation is likely to increase as the change process moves from gradual to dynamic. The role of human resources in change management, the need for specialized external assistance, the difficulty of reversing the decision, and the costs to implement the change also increase. While input from staff at lower organizational levels should be solicited, it is typically most required at times of gradual rather than during dynamic change.

How is the human resources function involved in organizational change? This issue is addressed in the following section.

ROLE OF HUMAN RESOURCES IN CHANGE

Figure 11.3 indicated that the role of human resources in change management increases as change moves from gradual to dynamic. You have learned that gradual

Human Resources Management:
CURRENT EVENTS 11.2

THE FUTURE OF ON-SITE HUMAN RESOURCES SPECIALISTS

While this chapter has emphasized the role of human resources personnel in the management of change, it is also true that the position of human resources manager in large hospitality organizations will likely change. In fact, a common stereotype of the human resources generalist in large operations may have a short-lived future.

More extensive use of outsourcing, information technology advances, and continuing pressure to minimize costs are among the factors that will make change in on-site human resources management inevitable. Consider, for example, that external recruitment organizations can help hospitality operations locate potentially eligible candidates for position vacancies. Information technology makes it easier and more effective to communicate with employees. Payroll and benefits administration are additional activities that will likely be outsourced even more in the future, because they are becoming more complex and require specialists to manage them cost effectively. Human resources managers in hospitality organizations will also need skills at developing strategies for and managing the outsourcing companies (service providers) that assist them.

In the future, many human resources professionals will work for outsourcers rather than for hospitality organizations. Those employed by the latter will likely become strategists to help ensure that their organization's human resources add value to the operation. Increased globalization also means that staff members in different countries with entirely different laws that impact the management of an international workforce will need to be coordinated.

As human resources managers realign their focus to more directly helping their companies to attain financial success, their influence in the organization is likely to increase. The goal of HR positions will be to help discover new and better ways to help the organization attain its business strategies.

Retrieved 11/16/06 from: Patrick Kiger, "The Changing HR Profession," *www.workforce.com/archive/article/24/51/85_printer.php*

change is often accomplished with relatively simple changes in operating procedures and work methods, revisions to policies, and modifications to service standards, among other tactics. Equipment and supplies may need to be purchased, staff may need to be trained, and new vendors may be required. Work schedule changes, new supervisory tactics, and new performance evaluation concerns may become important. The list of changes necessary to implement gradual changes can continue and become extensive. However, the primary point is that most gradual changes can be planned and implemented by the managers and staff members in the affected departments. Only supplemental, if any, human resources assistance will be required (e.g., obtaining or revising training materials, revising employee appraisal documents, and updating policy and/or procedure manuals).

The extent of human resources management assistance increases as the organization implements and reacts to intermediate-level change. Total quality management and the expanded use of teams for decision-making purposes (two of the examples noted in Figure 11.3) require organization-wide communication (top-down but also bottom-up and sideways) to ensure that all possible feedback is available. Training programs that address role-playing, dialog training, brainstorming, and other group decision-making processes are necessary. Those with human resources management responsibilities are among the likely choices to determine property-wide training needs, select training vendors and/ or develop and modify training materials, and conduct train-the-trainer sessions on applicable topics. Committee processes to address specific issues and to report back to top-level managers, planning and implementation schedules, the development and analysis of evaluation methods and input, and consideration of how new system philosophies impact existing policies and procedures must all be carefully coordinated. In large organizations with human resources personnel, some or all of these responsibilities may be centralized in this department because of the human resources focus required during planning and implementation.

Human resources staff in multiunit hospitality organizations must carefully coordinate company-wide initiatives. *Courtesy PhotoDisc, Inc.*

Figure 11.3 also provided one additional example of intermediate-level change: the use of outsourcing to replace some of the organization's employees with those provided by an external service provider. This topic will be discussed in depth later in this text (see Chapter 12), but it is easy to imagine the stress and anxiety created for both the staff members whose positions will be terminated and for those employees who will remain. (Employees may think: "Is my job next?" "All the managers think about is themselves, not their employees." "Money is more important to this organization than are the hearts and minds of those who work here.") Efforts to assist the employees who leave and those who will remain must receive a very high priority. However, human resources personnel may also assist with selection of a service provider, negotiation and administration of the agreement, and evaluation of the services provided under the agreement.

The extent of employee resistance to change will likely increase as individuals perceive threats and as change is seen to have a greater impact on themselves and the organization. Tactics to manage change resistance have obvious human resources implications, and their use suggests another responsibility of human resources managers.

When a hospitality organization is confronted with dynamic change, it can become a significant challenge to continue day-to-day operations. Managers at higher organization levels will be involved with numerous planning activities and with implementation tactics driven by their plans. These efforts will be required in addition to their ongoing assignments and can yield long workdays, the need to increase delegation to subordinates, and/or an inability to perform some tasks and an inability to ensure that required performance standards are consistently met. Each of the examples of dynamic change noted in Figure 11.3 (i.e., a new business model, business expansion, and reorganization) require significant management expertise and the time necessary for careful planning. Staff must "take up the slack" or, at least, otherwise work under a revised style of leadership direction. These changes, especially for those employees who appreciate the status quo, in addition to the uncertainty about what the organization will be like after the change, can lead to anxiety and stress, which can lead to numerous job-related issues.

Human resources managers must address these concerns while doing their fair share of the assignments applicable to preparing for the change. Meetings with staff at all organizational levels as they represent top-level leaders and the implementation of change tactics that require personnel interactions become priority responsibilities for human resources managers. Determining reporting relationships so organizational charts can be revised, working with higher-level managers to develop job descriptions, planning recruitment activities, and participating in selection decisions are examples of tasks that become important at this time. If new staff members, including specialists, must be employed as part of efforts to implement dynamic change, still more human resources responsibilities become evident.

Is the property unionized? If so, collective bargaining agreements may be affected, which will require renegotiation with, at least, significant upfront

Human Resources Managers Must Have Change Management Skills

Human resources and other managers who are most effective at helping their organizations confront and benefit from changes use numerous skills to do so that include:

- *Business skills.* An organization must be carefully managed before, during, and after changes are made. Revenues must be generated, costs must be controlled, product and service development efforts must continue, and the work of an organization's staff members must be facilitated. Effective change managers are good business managers.
- *Political skills.* Interpersonal relationships can become strained when, for example, managers compete for priorities, limited resources, and job security as the change process evolves. The organization's social systems must be understood, and judgments must consider the relationships with and personalities of those involved in the change process. Effective change managers are effective politicians.
- *Analytical skills.* One must be able to undertake an objective analysis of the conditions before and after change, and it is especially necessary to consider financial implications of change alternatives. Effective change managers are effective change analysts.
- *System skills.* Change managers know how employees in the organization's work sections, departments, and divisions, if applicable, affect and interact with each other. Those making change-related decisions in multiunit organizations further understand the relationship between individual properties and other levels in the organization. They consider how change will impact each element in the total system and how each component can be made better as a result of the change. Effective change managers are effective system managers.
- *People skills.* The types of communication and interpersonal skills required for successful change management have been discussed throughout this chapter. Those managing change must be able to minimize resistance to it, resolve conflicts as they occur, and, as the process evolves, utilize the best input from those affected by the change. Effective change managers are effective people managers.

input from human resources personnel. How are labor staffing levels and schedules affected? What about the need for training and retraining and for the numerous other HR-related activities that are required when the organization is confronted with change? This very short list of ways that change can impact those with human resources responsibilities should make this point: An organization's employees are affected by any type of change, and they must be considered as an integral part of the change process. Someone (human resources specialists in large organizations and managers with these responsibilities in smaller organizations) must undertake these tasks along with their other ongoing duties.

Human Resources MANAGEMENT ISSUES (11.1)

"**I**t just can't be done; it will never work. What does Susan think she is doing?" said Sam, the head cook at the Grayville Widget Company, an account managed by the Good Times Food Service Management Company. He was talking to Abhijit, the assistant cook.

Good Times had won the food service management account for the Grayville Company about two years ago. It had successfully negotiated the contract emphasizing high-quality food at reasonable prices for the employees with no required company subsidy. In fact, many of the menu items were high quality, but they were also convenience foods, and that was alleged to be the reason for a slow but steady decline in the employee participation rate.

Susan, the unit manager, analyzed responses from numerous surveys, focus groups, and suggestion box memos, and also conducted many face-to-face conversations with the employees. The conclusion was almost unanimous: the employees wanted freshly prepared foods or, at least, a lot more of them than were now available.

The head cook was responding to Susan's announcement about fresh food preparation at the meeting earlier in the day: "We don't have the staff, we don't have the time, we don't have the necessary storing and preparing equipment, we don't have the recipes, and many of our staff members don't have the skill. We just can't do it!"

"If I was neutral about this," said Abhijit, "I would say that I could see both sides of the situation. The employees want what they want, and we want what we think we can do. I'm glad I'm not Susan as she figures this out."

QUESTIONS

1. What, if any, role do you think that Susan's production staff played in the situation that has caused the present marketing challenge?
2. List tactics that Susan, as her facility's HR manager, should now use to involve her production staff in the decision-making process.
3. What are alternative ways that Susan can now work to minimize the production staff members' resistance to change?

Can All Changes Be Anticipated?

Effective leadership can anticipate many changes, but the need for change can also arise without any (or, at least, ample) time to plan. Some unanticipated change can be gradual. Assume, for example, that there have been an increasing number of member accidents around a private country club's swimming pool. Changes in the club's initial training for recreation and swimming pool staff will be required. The club's general manager requires that an applicable video on swimming pool safety be added to the training of those staff working in the pool area. Human resources personnel will likely be involved in training modifications for these affected staff.

Unfortunately, dynamic changes can also be unanticipated. At first, one might think there has been significant leadership failure if the need for big-picture change has not been anticipated. Hopefully, managers will at least see the need for dynamic change on the horizon, even if they don't plan the correct response to it. However, consider the need for multiunit hospitality operations to relocate their national or regional headquarters, and for almost all operators to deal with totally or extensively damaged units in the aftermath of Hurricane Katrina in the Gulf Coast area of the United States (August 2005). A second example is when threats or offers of buyouts of commercial hospitality organizations create concerns for staff members at all organizational levels because of the uncertainty about job security that arises. How can human resources and other personnel quickly develop and implement an effective communication program to provide current and often fast-breaking information to the staff members?

Effective managers know the benefits of getting ready for change by at least anticipating it. The alternative (reacting to change) may be defended by some hospitality managers who allege that current challenges provide little or no time for anticipating changes or the planning required in efforts to manage it. All hospitality managers, including those with human resources responsibilities, are busy, but their priorities must consider the need to look to the future as well as to deal with daily operations.

This discussion has emphasized that change, even that which is relatively minor and certainly that which is significant, impacts the hospitality operation in many ways. As change becomes significant, a greater number of employees across the organization are affected, and the concerns and needs of these staff members must be addressed. *Note:* Detailed information about two types of organizational change, downsizing and outsourcing, are discussed in Chapter 12. There you will learn about additional tactics that human

Business owners, including those with hospitality operations, cannot foresee disasters, but they and their employees will need to make plans in response to them.
Courtesy Corbis Digital Stock

resources managers can use to help facilitate the management of labor-related concerns during these changes.

Resistance to Organizational Change

4. **Explain basic issues that create organization-wide resistance to change, and explore human resources aspects of these issues.**

Numerous factors can influence the need for organizational change, and those with human resources management responsibilities should be involved in decisions about how the hospitality organization will anticipate and/or react to the changes. One might think that a well-thought-out response to pressure for organizational change would prompt everyone to unite and work together to promote meaningful change. In fact, this desired result of the planning process does not always occur. There are numerous potential reasons why employees at all organizational levels resist change.

One common concern relates to honest differences of opinion about the factor(s) suggesting the need for a change (or if there is even the need for a change!) and the best approach to address the change. Consider a problem of declining profitability in a hotel. Accounting records indicate that occupancy rates have been decreasing steadily. What is the reason? Top-level managers may have **brainstormed** potential issues that have created the problem. Assume potential reasons

Brainstorm: A decision-making approach in which group members suggest alternative potential causes and/or solutions to problems for group consideration.

include inadequate marketing messages, improper employee service attitudes, and untrained staff members who fail to meet performance standards, among others. Before change can be implemented, it is necessary to determine what must be changed (e.g., marketing, service, employee performance, and/or other things). Without a consensus (majority opinion; if not total agreement) of all top-level decision makers, resistance to any change is likely. For example, marketing personnel believe it is difficult to sell a property that fails to deliver what guests desire. Some department managers believe that service is a problem, but not in their own departments. They may also concede that some performance standards are not attained in their own departments. However, they allege that the reason relates to staffing reductions required because of lowered revenues that make it almost impossible to deliver training designed to increase output standards. In this example, without a consensus about the real problem, a unified response effort is not likely to occur.

Role of Human Resources Personnel in Problem Solutions

How can those with human resources responsibilities help with the resolution of problems? The answer is that it depends on the specific problem. Let's consider the potential problems just noted (i.e., inadequate marketing, proper service, and performance failures due to inadequate training):

- If the problem solution will involve marketing issues, there may be little, if any, human resources input that can be helpful, assuming marketing staff are competent. However, if the decision to hire an external marketing consultant is made, human resources staff may help to develop a Request for Proposal (RFP). If a resolution tactic involves securing the services of hospitality students or other part-time personnel to make cold calls to community businesses, then human resources personnel (in a large organization) can assist in these efforts. In a small property, marketing managers may assume these duties.
- If the problem is judged to be service-related, human resources managers might assist by developing (selecting) and implementing guest service training programs. They might also deliver leadership training to supervisors. The goal is to modify the relationship between supervisors and their employees in efforts to improve the staff members' attitudes about their jobs.
- If the problem relates to widespread job performance problems, this is a significant human resources concern. It begins when employees are selected, and it continues through orientation, training, and, again, the manner in which supervisors facilitate the work of their employees.

Human Resources MANAGEMENT ISSUES (11.2)

Drake and Thomas were sharing a cab to the Metropolitan Airport after attending a meeting of the top-level managers for their chain restaurant organization. Both were regional managers with responsibility for several dozen properties within a several-state area.

"These meetings are always good because they make us think beyond the scope of day-to-day operating concerns, and they allow us to consider the future, and how we might respond to it as a company," said Drake.

"Yes," said Thomas, "I agree. The old saying about 'the future is here now' is increasingly true, and we need to think about and plan for short- and long-term concerns even as we resolve today's operating challenges."

"You're right, Thomas," said Drake. "We both see the need for this, and we know we will give this responsibility a priority. I wonder, however, about our unit managers and their staff. Folks on the firing line really do have immediate issues. Their work is not easy, they work long hours, and they devote lots of creative energy to dealing with issues that take their mind off longer-term concerns."

"Yes, you're right," replied Thomas. "I wonder what we as their immediate supervisors can do about this."

QUESTIONS

1. What can Drake and Thomas say to, and do for, their unit managers that will help explain, defend, and justify the need to prioritize consideration of long-term challenges that will likely confront their property and their organization?
2. What are your specific recommendations about what Drake and Thomas can do to assist their property-level management team with their short-term planning needs?
3. Should managers at the restaurant organization's highest levels develop plans and then roll them down to the individual units or vice versa: should planning be done at the unit level with plans then rolled up to higher levels? Defend your answer.

There are numerous other potential reasons why good employees may resist change. Several, with applicable human resources tactics, include:

■ *Concerns about the change or the change process.* Top-level decision makers may question the need for change and may be defensive about making changes because of concerns that to do so would question the relevance of their earlier judgments. Territory (organizational chart reporting relationships), budgets, and the need to relearn and/or to significantly modify work practices are additional concerns that can prohibit buy-in to problem resolution strategies that will alter how the organization does things.

HUMAN RESOURCES TACTICS: Communicate (explain, defend, justify) the need for the change; indicate benefits to the affected staff members; solicit input from employees as changes are planned and implemented.

■ *Uncertainty about one's professional future.* "Will I still be needed?" and "How will I fit in?" are two obvious questions that can arise when significant organizational change is proposed, because this type of change will likely impact staff members at all organizational levels, including those at the top. "Why must I relearn everything if I will be retiring soon?" and "I don't think I can do things any other way" are two additional examples of concerns that can affect everyone at any organizational level as change is proposed and implemented.

HUMAN RESOURCES TACTICS: An ongoing relationship of trust and respect (which those with human resources responsibilities must earn) and the nurture of a corporate culture emphasizing high ethical standards will help satisfy employees who may wonder about any hidden agendas that prompt change. Managers who indicate that changes are needed and existing staff are important in their implementation will be believed when they have established a relationship of trust.

■ *Conflict between organizational levels.* The process of change may benefit some departments and staff members and negatively affect others. Outsourcing housekeeping responsibilities may ease the pressure on the accounting staff that must develop payroll reports and process employee paychecks. At the same time, stress is likely to increase for housekeeping and human resources managers, who may need to terminate staff and secure the services of and administer the contract for an external service provider. If the power struggles that can result from conflicting interests and impacts are not effectively managed, change will not occur or, at least, will not happen without significant offsetting problems.

HUMAN RESOURCES TACTICS: Communication is the key. Human resources personnel should be at the same organizational level as their department head counterparts. Their role in developing and implementing equitable policies and procedures, along with mutual efforts and agreements during executive committee meetings and at other times, help legitimize, promote, and assist with significant organizational changes.

■ *The organization itself.* Organizations with many management levels typically require a longer time to make decisions than do their flatter organizational counterparts. Some observers say this is good because decisions are more likely to be considered and carefully analyzed as they flow down through the organization's management layers. Other observers counter by noting that decision makers in small entrepreneurial businesses are much more able to quickly respond to and take advantage of changes that impact the organization because there are fewer management layers. With today's emphasis on less is better and doing more with less, many organizations are becoming less structured (centralized). Consider, for example, hotels that collapse the responsibilities of food and beverage manager and chef into one position, and that have eliminated assistant manager positions in other departments. Specialists in organizations with numerous levels of centralized authority are frequently more resistant to organizational changes than their peers in other organizations who have broader and more decentralized authority.

HUMAN RESOURCES TACTICS: The position analysis process with resulting job descriptions that is taught to staff members or that is facilitated by human resources managers can help define roles and develop defensible organizational charts.

- *The organization's culture.* Consider the cultural values of an organization that emphasize its reputation, history, the contributions of founders and early leaders, and quality and guest value. Contrast these values with others that emphasize "We go slow, and don't make mistakes" or "The best approach is to be conservative, and follow everyone else." While change for the sake of change is not always a virtue, an organizational culture striving to be its long-term best is certainly influenced by values that are very different from those in organizations where status quo and a dislike of change are emphasized.

Tunnel Vision Isn't Good

Despite the advantages of teamwork often cited by hospitality industry observers, well-intentioned managers can often take an "it's them—not me" posture to problem solving. Perhaps nowhere is this observation more commonplace than in large organizations with human resources departments. "If only HR would send me some good people" (a thought by line supervisors and managers) can be offset by "If only department managers would practice proper leadership tactics and not turn off so many staff members" (a typical corresponding thought by human resources specialists). Chefs say, "Let's increase food quality," while purchasing personnel work to reduce food costs. Maintenance engineers argue about how much new technology will save, while top-level managers are concerned about what it will cost. Marketing representatives talk about the long-term need for advertising messages, while they must work with a short-term advertising budget.

In their broadest sense, these and numerous other situations that arise almost daily in most hospitality organizations are human resources problems, because they concern people. Some, including the relationship between human resources personnel and department management personnel, should be of obvious interest to human resources managers. Others involving a **cost-benefit analysis** that equates cost and quality considerations of product and service alternatives may be less within their control. All, however, are important to the hospitality organization as it make changes in response to a wide range of external and internal pressures to do so. Everyone, including those with human resources responsibilities, should be involved in decisions about change, because they are all affected by the outcomes of the decisions.

Cost-benefit analysis: The process of evaluating alternative products and services based on cost and quality differences between each.

HUMAN RESOURCES TACTICS: The manner in which staff members are treated from time of recruitment to ongoing performance evaluation and while being supervised is a direct result of the approaches to human resources management utilized by the organization's leaders.

■ *Unfamiliarity with change details.* Groups of employees (teams) and specific individuals within departments may resist change when reasons have not been explained and justified, and if the impact on them is not carefully explained. *Note:* The factors influencing resistance to change in teams and individual employees, and procedures to minimize their impact on purposeful change, is beyond the scope of this book. These topics are addressed in many popular hospitality supervision texts.[1]

HUMAN RESOURCES TACTICS: Communication between managers and their staff members; input from affected personnel as changes are planned, implemented, and evaluated; and the recognition of employee concerns during the change process can be helpful.

HUMAN RESOURCES TERMS

The following terms were defined in this chapter:

Organizational change	**Dynamic change**
Niche marketing	**Data mining**
Strategy	**Total quality management**
Tactic	**Empower**
Strategic planning	**Condo-hotel**
SWOT analysis	**Brainstorm**
Rolling plan (long-range plan)	**Cost-benefit analysis**
Gradual change	

FOR YOUR CONSIDERATION

1. Figure 11.3 provides examples of gradual, intermediate, and dynamic changes that can confront hospitality organizations. What are additional examples that:
   a. Can be experienced by all hospitality organizations.
   b. Are specifically applicable to commercial and noncommercial foodservice operations.
   c. Are specifically applicable to lodging properties.
2. Figure 11.1 reviews examples of responsibilities and activities of human resources managers at each step in the strategic planning process. What are additional examples of duties that these officials might assume during the process to plan for dynamic change?

3. How, if at all, can global issues impact (become a mandate for change) those hospitality organizations that are part of large national chains? How about independently owned small hospitality properties in one specific location in the country?

CASE STUDY: HUMAN RESOURCES MANAGEMENT IN ACTION

Mindy and Stacey had grown up in the lodging business. Their family had owned a franchised property in an area that attracted family vacationers during the summer months. Over the years, occupancy rates during these months were always very high, even though more properties were (seemingly) always being built.

They and their families took over the operation of the property after their father had retired, and he had since passed away. During the intervening years, they perceived a decreased number of advantages to their property's franchisee affiliation. Mandated upgrades, many of which did not seem to be worth their cost, were an ongoing concern. The hotel did generate significant room nights through the centralized reservation system, but they also had a good base of repeat visitors. Also, they thought they could attract many more travelers with a marketing and advertising budget that could be funded from monies saved because franchise fees would no longer be necessary.

"I think we should just go ahead and do it, because the franchise agreement will be up within the next two years," said Mindy. "We can make more money, we won't have to endure so many hassles, and we can be successful by using lots of our own ideas instead of those of the franchisor, which don't always work."

"You might be right, Mindy," said Stacey. "We've talked about this a lot, and we have undertaken some feasibility studies that defend your position. Many people are coming through this area during the summer months, and I don't think we need to rely on our franchisor's reservation systems. We can also market to those coming here without reservations. Also, we talked about a water park that might attract people from within the region during our slow months. We've got lots of important things to consider and lots of decisions to make. Where do you think we should start?"

Dimension: Strategic Planning

1. Review steps in a strategic planning process that Mindy and Stacey might use to make decisions about the franchise affiliation issue. Emphasize the human resources management aspects of the process; focus on both the managers of the property and the employees.
2. How, if at all, is Mindy and Stacey's decision about an indoor water park related to their decision about franchise affiliation? What, if any, role should existing managers and their employees have in this decision, because it doesn't appear to be directly related to the existing business?

3. Figure 11.1 notes that competition is an external influence that impacts the planning activity. What competitive issues may impact the franchise affiliation decision that Mindy and Stacey must make? How, if at all, do these issues impact human resources?

Dimension: Employee Resistance to Change

1. When, if at all, do you recommend that Mindy and Stacey inform the employees in their existing lodging property about the decision to eliminate the franchise relationship, if this decision is made? What about their interest in considering an indoor water park?
2. Do you think Mindy and Stacey's employees are likely to become stressed and anxious about these pending decisions? Why? Defend your response.
3. What, if any, types of concerns might managers, front-office managers, and food and beverage managers in the property have?

Dimension: Human Resources Management

1. What, if any, difference do you think it will make in the way Mindy and Stacey recruit new staff members for their property if they are no longer affiliated with the chain organization?
2. What, if any, immediate changes relating to human resources will occur if the franchisor–franchisee affiliation ends?
3. What longer-term changes in human resources management might occur if the lodging properties become independent?

INTERNET ACTIVITIES

1. Want to review a Web site that provides a clearinghouse of information applicable to organizational change? If so, go to: *www.managementhelp.org. Note:* When you reach that site, click on "organizational change."
2. Managers can use numerous tactics to help support the need for change and to keep the process going as the implementation process evolves. To learn some specific suggestions, go to: *www.beyondresistance.com.*
3. The Internet provides numerous articles about organizational change and the role of human resources management in it. To learn much more about the topic of this chapter, type "human resources management and change" into your favorite search engine. You will discover many results that explore how change impacts human resources, and how human resources managers can assist their organizations in a planned and orderly change process.

ENDNOTE

1. See, for example: Raphael Kavanaugh and Jack Ninemeier, *Supervision in the Hospitality Industry*, 4th ed. East Lansing, MI: Educational Institute of the American Hotel & Lodging Association. In production.

CHAPTER TWELVE

Critical Issues in Human Resources Management

CHECKLIST OF CHAPTER LEARNING OBJECTIVES

As a result of satisfactory completion of this chapter, readers will be able to:

1. Explain how the responsibilities of human resources managers are affected when employees are unionized.

2. Discuss guidelines that are helpful in facilitating the work of staff members belonging to the Traditionalist, Baby Boomer, Generation X, and Generation Y age groups.

3. Provide tactics that may be useful when organizational downsizing and outsourcing strategies are planned and implemented.

4. Review basic procedures that are useful in the succession planning process.

5. Identify the benefits of and basic steps that human resources managers can use to develop and assist staff members with career planning activities.

Impact on Human Resources Management

Most hospitality organizations in the United States are not unionized, but some, especially large operations in metropolitan areas, do negotiate and administer agreements with one or more unions. This chapter addresses why employees are attracted to unions, how bargaining agreements affect management responsibilities, and procedures for collective bargaining.

Although many people believe that hospitality organizations are staffed by teenagers and young adults, there are, in fact, many persons of different ages working and enjoying careers in the industry. Should management and supervisory tactics be modified based on the age of staff members and, if so, how? Those with human resources responsibilities provide guidance and information to line supervisors and, in small properties, directly facilitate the work of employees. Therefore, a discussion of this topic is important for human resources managers.

The strategy of doing more with less while attaining performance standards is a concern of managers in every type of hospitality operation. When is downsizing (rightsizing) appropriate? What is the role of human resources managers in the process? and What are its potential effects on the organization? These questions are addressed in the chapter. Another tactic—outsourcing—is also increasingly being implemented and is considered in the specific context of the hospitality industry.

Even though hospitality managers are very busy with day-to-day concerns, they must also think about the short- and long-term future. To do so, they can use succession planning tactics to answer questions such as What and how many key management positions will be needed in the future and what competencies will be required for those in the positions? Once identified, career development programs and activities can be planned for incumbents in the positions and for those who aspire to the key roles.

This chapter addresses each of these topics to provide more comprehensive coverage of the types of concerns that confront contemporary hospitality human resources managers.

Unionization in the Hospitality Industry

Unions:
Organizations comprising employees who act together to promote and protect their mutual interests through collective bargaining; see *collective bargaining.*

1. Explain how the responsibilities of human resources managers are affected when employees are unionized.

Employee **unions** typically represent some hospitality organizations in metropolitan areas. Human resources practices in these operations must comply with the terms of the applicable **labor contract**, and managers work with other top-level officials to negotiate and administer these agreements. Those with line operating responsibilities may spend a significant amount of time ensuring compliance with the contract.

Labor contract: A written agreement covering a specific time that spells out management's expectations for employees and limits to management's authority; also called *collective bargaining agreement.*

Strategies to deal with employee unions from the time their representatives make initial contact with employees as a first step in the unionization process through negotiation procedures are developed by top-level managers, including those with human resources responsibilities. Because supervisors are likely to have more direct contact with union employees than are higher-level managers, they must learn the do's and don'ts of interactions with union employees. Top-level managers must also provide this union relations training to their supervisors.

REASONS FOR UNION AFFILIATION

There are several common reasons why some employees want to unionize. One relates to the employees' perceptions that their employer is unfair and, for example, shows disrespect, disciplines them unjustly, and/or does not correct problems in a reasonable or consistent manner. In other cases, workers believe (rightly or wrongly) that the profits made by the business owners are high, relative to the wages they (the employees) receive, and union affiliation will help spread the profit rewards more equitably.

Unions can increase the bargaining power of staff members because unified demands on the hospitality organization become possible. Unions also allow members to communicate and interact with higher-level managers in ways that would otherwise be different. For example, the **grievance process** spelled out in the union contract formalizes the communication procedures that dictate how managers interact with employees if problems arise.

Grievance process: A process to resolve a complaint that is spelled out in union contracts.

Union shop: The requirement that nonunion workers must join the union and pay applicable dues to it.

Equal treatment based on seniority replaces decisions, if any, made on the basis of personal relationships. Higher compensation levels, more control over work rules, greater job security, and peer influences are additional factors that some employees believe will be better addressed after union affiliation. Still other employees join unions because of **union shop** provisions of some union contracts: if all employees in a department are unionized, then new employees will be required to join the union and pay dues to it.

Interestingly, some hospitality organizations are pleased about their union affiliations because they enhance their business. Some large meeting groups only use unionized properties or, at least, will not do business with properties that are known to have union problems.

A BRIEF HISTORY

The historical purpose of labor legislation has been to maintain a balance of power between labor and management. Until the 1930s, unions were discouraged by court rulings as conspiracies in restraint of trade, because there were concerns that employee groups interfered with the right of employers to run their businesses as they desired. Most employees were hired with the understanding that they would not join unions or engage in union activities.

Some Employees Dislike Unions

Most hospitality industry employees are not union members. Unions do not generally attempt to organize small organizations with relatively few employees. Some employees are disinterested in unions because of:

- *Cultural and social reasons.* Some employees believe that professionals should not join unions.
- *Individual reasons.* Some staff members want to negotiate their own responsibilities and compensation because of their belief that they are in control of their own future as they do so. Basic human needs involving esteem and ego may contribute to this emphasis on individualism.
- *Promotional considerations.* Some staff members develop antiunion views in the belief that their affiliation with a union will hinder their career goals. While union membership typically results in increases in wages, benefits, and security for members, it is rare for rank-and-file union members to achieve the same levels of advancement (and income) within their companies as do talented individuals in nonunion operations.

During the Great Depression (1929 throughout most of the 1930s), many politicians began to believe that poor treatment of workers, especially low pay, was a significant factor that contributed to the nation's economic woes. In efforts to achieve a balance of power between labor and management, the National Labor Relations Act (1935), commonly referred to as the Wagner Act, was passed, and it prompted the growth of employee unions in the United States. Employees were allowed to affiliate with unions, union activities could be promoted, and union agreement violations could be reported without reprisal. Also, very importantly, employers had to undertake good-faith collective bargaining about three issues: wages, hours, and employment terms and conditions.

The Taft-Hartley Act (1947) amended the Wagner Act and removed some of the power given to unions by that earlier Act. Several unfair labor practices were identified. For example, unions could no longer:

- Force workers to join the union
- Mandate that the employer select specific grievance or bargaining representatives
- Refuse to bargain with employers in good faith
- Authorize strikes or boycotts for purposes the Act considered illegal
- Charge inappropriate fees (dues) to employees under union-shop contracts
- Operate closed shops (These occurred when employees joined a union and were trained by union personnel. When needed, employers requested employees from the union.)

Unions Affect Property Managers

When employees are represented by a union, property managers can no longer make unilateral decisions, and the decisions they do make will be applicable to all (rather than to specific) union employees. All staff members will need to be treated equally if they are in the same (or similar) positions regardless of their knowledge, experience, or skills. Frequently, **seniority** becomes the most important factor in many personnel decisions.

There may be some company benefits to unionization. For example, managers will develop and/or improve policies or procedures that affect relationships with line personnel, and use of these personnel management tools will likely benefit the organization. Managers will deal with one representative of unionized employees rather than with individual staff members. Top levels of management may need to recover some decision-making responsibilities delegated to supervisors. This can sometimes be beneficial, so centralized decision making represents another potential advantage to union affiliation.

Seniority: The status of employees based on their length of employment with an organization.

Union steward: A union member elected by other union members to represent the unionized employees within a specific department or work unit.

Grievance: An allegation that a work requirement or action taken by management violates the applicable union contract.

A local union is typically affiliated with a national-level union, and it can represent all unionized hospitality employees performing specific functions in a single community, or it may only represent members within a specific property. Local unions elect officers by a democratic vote of its members.

Full-time union officers are generally only found in large unions. Small employee unions have a president, whose responsibilities may include part-time union duties. Union members elect **union stewards** who represent the unionized employees within a department. Both the president and union stewards hold full-time jobs with the employer and are paid by the employer, and they typically use some job-related and their own time for union activities. Local union officials have numerous responsibilities, including negotiating labor contracts, filing **grievances**, ensuring that the bargaining agreement is complied with, and calling for work actions (such as strikes), if necessary.

Some unions have regional organizations that coordinate their affiliated local unions. They establish basic policies, provide necessary services, collect information, and administer strike and retirement funds. These organizations may employ staff specialists, such as attorneys and others, who carry on key responsibilities.

THE UNIONIZATION PROCESS

Employees become unionized as the result of a several-step process:

1. Initial contacts are made by employees to union representatives in their communities or vice versa: union representatives may begin a membership drive within an organization.

Authorization cards (union): A card signed by prospective union members specifying their interest in having a designated union represent them in employer negotiations.

Union recognition (voluntary): Union recognition that occurs when an employer agrees that signed authorization cards have been received from a majority of employees.

National Labor Relations Board (NLRB): An organization with responsibility to conduct union representation elections.

Union recognition (mandatory): Union recognition that occurs after the National Labor Relations Board conducts a secret ballot election and confirms that a majority of employees desire to be represented by the union.

Collective bargaining: The process of negotiating and administering written agreements between union and management officials.

Union security arrangements: Provisions of labor contracts that provide alternative tactics to attract and retain union members who pay dues.

Right-to-work law: A state law that prohibits a requirement that employees must join a union.

2. A campaign is undertaken to secure signed **authorization cards** from at least 30 percent of applicable employees requesting that a specific union should represent them in employer negotiations.

3. After the union has received signed authorization cards, the union or employees can request **voluntary recognition** of the union. The employer may comply or, alternatively, may request that cards be verified by a neutral third party. If voluntary recognition is granted, contract bargaining can begin.

4. If the employer refuses voluntary recognition, a petition is made to the **National Labor Relations Board** (NLRB) requesting an election to determine if the majority of eligible voting employees want the union to become their certified bargaining unit.

5. A union drive is conducted in which union advocates and management must comply with strict requirements about what they can and cannot do as they make their cases about why employees should or should not affiliate with the union.

6. If the union receives a majority vote, the NLRB certifies and recognizes the union as the exclusive bargaining unit for the employer. As this occurs, there is **mandatory recognition.**

What should (can) hospitality managers do during a union-organizing drive? Labor laws allow them to properly defend themselves against a unionizing campaign. Tactics include:

■ Remaining neutral if employees ask about their position about unionization
■ Allowing union-organizing activities during work hours if they do not interfere with ongoing operations
■ Refusing to let nonemployee organizers distribute union information in the property
■ Allowing employees to distribute union information during breaks
■ Avoiding opportunities to question staff members either in public or in private about union-organizing activities.
■ Not spying on employees' unionizing activities
■ Not making threats or promises about unionization
■ Refusing to discriminate against employees involved in unionization efforts
■ Keeping alert to union efforts to coerce employees to join or to commit otherwise unfair labor practices[1]

Sometimes union members become dissatisfied with their union and want to join another union or return to a nonunionized status. This is done as the union members petition the NLRB for a decertification election, and decertification will occur if a majority of the members vote to disaffiliate with the union.

THE COLLECTIVE BARGAINING PROCESS

Collective bargaining involves the process of negotiating and administering written agreements between union and management officials. A common stereotype

Do Employees Have to Join the Union?

Many labor agreements contain **union security arrangements** designed to attract and retain union members who pay dues. Under the most stringent arrangement, union shop, all employees hired for unionized positions must join the union or quit their jobs after a specified probationary period. However, approximately 20 states have **right-to-work laws** that, with few exceptions, do not permit union agreements in which employees are required to join or pay dues to a union. Under these laws, employees may resign from union membership at any time.

An **agency shop** arrangement requires nonunion employees to pay the union the equivalent of applicable fees and dues as a condition of continuing employment. With this plan, the union represents all employees regardless of whether they are union members.

The least desirable union security arrangement (from the unions' perspective) is the **open shop.** With this arrangement, union membership is voluntary, and those who do not join are not required to pay dues or fees.

Another desired union security arrangement relates to **dues check-off.** When used, the employer withholds union dues and fees from members' paychecks in much the same way that other payments such as taxes and insurance payments are withheld.

Agency shop: A security arrangement in a labor agreement that requires employees to pay union dues and fees even if they do not join the union.

Open shop: A union security arrangement in which employees are not required to join the union and do not need to pay union dues and fees if they are not union members.

Dues check-off: A process by which employers withhold union dues from the paychecks of union members.

of the contract negotiation process is one of labor and management attempting to win **concessions** from each other in an "I win, you lose" **distributive collective bargaining** strategy. This approach is used, for example, when a union attempts to bargain for increased compensation packages at a time when the organization cannot afford it. Management concessions negotiated during good economic times are infrequently given up during periods when profits are lower. Unfortunately, much of the hospitality industry goes through almost predictable profitability cycles tied to the nation's economy, and higher levels of compensation become very troublesome (sometimes disastrous) during down periods in the economy.

Integrative collective bargaining is a more cooperative effort that focuses on each party's interests, including those that are mutual, rather than positions that must be defended. The premise that a hospitality organization must be able to survive to benefit both parties becomes a foundation on which labor and management can work to "make the pie bigger," rather than to divide it up.

Significant time and effort is required by both union and management personnel to negotiate agreements. It is, therefore, common for contracts to span a several-year period. Both parties will be very interested about current compensation

Concessions (collective bargaining): The act of conceding (yielding) something as a labor contract is negotiated.

Collective bargaining (distributive): An "I win, you lose" approach to negotiation in which one party attempts to gain something at the expense of the other party.

Collective bargaining (integrative): An "I win, you win" approach to negotiation in which both parties benefit from the agreement.

Collective bargaining (mandatory items): Concerns over which labor and management must negotiate if either party wants to do so.

Collective bargaining (permissible items): Concerns that may be negotiated if both parties agree to do so.

Cost-of-living adjustment: An arrangement in which future wage increases are tied to the consumer price index that reflects changes in consumer purchasing power; often abbreviated COLA.

rates and the organization's current and projected financial position. Details about the current contract must be assessed, if applicable, and issues of concern to both parties must be considered in advance of negotiations. Union and organization representatives must, simultaneously, consider their going-in and fallback positions about their priority concerns.

Recall that the Wagner Act required employers to bargain in good faith about three mandatory issues: wages, hours, and employment terms/conditions. Additionally, grievance procedures are addressed in almost all labor contracts.

Labor contracts typically address concerns that unions make on behalf of their membership. Those that are most typically important relate to compensation, benefits, and job security. Bargaining issues generally concern one of two types. **Mandatory items** include those about which labor and management must negotiate if either party desires to do so, including wages, working hours, and benefits. **Permissible items** are those that can be negotiated if labor and management agree to do so (e.g., union veto power over a restaurant's hours of operation).

Employee unions are concerned about current and future compensation for their employees. They typically negotiate **cost-of-living adjustments** (COLAs) that tie wage increases to changes in consumer purchasing power.

Other typical union concerns relate to employee benefits, including retirement, paid holidays, and working conditions. Unions typically negotiate for employer payment of all or most employee insurance costs. Job security is another typical collective bargaining priority, and seniority is integral to this discussion. A wide range of other union-initiated issues are often considered. These include working hours and overtime pay policies, agreements about rest periods, differential pay for employees working on different shifts, and the use of part-time and temporary employees.

What happens if the union and management negotiators cannot agree on one or more contract clauses? One typically thinks about strikes and, unfortunately, these do occur, and they can cause significant disruption to hospitality operations and their guests. Other legal labor actions that unions can use to deal with labor disputes include **picketing, boycotts,** and **work slowdowns.**

Typical union agreements contain clauses addressing the following issues:

- Recognition of union
- Wages and benefits
- Vacation and holidays
- Working conditions
- Layoffs
- Management rights
- Working hours
- Employee seniority
- Arbitration
- Union renewal clause

Picketing: A legal labor action in which union employees promote grievances at the entrance to the employer's property.

Boycott: A legal labor action in which employees refuse to purchase the products or services of a specific employer.

Work slowdown: A legal labor action in which employees work at a slower-than-normal pace.

Arbitration (voluntary): An action in which both parties (organization and union personnel) submit a dispute to an external, disinterested third party for binding or nonbinding resolution after the presentation of evidence and related discussion.

Arbitration (compulsory): An action in which an arbitrator is appointed by the government to make a binding decision on the parties negotiating the contract.

Mediation: A nonbinding structured process in which a third party assists the management and union negotiators to reach an agreement.

Three conflict resolution tactics may be used when negotiations reach an impasse:

- **Voluntary arbitration.** An action in which both parties (organization and union personnel) submit a dispute to an external, disinterested third party for binding or nonbinding resolution after the presentation of evidence and related discussion.
- **Compulsory arbitration.** An action in which an arbitrator is appointed by the government to make a binding decision on the parties negotiating the contract. *Note:* This contract resolution tactic is not typically used in the United States to settle labor disputes in commercial hospitality operations.
- **Mediation.** A nonbinding structured process in which a third party assists management and union negotiators to reach an agreement. Advice, not a final, mandated decision, is the result.

CONTRACT ADMINISTRATION

After union and hospitality organization representatives agree to contract provisions, and the contract is ratified (approved) by the union members, communication and coordination efforts are required to ensure that the contract is understood by all parties. Even if changes are minor, significant communication, training and education, and meetings may be necessary so both parties understand all contractual terms. Changes involving work rules and hours, for example, can involve significant details that required focused explanation.

The union steward represents union employees, and managers represent the organization's interests. They must both consider each other's rights to work together cooperatively. If approved by the union steward, an employee may attempt to resolve a complaint through a formal grievance process that often includes the following steps, if resolution is not forthcoming at an earlier step:

1. The union steward and affected employee meet with the supervisor.
2. The employee, union steward, and chief steward meet with the supervisor and the organization's labor relations (human resources) specialist.
3. The employee, steward, and union grievance committee meet with labor relations (human resources) and the property's top management personnel.
4. Representatives of the national union or other top union officials meet with top-level organization management.

If the Step 4 grievance resolution procedure is unsuccessful, a final step will likely be arbitration. *Note:* In small organizations, the grievance process is often abbreviated. After Step 1, the property's senior manager or owner may become involved and, if still unresolved, the grievance may then move to arbitration.

The labor agreement should effectively spell out management's and employees' rights. The identification of management's rights is important, because they directly impact the ability of managers to operate the business. Those negotiating labor agreements and participating in grievance procedures should, respectively, ensure that contractual terms are properly worded and understood. Some of the numerous rights that managers should never negotiate away include:

- Terms and conditions for employee performance reviews
- The ability to develop schedules that manage overtime
- Employee assignment, reassignment, and promotion decisions
- Use of tests to assess employment qualifications
- Length of probationary periods
- Expected on-job conduct
- Discretion to administer work rules, policies, standard operating procedures, and performance standards
- Modification of job description tasks
- Implementation of tactics to increase productivity
- Decisions about staff members qualified for specific positions, merit increases, and promotions
- Property reorganization including the closure of departments or properties (in multiunit organizations)

Basic management rights are very important, and these topics should be addressed during employee orientation sessions.

McCormick Place: A Case Study in Union Problems and Their Resolution

Chicago's McCormick Place is the largest convention center in North America, with almost three million square feet of exhibit and related space. During the late 1990s, several major trade shows threatened to and actually did relocate annual exhibitions to other cities. A major reason related to high costs and exhibitor frustrations created by the four unions was represented at the facility. For example, exhibitors were prohibited from using hand tools to assemble booths, personnel from different unions were needed to lay carpet and decorate booths, and union personnel had to carry even relatively small packages throughout the trade floor areas.

Declining numbers of trade shows prompted numerous groups, including the mayor's office, Chicago Convention and Tourism Bureau, leaders of trade unions, and others, to work cooperatively to make the exhibition experience more hospitable for associations and their exhibitors. Their results were successful, and Chicago is still a major player in the country's convention and trade show market.

Union agreements affect other aspects of employee relations that should be addressed during orientation, including:

- Employees' rights and responsibilities
- Managers' and supervisors' rights and responsibilities
- Relations with supervisors and union stewards
- Union contract provisions and company policies
- Discipline and reprimands
- Grievance procedures
- Employment termination

Many employee and management rights and responsibilities may not differ significantly between unionized operations and their nonunionized counterparts. These special concerns relate to most employees, should be addressed during orientation, and should be administered equitably and consistently in all hospitality organizations regardless of union affiliation.

Unfortunately, some day-to-day interactions can create difficulty and significant differences between how things work in a nonunionized operation. For example, a major hotel in New York City has a person in the banquet and catering department whose only responsibility is contract interpretation. On one occasion, a banquet manager spent 30 minutes looking for an employee who could legally (according to the labor agreement) erect an eight-foot table at a meeting room entrance for guest use as a registration desk. No other employees could perform that task without a monetary penalty—additional wages for departmental employees

In a unionized hospitality operation, the bargaining agreement may specify that persons working in a specified position perform only very specific work tasks. *Courtesy PhotoDisc/Getty Images*

during that shift.[2] As a second example, some years ago, a public school district operated its school foodservice program under a union contract that prohibited the district from implementing convenience food or labor-saving equipment alternatives if productivity (meals produced per labor hour) increased.

Today, however, unions and employers often work cooperatively. For example, airline companies and their employees reduce labor costs to save jobs today and to share in mutual rewards tomorrow. While total union membership has been decreasing in the United States since the mid-1940s, renewed efforts have yielded some expansion of union membership in the hospitality industry (e.g., in Las Vegas and New York City). While the future is unknown, economic and/or organizational changes may increase the interest of hospitality industry employees in

Unfair labor practices: An action by either the hospitality organization or union that violates applicable provisions of the National Labor Relations Act.

IT'S THE LAW!

This chapter has identified several major legislative acts that impact the relationships among organizations, unions, and their employees who are union members. The bargaining process by which a union contract (collective bargaining agreement) is conducted must be within the restraints imposed by the National Labor Relations Act and the agency it created (the National Labor Relations Board). The NLRB administers required procedures for valid elections that determine whether employees want to become affiliated with a specific union. It also works to prevent and resolve **unfair labor practices** by organizations or unions.

Examples of unfair labor practices by hospitality organizations include:

- Discouraging attempts by employees to unionize
- Interfering with employees as they participate in union activities
- Discriminating against union members
- Terminating union members who participate in a legal strike

Examples of unfair labor practices conducted by union personnel include:

- Forcing employees to join or participate in a union
- Requiring employers to hire more workers than required
- Conducting an illegal strike (one that violates the terms of the collective bargaining agreement)

Numerous other laws and regulations require compliance by the employers and union officials.

Stephen Barth, Hospitality Law: Managing Legal Issues in the Hospitality Industry, 3rd Edition, John Wiley and Sons, 2008.

union membership. If this occurs, managers and supervisors with human resources responsibilities will be challenged to manage according to the labor agreement while addressing the needs of the guests being served.

A Multigenerational Workforce

2. **Discuss guidelines that are helpful in facilitating the work of staff members belonging to the Traditionalist, Baby Boomer, Generation X, and Generation Y age groups.**

Persons of all ages enjoy stimulating and interesting careers in the widely diverse hospitality industry. Writers from numerous disciplines have suggested that persons are fundamentally different because of their life experiences, which are impacted by the era during which they grew up, matured, and entered the workforce. These writers further suggest that these differences should be considered as persons are managed at work. This section summarizes some of the information presented and discusses its impact on managing hospitality human resources.

OVERVIEW OF THE GENERATIONS

Traditionalists (workforce generation): Persons with birthdates between approximately 1922 and 1945.

Figure 12.1 reviews basic demographics about the generations that comprise today's workforce.

While the names of each generation and the inclusive dates of birth sometimes vary, Figure 12.1 provides interesting information. For example, while there are few, if any, older **Traditionalists** still working, the youngest in that generation,

Name of Generation	Dates of Birth	AGE OF MEMBERS (2008)	
		Oldest	Youngest
Traditionalists	1922–1945	86	63
Baby Boomers	1946–1964	62	44
Generation X	1965–1978	43	30
Generation Y	1979–1994	29	14

From: Christine Zust, "Baby Boomer Leaders Face Challenges Communicating Across Generations." Retrieved on 11/13/06 from: www.emergingleader.com/article16.shtml.

Notes: Birth years vary slightly in the literature. Generation Y is also called the Echo Boomers and Millennial Generation.

FIGURE 12.1: Generations That Comprise Today's Workforce

Baby Boomers (workforce generation): Persons with birthdates between approximately 1945 and 1964.

Generation X (workforce generation): Persons with birthdates between approximately 1965 and 1978.

Generation Y (workforce generation): Persons with birthdates between approximately 1979 and 1994.

along with **Baby Boomers**, occupy a large number of senior management positions in hospitality organizations. Also, senior citizens (Traditionalists) frequently supplement retirement income with jobs in the hospitality and other industries. Older **Generation X** employees, especially those on the fast track, are also likely to be in the senior management ranks of hospitality organizations. Younger Generation X employees and some older **Generation Y** staff members are now advancing to middle-management positions. Other Generation Y employees are now assuming early management positions, while the youngest are just reaching the age at which they can begin working according to child labor laws.

In Chapter 1, you learned that it can be a mistake to generalize about (stereotype) persons based on nationality, ethnicity, and other factors. It is just as inappropriate to develop sweeping generalizations that must be applied to all persons of a given age group.

A detailed discussion about managing (supervising) employees goes beyond the scope of this book. Some observers note the advantages of, when possible, modifying your leadership style to accommodate different groups of individuals based on those factors that motivate them to be effective performers. Some writers, however, go on to say that, while this tactic is ideal, it is difficult at best to accomplish and, in fact, many managers use the same leadership style in most (all) situations.

This reasoning may also apply to the suggestion about modifying leadership styles based on employees' ages. This might be an appropriate tactic, and it is relatively easy to do when, for example, most staff members belong to a specific generation (think, for example, about quick-service restaurants and the majority of teenager/young adult employees who are employed by them). However, changing one's leadership style based on employee age is much more difficult to implement in other operations with many employees of differing ages. For example, a high-check average restaurant with Baby Boomer senior managers, Generation X production and service staff, and younger (Generation Y) employees in assistant production, server, and clean-up positions.

Wise human resources managers should be aware that employees may have different perceptions about work, its meaning, and their interest in it based on their age and other factors. Supervisory training sessions can address these topics, and the analyses of personnel-related challenges can consider these issues. Also, if possible, management–employee interactions can address the potential impact of generational differences in the employees' attitudes.

MANAGING THE GENERATIONS

It is difficult for some managers to interact with different generations, because doing so can challenge their own beliefs and values, force them to consider the impact of change and conflict, and create the need to modify their communication skills. Let's review some basic information about the work beliefs and characteristics of the four workforce generations in today's hospitality industry: Traditionalists, Baby Boomers, Generation X, and Generation Y. Figure 12.2 suggests general beliefs, characteristics applicable to work ethics, view of work, and personal and work traits of the workforce generations.

Work Characteristics	Traditionalists (1922–1945)	Baby Boomers (1946–1964)	Generation X (1965–1978)	Generation Y (1979–1994)
Work Ethics	Loyal	Driven	Balanced	Eager
View of Work	It is necessary	It is exciting	It is a challenge	It is done to make a difference
Personal Traits	Conservative	Idealistic	Practical	Politically conscious
	Respect authority	Not enough time	Flexible	High self-expectations
	Well-disciplined		Individualistic	Team builders
			Entrepreneurial	Tolerant of differences
			Interested in quality of life	Confident
				Desire challenges
Work Traits	Work hard; put in their time	The first workaholics	Don't like office politics	Want to know why
	Stay with company	Want to climb ladder of success	Have less loyalty to employer	Desire public praise
	Accept information dissemination on need-to-know basis	Want to be politically correct	Multitask workers	Enjoy a fun workplace
	May dislike but do not question directions of supervisors	Compete with peers	Like collegial work environment	Money is not a motivation; They can get it anywhere
	Work as they are told to	Performance measured by time in the office	Like to do projects	Want immediate responsibility
		Respect top-down authority	Are concerned more about job responsibilities than job titles	Want small goals with tight deadlines
		Casual attire means unprofessional	Performance measured by output	Work-life balance is important
			Do not like power structures	Do not seek longevity with a company
			Flexible with authority	High expectations of employers
			Casual attire is comfortable	Confident in their abilities

FIGURE 12.2: Work Beliefs and Characteristics of the Generations

Even a brief review of the generational characteristics noted in Figure 12.2 identifies some very interesting factors that differentiate members of each generation. *Note:* These differences often become much more noticeable when one considers persons at the midpoint of each generation. For example, when you think about differences between Generations X and Y, think about persons in their middle thirties (Generation X) versus those in their early twenties (Generation Y). Don't think about those who are 30 years old (the youngest persons in Generation X in 2008) and those who are 29 years old (the oldest persons in Generation Y in 2008).

When reviewing the work characteristics of Traditionalists (Figure 12.2), remember that they are familiar with hardship. The earliest members of the generation suffered through the Great Depression that began in 1929, and many were affected by World War II. They value consistency, respect authority, and are well-disciplined.

Baby Boomers have been called the "me generation." Their work incentives include money, position titles, and recognition for the work they do. When they entered the workforce, Baby Boomers wanted to build a significant career to enhance their reputation. They challenged the status quo, and those in this generation are responsible for many of the opportunities now taken for granted in the workplace. They became the first workaholics, and they believe that hard work and loyalty are a good way to get ahead. Many Baby Boomers sense that who they are is connected to their work and career achievements.

Workforce Generations Are Different!

Human resources managers should learn about the generations and their differences because:

- There are now four generations of employees working side-by-side in the hospitality industry.
- The industry is labor-intensive and will continue to need employees, regardless of their age, to staff the many available positions.
- The range of differences between earliest (Traditionalist) employees and the current (Generation Y) staff members is very wide.
- Differing values, experiences, lifestyles, and attitudes toward the future and life in general can create significant misunderstandings and frustrations.
- Those who better understand and appreciate each generation may gain ideas about how to motivate and retain persons within these generations, and will be better able to consistently work with individuals of differing ages.

Generation X employees are motivated by job satisfaction. They don't anticipate remaining in one job or with one company throughout their careers. They know they can jump jobs in efforts to attain desired compensation and other benefits and to receive increased opportunities for growth and personal fulfillment. They desire to provide input to their employers, and they have an interest in understanding how the company works, because they know this will influence their growth opportunities. Personal acknowledgment and job satisfaction are very important for this generation.

Generation Y employees want to know the why of what they are being asked to do; they want to know what's in it for them. They enjoy a fun workplace, and money is not a motivator, because they think they have numerous employment opportunities. They are also quick to speak their opinions and are not responsive to the do-it-or-else supervisory tactics that some hospitality managers use too frequently.

Should Managers Dwell on Generational Differences?

There are diverse opinions about how people should be managed. Some say that everyone should be treated the same. Others say it is important to emphasize or, at least, consider generational differences. Still others suggest that employees should be treated as individuals.

One writer has suggested several tactics that work equally well for employees in every generation, in every organization, at any time:

- Show employees that what they do matters.
- Tell employees the truth.
- Explain to staff members why they are being asked to do something.
- Learn the employee's language.
- Provide rewarding opportunities.
- Praise staff members in public.
- Make the workplace fun.
- Model the desired behavior.
- Give staff members the tools required to do their jobs.

While different generations may appreciate different leadership tactics, these best-practice techniques work with all staff members.

Retrieved on November 26, 2006, from: Carol Verret. "Generation Y: Motivating and Training a New Generation of Employees," *www.hotel-online.com*.

Human Resources MANAGEMENT ISSUES (12.1)

"Today's college graduates are sure a lot different than my generation," said Jason. He was talking to Bernice, another department head at the River Bank Conference Center.

"You're sure right about that, Jason," said Bernice. "We're both old-timers—Baby Boomers—and we've seen, first, the Generation X managers arrive and mature, and now we're seeing those in Generation Y join our organization. It seems there is a big difference between each generation of employees. I really think that's true, but maybe we're just getting old."

"I remember when I began my career in the hospitality industry," replied Jason. "I wanted to work hard, didn't mind the hours, and while I had respect for my bosses, I really thought I could do a better job than they were doing. Over the years, you and I and others in our generation have made lots of changes. Many were in response to the need to do so. I'm thinking about technology, cost minimization in an increasingly competitive industry, and the unprecedented labor shortages, among other things. Be honest, Bernice, do you think our industry is better serving our guests now as a result of our efforts or yesterday when our generation first started to influence the industry?"

"That's a tough question to answer, Jason, and I guess I really can't respond. You've mentioned some of the pressures that have influenced us, and I'd like to add one more: vastly changing differences in what our guests want. I know that everyone wants the basics—safety, courtesy and respect, and good price and value—but every organization must provide more than that to survive. Has our River Bend property just been lucky in our efforts to determine the products and services our guests want? Perhaps, instead, we have been lucky because we have been able to recruit and retain staff members from the later generations who can better keep up with changing guest preferences. I really don't know, but I think we should keep on doing what we are doing."

QUESTION

Think about some bosses you have had who have been 50 years old or older, others who have been in their mid-thirties, and those who have been younger. What, if any, differences have you noted in:

- Their leadership styles
- The procedures they use to make business-related decisions
- What they thought to be their greatest organizational strengths
- Their career aspirations
- Their ability to determine and deliver what the guests want and need
- Their interest in and approaches to help subordinate employees advance within their careers
- Their interest in remaining with their organization and in the hospitality industry
- The methods they use to communicate
- Their genuine interest in helping guests and in helping the organization (their employer) to succeed

Downsizing and Outsourcing

3. **Provide tactics that may be useful when organizational downsizing and outsourcing strategies are planned and implemented.**

Managers in hospitality organizations, like their counterparts in other industries, are consistently looking for ways to increase productivity (efficiency) without sacrificing required quality and quantity standards. Often, productivity increases yield some saved time that can efficiently be used for other purposes. This might even include some "we'll do it when we get around to it" work activities! By contrast, new work methods may be implemented that reduce the need for one or just a few staff members. At still other times, unfortunately, economic conditions may require a larger-scale reduction in the workforce. In these instances, human resources managers must use downsizing principles. Managers may also decide to use the services of external contractors for work that would otherwise be done by the organization's employees in a process called outsourcing. This section discusses both of these tactics that are commonly used to reduce the number of employees required by a hospitality organization.

DOWNSIZING TACTICS

Downsizing: The reduction of staff for the purpose of improving an organization's operating efficiency.

Downsizing refers to the process of terminating jobs in efforts to create greater operating efficiencies.

Some organizations confronted with financial difficulties because of increased costs and/or reduced revenues may need to downsize. Some of their counterparts may desire to proactively eliminate jobs to remain competitive and/or to avoid future problems. *Note:* Downsizing is not an all-or-nothing decision. An organization that is downsizing in specific positions may also be hiring other employees with required skills to implement new strategies.

All downsizing decisions are significant because (1) they impact both the staff members who are terminated and those who remain, and (2) because these decisions affect the organization's financial success and reputation. All downsizing alternatives have critical human resources implications, and those managers with these responsibilities must be very concerned about the human factors as they deliberate these options.

Because the impact of downsizing is difficult to reverse, at least in the short term, several alternatives to the termination of staff members should first be considered depending on the specific challenges confronting the organization. These include:

Succession planning: The process of considering the organization's future needs for key professional and other staff, and developing plans to select and/or to prepare persons for these positions.

- Careful review of alternative opportunities to reduce costs and/or to increase revenues
- Cross-training
- **Succession planning**
- Transfer within the organization (if a multiunit organization)

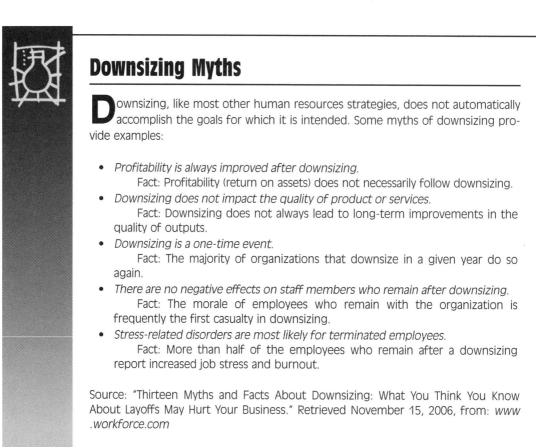

Downsizing Myths

Downsizing, like most other human resources strategies, does not automatically accomplish the goals for which it is intended. Some myths of downsizing provide examples:

- *Profitability is always improved after downsizing.*
    Fact: Profitability (return on assets) does not necessarily follow downsizing.
- *Downsizing does not impact the quality of product or services.*
    Fact: Downsizing does not always lead to long-term improvements in the quality of outputs.
- *Downsizing is a one-time event.*
    Fact: The majority of organizations that downsize in a given year do so again.
- *There are no negative effects on staff members who remain after downsizing.*
    Fact: The morale of employees who remain with the organization is frequently the first casualty in downsizing.
- *Stress-related disorders are most likely for terminated employees.*
    Fact: More than half of the employees who remain after a downsizing report increased job stress and burnout.

Source: "Thirteen Myths and Facts About Downsizing: What You Think You Know About Layoffs May Hurt Your Business." Retrieved November 15, 2006, from: *www .workforce.com*

Attrition: The reduction in an organization's workforce because of voluntary or involuntary employee separation.

- ▪ Reduced employee hours and/or wages
- ▪ **Attrition,** including the use of early retirement and/or employee buyout incentives and leaves of absence

Top-level managers, including those with human resources responsibilities, must be involved in downsizing decisions. Their assistance is needed to plan for and to defend this strategy to all employees, and to help remaining staff members adapt to the change. This is especially important because perceptions of remaining staff members about their future careers with the organization often cause them to begin job searches, and the best employees are among those that are typically first to leave.[3]

Human resources managers must address issues including attrition estimates, assessment of skills needed by the organization, and the determination of employees who have or can attain these skills. While the involvement of top-level managers is critical, affected staff members will most closely interact with managers and supervisors at lower levels, and these staff members must be committed to communicating and helping affected employees in the most appropriate manner. To do so requires ongoing communication about the status of downsizing plans.

Honest and ongoing communication is critical. Employees must know what, why, and when, and employers should advise employees about their rights, and what will be done to assist them. Advanced planning is important to create a better vision for the organization. Careful analysis of perceived benefits and potential problems is important, and input from employees will be helpful (and is likely required in unionized organizations).

Much internal and some external information is required for successful downsizing. Unfortunately, some of this information is not likely to be available, nor is a data collection system typically in place because it is not used for day-to-day operating decisions. For example, managers require information to plan for and monitor the downsizing process. Examples include demographic data about the existing workforce, information about employee skills that can be helpful in reorganizing, and information about staff members who are covered by federal, state, or other laws. (Minorities, women, disabled persons, and older employees may be disproportionally affected, and the impact of downsizing on these groups should be projected and monitored.) Employees will require information to help them plan their futures and, in multiunit organizations, information may include employee-related data that may help as transfer assignments are considered.

As part of the planning process, departmental plans should be developed to help show how each organizational unit will be able to operate effectively after downsizing. Department managers can also be asked to identify work processes that are not needed in the future, so affected positions can be targeted for elimination.

Several downsizing techniques can be useful as the process is implemented including:

- Attrition
- Early retirement and buyout incentives
- Involuntary separation (e.g., organizations bound by bargaining agreements must typically use seniority-based factors when deciding those employees to be terminated)
- Leaves without pay
- Flexible work arrangements (e.g., part-time, flexible work hours, variable workweeks, and job-sharing)

A wide range of useful activities can help staff members who will be laid off. Examples of these transitional services include the provision of:

- Career counseling to help staff members identify competencies and to assess skills necessary for future careers
- Personal counseling to help with stress reduction and to improve the affected employees' self-esteem

- Career transition training to enable employees to know what to expect during the downsizing process
- Assistance to help staff find other jobs or to enhance their skills for doing so
- Relocation assistance if staff can obtain employment in other locations where the organization has properties
- A career transition center to serve as a clearinghouse of information, services, and resources for affected staff members
- **Outplacement assistance** to help employees secure new employment (e.g., résumé writing assistance, access to necessary equipment, and information about Internet job placement sites)
- Paid time-off and/or child care assistance to staff while they search for new positions.
- Personal financial counseling

Outplacement assistance: The process of helping employees to secure new employment (e.g., résumé writing assistance, access to necessary equipment, and information about Internet job placement sites).

Human Resources Management:
CURRENT EVENTS 12.1

AD HOC AND ANNUAL DOWNSIZING ACTIVITIES

Many people think of downsizing when it occurs on an ad hoc (one-time) basis. For example, the Sands Hotel & Casino in Atlantic City was purchased, and plans were made to close, demolish, and replace the existing property with a larger hotel casino. Its 2,100 employees were to receive 60 days' notice and severance packages.*

For some hospitality properties, downsizing is an annual event. Consider, for example, private clubs in Florida and other southern states that lose members during the hot summer months and regain them in the fall when it begins to get cold in the northern states. The reverse is also true; consider hotels, resorts, and restaurants in northern locations, which enjoy high volumes of business during the summer but have significantly reduced revenues during the winter.

While employees in these properties are aware of their short-term employment opportunities (and some move north and south according to the seasons), human resources personnel at these properties face unique challenges as business slows down and, especially, as recruitment, orientation, and training activities are required for a large number of staff members during a relatively short period of time when business volumes increase.

*Suzette Parmley, "The Sands Atlantic City Hotel & Casino. Acquired by Pinnacle Entertainment; Plans to Close, Demolish, and Build a Bigger Casino Hotel—2,100 Employees to Receive 60 Days Notice and Severance Packages." Retrieved on November 6, 2006 from: *www.hotel-online.com/News/PR2006_3rd/Sep06_PinnacleSands.html.*

Results of the downsizing efforts are of obvious concern. Because cost reduction and productivity issues are typically among the primary reasons for downsizing, these factors must be addressed and can be done so by considering and measuring, if possible, the following:

■ Reduced number of employees (**full-time equivalents**) and associated labor costs
■ Impact on diversity goals
■ Extent to which revised budget goals are met
■ Compliance of legal/regulatory-mandated programs
■ Payback periods required to pay for early retirement or other incentive programs
■ Number of appeals (grievances) in union operations
■ Impact of guest service ratings

Those who survive the downsizing effort require special consideration. They must receive ongoing communication from top-level leaders to learn that the separated employees were treated equitably and that they are being helped to find new positions. Other tactics to minimize negative downsizing experiences include:

■ Top-level leaders must be visible and involved, and they must continually re-emphasize the organization's vision, mission, and goals after layoffs are completed.
■ **Survivors** must know where they fit in the reorganized structure and should be given assistance in planning their continued careers with the organization.
■ Appropriate rewards and recognition for the remaining employees should be provided.

Full-time equivalent: The total number of employees if all employees worked full time, calculated as: total labor hours divided by the average number of labor hours in a workweek. For example, three part-time employees working a total of 45 hours in a workweek represent 1.13 full-time equivalent employees (45 hours ÷ 40 hours) if there are 40 hours in a typical full-time workweek; often abbreviated FTE.

Survivor (downsizing): An employee who is not terminated and who remains with the organization after a downsizing process is completed.

Which Employees Should Be Laid Off?

The answer to this question is one of the most difficult that a manager will ever make. First, it can be helpful to be positive, and to rephrase the question: Which employees should I select (retain) to work in the redesigned positions?

This decision-making process can involve several steps:

● Think about the positions that will remain after downsizing is completed. Consider new work tasks to be added to, and existing work tasks that will be eliminated from, the position as it is modified.
● Consider the requirements, skills, and experience necessary to perform each task in the modified position.
● Study performance reviews and other information relating to the tasks that will be included in the position.
● Personnel selection positions must make sense to the manager, his or her superiors, and affected employees.

OUTSOURCING TACTICS

Outsourcing: A transfer of responsibility for performance of services that have been (or could be) performed by the organization's employees to an external service provider.

Offshoring: The transfer of jobs from an organization in one country to an organization in another country.

Outsourcing is a topic that is frequently discussed in the context of procurement, and much of the responsibility for it rests with those in hospitality operations who are responsible for purchasing. However, outsourcing also has a human resources dimension because its alternative (use the organization's employees to perform the affected activity) involves personnel.

Readers of general business publications find numerous references to outsourcing that discuss the transfer of jobs not only out of the organization but also out of the country. In the minds of many, the terms **outsourcing** and **offshoring** are almost the same. Some hospitality jobs have been moved out of the country. Examples include centralized hotel reservation operations for some companies and, more recently, quick-service restaurant (QSR) organizations that relocate the taking of drive-through guest orders to international locations. However, the terms do not generally have the same meaning for most hospitality organizations.

What jobs could be done by a hospitality organization's employees that are frequently outsourced? Examples are numerous and include human resources functions such as payroll and benefits administration, recruiting, training, and regulatory compliance monitoring. Accounting/bookkeeping activities (especially for small businesses), permanent or temporary security personnel, and technology applications are additional examples. Operations-related services such as cleaning kitchen exhaust systems, window cleaning, landscaping, maintenance, and janitorial services are often outsourced. Some lodging operations

This staff member may be an employee of the hospitality organization or, alternatively, may be working for an external service provider. *Courtesy Manchan/Photo-Disc, Inc./Getty Images*

utilize employees of external organizations to provide some or all of their housekeeping needs, and many healthcare, educational, business and industry, and other organizations outsource food services to contract management companies.

Priority reasons to consider and implement outsourcing alternatives typically relate to cost concerns and, often, to an inability to attract and retain qualified personnel to perform the necessary work. Some small properties, for example, contract for outside cleaning services. Their service providers employ many staff members and can obtain and provide medical and other benefits at lower costs than can the property using its own employees. This enables the service provider to attract and retain staff members, while their counterparts (small properties) must continually recruit to fill these high-turnover positions. The excessive time needed for recruitment, selection, and training of personnel, along with, frequently, the problems that arise when cleaning duties are not being completed (or as short-cuts must be taken) because of position vacancies prompts many organizations to consider outsourcing alternatives.

Core business strategies: The highest priority activities that are required to accomplish an organization's mission.

Outsourcing decisions must, at their most basic level, consider the organization's mission and **core business strategies**. What is it trying to accomplish? What are the most important things it does? Management goals must address these core business strategies, and some organizations then consider transferring noncore business functions to specialized service providers who can provide required products and services at similar (or higher) quality levels.

Those with human resources responsibilities should be part of the team that considers outsourcing alternatives to address questions including:

- How can an outsourcing alternative help the business by reducing costs, improving performance, and/or improving guest value?
- What internal expertise is available or must be acquired to select potential suppliers, to negotiate agreements, and to manage vendor relationships if an outsourcing alternative is used?
- How can the property identify and control costs, assess the accuracy of financial projections that are made, and consider the financial/nonfinancial costs and benefits to a service provider relationship?
- What is the impact on existing employees? *Note:* This issue is especially critical when existing personnel will be eliminated if activities are outsourced.
- What type of **escape clause** is needed? The hospitality organization may want to terminate the contract without significant harm if the products and services provided under the contract are unacceptable. It will also need to manage (perform) the function while the decision to use internal employees or external organizations for the service is reassessed.

Escape clause: A provision in a contract that permits one party to terminate the agreement when one or more specified events occur.

When should potential outsourcing solutions be considered? The best answer is that it depends on the severity of concerns that are prompting consideration of an existing outsourcing alternative. Factors that typically prompt an analysis include personnel issues, including unqualified/unwilling staff members, high turnover rates, loss of key personnel, and staff members' failure to use required practices. Other factors include an inability to meet standards with in-house personnel, the need to focus on core business strategies, and the belief that to do so will increase and improve financial results.

The process of making an outsourcing decision typically involves the following steps:

1. Determine exactly what is needed.
2. Review resources available in-house relative to those available externally.
3. Identify and evaluate potential bidders.
4. Develop and issue a **Request for Proposal (RFP)**.
5. Evaluate proposal responses.
6. Select a service provider and negotiate the contract.
7. Administer the service agreement.
8. Renegotiate or terminate the agreement at its expiration date.

Managers must consider the human resources impact of the outsourcing process when it affects employees. Examples of these times include:

■ When announcing that an outsourcing alternative will be considered
■ When evaluating outsourcing alternatives. Input from existing employees may be helpful, for example, as RFPs are developed and as proposal responses are considered.
■ When announcing the outsourcing decision
■ When transitioning to the service provider
■ When administering the service agreement
■ When continued use of a provider as an escape clause is being considered, or when the contract is about to expire

Many of the principles for communicating and interacting with staff members during downsizing activities (see the previous section) apply as outsourcing decisions are made. In both instances, managers must consider the staff members who are immediately affected (those whose jobs will be eliminated) and their counterparts who will remain with the organization. Much of the decision-making process involves cost and process analysis, legal issues, and the administration of day-to-day service delivery, which may not relate directly to human resources concerns. However, the human dimension is an important consideration, because the organization relies on employees to perform core service functions. Their interest in effectively doing so is impacted by the extent to which their perspectives are considered as management decisions are made.

A wide range of potential legal issues arise as contracts (agreements) for outsourced service providers are managed. Examples include risk management, intellectual property, privacy laws, compliance, disputes, litigation, and **Sarbanes-Oxley Act** requirements.

Request for Proposal: A document developed by a hospitality organization that requests price quotations for and suggestions and other information about the provision of products and/or services from suppliers deemed eligible to supply them; often abbreviated RFP.

Sarbanes-Oxley Act: The federal government's public company accounting reform and investor protection act that contains numerous provisions focused on improving the accuracy and reliability of corporate disclosures to investors.

Human Resources Management:
CURRENT EVENTS 12.2

OUTSOURCING AT DISNEY WORLD HOTELS

Baggage Airlines Guest Service (BAGS) operates Disney's Magical Express, the bus service that transports Disney visitors to and from the Orlando airport. That same company received a contract to provide bell, valet, and baggage service at the Disney World Hotels. It also recently contracted approximately 120 overnight custodian positions.

While union officials plan to protest, Disney was negotiating with the union to offer displaced workers other jobs with comparable wages, tip opportunities, and hours. One sticking point is that the union contract prevents the company from subcontracting services to save money. However, Disney officials indicated that the change was being made to improve quality.

The present outsourcing plans are the first that affect workers in direct contact with the public. Bell and baggage-service employees greet Disney visitors when they arrive, and valet workers assist guests in their hotel rooms.

Source: Scott Powers, "Walt Disney World Hotels to Sub-Contract Out 167 Bell, Valet, and Baggage-Service Jobs: Change Being Made to Improve Quality." Retrieved on 11/20/06 from: *www.hotel-online.com/News/PR2006_4th/Nov06_DisneyJobs.html.*

Succession Planning Activities

4. **Review basic procedures that are useful in the succession planning process.**

Succession planning is a process used by human resources managers to help ensure that they will continue to have the key professional and other staff needed to support their planned growth. To do so, they must consider numerous factors including attrition. As with any type of planning, the task is easier when it is done for the short term rather than for longer time periods. However, organization executives, human resources staff, and managers including position incumbents will do well to think about the future and to consider how, if at all, human resources needs are likely to change.

Figure 12.3 identifies steps that can be used for succession planning. Let's look at the steps in Figure 12.3 more closely:

- *Step 1: Identify priority positions for succession planning.* While all positions in the organization are critical (they should not exist if they are not), some

Staff Members Have Different Career Goals

Not every person in a hospitality organization wants to advance to positions with greater responsibilities and higher compensation levels. While some employees do, others do not and are content with their present responsibilities. A primary goal of every manager should be to provide the education and/or training necessary for staff members to become proficient to consistently attain performance standards in their existing position. Then managers should have another concern: to help interested staff members attain competencies that will allow them to assume new positions to further benefit themselves and their organization.

positions require more specialized training, experience, and/or skills than do others. These will be among those requiring special attention as future human resources needs are considered. Examples may include positions in which incumbents are responsible for specific multiunit locations in relatively small companies, and others in which incumbents have district, area, regional, or other responsibilities in larger organizations. Top-level executives and staff advisory specialists with human relations, accounting and/or procurement, and other responsibilities in small or larger organizations may also occupy hard-to-fill positions that require specialized expertise for which succession planning can be helpful.

▪ *Step 2: Update organizational planning tools.* Sometimes the urgency of ongoing business hinders opportunities to keep organization charts, job descriptions, and job specifications current. What is the relationship between the high-priority positions identified in Step 1 and others in the organization? (A current organization chart will indicate this relationship.) What are the current tasks in the priority positions? (Current job descriptions will answer this question.) What experience, skills, knowledge, educational, and/or other personal requirements are judged necessary for an incumbent in the position to be successful? (Current job specifications provide this information.)

Each of these organizational planning tools must be carefully analyzed and kept current, because they drive much of the succession planning process that follows. For example, will business volume and/or organizational structure change so that more, the same number, or fewer area managers will be required? How, if at all, will responsibilities of position incumbents change? Will responsibilities become more generalized or, alternatively, will positions become more focused with one or more of the current tasks being assigned to someone else?

▪ *Step 3: Determine the number of position incumbents needed.* Assume, for example, that a regional quick-service restaurant organization currently has four area managers, and that top-level managers are using a succession

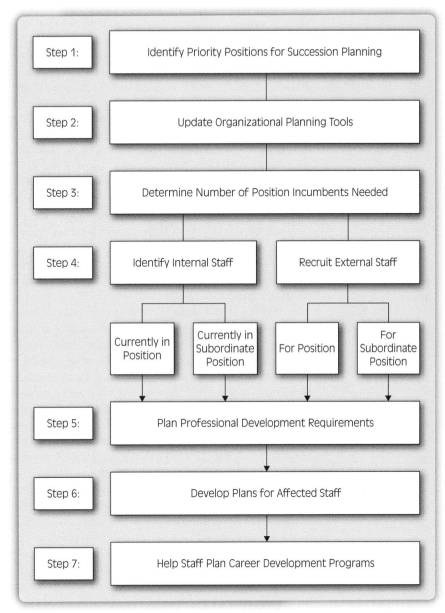

FIGURE 12.3: Steps in the Succession Planning Process

planning process to identify critical needs over the next five years. How many area managers will then be required? Concerns about anticipated organizational changes and business volume noted previously affect this decision. The increased role, if any, of technology and other means to increase productivity of those working in the positions, and to fulfill the communication needs of the organization, should also be considered as the number of future position incumbents is addressed.

Planners must also think about the number of vacancies likely to occur that will need to be filled. In this example, the organization currently has four area managers. Assume that planners (1) anticipate the need for six area manager positions in five years; (2) believe that one present incumbent will be retiring; and (3) plan to promote another area manager to a regional position within that time frame. Four area manager positions must be filled during the next years (i.e., 4 current managers – 2 managers leaving = 2 managers available; 6 managers needed – 2 managers available = 4 new managers required).

■ *Step 4: Identify internal staff and/or recruit external staff.* Some current incumbents in key positions may be available for these positions in the future. They may have expressed an interest in remaining in the position. Alternatively, they may be competent in their current position, but are not believed to be qualified for the position for which succession planning is being undertaken. Other staff members who are considered eligible for promotion to these key positions may currently occupy positions at subordinate (lower) organizational levels. The difference between the number of position incumbents needed (Step 3) and those currently in the position or who can be prepared for it (Step 4) represent the number of external staff to be recruited. As noted in Figure 12.4, external staff might be recruited for the positions as they become vacant. Alternatively, they might be recruited for a subordinate position with the assumption that they and some internal staff peers in these positions can be trained to assume the key positions.

■ *Step 5: Plan professional development requirements.* Current position tasks and applicable education and training requirements for those in the key positions should already be known based on, respectively, job descriptions and job specifications (Step 2). How can persons learn to attain current performance standards? What additional tasks or responsibilities are likely to be of concern? and How can one become competent to perform in the future? The answers to these and related questions help identify professional development requirements needed to prepare an employee for the future position.

■ *Step 6: Develop plans for affected staff.* Fortunately, incumbents currently in the position and external staff recruited for it will likely be competent in many (or even all) of the required tasks. Currently employed staff and their externally recruited counterparts retained for subordinate positions may also meet job specification requirements, and will be able to successfully complete many tasks required in the key positions. At this point, planners and affected staff members can develop specialized career development programs.

Staff members identified for these positions should be encouraged to participate in job enlargement and job enrichment programs. Special projects might be delegated that will also simultaneously assist the hospitality organization and prepare the staff members for their future positions.

■ *Step 7: Help staff plan career development programs.* Ideally, staff members identified in the succession planning process will be interested in a **career** with

Career: A sequence of professional experiences and positions in which one participates during a span of employment with an organization or industry.

the organization. Procedures helpful in training, implementing, and monitoring personal career development programs are discussed in the next section.

Every hospitality organization should be concerned about its future. While top-level managers can never predict the future with certainty, they can and should use their knowledge of the present to influence likely occurrences. They do so by (1) carefully considering a succession planning program that addresses human resources needs, (2) identifying existing talents, and (3) planning how deficiencies identified in the process can be addressed in professional development activities.

Career Development Programs

5. **Identify the benefits of and basic steps that human resources managers can use to develop and assist staff members with career planning activities.**

Career development program: A planning strategy in which one identifies career goals and then plans education and training activities designed to attain them.

A career development program (also called a professional development program) identifies training and educational opportunities to help staff members become more proficient in their current positions and to prepare them for career advancement. Much of the effort required to attain these objectives will have been expanded as basic training and education requirements applicable to each position were developed (see Chapter 6), and as the succession planning process (see the previous section) is completed.

ADVANTAGES

Advantages accrue to hospitality organizations that emphasize career development opportunities for their staff, including:

- *Reducing absenteeism and turnover.* Managers who help staff members prepare for the future show human relations concerns. These efforts can improve morale, which helps reduce absentee levels and turnover rates. While labor and other costs associated with absenteeism and turnover are difficult to quantify, they are real and significant. Organizations that improve their staff's morale do much to improve service to their guests and, in the process, to increase their bottom line.
- *Assisting with productivity increases.* Staff who are prepared for a new position can reduce the learning curve and be useful immediately when they assume the new position. The necessary transitional period before quality and quantity outputs attain performance standards will likely be reduced. Also, costs to provide necessary education and training programs today will likely be less than those in the future.
- *Emphasizing managers' concerns about their staff.* Showing respect for staff members, exhibiting a genuine desire to assist them, and providing open lines

Modern technology enables anyone desiring to participate in educational and training activities for career advancement to do so at any time in almost any place.
Courtesy Purestock

of communication are additional examples of ways that management concerns can be actualized through professional development programs.

■ *Preparing for future challenges.* Training alternatives such as cross-training, job enlargement, job enrichment, and job rotation programs have been noted (see Chapter 7). Organizations are better prepared for challenges that can arise when the range of job tasks that staff members can correctly perform is expanded. Professional development activities undertaken to improve performance in existing positions help improve product and service quality and reduce costs and increase profits.

■ *Addressing future labor needs.* As suggested in the previous section, succession planning tactics can help managers identify general education and work experience requirements that will likely be required for future successful performance. In the process, professional development opportunities needed by existing staff will be better known.

In addition to helping the hospitality organization, career development activities are of obvious benefit to those who undertake them:

■ *They allow staff members to learn and gain the experience necessary for promotional opportunities.* Many organizations utilize and many staff members appreciate promotion-from-within programs that recognize the potential for future contributions of existing staff and, in the process, help reduce turnover rates.

■ *They help reinforce the employment decisions made by new staff.* Corporate cultures that emphasize professional development opportunities allow staff members to enjoy on-job success and to feel positive about their employer.

PROCEDURES FOR CAREER DEVELOPMENT

You've learned that career development enables employees to plan for their futures within an organization or industry by identifying career goals and then developing plans to attain them. At the same time, it helps the organization to reduce turnover and related expenses because of the increased morale that typically occurs when affected staff members are given opportunities for career growth.

For many persons, career decisions are influenced by factors such as personal interests, likes and dislikes, and being at the right place at the right time. However, a staff member's career plans can also be influenced by opportunities presented by the employer. The mentoring, counseling, and encouragement provided by those at higher organizational levels can be significant influences on staff members' plans, aspirations, and the energy levels required for career advancement within the organization. You've also learned that opportunities to acquire greater levels of knowledge and skill can be addressed during performance appraisal sessions, as ongoing work responsibilities are assigned, and even as simple coaching conversations evolve.

Many staff members will not require significant encouragement to become involved in professional development programs, but others will. Employees will benefit

Professional Associations Assist with Career Development

Professional associations exist to assist members with numerous needs, including the provision of continuing education opportunities. Examples include the conduct of national conferences and the development and provision of training resources and services. Continuing education opportunities for group and/or individual study and the coordination of regional or other chapters that provide educational opportunities in local areas are additional examples.

Professional associations charge membership dues and fees to support their services. Typically, a significant percentage of the revenues generated is used to develop educational and training resources to improve the organization's members and the industry served by the association.

To review educational resources available from selected hospitality associations, review the Web sites of selected organizations, including:

- National Restaurant Association (Educational Foundation): *www.nraef.org*
- American Dietetic Association: *www.eatright.org*
- American Hotel & Lodging Association (Educational Institute): *www.ei-ahla.org*
- Club Managers Association of America: *www.cmaa.org*
- National Association of College & University Food Services: *www.nacufs.org*

Human Resources MANAGEMENT ISSUES   (12.2)

❝ **I** have an idea that will benefit our business and our employees, and that has no downside to it," said Joshua. He was the human resources manager for the foodservices operation at the Metropolitan Bank, one of the largest banks on the Eastern seacoast, and the largest bank in the United States with a self-operating foodservices program. Joshua was attending a meeting of department heads and had just returned from a national conference of hospitality human resources managers.

"I would call the program, 'We Care About You.' We would make an offer to all of our staff members: first become proficient in your existing position (and we could tie this to results of our performance appraisal procedures). Then we would assist them with career planning activities and provide them with ongoing professional development experiences. This would result in increased job skills and help prepare them for promotions to positions with greater responsibilities and more compensation."

"Joshua, that's sounds like a great idea, and I would personally support it in theory," replied Suzanne, the department manager. "I think we've implied this philosophy as we encouraged employees to do better and to learn more. However, we've never formalized a process, communicated it consistently and effectively, or really worked hard to encourage and help our employees to be better performers and stay with us."

"I guess it sounds like a good idea," said Raoul, the food production manager, "but I have two special concerns. First, it sure wouldn't look good if we make a big deal out of this now as we rolled out the program, and then de-emphasized it later. Also, do we really have time to do everything necessary to help all of our staff given the million and one things we must all do every day to keep the operation running?"

"I do like the general idea of the program, and I'm certain it will encourage spirited discussion as we consider it further," said Suzanne. "My suggestion is that we table the conversation for now, and let's all consider it over the next two weeks and then make it a primary agenda item at our next meeting."

QUESTIONS

1. What are the benefits to the Metropolitan Bank foodservices department if the "We Care About You" program can be implemented? The potential disadvantages?
2. What is the employees' likely reaction to the program?
3. What suggestions would you make to Suzanne, Joshua, and the management team as they consider implementation of the program?

from their employer's efforts to encourage them to prepare for promotions, and they can do so by participating in well-planned education and training activities.

Documentation of career development plans and accomplishments can help one to further prepare for the future. Figure 12.4 shows specifics that can be identified in a career development plan.

Name: _____   Date: _____

Employer: _____

Position: _____

Time in current
position: Years _____   Months: _____

Current
Supervisor: _____

Personal/Professional
Interests: _____

_____

_____

Education: High School Graduate or   Yes   NO
              GED: Circle one.
              College   Yes _____   NO _____
              If yes, circle one: GRADUATE   ATTENDING   ATTENDED
              Other Formal Education: _____

CAREER
GOALS:

To what position do you aspire: New competencies needed to attain this
                                               career goal:

In one
years: _____   _____

_____   _____

_____   _____

In five
years: _____   _____

_____   _____

_____   _____

In ten
years: _____   _____

_____   _____

_____   _____

FIGURE 12.4: Career Development Plan

EDUCATION LEARNING METHOD

Required Competencies	On-Job Training	Ongoing Staff Meetings	Independent Learning Course	Group Study Course	Local Chapter Program	College Course	Other (Indicate)	Completion Date Planned	Completion Date Actual

Other Education/Training Plans:

FIGURE 12.5: Training and Education Planning Worksheet

Figure 12.5 illustrates a worksheet that can be used to identify the planned methods by which the required competencies identified in Figure 12.4 can be obtained. It also allows the career planner to indicate scheduled and actual completion dates.

Figure 12.6 provides a detailed summary of information about how and when the required competencies identified in Figure 12.4 were actually acquired.

As a final example, Figure 12.7 shows a format for a career progression record that comprises the experience portion of one's professional résumé.

Activities integral to one's career comprise a significant part of the waking hours of many persons. Those who enjoy their careers are, therefore, very fortunate. Organizations with a culture that allows (encourages) staff members to enjoy what they do provide a win-win situation for all constituencies. Managers in these organizations plan professional development programs to help their staff members become competent in future positions. The personal career development programs driven by them benefit the guests, the hospitality organization, and its staff members.

Name: _____

Intermediate Career
Goal: _____

_____

New Competency: _____

_____

_____

Date
Completed: _____

Name of Institution/Training
Organization: _____

_____

Certificate Awarded: YES   NO   **Type:** _____

_____

Other
Details: _____

_____

_____

FIGURE 12.6: Competency Score Card

NAME:

CAREER GOAL:

Starting Date	Ending Date	Position	Name of Organization	General Position Responsibilities

FIGURE 12.7: Career Progression Record

HUMAN RESOURCES TERMS

The following terms were defined in this chapter:

Unions
Labor contract
Grievance process
Union shop
Union steward
Grievance
Seniority
Authorization card (union)
Union recognition (mandatory)
National Labor Relations Board (NLRB)
Union recognition (voluntary)
Union security arrangement
Right-to-work law
Agency shop
Open shop
Dues check-off
Collective bargaining
Concession (collective bargaining)
Collective bargaining (distribute)
Collective bargaining (integrative)
Collective bargaining (mandatory items)
Collective bargaining (permissible items)
Cost-of-living adjustment
Picketing

Boycott
Work slowdown
Arbitration (voluntary)
Arbitration (compulsory)
Mediation
Unfair labor practices
Traditionalists (workforce generation)
Baby Boomers (workforce generation)
Generation X (workforce generation)
Generation Y (workforce generation)
Downsizing
Succession planning
Attrition
Outplacement assistance
Full-time equivalents
Survivor (downsizing)
Outsourcing
Offshoring
Core business strategies
Escape strategy
Request for proposal
Sarbanes-Oxley Act
Career
Career development program

FOR YOUR CONSIDERATION

1. Assume that you were beginning your first (entry-level) management position at a hospitality organization that is unionized. How, if at all, do you think your initial work experiences would be different than if your initial employment

was with a nonunionized property? Which type of beginning management position would you most like? Why?

2. How do you think your perspectives about an organization would be affected if you were an employee and you heard rumors about the possibility of downsizing? What kind of facts would you want to know about the situation? What would be your priority concerns if you were to be terminated? If you were a survivor?

3. How, if at all, could a career development process such as that noted in this chapter benefit you if you were just beginning your hospitality management career? If you were in an entry-level (nonmanagement) position in an operation? If you were in a middle-management position with an organization?

CASE STUDY: HUMAN RESOURCES MANAGEMENT IN ACTION

"Last night wasn't a very good night, was it?" asked Maureen, the foodservices director for the school district. She was meeting with Francine, the business manager of the public school district in a large and affluent suburb of a major metropolitan city.

"No, it wasn't a very good evening; in fact, it was a disaster!" replied Francine.

The two professionals were discussing the results of a school board meeting in which the local union representing the foodservices workers and the custodians outnegotiated the school district's representatives. The union had obtained a collective bargaining concession that, in the opinion of Maureen and Francine, went too far.

"I just can't believe it," said Francine. "Now there's no way we can increase productivity because the labor contract specifies a required number of union employee labor hours for every 100 meals we serve, and it even defines our á la carte operations to ensure that the mandated productivity level is controlled."

"Yes, that certainly is the most significant challenge," replied Maureen. "In addition, we have to deal with lots of other issues that, in total, create pretty big obstacles. For example, isn't it ironic that we just spent $80,000 for trash compactors? In part, our payback analysis indicated that the equipment costs would be recovered in only 11 months because of reduced fees from waste pickup. Now the labor agreement specifies that workers can't handle anything weighing more than 35 pounds, so the compactors won't be able to help reduce costs at anywhere near their capacity to do so. Another example is that when it's time for an employee break, it's really time for the break! Ten o'clock means ten o'clock, not five after ten or another time shortly after ten, which enables a work task in process to be completed."

"Our list of examples could go on, couldn't it, Maureen?" asked Francine. "One thing I know is that, even while the school board wants us to increase the quantity and quality of our outputs, they have really limited our ability to do so."

Dimension: Collective Bargaining Process

1. Assume the union had represented the employees for the last several years. What kind of financial- and employee-related information should Maureen and her foodservices management team have provided to the school board committee negotiating with union representatives?
2. What are the most important management rights that remain and, hopefully, will not be lost by the school district?
3. What, if any, impact do you think the results of this bargaining process will have when the agreement is next negotiated?

Dimension: Supervision

1. What procedures should Maureen use to educate her supervisors and managers about the terms of the new agreement?
2. What are the most serious consequences of the new contractual clause that ties input (labor hours) to output (number of meals/meal equivalents served)?
3. What, if any, types of employee scheduling tactics can be used when specified employees must take breaks at specified time periods?

Dimension: Financial Management Concerns

1. What tactics, if any, are available to Maureen in her efforts to manage her labor costs given the contractual clause relating to productivity restraints?
2. What are the priority alternatives available to Maureen as she develops future operating budgets and attempts to manage future operating costs?
3. What, if anything, can Maureen do to help reduce the stress and anxiety of the foodservice managers in each school as they attempt to cope with the new operational and financial constraints?

INTERNET ACTIVITIES

1. Would you like to review an excellent report presenting detailed information about the U.S. hotel industry and its employees? The AFL-CIO Working for America Institute has published a report providing excellent background information, policy recommendations, and extensive footnotes that refer readers to additional information. To view this information, go to: *www.hotelonline.com* When you reach the site, enter "afl-cio working for america" into the search box."
2. This chapter has identified several critical issues that confront human resources managers in the hospitality industry. One topic that is of increasing interest to the industry and to the entire country relates to immigration. If you want to learn more about immigration and its impact on the hospitality industry, type "Immigration and Hospitality Industry" into your favorite search engine. You'll discover Web sites discussing current events, historical trends, services

of firms assisting hospitality organizations with specific concerns, and a wide variety of other information.

3. Managers in the hospitality industry may be involved in many more outsourcing alternatives than you might have initially imagined. Two Web sites that can help you explore the present and future of outsourcing in the hospitality industry are:

- ▪ *www.findarticles.com* (When you reach the site, type "Outsourcing in hospitality industry" into the site's search box.)
- ▪ *www.hotelresource.com* (Enter "outsourcing" into the site's search box. You'll find results categorized by "Industry News," "Industry Trends," and "Web Directory.")

ENDNOTES

1. Information about do's and don'ts during union drives is adapted from: David DeCenzo and Stephen Robbins, *Fundamentals of Human Resources Management,* 8th ed. Hoboken, NJ: John Wiley and Sons, 2005.
2. The authors wish to acknowledge and thank Mr. Steven H. Siegel, Associate Professor, College of Hospitality and Tourism Management, Niagara University, New York, for suggesting this example of a requirement imposed by a labor agreement in a hospitality organization.
3. The information in the remainder of this discussion on downsizing is adapted from: National Performance Review, "Serving the American Public: Best Practices in Downsizing." Benchmarking Study Report, 1997.

CHAPTER THIRTEEN

Human Resources: Planning for Global Expansion*

CHAPTER OUTLINE

CHAPTER LEARNING OBJECTIVES

As a result of successfully completing this chapter, readers will be able to:

1. Explain the increased need for hospitality organizations to have a presence in the international marketplace.

2. Review how cultural factors affect the conduct of international business.

3. Discuss the process of and challenges involved in a successful international assignment: selection, preparation, on-job issues, and after-assignment return.

4. Describe important considerations when managing hospitality employees in a foreign country.

---

*This chapter was authored by Dr. A. J. Singh, Associate Professor, The School of Hospitality Business, Michigan State University.

Impact on Human Resources Management

Hospitality and tourism is truly a global industry. Transportation has made it much easier for people to travel, and businesses of all kinds have become much more dependent on each other. In the process, the hotel and restaurant industry has grown as the world has shrunk. Large hospitality organizations headquartered in the United States own and/or manage properties in the United States and throughout the world. Hospitality organizations owned by Asians, Europeans, and those of other nationalities increasingly own and/or manage hospitality businesses in their countries, in the United States, and throughout the world. Many domestic hospitality managers will have opportunities for international assignments during their careers, and effective management of staff members in these locations is just as important as in domestic operations. How should companies prepare their executives to be effective in these global assignments? What skill sets and competencies are important to be a successful expatriate manager? What are special considerations when organizations manage people in foreign locations? These are among the critical questions addressed in this chapter.

The Global Imperative: Why Hospitality Companies Expand Internationally

1. Explain the increased need for hospitality organizations to have a presence in the international marketplace.

During periods of increasing competition and shrinking market share, hotel chains can grow domestic market share, create new products (brands), and/or expand globally. Initially, U.S. hotel companies expanded into neighboring Canada, Mexico, and the Caribbean, and since the mid-1990s, they have expanded around the globe. Similarly, European and Asian chains initially expanded within their regions, and later focused on more distant and developed markets. Figure 13.1 illustrates the intensity of internationalization by some leading hotel companies.

The intense natures of domestic competition and market saturation have prompted restaurant chains to expand globally as well. For example, McDonald's Corporation operates in more than 100 countries. Subway Restaurants has almost 27,000 restaurants in approximately 90 countries. Burger King has more than 200 restaurants in Asia, 350 restaurants throughout Australia and New Zealand, 2,000 units in the European and Middle East regions, and 700 restaurants in Latin America and the Caribbean. Wendy's International operates more than 3,000 international units.

Hotel Company	Hotel Brands	Countries in Operation
Intercontinental Hotels Group	Intercontinental Hotels & Resorts, Crowne Plaza Hotels & Resorts, Hotel Indigo, Holiday Inn Hotels & Resorts, Nickelodeon Family Suites by Holiday Inn, Holiday Inn Select, Holiday Inn Sunspree Resorts, Holiday Inn Express, Express by Holiday Inn, Staybridge Suites, Candlewood Suites	100
Accor	Sofitel, Novatel, Mercure, Dorint, Suitehotel, All Seasons, Ibis, Etap, Formule 1, Red Roof, Motel 6, Accor, Thalassa Accor, Vacances, Studio 6	90
Starwood Hotels & Resorts	Four Points by Sheraton, Sheraton, Aloft Hotels, W Hotels, Le Meridien, Luxury Collection, Element, Westin, St. Regis	82
Best Western International	Best Western Hotels	80
Hilton Group PLC	Conrad Hotels, Doubletree, Embassy Suites Hotels, Hampton Inn, Hampton Inn & Suites, Hilton Hotels, Hilton Garden Inn, Homewood Suites by Hilton	78
Carlson Hospitality Worldwide	Regent Hotels & Resorts, Radisson Hotels & Resorts, Park Plaza Hotels & Resorts, Country Inns & Suites by Carlson, Park Inn Hotels	70

*Adapted from: Hotels' Giants Survey, 2005.

FIGURE 13.1: Hotel Companies in Most Countries*

There is significant international growth in the casual-dining restaurant segment as well. Examples abound:

- Ruby Tuesday, Inc., has entered into a Middle Eastern franchising agreement to open four units in Saudi Arabia. (The company is already in 13 foreign countries and has 35 franchised units that operate internationally.)
- Bennigan's Grill and Tavern has approximately 30 units in South Korea and has almost 50 locations in 10 countries.
- T.G.I. Friday's has approximately 50 properties in South Korea. (It opened its first unit in England more than 20 years ago.) It also has stores in Saudi Arabia, the United Arab Emirates, Kuwait, Egypt, and Lebanon.[1]
- Pizza Hut has more than 4,100 units in 85 countries.
- Domino's Pizza operates more than 2,500 units in 50-plus countries (including nearly 500 locations in Mexico).[2]

Would you like to do some of your shopping here? This public market is just one example of how one's personal lifestyle is likely to change after he or she accepts a global assignment.
Courtesy Flat Earth

Foodservice management companies operating in the noncommercial segment also have significant international operations. For example, Aramark Corporation, the largest revenue-producing company, operates in 17 countries, and Compass Group North America, part of Compass Group PLC (a UK-based company), operates in more than 90 countries. Sodexho's North America Division operates in 76 countries.

STAGES OF GLOBAL EXPANSION

Figure 13.2 reviews several ways that hospitality operations can evolve in the international marketplace.

As seen in Figure 13.2, most hospitality organizations begin to operate and grow domestically. They initially expand by adding locations in the same or different cities, and then open properties in other states. At some point, successful organizations may expand to foreign markets (Stage 2), and basic operating concepts, hopefully modified to meet the needs of the foreign marketplace, are transferred to international locations. However, top-level operating decisions are still typically made in the United States, and top-level managers in global units are generally U.S. expatriates.

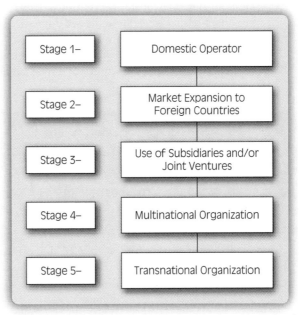

Stage 1–	Domestic Operator
Stage 2–	Market Expansion to Foreign Countries
Stage 3–	Use of Subsidiaries and/or Joint Ventures
Stage 4–	Multinational Organization
Stage 5–	Transnational Organization

FIGURE 13.2: Hospitality Organizations in the International Marketplace

Mode of entry: The process by which a hospitality organization begins a business in another country.

Subsidiaries: A foreign company operated by a domestic hospitality organization with majority (more than 50 percent) ownership by another (parent) company.

Joint venture: A foreign branch partially owned by the domestic organization and partially owned by an entity in the host (foreign) country. Ownership could be a company, several companies, one or more individuals, and/or the government.

Multinational (organization): A hospitality organization with operating units in many countries and regions of the world.

Most hospitality firms that operate internationally negotiate franchising contract or management agreements with individuals or companies in the global location, especially when organizations from developed countries expand to emerging countries (e.g., a U.S.-based company expanding to China). By contrast, when an organization expands regionally (e.g., from Canada to the United States), there is the added possibility of an equity investment.

Decisions about the **mode of entry** into another country depend, in part, on the perceptions of executives in expanding organizations about whether trustworthy and qualified investors are available locally. If so, the hospitality organization is more likely to use a franchise or management contract arrangement rather than outright ownership. Advantages of the latter include more control and an ability to maintain a desired corporate culture. However, a disadvantage includes the company's significant commitment of financial resources associated with ownership.

As hospitality organizations evolve to Stage 3, the organization may collaborate with a host country, organizations, and/or individuals, and foreign divisions, **subsidiaries,** or **joint ventures** may develop. Expatriates still often assume unit management responsibilities in the host locations. Stage 3 organizations increasingly focus human resources efforts on the selection, training, and placement of staff, and on implementing personnel-related policies for local employees.

Hospitality operations become **multinational** (Stage 4) in scope when they expand to several (or more) countries and regions throughout the world. Decision making becomes more decentralized and more applicable to each international location, but final operating control is still from domestic headquarters. Broad personnel-related issues are addressed domestically, often by an international human resources department. Many local locations are still managed by expatriates, and human resources practices become complex because of the number of expatriates in different countries and the number of diverse cultural groups in an increasing number

Human Resources Management:
CURRENT EVENTS 13.1

CASE STUDY: MCDONALD'S CORPORATION ENTERS A NEW COUNTRY

Plans to open a McDonald's unit in a new country begin with exploratory visits that may be conducted several years before the unit is built. Much of the information collected is marketing-related: Can the restaurant be supported? Who will be its competitors? What is the probability of success?

Human resources issues are also important, and numerous employment-practice questions must be answered, including:

- What are the applicable labor laws?
- Can the company establish part-time and flexible work schedules? (Flexible or part-time scheduling is a new concept for many countries, and discussions with labor ministries and other local businesspersons are often required.)
- How many hours are employees allowed to work?
- What are youth-related employment laws?
- What benefits must the company provide? (In central Europe, for example, employee shower and locker areas are required.)
- Are support service personnel, including engineers, construction personnel, and experts with knowledge of food and agriculture requirements, available?

New local human resources managers and other personnel must receive training, and this is often done in a country with established restaurants. To do so requires visas and work permits that allow managers in training to cross country borders regularly. As well, local attorneys with knowledge of applicable labor laws must work with company officials to establish personnel policies, because all local employment practices, policies, and regulations must be met.

The company's name recognition makes it relatively easy to recruit staff members, and it becomes an employer of choice by paying top wages and providing enviable benefits packages. Store manager applicants who successfully complete initial screening typically work several days in a property as part of the selection process. Then applicants can consider their interest in the position as the company further evaluates them.

Adapted from: C. Solomon, "Big Mac's McGlobal Human Resources Secrets," *Personnel Journal* 75, No. 4, April 1996.

of countries. *Note:* Most of the restaurant and hotel organizations discussed in the previous section would likely be considered multinational organizations.

Transnational (organization): A company with operations throughout the world that features highly decentralized decision making, is less aligned with its country of origin, and that may have weak ties to any specific country.

Finally (in Stage 5), organizations become **transnational** in scope. Highly decentralized governing boards comprise people from different countries, and staff members from anywhere in the world may be recruited for positions at all, including the highest, organizational levels.

One example of a transnational hospitality organization might be Sodexho Alliance. It provides food and management services to almost 2,500 locations in more than 75 countries throughout the world. Its business focus emphasizes the provision of services worldwide; it has major organizational divisions throughout the world; and it implements programs that contribute to the economic and social development of its host countries. (*Note:* To learn more about Sodexho, go to *www.sodexho.com.*)

GLOBALIZATION AND EFFECTIVE HUMAN RESOURCES MANAGEMENT

Today, many observers believe that the globalization of markets and production has reached a tipping point in which the world economy has moved from self-contained entities to an interdependent global economic system. As hospitality corporations grow internationally and, as individuals increasingly work across borders in this interdependent global arena, organizations must conceptualize and implement human resource practices to remain effective.

We have already considered some dimensions of international human resources management in this text. Recall that domestic managers must increasingly facilitate the work of persons with varied cultural backgrounds. The principles to do so in domestic operations are basically the same as those required when the manager lives and works in another country. In both instances, managers will learn that people typically share many human concerns. At the same time, a person's cultural background can influence his or her perceptions of and reactions to personal and workplace concerns. Therefore, effective hospitality managers working on a domestic or international assignment must recognize the influence of a person's culture and consider and modify management and supervisory tactics accordingly.

Hospitality operators are increasingly dependent on the political actions, economies, and other influences that affect countries throughout the world marketplace. This is of obvious importance in the hotel industry, which enjoys high or suffers through low occupancy periods based on economic conditions. Guest counts in commercial foodservice operations depend on the disposable income levels of potential guests, which are affected by their employment (which is impacted by local, national, and world economics). Business travelers are also a primary market of many foodservice operations.

During good economic times, foreign citizens may seek healthcare services in the United States, and operating costs become more manageable as revenues increase in healthcare foodservice operations. Worldwide economic conditions also influence foodservice operations in postsecondary educational institutions that encourage enrollments of international students. Amusement and theme parks, casinos, sports and recreational food services, cruise lines, and numerous other venues in the tourism industry benefit from a growing international economy and are negatively affected as the worldwide economy retracts.

Global influences, then, are an important concern to hospitality managers, because they influence the number of guests who come through their doors. At the same time, managers must facilitate the work of their staff members. Managers require general knowledge about the factors and concerns that influence the perceptions and actions of their staff members. While managers cannot influence the world economic situation, what they do (and do not do) can have a significant impact on their guests and staff members.

Cultural Factors Impact International Operations

2. **Review how cultural factors affect the conduct of international business.**

CULTURAL CONCERNS ARE IMPORTANT

Culture: A set of learned beliefs, values, and behaviors that influence the way of life shared by the members of a society.

Organizational culture: A set of understandings shared by members of an organization that are relevant and distinctive, that are passed on to new group members, and that influence organizational decision making.

The thoughts, words, and actions of employees are typically affected, in part, by their **culture:** the collective programming of common beliefs, values, behaviors, and other factors that influence what an individual believes and how a person acts. Today, people are becoming more individualized, and it is challenging to explain the components of, for example, an Eastern or Western culture, or even general beliefs of those living in a specific country, region, or state. Difficulties also arise in the business world as one attempts to define an **organizational culture.** However, it is still important to recognize that an employee's cultural background may influence his or her reactions to even the most well-intentioned management actions. The manager who asks the question, "How would I react to a specific leadership style, policy, or procedure?" may not generate a response providing meaningful operating tactics for employees with different cultural backgrounds.

Traditions and customs often evolve, perhaps at an accelerated pace, as the generations change. One example is that the tradition of the extended family living together in the United States has changed as family members move, often around the world, for career advancement or for other reasons. Many more young people in China, Japan, and Korea prioritize financial success than did their counterparts in earlier generations.

Keeping this point in mind, one's cultural background can impact how he or she views and reacts to life's special concerns, including personal relationships, attitudes about time (which is more important: the past, the present, or the future?), and the environment (how important is nature, and how powerful is it?). Persons living in the same society do tend to respond similarly to at-work leadership. Managers should anticipate likely responses and incorporate their knowledge of cultural differences into the way they facilitate work. At the same time, they must realize that this knowledge must be modified for the specific situation.

McDonald's Expands to India: A Cultural Dilemma

The world's largest hamburger chain had a unique challenge when it expanded to India in the late 1990s: cows are considered sacred there, and the consumption of beef is thought to be a sin. There is also a large Muslim population (they do not consume pork) and a very large vegetarian population. The solution was that McDonald's inaugural plans called for a Maharaja Mac made from mutton (sheep), and some chicken and vegetarian items.

For a short time, the Indian menu seemed to be acceptable. Then a lawsuit was filed in reaction to the company's claim that it used only 100 percent vegetarian oil for its french fries. In fact, the oil did contain a small amount of beef extract. McDonald's settled the lawsuit for $10 million, an apology, a promise of better ingredient labeling, and cooking oil that did not contain beef extract.

Reactions in India to the cooking oil revelations included vandalism of a McDonald's restaurant, picketing of the company's headquarters, and requests to the government to close all McDonald's restaurants. The company's long-term expansion continued after this problem was resolved. Indian customers indicated that their children enjoyed the American experience, the food was of consistent quality, and the restrooms were clean.

Adapted from: L. Handing, "Give Me A Big Mac—But Hold the Beef," *The Guardian,* December 28, 2000 (pg. 24); and "Indian McAnger," *The Guardian,* May 7, 2001 (pg. 1). Also A. Dhillan, "India Has No Beef with Fast Food Chains," *Financial Times,* March 23, 2002 (pg. 3).

The society in which one lives also establishes norms and values that impact conduct. For example, laws mandate many acceptable (and unacceptable) actions, and many people in that society share common and basic beliefs about family values and ethics, and may share common purposes and interests.

Sociocultural:
Relating to social and cultural matters.

We have discussed how a person's social and cultural background may influence one's thoughts and behavior. Together, these **sociocultural** factors are a constant influence on—and off—the job.

Numerous sociocultural factors influence how persons react in specific situations. Consider the role of incentives to encourage work performance. Staff members from Western backgrounds such as the United States typically react favorably to incentives based on individual achievement. However, in Eastern countries such as Japan, group-based performance has traditionally been viewed as most important.

Communication issues should also be addressed in the hospitality workplace. Many nations (including the United States) have vast numbers of people who speak different languages. An interesting observation is that many challenges in business are thought to be caused by communication problems. If these occur when all persons speak the same language, how much more difficult will problem solving become when the organization employs numerous persons speaking different languages?

Should one be authoritative or participatory as decisions are made, and objective or impulsive as problems are resolved? Effective managers understand the likely impact of these alternatives as they interact in the environment of their host country. Norms relating to social distance should be observed as people talk, and the exactness of meeting times can differ among staff members with diverse backgrounds. Protocols, if any, for giving gifts (and even bribes), and the importance of personal trust and friendship versus performance-based written contracts, are other sociocultural factors of which expatriate managers must be aware.

Human resources policies affecting holidays, sex discrimination, job advancement, retirement, work breaks, and employee selection (among many others) can be influenced by religious factors that are integral to the dominant culture in many locations. Clearly, hospitality managers cannot stereotype any individual from any culture, but these examples suggest that culture is important in the way that the art and science of human resource management should be practiced.

CULTURAL DIMENSIONS IMPACT HOSPITALITY OPERATIONS

Country cluster:
The notion that some countries can be grouped together based on their population's characteristics, such as language, location, ethnicity, religion, and economic status.

The concept of a **country cluster** suggests that some countries can be grouped together based on their population's similar characteristics, such as language, location, ethnicity, religion, and economic status. Examples of these clusters are shown in Figure 13.3.

One potential use about knowledge of country clusters arises as hospitality managers consider expansion alternatives. There are likely to be fewer cultural issues as they enter markets of countries within the same cluster compared to countries in different clusters. Consider, for example, the differences in human resources planning that are likely to be required in moving an operation between the United States and Canada, and between the United States and Bahrain.

Culture	Country Examples
Near Eastern	Turkey, Greece
Nordic	Norway, Sweden
Anglo	United States, Canada
Latin European	Spain, Portugal
Latin American	Colombia, Brazil
Far Eastern	Taiwan, Singapore
Arab	Kuwait, Bahrain

FIGURE 13.3: Examples of Country Clusters

Geert Hofstede[3] suggests that there are five major dimensions to culture and illustrates how characteristics of an organization and human resources tactics used within it are driven by these cultural dimensions.

Hofstede's five cultural dimensions are:

- *Power distance.* The extent to which the organizational structure emphasizes differences between entry-level staff and top-level managers.
- *Individualism.* The extent to which personal goals, autonomy, and privacy are more important than group loyalty, belief in group norms, and extensive socialization.
- *Risk avoidance.* The extent to which the society emphasizes the reduction of risks.
- *Rigid gender roles.* The extent to which the society views assertive (masculine) behavior to be necessary for success and emphasizes rigid gender stereotypes.
- *Past, present, and future orientation.* The extent to which the society's values focus on the past, present, or future.

Cultural intelligence: The process by which one learns about a culture and adjusts thinking and behavior responses when interacting with persons from the culture.

Figures 13.4 through 13.8 review these five cultural dimensions. They suggest examples of an organization's cultural values and characteristics, and they note examples of on-job rewards and how basic human resources issues are addressed.

These figures suggest that cultures differ, as do the people within them. While one cannot stereotype all people from a specific culture to fit into a specific space on a high-value to low-value continuum, it is also ineffective to believe that every person is the same. Successful managers understand basic norms in the culture within which they work, and they use this information to help with human resources decision making.

Be Careful with Stereotypes!

While this section addresses cultural workplace differences around the world, consistently accurate generalizations and stereotypes are not possible to develop, and there will always be innumerable exceptions. For example, do all of the people in your state, city, and neighborhood (and perhaps, even in your family) have the same beliefs about ethical behavior, and do they share the same political views? The answer to this question is "no." Similarly, generalizations about cultural dimensions applicable to organizations based on their country location may be helpful but are not indicative of every organization within a country. Many companies in a specific country, for example, consciously develop corporate cultures that establish values on both sides (and in the middle) of a cultural dimension continuum. As well, cultural impacts on a society and the organizations within it evolve. As you have learned, globalism does not isolate but, instead, plays a role in changing views about the workplace, management of employees, and the wants and needs of an organization's markets.

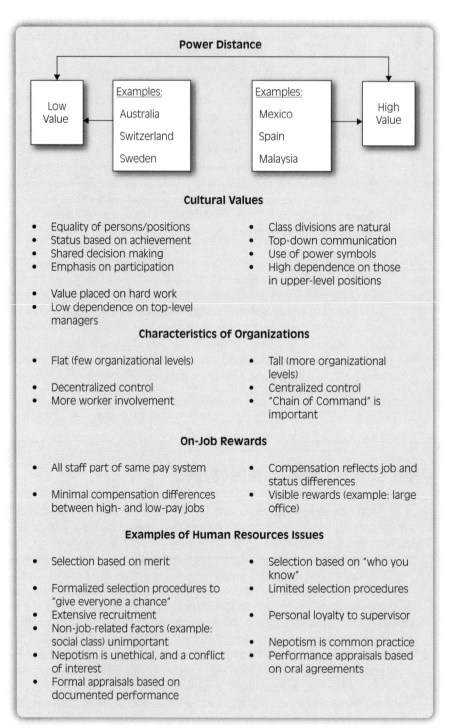

FIGURE 13.4: Power Distance and Human Resources Management

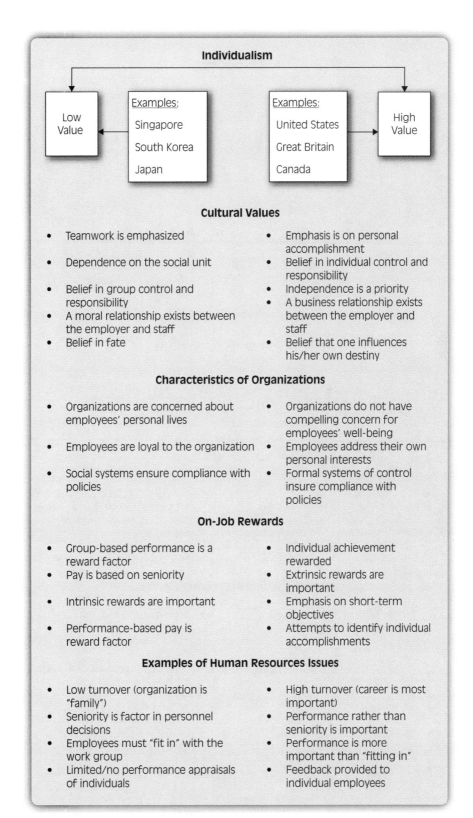

FIGURE 13.5: Individualism and Human Resources Management

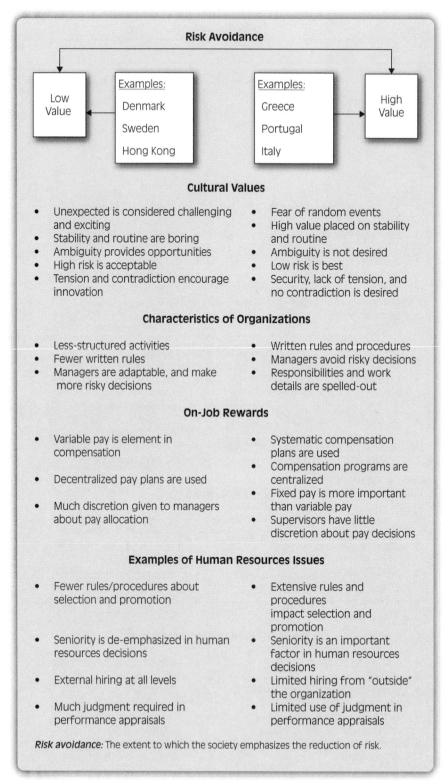

Risk Avoidance

| Low Value | Examples: Denmark, Sweden, Hong Kong | Examples: Greece, Portugal, Italy | High Value |

Cultural Values

- Unexpected is considered challenging and exciting
- Stability and routine are boring
- Ambiguity provides opportunities
- High risk is acceptable
- Tension and contradiction encourage innovation

- Fear of random events
- High value placed on stability and routine
- Ambiguity is not desired
- Low risk is best
- Security, lack of tension, and no contradiction is desired

Characteristics of Organizations

- Less-structured activities
- Fewer written rules
- Managers are adaptable, and make more risky decisions

- Written rules and procedures
- Managers avoid risky decisions
- Responsibilities and work details are spelled-out

On-Job Rewards

- Variable pay is element in compensation
- Decentralized pay plans are used
- Much discretion given to managers about pay allocation

- Systematic compensation plans are used
- Compensation programs are centralized
- Fixed pay is more important than variable pay
- Supervisors have little discretion about pay decisions

Examples of Human Resources Issues

- Fewer rules/procedures about selection and promotion
- Seniority is de-emphasized in human resources decisions
- External hiring at all levels
- Much judgment required in performance appraisals

- Extensive rules and procedures impact selection and promotion
- Seniority is an important factor in human resources decisions
- Limited hiring from "outside" the organization
- Limited use of judgment in performance appraisals

Risk avoidance: The extent to which the society emphasizes the reduction of risk.

FIGURE 13.6: Risk Avoidance and Human Resources Management

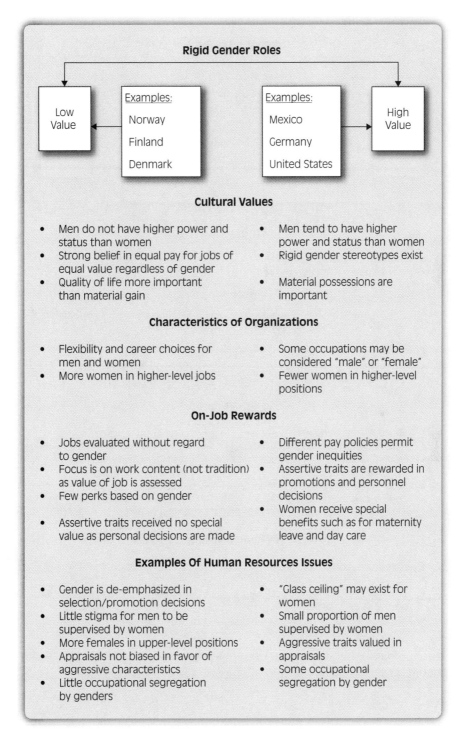

FIGURE 13.7: Rigid Gender Roles and Human Resources Management

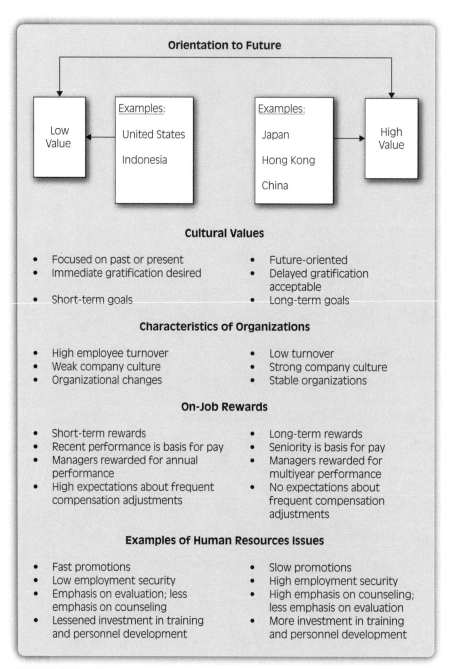

FIGURE 13.8: Orientation to Future and Human Resources Management

Acquiring Cultural Intelligence

The examples of cultural characteristics described in this section provide some information that can be used to anticipate behavior based on one's cultural background. A significant progression beyond these stereotypes occurs as one acquires **cultural intelligence,** in which he or she:

- Learns about a culture and how it impacts behavior.
- Considers the appropriate reactions to those with a specific cultural background.
- Acts in concert with this cultural knowledge and insight in situations that are encountered.

The process of cultural intelligence is progressive: each interaction adds to one's background of cultural awareness and increases the ability to respond appropriately in future situations. It has been said that "Experience is a good teacher," and this observation applies to expatriates as they learn how to best interact with persons in their host country.

Universal Truths about Human Resources Management

One universal truth in managing human resources is: There are few universal truths! While it is not possible to accurately stereotype persons based on their cultural background, here are three examples of generally accepted truths in the United States that are *not* universal:

- *Pay for performance is best.* Hospitality managers in the United States typically believe that one's pay and performance are correlated. A review of Figures 13.4 through 13.8 disprove this truth, because numerous cultural issues impact the sequence, timing, and basis for on-job rewards.
- *Formal objectives should drive management actions.* This truth is prevalent in many Western business organizations, but it is less relevant for managers and their employees (1) who don't conform to the abstract nature of preconceived guidelines; (2) to others who emphasize the past and present; and (3) to those who believe that decision making is a shared, if not equal, responsibility between managers and their employees.
- *Human resources can be managed.* Even the topic of this text can be controversial! In some countries, people do not like to be considered resources that can be managed like money or products. Also, some cultures have a reduced emphasis on a person's unlimited capabilities for individual progress that is a cornerstone for some professional development programs.

Focus on International Assignments

3. **Discuss the process of and challenges involved in a successful international assignment: selection, preparation, on-job issues, and after-assignment return.**

BACKGROUND

Hospitality managers who are potentially interested in an expatriate position must consider numerous professional and personal challenges before deciding to seek the assignment. Several concerns impact the prospective global candidate professionally and personally, including:

■ *The political environment.* Governments in some countries are not stable, and problems can arise quickly, even in countries with long-term leaders and political organizations in power. Revolutions can occur, and coups can change governmental structures and leaders overnight. Travel restrictions can be imposed that can create great concerns about the welfare of expatriates and their families.

■ *Economic concerns.* The costs of conducting business and living in other countries create challenges. Tax laws differ, **exchange rates** and **inflation** must be considered, and this knowledge must be factored into compensation plans that are negotiated for service abroad.

■ *Cultural environment.* Managers relocating to a country in which the culture and its norms are significantly different from those of their native country may suffer **culture shock** unless they and their families have been prepared in an extensive predeparture training and counseling program.

Managers who are likely to have successful expatriate experiences will:

■ Be able to adapt to and accept change.
■ Have an interest in living in another country or region of the world.
■ Know (or have an interest in learning about) the culture and language of the people of the host country.
■ Have the knowledge and skills needed for the assigned job.
■ Be fully supported by their families and, if the family will accompany them, members are equally willing to accept and adapt to the international assignment.
■ Have an interest in understanding the perspectives of persons from other cultures.

Figure 13.9 identifies factors that are important in a successful global assignment. These factors should be of concern to hospitality managers who are considering this career alternative and to human resources managers who plan programs for them.

Exchange rate: The rate at which the money of one country is exchanged (traded) for that of another country.

Inflation: The economic condition that exists when prices charged for products and services increase throughout a country.

Culture shock: The feeling of disorientation and an inability to adjust to a cultural environment that is different from one's own.

What Types of Skills Are Important for International Hospitality Managers?

One research study* explored the types of skills required for successful international hospitality management. Perhaps surprisingly, functional and technical skills were at the bottom of the list. Following are the skills ranked from most to least importance:

- Cultural sensitivity
- Interpersonal skills
- Managerial flexibility
- Adaptive leadership
- International motivation
- Intercultural competence
- Ability to work with limited resources
- Understanding of international business
- Interest
- International etiquette
- Stress management
- Functional skills
- Technical skills

*Kriegl, U. "International Hospitality Management," *Cornell Hotel and Restaurant Administration Quarterly* 41, No. 2, April 2000.

Let's see what Figure 13.9 tells us about the stages in a global hospitality work experience.

SELECTION ISSUES

Tens of thousands of dollars (probably much more!) will be invested in the relocation and support of the expatriate at the global location. Even more importantly, at least from a financial perspective, is the manager's impact on the business. Will it thrive and grow or, alternatively, be overcome with operating problems that do significant harm during his or her watch?

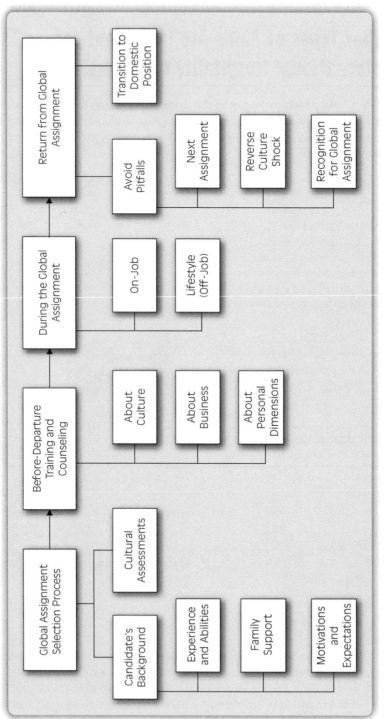

FIGURE 13.9: Overview of a Global Work Experience

Unfortunately, the importance of the candidate selection decision and a formalized selection process has not been a significant historic concern for some hospitality organizations. Concerns often focused on who wanted to go, rather than on selecting a person with the proper qualifications who could be most effective in the position. The result is that neither the candidate nor the organization met global operating objectives, and financial and other setbacks often occurred.

Figure 13.9 indicates that a formalized selection process is important. The candidate's experience and ability should be of special concern. Does his or her work experience suit the needs of the position to be filled? This issue addresses required competencies, and the expatriate must have the cultural sensitivities to make decisions in an unfamiliar environment. He or she must also be able to interact with staff members at all organizational levels from different sociocultural backgrounds.

Does the candidate's family fully support the assignment? Many early returns result from family problems. These can easily arise if spouses and families do not accompany the expatriate, but significant problems also occur when families do relocate, but cannot adjust to lifestyle changes, including housing, transportation, shopping, educational programs for children, and numerous other activities that become a new part of everyday life.

The motivations and expectations of the candidate are another concern identified in Figure 13.9. One who must relocate to help an employer, or who is doing so because it is judged necessary for career advancement, may not have significant positive motivating influences. Other inappropriate reasons for selecting a global assignment include "because it appears exciting," or when perceived problem staff members are relocated to "get them out of the way."

Cross-cultural adaptability: The extent to which a person can be comfortable in a different culture.

Instruments to assess the **cross-cultural adaptability** of the potential expatriate and his or her spouse and family can be useful in assessing attitudes judged important for successful cultural adjustment.

Counseling sessions can help persons anticipate lifestyle and other situations in which they will likely find themselves, and can help ensure that persons interested in global assignments know what to expect if they are selected.

PREPARATION ACTIVITIES

Figure 13.9 indicates that before-departure training provides additional information about the culture of the host country. Explanations about how business is conducted within the country of the assignment also become important. This training must also provide details about personal aspects, such as norms of dress, local costs, availability and quality of schools, the local currency, and (seemingly) innumerable other matters involved in adapting to the new environment.

Interviewing and counseling sessions with the candidate and family will be helpful in identifying and anticipating situations that are likely to occur, and they can further minimize the possibility of surprises that create stress.

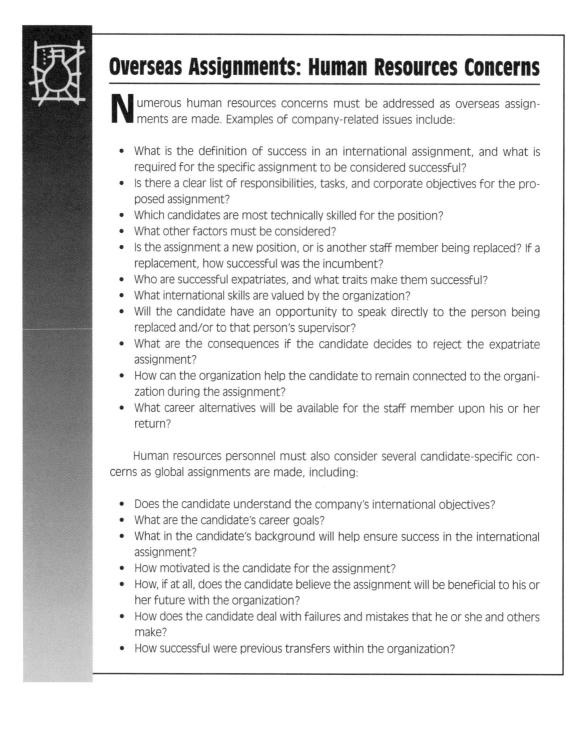

Overseas Assignments: Human Resources Concerns

Numerous human resources concerns must be addressed as overseas assignments are made. Examples of company-related issues include:

- What is the definition of success in an international assignment, and what is required for the specific assignment to be considered successful?
- Is there a clear list of responsibilities, tasks, and corporate objectives for the proposed assignment?
- Which candidates are most technically skilled for the position?
- What other factors must be considered?
- Is the assignment a new position, or is another staff member being replaced? If a replacement, how successful was the incumbent?
- Who are successful expatriates, and what traits make them successful?
- What international skills are valued by the organization?
- Will the candidate have an opportunity to speak directly to the person being replaced and/or to that person's supervisor?
- What are the consequences if the candidate decides to reject the expatriate assignment?
- How can the organization help the candidate to remain connected to the organization during the assignment?
- What career alternatives will be available for the staff member upon his or her return?

Human resources personnel must also consider several candidate-specific concerns as global assignments are made, including:

- Does the candidate understand the company's international objectives?
- What are the candidate's career goals?
- What in the candidate's background will help ensure success in the international assignment?
- How motivated is the candidate for the assignment?
- How, if at all, does the candidate believe the assignment will be beneficial to his or her future with the organization?
- How does the candidate deal with failures and mistakes that he or she and others make?
- How successful were previous transfers within the organization?

Human Resources MANAGEMENT ISSUES (13.1)

Victor had grown up in a home where Spanish was spoken almost as much as English. He graduated from college with a degree in hospitality business. Over the years, he had worked his way up in food and beverage positions to his current role as food and beverage director for one of the largest properties in his organization. His goal was to become a general manager, and the food and beverage track was a popular route to the top for many of his peers.

One afternoon, Victor was summoned to the office of the general manager at the hotel where he worked. After a few minutes of shop talk, he learned the purpose of the meeting and why the company's regional director of operations was present.

"Victor, you're aware of the joint venture we have with Travel Days Lodging to renovate and operate several first-class hotels in China," said the general manager. "We need someone to oversee the design and layout of the kitchens, restaurant outlets, and banquet facilities, and to begin establishing food and beverage operating procedures. Are you interested?"

Victor was surprised, and had no idea the company was interested in considering him for this overseas assignment. His most immediate thoughts were:

- I think I can do it.
- I would like to do it.
- I'm not certain my family would share my interest in doing it.
- I want to achieve a top-level position in my company, and I don't want to do anything that hinders my opportunity to do so.

After these almost instantaneous thoughts, Victor replied, "I'm really flattered that I would be considered for this opportunity, and I know it is a great one. However, I need to learn exactly what you want me to do. Then I need to talk to my family before I know exactly how we will be affected."

QUESTIONS

1. What are the most important factors that Victor should evaluate about this opportunity? What questions should he ask about each factor?
2. How, if at all, will Victor's ability to speak Spanish in the United States impact his ability to supervise and facilitate the work of managers and employees in China?
3. How might Victor assess the extent to which this career move will help him to become a large-property general manager with his organization? How important should this long-term career concern be in his immediate decision?

Much information must be provided to help managers and their families adapt to life in the new country. Examples include:

- Information about the form of government and the role it plays in business
- Overview of the prevalent religion(s)
- Examples of important social and cultural standards
- Significant information about nonverbal communication
- Basics of legal concerns that may differ from those in the United States
- Size, population, history, holidays, recreational activities, and related country-specific information
- Information about medical facilities and how to access quality medical care
- Costs for housing, food, and all other likely purchases, and information about currency and exchange rates

Basic language training, if applicable, will also be of great assistance.

ON-JOB CONCERNS

Additional training and adjustment to the new organization and position will be required when the expatriate arrives in the host country. Personal lifestyle concerns such as living arrangements and social interactions that will influence the manager's and his or her family's perceptions of the assignment must also be addressed.

About Compensation for Global Assignments

Compensation concerns are of critical importance to staff members who go on international assignments. Typically, salary decisions first consider the prevalent compensation for a similar domestic position. Then a significant amount of additional pay is typically provided to adjust for differences in housing, food, and other living costs in the host country. Additional monies are also frequently granted to offset the family's educational expenses for children, and medical concerns (access to quality care and costs associated with medical care, if needed) will also be an important consideration. Benefits such as relocation expenses to and from the assignment country will be incurred, and reimbursements for a specified number of trips to the incumbent's home location must also be considered.

Many organizations provide an additional incentive for those who accept an international assignment. This incentive may be in the form of a sign-up bonus, an increase over base pay during the assignment, and/or a bonus when the assignment is completed.

The chances of successfully completing an "out-of-country" assignment are enhanced when the entire family supports the manager's appointment.
Courtesy Purestock

Learning about and adapting to the work and the new culture will be continuous during the assignment. For example, numerous fundamental and basic changes in human resources practices will be required from those used in domestic assignments. Those who are properly motivated will find this aspect of the assignment to be enjoyable. By contrast, those who are less prepared may be confronted with the culture shock discussed earlier.

AFTER-ASSIGNMENT FOLLOW-UP

Figure 13.9 indicates that several concerns (pitfalls) can arise when an expatriate returns from a global assignment:

- *Next assignment.* A global manager may return to headquarters without knowledge of his or her next assignment. Sometimes this problem occurs because top-level managers have not thought about the issue. Others return to discover that career opportunities have actually diminished, and their peers have received significant promotions with increased responsibilities during their absence. Frustrations about the worth of the relocation will likely arise, as can concerns about one's future with the organization.

Charles has recently relocated to the Republic of the Fiji Islands (Fiji) from a major city in the Eastern United States to manage a resort for a West Coast hotel chain that is just beginning an international expansion. His company had the best intentions of adequately preparing him for his new assignment. His background and motivations were considered, and cross-cultural adaptability tools suggested that he and his family would adequately adjust to the new culture.

Before departing, Charles and his family had learned background information about the culture and knew what to expect about personal issues such as housing, education, and access to medical services. Charles had also received some general information about conducting business in Fiji. He had not, however, learned details about hotel management protocols in the country, because his company was not able to locate persons with this background who could or would provide basic information for a reasonable fee. The consensus was that this was not a major problem because, in its most general sense, the hotel would be managed and operated in the same way as any other business in the country, and this information was utilized.

Charles and his family arrived in Fiji and were pleased to learn that their predeparture preparation experiences were of great value. They knew what to expect, and there were only a few minor surprises to which they were able to adapt without significant hardship.

Charles's experiences on the job, however, were different. All of the employees spoke English (as he knew they would), and communication did not seem to be a significant issue. However, there were two concerns that he did not expect. One involved the fact that most of his staff members lived in the same tribal village. Numerous awkward situations arose when persons of different tribal rank and/or familial relationships were required to supervise, or to be supervised, by each other. Problems arose when, for example, a family patriarch in the village was supervised on the job by a junior nephew.

The second concern was, normally, one that he wished he could have experienced in his domestic positions: entry-level staff members wanted (almost excessively) ongoing training. Charles liked this request, wanted to provide the training, and realized its long-term benefit to the organization. However, he was concerned about the time needed for these staff members to learn tasks required for their present position. The time available for additional training for future positions was minimal because of the significant amount of hotel start-up work that was necessary.

Charles wished that he would have been prepared for these issues so he would have known how to deal with them better.

QUESTIONS

1. How can Charles deal with these issues in a way that is acceptable for both the organization and the employees?
2. What, if any, general assistance can his organization headquartered in the United States give him as he addresses these concerns?
3. How should future training of expatriates be modified based on Charles's experiences?

Reverse culture shock: Emotional and physiological readjustments that can occur as one returns from an international assignment.

- **Reverse culture shock.** Reverse culture shock can cause problems for those who have learned and worked in another culture.
- *No recognition for global assignment.* If the hospitality organization is focused on domestic operations, returning expatriates may not be recognized for their newly acquired knowledge and skills. Frustration can also arise if these managers believe that they have new knowledge and skills that are not used or that are underused in their next domestic assignment.

Hopefully, the organization will provide a systematic transition as the manager returns to a new domestic position. Career planning activities can begin with the manager's current status in the organization. Access to mentors who have served in expatriate management positions can be helpful, as can a formal process of recognizing the returning manager's international contributions. The after-assignment process is easier if the expatriate has received regular communication and updates from headquarters during the time of the international assignment.

Wouldn't it be wonderful to manage this resort in paradise? The answer is "yes" or "no" depending on one's motivations for accepting the assignment and the amount of predeparture assessment and personal/business background information the expatriate manager has received. *Courtesy The Four Seasons, photo by Robert Miller of Robert Miller Pictures*

IT'S THE LAW!

Hospitality managers in the United States know that there are (seemingly) innumerable legal concerns to be addressed as decisions are made about recruitment and selection, compensation including mandatory benefits, and modification of work tasks to meet the needs of those with selected disabilities. Interactions with unions, implementing performance appraisal programs, and protecting employees are among many other examples.

This chapter has noted some legal aspects of human resources management in selected countries, and even a cursory review notes major differences between laws in these countries. Expatriate managers must know and consistently comply with legal requirements applicable to their locations. These laws may be difficult to locate and/or understand and, as in the United States, they may also change. It is, therefore, typically necessary to utilize the services of attorneys and/or government officials knowledgeable in the applicable area with experience in administrating the labor laws in the specific location.

Following the letter of the law in the foreign country is, often, not the same as following the spirit of the law in the United States. Hospitality human resources managers may encounter numerous problems relating to gender inequity, employment of child labor, working hours and working conditions, and occupational health concerns, among others, that are outrageous by standards of domestic laws, but that are acceptable (or, at least, are overlooked) under local laws. These problems may occur in hospitality organizations and/or may be practiced by the suppliers of products and services to the organization. In both cases, they impact the lives of the affected employees and can irreparably harm the reputations of the hospitality organizations that permit them to occur.

It is relatively easy and necessary to develop policies supported by domestic laws and personal concerns for persons victimized by these practices. At the same time, it is difficult to compete with other organizations that take advantage of legal oversights or loopholes and misuse employees and others for their organization's financial gain. These concerns represent just a few of the many legal challenges that can confront expatriates with human resource management responsibilities.

Managing Employees During Global Assignments

4. Describe important considerations when managing hospitality employees in a foreign country.

Most hospitality personnel involved in international assignments will have management and operating responsibilities that include the management of subordinates. Hopefully, the new expatriate manager participated in transitional training and will know and practice basic background information about the do's and don'ts of managing personnel in the new location.

USE LOCALS OR EXPATRIATES?

Most employees in a typical hospitality operation are entry-level and supervisory personnel. The former can be trained as they begin their positions, and many of the latter have occupied entry-level positions before being promoted to their supervisory position. These staff members are typically recruited from the local employee market and are citizens of the host country. Expatriate employees are generally those required for higher-level management operating positions. Others will have short-term responsibilities such as planning for new business ventures and openings, acquiring technology, coordinating operating systems, increasing profitability (business turnaround), and other specialized activities. This expertise may not be available locally, and these positions represent those for which expatriate managers are typically desired.

Figure 13.10 reviews some advantages and disadvantages to the use of local and expatriate staff members in a foreign location. While many of these factors appear obvious, some are difficult to assess, and all must be considered relative to the specific situation.

	Advantages	Disadvantages
Use Locals	➤ Lower compensation ➤ Increased acceptance of hospitality organization in the community ➤ Easier to incorporate local concerns into the decision-making process	➤ Can be a challenge to merge local employment demands with the organization's concerns and needs. ➤ May be difficult to recruit qualified applicants for vacant positions. ➤ Can reduce the organization's control of labor.
Use Expatriates	➤ Culture is similar to that of the hospitality organization. ➤ Closer operating control will be possible. ➤ Provides the organization's employees with international management perspectives.	➤ Will likely involve significant compensation expenses. ➤ Makes it more difficult to adapt the organization to the local culture. ➤ Can have a negative impact on the morale of local employees. ➤ May need to address government regulations about expatriate employment.

FIGURE 13.10: Locals or Expatriates for Global Positions?

Futuristic Strategies to Manage a Global Workforce

There are potential alternatives to the traditional expatriate assignment in which a domestic manager is prepared for and then assumes a management role in a host country before returning to his or her home country, including:

- *Global career personnel.* This tactic uses persons who desire to live and work in multiple countries over their careers. Some move from country to country, and others have a home base but frequently travel away from it. These managers develop an in-depth understanding of global operations because they have managed in different cultures and understand how cultural backgrounds impact work. They also have useful international networks of contacts who can add diverse viewpoints to problem-solving and decision-making activities.
- *Awareness-building assignments.* Some managers can be given relatively short-term assignments of 3 to 12 months' duration. *Note:* Families do not typically relocate for these short-term assignments, so home visits are important. These singular assignments are typically made early in one's career and are not usually repeated. The purpose is to provide international perspectives to and experience for young managers. Some organizations may also use these assignments to give local managers advanced experience in another country. Upon completion, they can then return home to manage a local operation using the knowledge and skills learned during their relatively brief global assignment.
- *SWAT teams.* This strategy involves the use of mobile expert teams who travel to foreign sites on a short-term basis to address a specific concern or to complete an identified project. After a team is organized, the team can be deployed on an ad hoc basis where and whenever it is needed.
- *Virtual alternatives.* In some situations, technology can replace the need to send managers across international borders. Intranets and the Internet, videoconferencing, and the use of electronic databases are examples of tactics that can be low cost and effective alternatives to more labor-intensive solutions. Projects can be worked on around the clock as teams pass projects through global time zones. Distance learning, e-mails, and worldwide job posting systems are other examples of how technology can, in some instances, replace or supplement face-to-face interactions.

*From: Roberts, K. et. al., "Managing the Global Workforce: Challenges and Strategies," *The Academy of Management Executives* 12, No. 4, November 1998.

BASIC CONCERNS ARE IMPORTANT

Human resources policies must consider the context within which they will be used, and to do so requires knowledge about the culture of affected staff members. Inconsistencies between cultural influences and the policies and procedures will almost certainly be detrimental to the organization's goals. Depending on the location, obvious tactics such as using a leadership style that emphasizes teamwork and empowerment, and even establishing employee recognition programs, can be met with resistance. Therefore, training is needed to enable managers without the appropriate background to make effective at-work decisions in many locations around the globe.

Figure 13.11 compares several human resources concerns and governmental (legal) regulations in selected countries with many hospitality and tourism businesses. Expatriates are frequently used in top-level management positions in these countries. As you review this information, consider:

- How these concerns differ from those with which you might be familiar in the United States.
- How they illustrate cultural influences on the management of human resources.
- How an expatriate manager can learn about these important influences on hospitality operations in each country.

DETAILS! DETAILS!

Successful hospitality managers must also know about and utilize numerous details that are driven by culture, custom, precedent, and a long history of how business is conducted. Figure 13.12 reviews examples of protocols useful in the conduct of business in selected countries. *Note:* Information about the United States is added for comparative purposes.

Even a quick review of Figure 13.12 reveals differences in the details of how business is conducted in foreign countries. Hospitality managers will likely be involved in business meetings and negotiations, and may be responsible for business entertaining. Simple greetings and the giving of gifts are also natural activities in business and personal situations. It takes some time to learn about these and other traditions, but successful businesspersons take the time to do so. Then they consistently practice these protocols to enhance their business and off-work relationships with persons from the host country.

Country	Human Resources Concerns	Governmental (Legal) Regulations
China	⋏ Labor disputes are encouraged to be settled by negotiation or mediation. Compulsory arbitration is required before legal proceedings can occur.	⋏ Laws are in effect to address employment contracts, wages, work conditions, safety and health, women in the workplace, and resolutions of disputes.
	⋏ There is a shortage of talented managers, which increases compensation costs to attract and retain the managers.	⋏ Labor practices vary among regions of the country.
	⋏ Benefit costs double basic compensation costs.	⋏ Chinese employees can be recruited directly or through local employment centers. Expatriates are approved after demonstration that locals cannot fill the position.
	⋏ Chinese workers want training and are attracted to multinational enterprises to obtain it.	⋏ Laws relate to wages, employment of minors, and maternity benefits.
		⋏ Regular overtime is 1.5 times the contractual hourly wage. If workers must work on their regular days off, the minimum rate is 200 percent of normal wage. Overtime or statutory holidays require payments of 300 percent of normal wage.
		⋏ Businesses must participate in and pay social insurance premiums on behalf of an employee's account.
France	⋏ Compensation for hospitality industry personnel is lower than in alternative employee markets. This makes it difficult to attract and retain motivated employees.	⋏ Labor laws are expanding and place a compliance burden on many hospitality operations.
	⋏ There are perceptions of low status and long work-hour positions.	⋏ A legal workweek is 35 hours, and employees receive five weeks' paid leave annually. The hospitality industry may be treated as a special case, and managers are attempting to increase the number of industry employees and productivity levels of existing staff.
	⋏ Employees may join trade unions or "house unions."	

FIGURE 13.11: Comparative Human Resources Overview of Selected Countries*

➤ Employee strikes are common and are considered the rules of the game in collective bargaining efforts.

➤ Many employees work under annualized contracts that allow work to be spread over the entire year to avoid paying overtime. (These must be negotiated with and agreed to by unions.)

➤ Fixed-term, including seasonal, contracts are also used, and are carefully regulated.

➤ Extensive legal procedures are typically necessary to terminate employees, and prior notice and severance allowances are typically required. Employees must be interviewed while in the presence of another employee representative before they can be terminated.

➤ Annual negotiations between management and unions are required. If there is no union, negotiations then occur between managers and employee representatives.

➤ Business and employee contributions fund a generous security package to help ensure acceptable living conditions and medical coverage for the population. Social charges for businesses are among the highest in the world.

➤ Businesses pay a special tax that is used to fund training beyond that normally provided by the company.

Korea

➤ Employee work schedules can include 24-hour work shifts with breaks for meals and naps throughout the shift. This is followed with 24 hours off of work, and then the cycle begins again for several weeks until the employee receives a 48-hour break.

➤ The legal workweek is 44 hours, but employees may be scheduled for additional hours, and overtime pay may not be regulated.

➤ Korea has nationalized health insurance and social security (retirement) systems that are mandatory.

FIGURE 13.11: (Continued)

Country	Human Resources Concerns	Governmental (Legal) Regulations
	∧ Bonuses for profitable years can be as much as 150 to 200 percent of salaried workers' yearly pay, and hourly employees may receive a bonus equal to one to two months' pay.	∧ There is no minimum wage, so wages are set by the employee marketplace.
	∧ While there is no longer lifetime employment, loyalty is high among full-time employees.	∧ Short-time employees are subject to taxation.
	∧ While sex discrimination in the workplace has been abolished, most management positions are occupied by men, and there are fewer long-term careers for women.	
	∧ The labor force is highly unionized on a by-company basis. Unions typically have indirect influence on hotel operations based on their impact on the parent company that owns the hotels.	
	∧ Expatriates may manage large hotels owned by unionized businesses, and middle-level managers are referred from businesses owned by those organizations.	
Mexico	∧ Employees may join labor unions, and union relationships are very complex. Expatriates require advice and counseling about them.	∧ Federal laws prohibit racial, sexual, age, religious, social, and political discrimination.
	∧ Companies work with each other through interchange groups, which share personnel databases.	∧ Annual training courses for employees are required that must be reapproved each year.
		∧ Laws regulate the hiring and employment of children.
		∧ Legal stipulations describe the conditions under which staff members may be terminated.
		∧ The workweek is six 8-hour days, but night shifts are 7 hours.

FIGURE 13.11: (Continued)

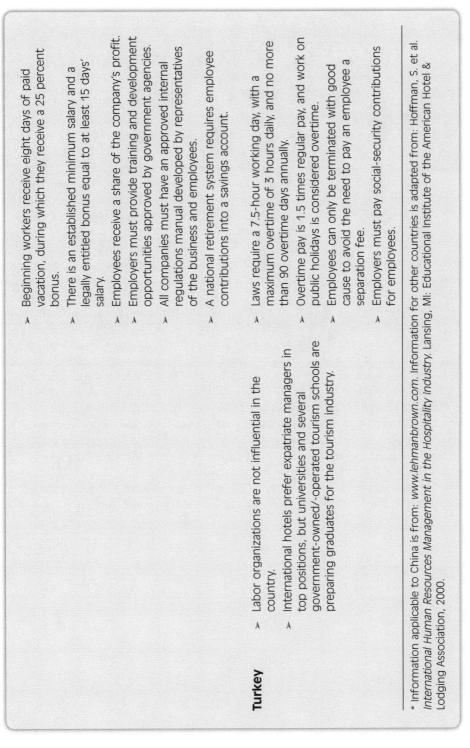

> Beginning workers receive eight days of paid vacation, during which they receive a 25 percent bonus.

> There is an established minimum salary and a legally entitled bonus equal to at least 15 days' salary.

> Employees receive a share of the company's profit.

> Employers must provide training and development opportunities approved by government agencies.

> All companies must have an approved internal regulations manual developed by representatives of the business and employees.

> A national retirement system requires employee contributions into a savings account.

> Laws require a 7.5-hour working day, with a maximum overtime of 3 hours daily, and no more than 90 overtime days annually.

> Overtime pay is 1.5 times regular pay, and work on public holidays is considered overtime.

> Employees can only be terminated with good cause to avoid the need to pay an employee a separation fee.

> Employers must pay social-security contributions for employees.

Turkey

> Labor organizations are not influential in the country.

> International hotels prefer expatriate managers in top positions, but universities and several government-owned/-operated tourism schools are preparing graduates for the tourism industry.

* Information applicable to China is from: *www.lehmanbrown.com*. Information for other countries is adapted from: Hoffman, S. et al. *International Human Resources Management in the Hospitality Industry*. Lansing, MI: Educational Institute of the American Hotel & Lodging Association, 2000.

FIGURE 13.11: (*Continued*)

Human Resources Management:
CURRENT EVENTS 13.2

EXPATRIATE SAFETY AND SECURITY CONCERNS

Expatriate management assignments can change from being rewarding to terrifying in a very short time. Ever-present terrorism concerns and political or military-inspired events can create serious safety situations for those working in global locations.

Events creating the need for emergency solutions have, unfortunately, occurred for many years and in many locations. Terrorist bombings in London, the need to remove employees from Lebanon and Indonesia, and recurring dangers in Israel and other Middle Eastern locations are just a few examples.

Hospitality organizations utilizing the services of expatriate managers must be aware of the potential need to provide security for all of its employees in the host country sites, including both U.S. expatriate managers and their employees from the host country.

The U.S. Department of State maintains an extensive library of information that is important to U.S. citizens living or traveling abroad. For example, its Bureau of Consular Affairs provides a wide range of services during emergencies and crises. The State Department also issues and updates travel warnings with recommendations for Americans to avoid certain countries. These are issued when officials decide, based on relevant information, to recommend that Americans avoid travel to a certain country. It also issues public announcements to disseminate information about terrorist threats and other relatively short-term and/or transnational conditions that may pose a significant risk to the security of Americans abroad. These announcements are typically issued during short-term coups, violence by terrorists, and for anniversary dates for specific terrorist events.

To review current information, type: "US Department of State" into your favorite search engine. Then click on the applicable titles in the "Travel and Business" section.

BUSINESS PRACTICES

Country	Official Language	Appointments	Negotiating	Business Entertaining	Greetings	Gifts
Australia	English	Be punctual. Business hours: 9 A.M. – 5 P.M., Monday – Friday; 9 A.M. – Noon, Saturday	Directness is appreciated. A business case should be presented by noting "good" and "bad." Be modest and casual. Don't digress or provide details. Spend a brief time before the meeting with small talk.	Don't make unannounced visits. Each person pays for a round of drinks. Sports are a good topic of conversation. Australians respect people with opinions, even if they conflict with their own.	Shake hands at the beginning of a meeting. Present a business card, but remember that many Australians do not have them.	Gifts are not generally given in a business context.
China	Chinese with a Mandarin dialect. *Note:* English is spoken by many businesspeople.	Punctuality is a must.	A business presentation will likely be made to many groups at different levels. When entering the meeting, the most senior official should lead the way. Do not use colored presentation materials. Negotiations can become lengthy and time consuming.	Surpass the host in terms of lavish restaurant banquets. Arrive 30 minutes before the guest. If you are the guest, arrive promptly; do not discuss business. Don't begin to eat or drink before the host.	Introductions tend to be formal and courteous. Chinese workers nod or bow slightly, although handshakes are common.	Avoid giving any gift of value in front of others. Make it clear that a gift is from your company to the Chinese organization. Present the gift to the leader of the Chinese group.

FIGURE 13.12: Business Protocols in Selected Countries*

BUSINESS PRACTICES (continued)

Country	Official Language	Appointments	Negotiating	Business Entertaining	Greetings	Gifts
			A better deal can be sought even after a contract is signed. Don't exaggerate an ability to deliver. Patience is required: negotiations may not be finalized for several trips. Business cards should be translated into Mandarin Chinese on the reverse side. Don't put a business card in your wallet and then put the wallet in your back pocket; this is considered to dishonor the person who gave you the card. It is expected that business will be conducted by senior leaders on both sides. At the end of a meeting, leave before the Chinese representatives.		Wait for the Chinese person to first extend a hand.	When giving or receiving a gift, use both hands. Do not open a gift in the presence of the giver. Chinese people traditionally decline a gift three times to avoid appearing greedy. Continue to insist, and indicate that you are pleased after the gift is accepted. All negotiations should end before gifts are exchanged.

France	French	Make appointments for business and social occasions. People are more relaxed about time in southern France.	Eye contact is frequent and intense. Negotiations are typically formal and reserved. Strict hierarchies are followed. Don't ask personal questions. Don't mistake a high-pitched voice or excited gestures for anger.	Business can be conducted at any meal. Be excited about the food before beginning business discussion. Whoever initiates the occasion is expected to pay for it. Keep both hands on the table at all times. Don't drink hard liquor between meals or smoke between courses.	Shake hands when being introduced and when leaving. French handshakes are not as firm as in the United States.	Don't give a business gift at the first meeting. Avoid gifts with a company logo. Do not include your business card with a gift. Do not bring wine, but send a thank-you note, flowers, or fruit basket after the event.
Hong Kong	Chinese and English	Punctuality is important.	Age is respected; the chief representative should be 50 years of age or older. Present all materials and ideas in a modest and patient way. Don't confront a Chinese person with an unpleasant fact in public.	Entertain at first-class restaurants and banquet halls. A celebration may require 8 to 12 meal courses.	Bows are traditional. Sincere compliments are given, but it is considered poor manners to agree with a compliment.	Gifts such as clocks and books can offend. Do not open gifts in the presence of the giver. Accept and give gifts with both hands.

FIGURE 13.12: (Continued)

BUSINESS PRACTICES (*continued*)

Country	Official Language	Appointments	Negotiating	Business Entertaining	Greetings	Gifts
			The word "yes" means "I heard you," not necessarily "yes." Do not say "no." Instead, a phrase with a similar meaning is, "It would be difficult." Prepare many alternatives to give the Chinese negotiator options. Don't direct all information to the senior negotiator. (The presence of some officials may be ceremonial.)	If a banquet is offered, it must be reciprocated. Pace yourself, and eat sparingly. Know how to use chopsticks.	Greet the most senior or elderly person first.	
Japan	Japanese	Be punctual. *Note:* Although office hours are from 9:00 A.M. to 5:00 (or 5:30) P.M., many persons go to dinner, and then return to work until 9 or 10 P.M.	Negotiations begin at the executive level and are then continued at the working level. Connections are helpful in Japan. If there are none, a personal call is better than a letter. Agreements of confidentiality are vague.	If you are invited out, the host will treat. Allow the host to order for you. Business can be discussed during the evening.	A bow is the traditional greeting, but handshakes are often used. If someone bows to greet you, bow to the same depth as he or she does, because this indicates	Give business gifts at midyear, at year-end, and often during the first business meeting. The ceremony of gift giving is more important than the objects being exchanged.

	A workweek is generally 40 to 48 hours without overtime pay done over 5.5 working days.	Contracts are not perceived as final agreements. Show the greatest respect to the oldest member of the Japanese group. The group (not the individual) is rewarded, so there will not be compliments to individuals. Don't directly refuse anything.	Use both hands to fill a cup or bowl that you wish to have refilled.	Japanese people do not open gifts when they are received. Avoid giving gifts with an equal number of elements (such as an even number of flowers in an arrangement).
Kuwait	Arabic is the national language; English is widely spoken among businesspersons.	You should be prompt, but a client may be late or not show up; it is standard practice to keep foreign businesspersons waiting. There may be several meetings of small talk before a business presentation can be made. Business cards should be printed in English and in Arabic. The card should be handed with your right hand to the Kuwaiti with the Arabic-language side up. You may need to compromise on some issue just to protect someone's ego.	Follow the lead of your host to decide if shoes should be removed before entering a building. Alcohol and pork consumption are illegal, and eating is done with the right hand only.	Allow your Kuwaiti counterpart to greet you first. Then use the same style of greeting. It is not traditional to introduce a veiled Kuwaiti woman who is accompanying a Kuwaiti man. Avoid images or pictures of people or dogs. Engraved pens, pencils, finely made compasses, and business card cases are examples of appropriate gifts.

FIGURE 13.12: (Continued)

BUSINESS PRACTICES (continued)

Country	Official Language	Appointments	Negotiating	Business Entertaining	Greetings	Gifts
Mexico	Spanish	Punctuality is not strictly adhered to.	Business atmosphere is friendly and easygoing and of a slower pace than in the United States. Personal friendships are important when doing business in Mexico. Be warm and personal. Avoid saying "no." Better terms are "maybe" or "we'll see." Emphasize trust and the mutual compatibility of the two companies when negotiating. At least one member of the team should be from higher-level management.	The oldest person in the group typically pays for a group's meal. Minimize heavy eating, drinking, and smoking.	Men shake hands when greeting. There may be hugs on the second or third meeting.	Giving gifts in a business context is not required. Small gifts such as items with a company logo are appreciated. Secretaries in the private sector should be given a gift on a return visit. Avoid giving gifts of silver.
Singapore	While there are four official languages, English is the language of business and government.	Punctuality is important.	The pace of negotiations is slower than in the United States. Several trips over several months are typically needed to complete an agreement. The word "no" is rarely used.	A successful business relationship requires an established social relationship. Respond to written invitations in writing.	A handshake is a common form of greeting for younger, foreign-educated persons. (It is a handclasp lasting for 10 to 20 seconds.)	Gifts are given between friends. Do not give a gift before you have established a personal relationship. Gifts are not unwrapped in the presence of the giver.

	Language	Business Practices	Social Occasions	Greetings	Gifts
		Singapore businesspersons are most comfortable dealing with a person rather than a company. Politeness is a critical attribute for successful relationships.	Social occasions always involve food.	Singaporean Chinese people use a traditional bow, a handshake, or both. Only Westernized Hindus shake hands with those of the opposite sex.	Gifts are traditionally declined three times before they are accepted.
United States	English	Punctuality is emphasized. Business is conducted quickly relative to many cultures. Deals are often made during initial meetings. Financial concerns, technology, and short-term rewards are normal negotiation issues. There is little small talk. Compliments are exchanged, but personal questions are minimized if persons do not know each other. Smoking is increasingly prohibited in public areas. Business cards are not exchanged unless future contacts are desired.	Many business meetings are held over lunch, and early-morning breakfasts are also common. The business host typically pays for meals.	A firm handshake is used in business situations. In casual situations, a smile, nod, and/or verbal greeting is appropriate.	Expensive business gifts are discouraged (a maximum of $25 tax deduction for gifts is permitted). Thank-you notes are often appropriate. Gifts are unwrapped when presented and shown to all persons who are present. A meal or entertainment is a common gift.

*Source: Morrison, T. et. al. *Kiss, Bow, or Shake Hands: How To Do Business in Sixty Countries*. Holbrook, MA: Adams Media Corporation, 1994.

FIGURE 13.12: (Continued)

HUMAN RESOURCES TERMS

The following terms were defined in this chapter:

Mode of entry	Country cluster
Subsidiaries	Cultural intelligence
Joint venture	Exchange rate
Multinational (organization)	Inflation
Transnational (organization)	Culture shock
Culture	Cross-cultural adaptability
Organizational culture	Reverse culture shock
Sociocultural	

FOR YOUR CONSIDERATION

1. Would you be interested in an expatriate management position in the hospitality industry? Why or why not?
2. If possible, interview a hospitality manager with expatriate experience (ask local managers or faculty members for referrals). Ask the following questions:
   a. What were the main reasons that you accepted the assignment?
   b. How did you prepare for the assignment?
   c. What, if any, surprises arose as you managed the operation?
   d. What is your advice for someone considering an expatriate management position?
3. Do you think that managing employees with diverse cultural backgrounds in the United States is helpful experience for someone planning to be an expatriate manager? Why or why not?
4. Would business or personal living adjustments be the most difficult if you assumed an expatriate position? Why?

CASE STUDY: HUMAN RESOURCES MANAGEMENT IN ACTION

Rio Grand Services Management operates contracted food services for about 25 relatively small healthcare facilities throughout south Texas. Recently, company officials have been approached by two government-operated hospitals in Mexico about the possibility of managing their facility's foodservice departments. Company officials had also met with several representatives of small hospitals from Central American countries who had similar interests. Rio Grand Services officials thought they might have discovered a market niche that was not being served by large contract management organizations.

Top-level Rio Grand Services managers decided that they would negotiate a contract for the two facilities in Mexico with the longer-term intention of learning more to help them decide about the potential worth of concentrated expansion throughout Mexico and Central America. Their reasoning was that it is not possible to plan a market expansion effort without knowing what to expect. A few initial operations would, therefore, provide input that would be very helpful with longer-term planning.

Dimension: Strategic

1. What are examples of basic human resources management concerns that should be addressed as Rio Grand Services officials consider international expansion?
2. Company officials hope they will learn something about human resources management concerns through their limited operation of these two health-care facility accounts. What additional sources of information can help company officials to anticipate human resources challenges?

Dimension: Expatriate Selection

1. What factors should Rio Grand Services officials consider as they determine whether a local citizen or an expatriate should be retained to manage the first two accounts in Mexico?
2. Assume that expatriate managers must be retained. How should officials determine if an existing manager should be utilized or a new staff member (e.g., someone with experience in healthcare foodservices management in Mexico) should be employed?

Dimension: Expatriate Placement

1. Where can company officials locate persons or companies with expertise in expatriate manager selection and cultural adaptation information?
2. How can company officials learn about the do's and don'ts of managing a business in general and administering a healthcare foodservices operation more specifically in Mexico?

INTERNET ACTIVITIES

1. Grovewell, LLC (*www.grovewell.com*) is a leader in providing global leadership training. Review this company's home page. What kind of services does this organization provide? What have you learned about global leadership?
2. Many companies provide expatriate management assessment and preparation programs. To review the Web sites of many of these organizations, type "expatriate manager assessments" into your favorite search engine.

3. Do you want to learn more about international business protocols? If so, type "international business protocols" into your favorite search engine. Also, review an especially useful resource: *www.kwintessential.com.*

4. If you are interested in a Web site to locate international business resources that address the needs of academics, including researchers and graduate students, go to: *www.globaledge.msu.edu.* When you arrive at the site, click on "Academy."

ENDNOTES

1. Ruggless, R. "Global Ambitions. Segment Study: Casual Dining." *Nation's Restaurant News,* September 18, 2006.

2. Garber, A. "Operators Across the Globe Hungry for Slice of Domino's Pie." *Nation's Restaurant News,* January 19, 2004.

3. Hofstede, G. *Culture's Consequences: International Differences in Work-Related Values.* Beverly Hills, CA: Sage Publications, 1980.

Index